3-

Sight Unseen

Science, UFO Invisibility and Transgenic Beings

Budd Hopkins
Carol Rainey

ATRIA BOOKS

New York   London   Toronto   Sydney   Singapore

ATRIA BOOKS
1230 Avenue of the Americas
New York, NY 10020

Copyright © 2003 by Budd Hopkins and Carol Rainey

Drawings on pgs. 54, 62, 87, and 176 by Michael Esposito

ISBN: 0-7434-1218-4

First Atria Books hardcover printing September 2003

10   9   8   7   6   5   4   3   2   1

ATRIA BOOKS is a trademark of Simon & Schuster, Inc.

Printed in the U.S.A.

For information regarding special discounts for bulk purchases,
please contact Simon & Schuster Special Sales at 1-800-456-6798
or business@simonandschuster.com

We dedicate this book to our colleagues in the Intruders Foundation (IF), who have, over the years, unstintingly given of their energy, their time, and their creativity, thus making possible serious research into the UFO abduction phenomenon. Volunteers as well as the members of IF's advisory committee have shown great dedication to this important work, and we, the authors, extend our deepest thanks to:

Sal Amendola
Dennis Anderson
Ted Davis
Cathy Del Grosso
Robert Fischer
Oliver Kemenczky
Lisa Langelier-Marks
Bob Long
Ed Martin
Agnes McGarrigle
Joe Orsini
Peter Robbins
Greg Sandow
Jed Turnbull

Acknowledgments

M y coauthor, Carol Rainey, and I owe an enormous debt of gratitude to the many people who contributed to the shaping of our book, helping to keep it as error-free as possible and as rich in new scientific and abduction information as we ever dared to hope.

First, we would like to thank the many abduction experiencers whose intimate and revealing accounts are included in the following pages. One abductee, Katharina Wilson, has gone so far as to allow us to use her name, a brave decision in this contentious field. Many other abductees whose UFO encounters are included in these pages have generously allowed us to use their accounts under pseudonyms, and to each of them we also offer our profound thanks. They have made vital and courageous contributions to the world's understanding of the UFO abduction phenomenon.

A number of scientists have also been extremely helpful and conscientious in reading the manuscript and offering professional advice. Among these scientists are many friends and colleagues, including, especially, Michael Swords, Stanton Friedman, Bruce Maccabee, and John Altshuler. Historian and pioneering abduction researcher David Jacobs has been centrally helpful in giving the manuscript a wise, critical reading, as has my close associate, Ted Davis.

Jerry Clark, through his invaluable writings, has been, as always, a reservoir of useful information. We have also received significant leads and assistance from Anne Ramsey Cuvelier and Michael O'Connell. Carolyn Longo also gave unstintingly of her time in transcribing our extensive interviews.

We would especially like to offer our gratitude to Phyllis Wender, my agent of more than twenty years, who has shepherded me through the rigors of three previous books as well as this current work, *Sight Unseen*. She has been enormously helpful to us both. Our editor, Mitchell Ivers, has done a superb job of aiding in the clarification of a great deal of intricate information, and if the book flows smoothly, he deserves a great deal of the credit.

Throughout the research and writing of *Sight Unseen,* we have felt ourselves blessed by the support of friends, fellow UFO researchers, and literary colleagues too numerous to mention, and to all of them we wish to extend our profound gratitude. In so many ways, their gifts of critical intelligence and generous affection have helped make this book possible.

Contents

Budd Hopkins

In the year 2001, I marked a quarter-century of investigation into the UFO abduction phenomenon. When I first began to examine accounts of alien abduction in 1976, researchers were aware of only a handful of these bizarre and intriguing reports. Although these accounts of alien abduction were apparently unrelated, they were often made by highly credible witnesses. As the years passed I received thousands of reports and was able to closely investigate hundreds of accounts with striking similarities. Unrelated individuals each described similar specific details, further adding to the credibility of the witnesses. As I examined and compared these cases, I was able to detect many recurring patterns. Portentous in the extreme, these patterns seemed to point inexorably to one plausible interpretation: Intelligent, nonhuman beings possessing a technology vastly superior to our own have arrived on our planet.

Even more disturbing, these enigmatic visitors have apparently embarked upon a covert, highly systematic program in which thousands of our men, women, and children are repeatedly lifted out of their everyday lives. They are removed from their cars, backyards, beds, and schools and subjected to a methodical regimen of examination, study, and sample-taking. Though UFO investigators have amassed a great deal of information about the UFO occupants' methods and the nature of their interest in us, we are still uncertain as to their ultimate plans, for our planet and for the human race. Various scenarios been proposed; few offer much peace of mind.[1]

It has taken years of careful comparative research to isolate scores of highly specific recurring patterns within what had at first seemed an idiosyncratic, almost random collection of incidents. At the present time we can confidently define the abduction phenomenon as a distinct body of hard-edged, precisely detailed, mutually corroborative recurring events that have involved thousands of individuals from all over the world.

As I looked into case after case, one common pattern that I discovered has to do with particular types of scars found on individuals after abduction experiences, apparently the result of quasimedical sample-taking procedures carried out by the UFO occupants.[2] These telltale lesions are of two main types: circular "scoopmarks"—depressions one to two centimeters in diameter and several millimeters deep—and neat, straight-line, "surgical" cuts ranging from two to nine centimeters in length. I have seen perhaps one hundred scoop marks—the more common of the two types and often appearing on the lower leg—and scores of straight-line cuts. Several physicians have noticed the similarity of scoop marks to the scars left by punch biopsies, but X rays and other forms of medical examination have not yet led to a consistent theory as to why these marks were made.

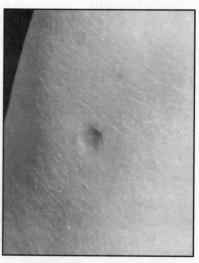

The "screen memory" phenomenon is another pattern that I uncov-

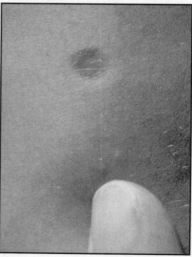

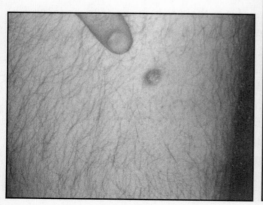

ered shortly after I began my investigations.[3] A "screen memory" results when UFO occupants somehow substitute more palatable conventional imagery for an abductee's traumatic recollections. Instead of recalling unnerving alien faces with large, impenetrable black eyes and gray, hairless skin, abductees have frequently reported conscious, prehypnotic memories of such things as five-foot-tall wingless owls; gray, hairless, upright cats; or deer with expressive black eyes that communicate mind-to-mind. In one case, what was first perceived as a pileup of six wrecked automobiles with their headlights ablaze eventually revealed itself as a landed UFO, and in another case, a huge, motionless silver airplane initially stood in for a UFO in the sunny sky. The idea that these images are not self-generated but are implanted in the minds of abductees by their captors is supported by the fact that two or more people in the same encounter saw exactly the same (impossible) five-foot-tall owl staring at them, the same pileup of six empty cars on a deserted road, or the same telepathic deer.

Scoop marks, straight-line scars, and screen memories are just a few of the many recurring patterns that have been documented by researchers in literally thousands of abduction cases throughout the world. Among the more than five hundred abductees I have personally worked with over the past quarter century, there are African-Americans, Catholics, musicians, a NASA research scientist, Mormons, medical doctors, Japanese, Muslims, Scotsmen, farmers, Israelis, nurses, Orthodox Jews, Brazilians, Protestant ministers, Australians, scientists, Hispanics, policemen, Hindus, actors, Canadians, psychiatrists, airline pilots, military officers, businesspeople, engineers, artists, students, professors—and even a prostitute or two. Their encounters with non-human occupants of UFOs have taken place in the city and the country, in forests and front yards, in groups or individually. These encounters are neither imaginary nor "imaginal"—whatever that portmanteau word actually means. They are not the results of hallucinations, sleep paralysis, or hoaxes. The skilled UFO researcher has learned how to identify such mundane explanations, thus avoiding pursuit of any vague, dubious, and unsupported accounts.

Out of the mass of credible reports that remain, the supporting physical, medical, and photographic evidence is so consistent that *none* of the debunkers' psychological or psychosocial theories can begin to explain it away. Over the years, for better or for worse, I have come to believe that UFO abductions are real, event-level occurrences. They constitute a truly extraordinary phenomenon, and it would seem a truism that an extraordinary phenomenon *demands* an extraordinary investigation.

This brings us to one of the truly great human mysteries: that five decades of these consistent and alarming findings have escaped the attention of mainstream science. Not one penny of the National Science Foundation's budget or the National Institutes of Health's (NIH) $20.3 billion research budget has ever been applied to investigation of the UFO abduction phenomenon. (The NIH confidently predicts congressional approval to double that research budget by 2003.) Not one academic institution takes the phenomenon seriously enough to develop an accredited program of study around it. There have been, certainly, a few courageous individual scientists and scholars who have hacked paths into the tangled UFO jungle of skeptical hyperbole, myth, ridicule, and misidentification and found their way into the broad clearing of credible eyewitness reports. Unfortunately, many of those who have publicly announced themselves as being seriously interested in investigating the UFO mystery have paid dearly for their courage with professional careers that have been blighted by intolerant, even outraged colleagues.[4]

Researcher Richard Hall has said that we have two possibilities of obtaining meaningful answers to the UFO dilemma: one; if science and government wake up and begin to support its thorough investigation; and two; if the aliens decide to communicate their intent to us and make their presence undeniable. But, unfortunately, none of the parties involved seem very partial to either of these possibilities.

One would think that the implications of the UFO mystery—which include the possible end of human culture and existence as we know it—would evoke a terrible outcry, a groundswell of demands to look into these reports. But this is not happening, especially at the governmental and scientific levels, where scorn and disavowal of interest in the subject prevail. We believe this is due less to concern about the potential danger of covert extraterrestrial presence than to the widespread tenet in the realms of government, science, and the media that it is just not possible.

As for the aliens, rather than the proverbial broadcast from the White House lawn, the aliens seem quite content with their program of secrecy. And why not? Whatever their ultimate purpose, they are able to dip in and out of our world with impunity. They don't have to tell us what they are doing, because—to the best of our knowledge—no government, no power on earth is holding them accountable.

In *Sight Unseen*, my wife, writer and filmmaker Carol Rainey, and I propose to look directly at the question of what is possible—and what is not—in the so-called "impossible" UFO phenomenon. For instance, how can a flying disc fifty feet in diameter simply vanish? Is it feasible that two little girls in a major city could be abducted from their cellar playroom in broad daylight with no one seeing it happen? Or, if nature has established a powerful barrier against interspecies breeding, how could we be receiving so many reports of human-alien "hybrids"? How could a car, a cow, or even a person, "levitate" up a beam of light? Is there any credibility to abductee reports of having their behavior and emotions controlled by the UFO occupants? Is there any concrete science that we can refer to in exploring these seemingly paranormal events?

We believe that by looking at some fascinating theoretical twists and turns as well as several quite bizarre discoveries in modern science, particularly in the field of physics, we can show how UFOs and their occupants may actually obey, not defy, the laws of physics and the natural sciences. We will demonstrate, once and for all, how phenomena conventionally thought to be impossible might actually be occurring now, presently, in our lifetime.

But while we may find intriguing analogies between the mysteries of the UFO phenomenon and the kaleidoscopic new findings in biotechnology, neurophysiology, and quantum physics, we'll resist the temptation to assume that likeness constitutes proof of the existence of radical UFO technology. For several reasons, applying scientific principles to UFO research through the time-honored methods of science has always been a problematic undertaking. Most often the researcher is not a direct observer of the UFO event or abduction and instead has to depend on the testimony of credible witnesses—on secondhand observations. However, as we have seen, specific details, reported over and over by individuals from different countries, ages, and backgrounds, form distinct and compelling patterns, and it is by thorough examination of those patterns that our knowledge of the UFO phenomenon advances. Furthermore, we believe that both our current and emerging scientific ideas will shed light on the UFO mystery, and light is what will ultimately give the UFO phenomenon plausibility and corporeal reality in the doubting eyes of the world.

In the following chapters, we will explore several newly isolated abduction patterns that are both extraordinary and deeply unsettling. The consistencies of these cases form perhaps the most radical and disturbing aspects of the UFO phenomenon yet to be openly discussed. We don't yet fully understand these events, nor are we able to prove their occurrence in the usual scientific manner. However, these events can newly inform a dialogue between abduction data and our earthly science's fresh gleanings about the nature of reality. It is in this exchange between the elusive mystery of UFOs and, for instance, the eerie world of quantum particles that some common language may be found.

A recent example of scientific support for "impossible" alien capabilities has to do with what I term "alien co-option." In *Witnessed: The True Story of the Brooklyn Bridge Abductions,* I described how the abductee Linda Cortile seemed to have been temporarily "taken over" by the UFO occupants, behaving as if she were in complete sympathy with them, wholly accepting their goals and methods. Her behavior went far beyond what has been called the Stockholm syndrome, the tendency for long-term captives to identify with their captors. As revealed in a hypnotic regression, in less than an hour Linda changed from a reluctant prisoner to a forceful ally of the aliens, showing outright contempt for her fellow abductees. Even more remarkable, she scolded them about reckless human damage to the environment, mentioning specific materials such as basaltic lavas and the effects of pollution on the health of certain sea creatures—issues about which she apparently had no conscious knowledge. When the abduction ended, she changed from Mr. Hyde back to Dr. Jekyll and resumed her normal stance as a frightened, angry abductee who despised what the aliens had done to her and her companions. Her temporary co-option by the aliens had ended. "You know, Budd," she said later, "I flunked science in high school. I don't know how I knew about these things."

At the time, as is my custom, I did not write or speak about what seemed to be a onetime report of a new element in an abduction account. But after a number of similar reports surfaced, I had to acknowledge that a new pattern had emerged. In several cases the co-opted abductees described themselves as dressed in smooth, blue, formfitting one-piece "alien" garments with no noticeable fasteners—garments they do not remember putting on or taking off. All felt both a deep-seated anger and a sense of profound humiliation after their experiences, in which their wills had somehow been completely overridden. All hated the fact that they had been used as involuntary conscripts, either to ease the fears of other frightened abductees or, as in Linda's case, to preach a demeaning alien message.

How is such a thorough co-option of abductees possible? Is it the result of a patient, long-drawn-out *Manchurian Candidate* type of alien brainwashing? Is it a chemical or psychological process? Or is it perhaps something more direct: a neurological shortcut that can be utilized as easily as pressing a light switch?

In her perusal of the scientific literature, Carol Rainey has discovered a fascinating mystery involving a particular kind of spider that suggests, on an infinitely more primitive level, a parallel with alien co-option. She explains:

> One of the creepiest images that science fiction has planted in our cultural psyche is the idea of alien invasion of one's mind and body—being taken over by another creature and made to do its terrible bidding. But scientists have recently discovered that at least one form of bizarre "mind control" is not just science fiction: It actually occurs on a regular basis deep in the rain forests of Costa Rica. As reported in the journal *Nature* by spider expert Dr. William G. Eberhard, scientists have discovered a parasitic wasp with the ability to manipulate its host's behavior.[5]
>
> Here in the deep-shadowed jungle, the ichneumon, or parasitic wasp, preys on the industrious orb-weaving spider, so named because of the perfectly round web it regularly spins. The distinctive web results from a five-step process: In the first two stages, the spider lays lateral cables as the web's structural framework; it then interweaves row after row of delicate circular strands around the lateral frame. When the wasp attacks, it temporarily paralyzes the spider before laying an egg on the tip of the spider's abdomen. With

the "alien" wasp egg awkwardly out of its reach, the spider dutifully resumes its daily web-spinning. For two weeks the spider's activities go on as before—except for the wasp larva clinging to its belly, slowly sucking the life out of its host. Up to this point it's your typical unsavory bodily-fluid-loss parasite story.

But here's the twist: The night before the wasp larva finally kills the spider, it somehow directs the spider to construct *a totally different web*. Like a zombie, the spider suddenly stops the daily rebuilding of its delicate, round web. With hours or minutes left to live, the spider host spins two thick, cablelike strands with strong crossbraces between them—a resting place for the stately, heavier wasp; a durable platform resistant to wind and rain, high above the marauding ants on the ground below.

Mission accomplished, the wasp larva kills the spider and spins its own cocoon on the suspended platform especially constructed for it by its co-opted victim. Dr. Eberhard postulates that the spider has literally been reprogrammed, most likely by the wasp's having injected some chemical into its host. But the internal target is clearly specific and alters the spider's normal behavior at just the right time to benefit the wasp. Essentially, the larva has manipulated a specific subroutine in the spider's web-spinning program. Instead of its usual five-step process, the spider—under larval direction—can only perform the first two *lateral* steps over and over.

Another interesting twist: When Dr. Eberhard experimented by removing the larva from the spider right before it was killed, the spider continued to build the platform-style web for only a short time. Within hours, it reverted to weaving its usual orblike web. "It's as if," Eberhard says, "the spider is recovering from strong drug."

At this early point in the study, goals are to isolate the chemical and the larval gland that secretes it and determine how it targets specifically the web-spinning operations of the spider. Other scientists have previously reported on various ways that parasites shape their hosts' behavior. But according to Dr. Jay Rosenheim, an expert on parasitic wasps at the University of California at Davis, this example is astounding, both for the detailed way that the host's behavior is manipulated and how little is known about the means by which it is accomplished.

"I think biology is one of our last great frontiers," said Dr. Ian Gauld at the Natural History Museum in London.[6] "We have got no idea about what there is on earth with us, let alone what it is doing or how it is doing it."

Little, indeed, do Dr. Gauld—or many other scientists—know what is on earth with us. Or what it is doing. Or how it does it.

With regard to alien co-option and Linda Cortile, the sudden changes in her behavior, coupled with the surprising new breadth of her vocabulary and knowledge of technology, suggest a kind of temporary alien control similar to, but far more complex than, the wasp's effect on the orb-spinning spider. And as in the spider's situation, when Linda was removed from the controlling alien milieu, she resumed her normal anti-alien posture as well as her usual modest range of scientific knowledge. Is one of these two very strange phenomena any easier to explain than the other? We know for certain that one phenomenon—the temporary co-option of the spider by the wasp—is not only possible but observably real. By some analogous process, might not alien co-option of abductees be equally possible, equally real?

The structure of this book is deceptively simple: I will present newly observed patterns within the abduction phenomenon, and Carol Rainey will present recent developments in various fields of science—such as the story of Dr. Eberhard's wasp—that appear relevant to these startling UFO abduction cases.

We have titled our book *Sight Unseen* for a very specific reason. The first section "Unseen," deals with the aliens' successful methods of concealing their worldwide program of human abduction, while the second section, "Seen" will explore newly recognized patterns of extreme alien *visibility*. In each part of the book we will be presenting case material that is almost totally unknown to the general public, as well as unfamiliar and radical new scientific thinking and experimentation in fields such as physics, neurobiology, and genetics that will help the reader further understand the plausibility of UFO technology.

For too long the idea has persisted that the UFO phenomenon and science as we know it are absolute adversaries. Fed by eager skeptics, the illusion persists that science is rational while everything having to do with UFOs is irrational—that scientists "know" with certainty what is possible and what is ultimately impossible. In *Sight Unseen* we intend to show how that blinkered view needlessly narrows our conception of the physical world and blinds us to what may well be the most important event in human history—the unheralded arrival on our planet of intelligent, nonhuman beings.

Carol Rainey

The first time that I ever heard about UFO abduction cases, I was leaning into the wind on a Cape Cod beach that was sparsely dotted with companionable groups of summer people enjoying their last few days at the shore. It was the fall of 1995, and my neighbor, Sally Fleschner, and I had just driven down from the Boston area where we lived to join some of Sally's New York friends—writers, painters, psychiatrists, professors, restaurateurs, and patrons of the arts. One of the painters I was introduced to was an animated, slender man with silver hair, a natural-born raconteur by the name of Budd Hopkins. As his stories unfurled one after another that afternoon, it became apparent that this artist was also the "UFO investigator" that Sally had told me about on the drive down. As a pragmatic attorney, she had thought the UFO subject was "a little kooky" but told me not to worry about it, that I'd like Budd. Everybody liked Budd. A few hours later, seeing him surrounded by friends at the water's edge, I was also drawn to this man's lively wit. But as I listened that day to Budd's account of a UFO case right there on Cape Cod, I clearly remember the confusion of my thoughts. I'd never thought of UFOs, I'd never even heard of "alien abductions," and I had no idea that intelligent people took these ideas seriously.

At first I felt slightly stunned. Budd had launched into an account about an enlisted man, Bob, who'd been abducted by a UFO in Truro, the next town over from the beach we stood on, right in front of Dutra's Grocery, a mom-and-pop store I knew well. Two hours later, according to Budd, Bob was returned to the road in front of the store, disheveled and confused. When he called his destination, the North Truro Air Force Base, he discovered that a jeep had been sent to pick him up at the store an hour and a half earlier and hadn't found him there. Bob later had scattered memories of bulbous-headed creatures with big eyes inserting something in his nose.

I looked quizzically at my friend Sally, thinking: *What have you gotten me into this time?* She laughed and waved me away as Budd managed to steer me apart from the others and into a stroll down the beach. That's when my innate skepticism kicked in. Almost shouting to be heard over the wind and the waves, I fired a volley of questions at this affable, gentle man. Budd was more than implying that UFOs actually existed. How could that be possible? Why would he believe these people's stories when science was silent on the subject? Furthermore, if this was even partially true, what would be the implications for humans as a species? And how did he propose to deal with the terrible shakeup of human beings coming to terms with the idea that we might not be the pinnacle of all earthly creation, as we'd naively assumed ever since man became a sentient being?

Looking back, I realize now that my anger on that brisk, salt afternoon was coming from a familiar place. I was feeling foolish and clueless because I had no way to evaluate the truth of what had been placed in front of me. My childhood had been sprinkled liberally with similar moments of stinging helplessness and frustration. Growing up as I did, inside a clan of fundamentalist Plymouth Brethren in central Illinois, tended to limit one's knowledge of popular culture, which this UFO thing seemed to be. I'd grown up in the sixties without television or movies or popular literature; we didn't dance, smoke, drink, fornicate, or divorce. I couldn't have identified Elvis from Opie or H. G. Wells from Orson Welles. During my high school science class, on certain days I often found myself seated outside in the hallway on a chair placed there just for me. The topic under discussion inside, I vaguely gathered, was blasphemous about the truth of Genesis—that God had created the heavens and the earth in six days.

After blasting a painful exit out of my family at age nineteen, I'd set about to deliberately change every major aspect of my life and consciousness. Rather than be separate from the world, as I'd been taught was right and good, I wanted to immerse myself in knowledge of the world—both in this universe and in other possible universes. After many years in graduate school, it was this yearning that finally led me into doctoral work in Future Studies, one of the last advanced generalist degrees left in the country. We studied such futuristic subjects as the shocks to the system brought about by a rapidly changing, technological society, alternative energy, and the possibility of living off-planet one day. Eventually, I went on to make documentaries and other television programs, mainly films about science, with scientists. My life was filled to the brim with intellectual friends, literature, scholarship, and art. So, twenty-six years later, how was it possible to find myself stranded again by my own cultural ignorance? Over the past quarter century of moving about freely in "the world," I could not consciously remember ever hearing the phrase *alien abduction phenomenon*. And the only vague association I had for the term *UFO* was a light, dismissive tone in someone's voice. It certainly wasn't a subject anyone I knew in Boston talked about.

Why I didn't automatically dismiss the ideas I was hearing for the first time on that Cape Cod beach I wouldn't understand until several years later. But I didn't dismiss them: I let the ideas sit and simmer. The patterns that began to emerge from the reports—certain details of the experiences repeated over and over by people who didn't know one another—stirred my sense of wonder. In some odd way, my earlier academic life in Future Studies had prepared me to take this thing on. If I was going to continue a friendship with Budd Hopkins—was going to continue to discuss a topic as outré as people abducted by UFOs—I knew what I had to do. I had to go back and look at the underpinnings, the background, of a topic that included people levitating up light beams, people "switched off," their memories seemingly manipulated from afar, and the on-again, off-again visibility of airborne objects larger than houses and even football stadiums. Just how solid was the ground that Budd was standing on? Was there any scientific evidence or theory that explained such "paranormal" events?

So it was a secret project of my own that I took on that fall of 1995. I didn't mention to anyone how I spent my evenings and weekends— reading books with titles that I hid in public: *UFOs Over the Americas* and *Flying Saucers: Top Secret*. Starting with some of the earliest literature from the 1950's and 1960's that dealt exclusively with craft sightings, I planned to methodically work my way toward my new friend's more recent abduction-related books.

I remember the night I made the decision to fully commit to the study of the UFO phenomenon. As I opened yet another book on the subject, I sensed that it was more than an autumn chill that was causing my discomfort. I suddenly recalled a favorite professor of mine who'd been fond of quoting British philosopher Alfred North Whitehead whenever one of her students felt confused and tangled up in the various threads of writing an essay or short story. "Just hold on to the idea and trust it," she'd say, "because the creative process, like a new relationship or any discovery, always begins in that " *'state of imaginative muddled suspense.'* " And after the chaos and discomfort, continued the unspoken promise, there would come the understanding, the synthesis and breakthrough.

I turned on the lamp and pulled a comforter around me as I started reading. Opening the yellowing pages of a 1955 book by retired Marine Corps major Donald Keyhoe called *Flying Saucer Conspiracy* that I'd borrowed from Budd, I set out on the first leg of my life's most unusual adventure yet. As far away from Normal, Illinois, as I'd come, I had a distinctly eerie feeling that there was somewhere else I was supposed to go—but where that place was, I didn't know. The danger was that the territory was so strange, so unknown, that I'd get lost. *In fact, plan on it,* I thought with a grim sort of humor. *Just count on it.*

In *Sight Unseen,* the science chapters record my own journey into the mazelike heart of the UFO phenomenon. Along the way, I share insights I've gained from holding up abduction reports to the light of contemporary science. By taking a look at both our current and emerging sciences, we can begin to understand how UFOs seem to exist in a realm that is hard-edged and material part of the time and immaterial and ghostly at other times. Although some explanations for aspects of the UFO phenomenon come directly from mainstream science—such as military stealth technology and the limitations of our own human senses—most of the possibilities we'll explore are so cutting-edge that the public is not yet aware they exist in the objectively tested, documented world of science. Some of the new technologies and discoveries that we'll examine might have seemed magical even ten years ago. They include:

- levitation of objects, including live frogs and balls
- laser light beams that lift objects

- the dropping of the genetic barrier between species
- transplanting a specific behavior from one species to another
- the development of targeted gene transfer—implanting a salmon gene into a tomato, for example
- teleportation achieved in the laboratory, not on *Star Trek*
- stopping light in its speedy tracks before sending it on its way again
- the real possibility of time travel
- the probability that we are surrounded by an infinite number of other universes.

I hope that the exploration of these and other new discoveries will help to create common ground between scientists and people intrigued by UFOs. Although it often seems so, this is not an impossible goal. After all, as psychoanalyst Salvatore Guido, a fellow futurist of sorts, once said: "Nature does not deceive or surreptitiously change its mind: we can count on the eventuality that it will not secretly change the rules of the game. It is only our knowlege that is limited. In the quest for scientific knowledge, the resistance to be overcome is on the side of the scientist."[7]

PART I

UNSEEN

Chapter 1

THE ALIEN ABDUCTORS:
HIDING—AND SOMETIMES SHOWING OFF

WHEN DETAILS OF THE FIRST thoroughly investigated UFO abduction report—the now famous Betty and Barney Hill case—came to wide public attention in 1966, researchers made several deductions about the aliens' modus operandi. Since the incident occurred at night in a sparsely populated area of New Hampshire's White Mountains, it was assumed that the aliens had selected the time and location in order to reduce the chance of accidental witnesses. The full story of the Hills' abduction story has been told elsewhere and need not be repeated here, but for our purposes it is important to point out that in 1961, the year the incident actually occurred, investigators thought of it as a kind of cosmic commando raid in which speed and maximum concealment were central concerns.[1] And when I later read about it in John Fuller's classic account and eventually accepted its validity, I agreed with this simple, military-type analysis.

Similar UFO abductions, if they happened at all, were most likely to be extremely rare, investigators later hypothesized, almost always taking place at night, in rural settings, so that they could be carried out unobserved. And among those who took the case seriously, most assumed that the Hills' abduction might well be the only such incident that had ever occurred. Apart from this unlucky couple who were in the wrong place at the wrong time, human beings were probably safe from such experiences.

As it turned out, all of these assumptions were wrong.

By the 1970's, as a few more abduction cases were reported and investigated, another pattern emerged that radically changed our thinking. In these accounts, several abductees reported that when the UFO occupants first approached them, people in their immediate vicinity suddenly appeared to have been "switched off" and put into a comalike state. These switched-off individuals were often described as sitting or standing rigidly in the postures they had been in when the aliens arrived on the scene. Their eyes were open, but they were obviously not registering what was taking place. Later, when the abduction ended, these potential witnesses began to move normally, recalling nothing of the incident but often aware that, mysteriously, several hours—of which they had no memory—had elapsed.

Thus we had a major new factor to consider in the aliens' ability to maintain the covert nature of their operations. They apparently possessed a technology by which potential witnesses could be prevented from seeing UFO occupants and observing the abduction of someone in their immediate vicinity—even someone traveling in the same automobile. As an example of this newly discovered factor, one highly credible woman I once worked with, a mother of two and by profession an obstetrical nurse, described an experience she had had as a young student. In 1973, "Karen" was at a small party with about ten other young people, some of whom were also student nurses. Karen recalls that she was seated cross-legged on the couch, talking with her friends, relaxing, and listening to music. Though the young people were drinking beer, none of the student nurses were intoxicated.

In Karen's very next conscious memory she was in her car, driving along a local road just after sunrise, completely confused and disoriented. She stopped at a coffee shop and went in to try to calm herself, but the more she pondered the mystery of the nearly five missing hours, the more upset she became.

Later, when she was in her apartment and feeling less frightened, she called a friend who had been present at the party. He asked where she had gone. "I looked around and you weren't there. Nobody remembers seeing you leave. We figured you had just slipped out and gone home."

Some ten years later, Karen read *Missing Time*—an apt title for her disturbing experience—and wrote to me. We met in my studio on Cape Cod for a hypnotic regression session to explore the incidents of that night. We began with the party itself, when Karen sat cross-legged on the couch. Suddenly she felt herself begin to move involuntarily. Frightened and confused, she floated forward off the couch with her legs still folded in front of her. She tried to grab something to stop herself but realized that she could not move her arms. She was paralyzed and helpless.

Though she could not turn her head, her vision was unimpaired. All of the other people in the room were absolutely frozen in fixed positions. No one spoke. There was an eerie, total silence. She floated to, and then *through,* the closed front door. Several small alien beings were waiting outside and accompanied her into a UFO hovering above the street, and the abduction commenced.

UFO investigators have received hundreds of such reports in the past few decades, incidents in which abductees have described friends, family members, or even passing strangers as seeming to be switched off in just this manner, unaware of the abduction that is taking place in their presence, but often aware of an unrecalled period of missing time. Some people have noted particular physical consequences to having been "frozen" for an hour or so. In one case, "Ann," a young college student, was apparently switched off while her companion was abducted. Afterward, when things returned to normal and Ann could move, her eyes hurt so badly that her contact lenses felt like sandpaper. As she removed the lenses and lubricated her eyes, she wondered why this painful condition had developed so suddenly, seemingly in an instant. Years later, in separate hypnosis sessions, we explored the experience shared by Ann and her companion and she learned for the first time that she had been switched off—unmoving and unblinking—for an hour or so. Our eyes are naturally lubricated by a layer of moisture and the regular blinking action of the eyelids, so when that process was stopped, painful dryness resulted. This same condition has been reported to me by a number of other switched-off wearers of contact lenses.

To complicate the issue of abduction concealment even further, in later years a pair of extremely unusual UFO abductions have come to light that cast an interesting light on the patterns we have been considering. In these incidents, witnesses were not switched off but in fact saw and remembered the abduction—or at least certain parts of its basic scenario. For some reason, in these cases the UFO occupants made virtually no attempt to hide their activities and in one instance— the Linda Cortile case of 1989—apparently arranged things deliberately so that the abduction would be seen by numerous people, including several important political figures.[2]

Earlier, in the 1975 Travis Walton case, seven young men in a double-cab truck were returning from work in a remote area near Snowflake, Arizona, when they sighted a large UFO hovering above the treetops off to one side of the road.[3] The driver stopped and Walton, a passenger, jumped out for a closer look. As the men in the truck yelled for him to get back in, they saw a blue beam of light shoot from the craft and hit Walton, lifting him off the ground and knocking him backward. Terrified, the men drove off, only to collect themselves after a few minutes and return to search for their comrade. Walton had disappeared.

Frightened and in a state of near panic, Walton's fellow workers reported the incident to the police and a fruitless search was begun. Ultimately the witnesses were tested by an experienced polygraph operator and none showed any signs of deception. Five days later Travis Walton returned, dehydrated and disoriented, having been deposited by the UFO beside a nearby highway. Eventually he, too, passed a polygraph test about his abduction. Two decades later, in a reinvestigation of the case, the men were once again given polygraph tests. All passed.

What is important about the Walton case for our purposes is that it demonstrates what might happen if abductions were regularly observed and consciously recalled by independent witnesses, especially close friends or family members. Panic, terror, and an immediate call for help would be their predictable responses—all of which run counter to the aliens' apparent need to operate covertly.

The Linda Cortile case, the subject of my book *Witnessed: The True Story of the Brooklyn Bridge UFO Abductions,* is an even more important instance of an abduction seen by numerous witnesses who also were not switched off but were able to watch Linda—the abductee—and three small alien figures float out the window of her twelfth-floor apartment and up into a hovering UFO. The story is extremely complex, with independent witnesses at six separate locations seeing all or part of the initial abduction events. Furthermore, each of these witnesses has described *other* witnesses to this abduction who were either switched off and do not remember the incident or, for one reason or another, have not wished either to contact me or to make themselves known. (Humiliation and ridicule, debunkers' basic methods of intimidating witnesses, are extremely effective.)

So we can assume that even though this incident took place around three A.M. and lasted only a minute or so, there must have been many people—perhaps hundreds—who also saw a truly "impossible" sight. Though it is difficult to put ourselves in the place of such witnesses, many rationalizations for not calling the police or the news media present themselves. One woman I interviewed, "Janet Kimball," was driving across the Brooklyn Bridge when the craft turned on all its lights. She said that as the clearly visible UFO hovered above the building, shining down a bluish-white beam of light and levitating Linda Cortile and the aliens up into it, she thought she must be watching a movie being made. *These are special effects,* Janet thought to herself. "Someone's always shooting a movie in New York," she told me. "It was so real, it looked fake."

The Linda Cortile case and the Travis Walton abduction suggest that the switching off of potential witnesses to conceal abductions is perhaps not always a viable tactic. But these two cases surely demonstrate that if people are allowed to observe and recall what they have seen, the basic alien strategy of concealment is dramatically undercut. As I stated earlier, I have investigated hundreds of reports from New York and other large cities, including Washington, D.C., London, Los Angeles, Chicago, Paris, Istanbul, and Rio de Janeiro—cases in which abductions were carried out successfully and covertly, even though there were hundreds, perhaps thousands, of potential witnesses.

And so we come to the first question we must try to answer: If we accept the premise that it is preferable—if not always possible—for UFO occupants to carry out abductions covertly, by what methods do they effectively conceal their frequent abductions of city residents? How do operations that normally should be witnessed by thousands remain unseen?

Chapter 2

MISSING CHILDREN, A THREE–STORY FALL, AND AN AIR FORCE FIRE TRUCK

L ET US BEGIN TO ATTEMPT to answer the question posed at the end of the last chapter by examining the following three cases, which demonstrate some of the perplexing issues faced by skeptics, debunkers, and open-minded investigators alike. Beyond any doubt, a major aspect of the abduction mystery lies in such vivid *initial* accounts as these, all three of which preceded by decades any associations the witnesses made between these experiences and UFO phenomena. In fact, the incidents occurred in 1948, 1957, and 1974, respectively, when almost no one was familiar with what we have come to know as the signature patterns of the UFO abduction phenomenon.

At the time these mysterious incidents occurred, the participants could make no logical sense of them. Therefore, each account eventually became part of the family lore, told, retold, puzzled over, and discussed again and again by close friends and family members. Twenty, thirty, even forty years passed before any of those involved sensed that these experiences might be connected to the UFO abduction phenomenon and consequently got in touch with me. As we shall see, the factors that caused them finally to make that association vary from case to case, but the central issue was their belated recognition of clear-cut UFO sightings and alien and "missing time" encounters later in their lives—literal, anomalous events that seemed connected with their earlier experiences.

The reasons for the crucial importance of these early recollections are obvious. First, none of the witnesses can be accused of having invented a UFO report for personal gain or notoriety, because, in addition to their current insistence upon complete anomymity, these original accounts had no UFO component: They were simply unexplainable experiences. Decades later, all of them remain truly bizarre, and debunkers—whom I define as true believers in the nonexistence of UFOs—are hard-pressed to come up with any plausible, mundane theory to explain them away.

Eventually, I investigated each of the following three cases through extensive witness interviews and hypnotic regression sessions. (Because these encounters took place decades ago, on-site visits and the search for additional witnesses were rejected as unlikely to turn up relevant information, as they had in the recent Linda Cortile case.) The hypnosis sessions and witness interviews provided coherent explanations for what happened to the abductees during the "missing time" portions of their recollections—explanations that are fully consistent with what we now know about the UFO abduction phenomenon. However, in none of the following accounts will I dwell extensively upon the hypnotically retrieved memories, because much of that information is not immediately relevant to the issues we are exploring here. The strangeness of these experiences is fully revealed by what each witness remembered consciously from the time each incident first occurred.

A Three-Story Fall

"Joan" is a forceful, active woman in her late seventies. She is clear of mind and perceptive in her judgments. Her daughter, "Molly," a widow and an attractive redhead in her middle fifties, has had numerous UFO experiences, as have other members of her family. I met Molly in 1993 when she wrote to me for the first time as a result of reading my book *Intruders.* In her letter she decribed a virtual lifetime of anomalous events involving herself and other family members: strange figures in her room, episodes of extended physical paralysis, "missing time," and other experiences typical of UFO abductions. Significantly she did not mention her childhood fall-from-the-window incident until I asked if she remembered any other odd occurrences from her early childhood. Perhaps because she and her brother were so young at the time, until that moment she had never thought about the window experience in context with the other more obviously UFO-related anomalies.

The incident of interest here occurred in a suburban neighborhood called Price Hill in Cincinnati, Ohio, in the summer of 1948, only one year after the first major UFO wave in the United States and thirteen years before the landmark Betty and Barney Hill abduction. At the time Molly was four and her brother, "Danny," was six. Joan had put the two children down for their afternoon naps, when something—a sound, a feeling—caused her to check their bedroom. They were not there. The window was open. With a sense of panic Joan ran downstairs to search for them. Forty-two years later, as Carol and I sat in Molly's dining room sipping coffee, she and her mother spoke to us about the experience:

> Joan: Well, I can date it, because I was expecting my fourth child at the time. That's Bill. I had taken the other three to the doctor's for their general checkup and they turned out real good, thank goodness. We came home and I told Danny and Molly to lay down—I put the baby in the crib—because they were to take naps. They were on the second floor of the building. I had to go change the baby . . . she had to have her didie rinsed out because in those days we weren't privileged to have throwaway Pampers. All the people now that complain, shame on them. They don't know what work is. Anyhow, I had to go into the bathroom and put the didie in to soak so that I could get it ready for the laundry, when I heard something or . . . had a feeling, I don't know what, and I went to inspect. There wasn't anybody in the bedroom, just the screen was gone out of the window and there were no kids in the bedroom. I went flying downstairs.
>
> I went outside and there at the foot of the basement steps were the children. Danny and Molly. It all happened so darn fast. I saw Molly and I scooped her up and went tearing upstairs. There was a tailor shop underneath us. The tailor realized something was radically wrong [and] came to see. He scooped up Danny and said, "Don't go all the way upstairs! The lady downstairs will take care of

your other kids and I'll take you to the doctor." And he did, he piled us into his car, because I didn't drive at that time, and took us back to the doctor's. The kids weren't crying. They didn't seem hurt, but they weren't moving. They fell out of the second-story window down into the basement. They had fallen on cement steps, you would say three floors down, from the second floor, past the first floor, down into the basement. Onto cement steps! Not just flat cement, cement steps! Danny was on the bottom, Molly was on top of him. They landed on the bottom portion of the cement steps. They fell on something jagged. If you had been there, you would have said their angels took care of them. You certainly would have.

Anyhow, the doctor examined them thoroughly from the top of their heads to the bottom of their toes, even wiggling them. Not a bump, a scratch, or a bruise. He said, "There's nothing wrong with these kids. They might have gotten shook, that's all." He said, "How are you, Danny? Do you hurt anywhere?" [Danny] said no. And so we were all brought home and went on about our business and I thank God for my babies.

I asked Danny what happened, and he was delighted to tell me. "Mama, there was a plane going overhead and I had to see it. Molly said, 'Let me see, let me see, let me see,'" and she pushed in on top of him and she pushed so good that they both went flying out. He wanted to see that plane. Molly remembers that plane, that big airplane. Danny was crazy about planes. So was she 'cause Danny was. This plane was low enough they could see it. A big silver plane. I never heard any airplane.

When I found them, they were not screaming, they were not crying. They were down, like they had the wind knocked out of them, I guess, would be the best way to describe it. And I just scooped Molly up and then I was shocked, my God, there's Danny too! And then the tailor came and he scooped Danny up. And then he said, "Agnes, will you watch her two little ones?" and Agnes said, "Yeah, go on and go." So he took us to the doctor's and Dr. Mackay checked them—he had checked them earlier, and so now he checked them again—from the top of their heads to the bottom of their toes. He said, "They do not even have bumps or bruises." I was blessed. I firmly believe that their guardian angels were with them.

When I picked Molly up, when I had her in my arms, she didn't say anything, she wasn't gasping, she was breathing normally. When I asked them, "Why did you fall out the window? What happened? Why were you . . ." and Danny said, "I had to see the airplane," and Molly said, "I had to see the airplane too. Me too."

BH: *Did the doctor feel there was something really unusual about the fact that they had fallen three floors onto cement and weren't bruised?*

Joan: What he said was, "They either kill themselves or they get up and dust themselves off and go." He was old-fashioned, he was wonderful. His name was Mackay, but whenever there were sirens that went past his office, he left and he was the first one along with the fire department to any dire emergency, be it a fire, be it a baby born, be it somebody that needs a hospital. But he didn't find a bump, a scratch, or a bruise on my babies. No matter what anybody says, I fully believe in angels and I believe their angels took care of them.

At this point in our interview, Molly brought in more coffee and joined us to add her recollections to her mother's:

Molly: I don't remember falling out the window. I remember we were looking up, trying to look up at it. It got kind of dark out and we were looking up at a silver-colored plane or whatever. My brother remembers bits and pieces of it and now he doesn't even want to talk about it. He said he remembers this big silver airplane that was above the house. He said it was huge but the thing that caught his eye was the fact that it was practically on the house, and it was huge, and you just don't see airplanes down that low. It wasn't noisy at all. It was straight up . . . it wasn't like you look out the window and there it is over there. It was *up*. It was over the house and it also put a shadow over the house. The sun was out and then there was a shadow over the house and we were trying to look up, my brother and I.

I don't remember falling out of the window: I remember going out the window, but not falling. We were floating. Nobody saw us fall out the window. Nobody. And it was daytime. The sun was out except for when it got cloudy when the plane was overhead. It was just dark where we were. The sun was still out. As a matter of fact, the sun was so bright, it was, like, blinding. It killed your eyes.

The next thing I remember, we were on the ground and somebody was picking us up . . . and I do remember you were there, Mom, and I remember the cat. We had a cat that had babies that day. I remember the cat was totally traumatized. I don't remember the cat being under us, although Mom said the cat was under us or near us or whatever.

Joan: Not under you.

Molly: No, if I fell on the cat she would have been squashed. I was on top of my brother. Down at the bottom of the cellar steps. There's, like, a square at the bottom, you know, with the wall.

BH: *Do you remember the pain when you hit?*

Molly: No. No pain. I don't remember hitting. My mother and a man were there. I remember that. Exactly who picked me up, I don't remember. I didn't say anything because I *couldn't* say anything. I guess I was shocked or whatever. I couldn't say anything, couldn't move, couldn't do anything.

BH: *Did you feel the wind was knocked out of you? And were you crying?*

Molly: No. Neither was Danny. Neither one of us moved or cried or did anything. I couldn't talk. I remember trying to talk to my mother, but I couldn't talk. I didn't feel the wind was knocked out of me. I was breathing normally. I just couldn't move or talk. I had no pain, I wasn't hurt in any way. I remember when somebody picked me up, my leg hit the side of the wall. It was kind of rough concrete. I remember it dragging on my leg a little bit. It kind of scratched my leg. But I think we were in shock, my brother and I. Mom, don't you think we were in shock?

Joan: It's possible. But I still remember Dr. Mackay and what he had to say. He checked each one of you—you first and then Danny—and he said, "There is absolutely nothing wrong with these children. These kids, when they have a traumatic experience like this, they're either dead or they pick themselves up, dust themselves off, and go on their way." They didn't cry, either one of them. They didn't complain. I was the one who was terribly upset and got to the doctor's as fast as I could and was grateful to God when the doctor said what he did.

BH: *Do you think there is any possibility that the children could have slipped out of the house and run downstairs?*

Joan: Absolutely none! They would have had to get past me in the first place and in the second place, to find Danny laying at the bottom and Molly on top of him, no, that's not possible.

Molly: Not to mention we used to have a high latch on the apartment door that we tried to reach. We couldn't open it. You would have to unlock the door in order for us to get out, to go downstairs. We tried sometimes with the chair. We'd pull it over and try to unlock it but we couldn't reach it.

We were three stories high, and then we went down in the cellar, down the concrete steps to the basement. And the cellar steps weren't directly under the window. Say, here's the building [gestures, indicating about an eight-foot difference]. Here's the window. The cellar steps were over here, not under the window. The window was over here. But we ended up down at the bottom of the cellar steps.

And I just couldn't move, I couldn't, couldn't move. They took us to the doctor's because they thought there was something really wrong. But I didn't have any injuries at all. None! Danny didn't, either. The neighbors couldn't figure out why we weren't even bruised. The doctor said we should have been dead.

BH: *How did your mother ever explain any of this to herself?*

Molly: She didn't. She just accepted the fact that we were alive, and thanked God.

In the course of our investigation, hypnotic regression sessions with Molly revealed the chronological details of the window experience: the childrens' abduction into a huge UFO—the "big silver airplane" that cast the building into shadow. Molly recalled floating out of the bedroom window into a bright beam of light and then levitating, along with her brother, up into the hovering UFO. She remembered the appearance of the examining area, the demeanor of the aliens, and many other details.

However, for our immediate purposes, we will focus upon a few highly significant abduction patterns present in the two womens' *pre-hypnotic* recollections. First of all, it is highly unlikely for two children to fall three stories onto jagged cement steps without sustaining even a bruise. As a general rule of thumb it is assumed that anyone falling three stories has only a 50-percent chance of *living through it*, and the absence of broken bones, internal injuries, or even bruises after such a drop is unthinkable. Molly initially remembered *floating* out the window but had no sense either of falling or of hitting the cement steps. And to make an accidental fall even more unlikely, the cellar steps were seven or eight feet away from the area directly under the window. People, even children, do not fall diagonally, unless they are propelled by some force.

There are many cases in the abduction literature in which individuals are floated out of their second-story bedrooms and later deposited on the ground or even several miles away. It is a familiar pattern. Automobiles and their passengers have been lifted up and put down in the middle of a field or on a different highway, sometimes gently, sometimes heavily. In one English case a police car was even replaced on the road wheels up, top down, and severely damaged although the constable abductee inside was unhurt.

In another case that I suspect was a hidden abduction, unremembered by the abductee and as yet uninvestigated, a small boy apparently "fell" from a sixth-floor apartment window onto a fenced-in and padlocked cement courtyard, and though he exhibited a few small bruises, he was absolutely unhurt. After reading about this event in a newspaper, a neurosurgeon friend of mine flatly declared, "He didn't fall. Period. He would have died." In the context of familiar UFO abduction patterns, however, this well-documented incident—and Molly and Danny's painless diagonal descent onto the concrete—make sense.

Another ubiquitous abduction pattern appears in Molly and Joan's mutually corroborative testimony indicating that the children were paralyzed when they were found at the foot of the cellar steps. In Molly's words, "I just couldn't say anything, couldn't move, I couldn't do anything." Joan stated that when she found them, "the kids weren't crying. They didn't seem hurt, but they weren't moving." This kind of (apparently) alien-instituted paralysis gradually wears off, but it is one more example of a by now well-documented abduction pattern.

Finally we come to another, even more "impossible" situation raised by the childrens' experience. This inescapable aspect of the abduction phenomenon is almost invariably skirted, denied, or ignored by abduction researchers because it presents such outright challenges to both common sense and the basic laws of physics. Simply stated: How can such an event take place in a busy commercial neighborhood and not be seen?

Molly and Danny's abduction took place on a sunny afternoon—presumably in the summer, because the window was open during naptime—and the buildings on the street were close together. According to Joan, among the modest homes and small apartment houses of their neighborhood, the ground floors often contained shops and commercial businesses—a fruit and vegetable store, a tailor shop, and so on. Obviously, within the city of Cincinnati, where there are stores such as this in and around small apartment houses, there are customers, traffic, pedestrians, activity. In short, there are hundreds of potential witnesses to a UFO abduction.

Molly said that just above the building was a huge silver craft flying or hovering so low that it cast their building into a shadow which lasted long enough for the two children to get to the window to look up. Obviously, had it actually been a large, low-flying airplane, its house-darkening shadow would have flashed by in a split second.

But Molly's description contained yet another, rather different anomaly. "The sun was out," she said, "except for when it got cloudy when the plane was overhead. . . . As a matter of fact, the sun was so bright, it was, like, blinding. It killed your eyes." In the middle of a normal sunny day, abnormally blinding bright light such as she describes is yet another frequently reported abduction pattern. This extraordinary and unnatural light is apparently emitted by the UFO, usually in the form of a beam.

Joan said that she never heard the "airplane," which should have been audible if it had been a normal craft flying as low as the children reported. Also, she apparently did not see either the shadow over the building or the blindingly intense light. None of the neighbors, shopkeepers, or passersby seem to have reported seeing or hearing the huge low-flying "airplane" or seeing a shadow or the intense light, and no one reported seeing the children fall (or float) out of the window.

One is immediately tempted to say that together these facts prove that the incident never happened the way Molly, her brother, and her mother claim. The absence of corroborating testimony from others who were at the scene—in broad daylight, in a city neighborhood—must mean that the story is a hoax, a lie, a joint hallucination—anything but a real event. But in the light of more than fifty years of consistent reports of "impossible" UFO maneuvers, coupled with supporting radar returns and photographic evidence, should we not be asking ourselves if the answer to this enigma is nothing more than another example of an alien technology so advanced that the UFO, its shadow, its light, and the floating children *could not be seen* by any witnesses in the area? Is it possible that for a short time, Molly, Danny, and the hovering craft were all temporarily invisible?

The Missing Children

In 1990 I was contacted by "Marianne," a resident of Queens, New York, and shortly thereafter began to investigate a number of partially recalled abduction experiences dating back to her childhood. Marianne is a very slight, delicate, almost doll-like woman now in her early fifties, a divorcee with one child, a son, who had recently graduated from college. She speaks with a quick, nervous quality, laughs easily, and, though far from gregarious, has long maintained close friendships with several men and women. Currently she lives in New York City in an apartment with her aged mother, who requires extensive at-home care.

One of the experiences we explored through hypnotic regression concerned an abduction that took place when she was seven or eight years old. She and her best friend, "Angie," a little girl who lived down the street, were abducted simultaneously in what emerged as a very traumatic childhood experience. It is important to note that Marianne mentioned the incident at Angie's house only after I asked, in an extensive early interview, if she had ever been lost as a child. Until that moment, she said, she had never considered this incident to be a possible unrecalled UFO abduction.

The following is Marianne's account of what she remembered consciously, before hypnosis, about that incident:

Marianne: I was on my block in Fresh Meadows, a residential area with private homes. I was at my friend's, which is on the other side of the street and about five houses up. We were in the basement—which is the way we usually ended up playing in the house—and coloring pictures. Craypas, as a matter of fact, is what we used to use, and I was coloring my favorite scene at the time that I colored over and over, sort of an island tropical scene on a beach, palm trees, very bright oranges and yellows, sunset time in the sky, and I usually tried to throw in a few little birds up in the sky as well.

We were there probably at least three or four times a week, in the basement. This was during the summer, school was out, so we spent a lot of time together. If we were not outside playing, then we would be usually in the same room, in the basement of her house. It was a partially finished basement made into a combination playroom-lounge-bar area. There was a couch, a small coffee table in front of the couch. There were linoleum floors, if I remember correctly, but there was a rug under the area where we would sit by the couch. There was a bar area over on the other side of the room, a TV, and sometimes they had a Ping-Pong table set up down there as well.

Angie had some toys there. She kept a lot of things up in her room, but she did have some things that she played with more often in the basement. Some dolls, building things, games, board games—that sort of thing would be kept in the basement. And we were sitting there on this day, a very common thing for us to be doing, sitting there drawing the pictures. I remember we were kneeling or sitting on the floor, not on the couch, coloring on the coffee table, and I was drawing my same picture of the island.

I'd say we were there probably a couple of hours. At some point—

it was around, I think, late afternoon, probably a little before dinner-time—we decided to go outside. So we went up the steps from the basement, went out the back door, which was off an enclosed porch area that they built on the house, and walked down the driveway. As we got down the driveway, we saw Angie's mother across the street. My mother was standing on the other side of the street, and several neighbors from up the block were standing and there was a police car parked out front. Then we noticed the police were walking back and forth and talking to some of the people. We came down the drive-way, and I believe it was Angie who asked her mother what was going on. Her mother looked absolutely shocked when we started walking down the driveway. When she turned around and finally saw us, she started carrying on almost hysterically, asked us where we had been the whole time. We told her: In the basement, where we'd been all afternoon. I don't recall the exact words or the exact conversation, but she swore that we were not in the house, that she had checked the house—the basement and the whole rest of the house—and then had called the police. She thought we had left for some reason without telling her and taken off somewhere.

They had checked the little park that was about a block and a half around the corner from where we lived, a little neighborhood park. There had been some talk of a man that had been hanging around the park recently at that time who seemed to be a little suspicious, and a few of the neighbors had reported him. And I think they were a little afraid that possibly we had run into foul play if we had gone over to the park. The thing that struck me as strange, too, is neither one of us were the types of kids who would take off anywhere with-out at least telling our parents or even asking permission to go. So it seemed odd to us that Angie's mother would have even thought we left the house. But everyone swore up and down that she checked the entire house.

I would imagine that the police checked the house as well when they were called in, and she swore we were not in the house. We were never able to figure it out. It always struck us as odd because we had been in the basement the whole afternoon until we decided to come out. It was getting near dinnertime and we walked down the driveway to find this scene out there.

The police looked surprised also. I remember the one police officer asked us, "Did you go anywhere?" and we said, "No, we've been in the basement the whole time." At which point I recall the officer—there were two of them at the time—kind of exchanging looks between them and looking at Angie's mother, and I think they were wondering a little about her mother, quite frankly, and why she couldn't find us in the house. I think, after they had questioned us, our reactions of being totally puzzled let them know that we were not lying about where we had been. They figured we had been in the house. None of us could figure it out. My mother sort of chalked it off as Angie's mother being overly alarmed or just not really checking the house and saying she did.

But the incident has been brought up a number of times over the years as one of the things when neighbors get together, or people in the family get together, and talk about odd incidents. Every so often this will come up: "You remember the time you kids were in the house and Angie's mother called the police swearing you were gone?"

BH: *Do you think that anybody else searched the house besides Angie's mother?*

Marianne: Well, to my recollection, her father was working, so he wasn't home during all of this. I believe Angie's mother was the only one in the house. Angie had a brother but he was not home that day. In fact, I believe that Joey went to camp during the summer. I would assume the police did check through the house. I can't imagine a mother calling and saying her child and friend are missing and the police not checking the house to see where they were before they took off someplace else.

We never moved, we never went anywhere. We had been known to be able to sit for hours doing the same thing. Then we got up, we walked out the back door, we walked down the driveway to this scene of people trying to figure out where we were. I was only a seven- or eight-year-old child. I would not have wanted to say anything bad about my friend's mother, but I was thinking it. I believe my mother was thinking it as well, and probably the other neighbors. We just thought her mother was a bit of a flake for having done this.

Later, I brought it up once or twice with friends. If you were sitting around, just talking about odd incidents in your life, this would be one of a few incidents I had in my life that I would bring up and say, "Yeah, I had this strange thing happen to me," that kind of thing, yeah. I always wondered how someone could check a house for two kids and not see them there in the basement the whole time they were there. I just found it odd.

BH: *When did you first connect this with a possible UFO incident?*

Marianne: Actually, not until many, many years later. Until you asked if I had ever been lost, I had never made any connections with it.

BH: *Tell me a little about the neighborhood. On a summer afternoon, were there other people, children, out on the street?*

Marianne: At the time, there were quite a few kids on the block. Most of us were approximately the same age, give or take a year or so. Several of us played together on a regular basis—in the summer, pretty much every day. At least two or three of us would be together. The kids were home from school. It was a quiet area, but there certainly would have been people going in and out, cars going down the block. It was sunny, warm, very bright outside. A typical summer day.

BH: *Do you think a UFO could have flown over the house and not been seen?*

Marianne: I would highly doubt that [laughs]. I would highly doubt that. Somebody would have had to see something, yes.

As with Molly and her brother's falling, unhurt, some thirty feet onto concrete steps, Marianne and Angie's claim that they never left the basement playroom—despite Angie's mother's frantic search—also strains credulity. The place the mother would have searched first—

the girls' habitual downstairs playspace, was empty. One can easily picture her calling for the children, her worry deepening as she searched
the house from top to bottom. And one can easily imagine the panic
that led her, finally, to phone the police for help.

Common sense tells us that no one searching a restricted area for
suddenly missing children—or dogs, cats, friends, relatives, whom-
ever—does so without calling out their names with increasing agita-
tion. But Angie and Marianne claimed that they neither left their play
area nor heard anyone—mother, neighbors, or police—calling for them.

Under hypnosis, Marianne, to her later surprise, recalled a complex
abduction in which the two children were separately floated out of the
house and up into a hovering UFO, a bizarre but otherwise logical
explanation for their disappearance and their inability to hear anyone
calling for them. The content of her hypnotic recall of their joint abduction conforms to the familiar patterns of UFO abduction experiences
worldwide but need not concern us here, though Marianne's recollections of the way the encounter began and ended are worth quoting:

> I recall a feeling that kind of came over the room, and at some point
> Angie not being there. I assumed she left to go upstairs to go to the
> bathroom or something like that. But I started to get nervous. . . .
> There was a different feeling in the air and I recall something com-
> ing from the area that was not finished . . . where the boiler and the
> washers would have been, where I hardly ever had reason to go, but
> there seemed to be something that changed in the room, some kind
> of a difference in the lighting.

Marianne was then floated up the basement stairs and in a few
moments found herself inside the craft. Her account of her later return
to the basement playroom is particularly interesting:

> I recall what happened when I came back to the house, which is
> where it got really odd, because at some point I was actually caught
> somewhere in the actual structure of the house, the wood from
> where you would go from the kitchen, the top of the basement
> stairs, down the stairs to the basement—I was caught somewhere in
> that structure of wood, coming through the wall as if I would be

coming back down. From that point there was some sort of a jump to being back down in the basement, where we had last remembered sitting, coloring, and then it became quite normal again. Angie was there. And the only thing that I remember thinking at that time was that we were now going to go upstairs and leave the house.

And then we were walking down the driveway, to be met by this scene of Angie's mother upset and hysterical and my mother across the street, other neighbors on the block, and the police.

There are two alternative non-UFO explanations for Marianne and Angie's alleged disappearance that must be considered: first, that they never vanished, but instead were hiding from Angie's mother for some reason and only came out of hiding when the police arrived and the situation became more serious. The problem with this theory is that when Marianne first told me about their disappearance, she was a grown woman with a college-age son. It is hardly likely that she would still be afraid to tell the truth about a childhood prank involving her friend's mother. And why, if she *were* afraid of revealing their prank, would she have mentioned the incident to me in the first place?

Next, there is the possibility that she invented this story out of whole cloth as part of a subtle collection of lies designed to convince me that she was a UFO abductee. Over the years I have investigated ten abduction incidents Marianne experienced at different periods in her life, several of which involved other people whom I was able to interview separately. Through all of these investigations I never found a reason to doubt her essential truthfulness, nor could I imagine a plausible motive for a hoax in which she would have had to enlist and train several confederates. Marianne has never sought media attention and has never seemed to be anything but genuinely frightened by her UFO experiences.

But if the two little girls did vanish and were floated up into a hovering UFO, there is, once again, another, more central issue we must consider: the time and location of their abduction. As in the case of Molly and Danny, this incident took place in the middle of a summer afternoon, not in an isolated area but on a street where children played, automobiles passed by, and undoubtedly an occasional pedestrian walked along the sidewalk. When I asked Marianne if a UFO could have flown over the house without being seen, she had said, "I would highly doubt that. [She laughs.] I would highly doubt that. Somebody would have had to see something."

And so we come back to the problem we faced with Molly and Danny. At such a time of day, in such a location, the UFO should have been seen and heard by scores of people—and not only the hovering UFO but also, as in the case of Molly and Danny, the levitating children. But again, because of these circumstances, we must ask ourselves if the craft and the ascending children were actually "seeable." Or, by some as yet unknown technology, were they temporarily invisible? Is temporary invisibility or an extraordinary kind of "cloaking" capability the means by which such abductions take place unobserved, even in the midst of a large city?

Dennis, B.J., and the Air Force Fire Truck

In 1974, at the age of twenty-one, "Dennis" was a recent enlistee in the United States Air Force. He was stationed at a North American airbase where, though the war in Vietnam had recently ended, young fighter pilots were still being trained for combat.

Dennis had been assigned to a fire and rescue unit, part of the extensive support and service system that exists at any airbase. But unlike the crash equipment standing by at most major commercial airports, his unit was actually called out from time to time when student pilots inevitably made errors landing or taking off.

At the time of this disturbing 1974 incident, Dennis's young wife had just left left him, a situation that made his military friendships, such as that with B.J., even more important to him.

> Dennis: On this particular night I was assigned to a first-response team with my sergeant, B.J. We were good friends. B.J. had been in 'Nam and was about six or eight years older than me. We got along real well. We drove up to the flight line in our truck and parked in position. We set out our gear, our boots and stuff, and arranged them on the ground outside the doors of the truck so that we could get into them in a hurry if we had to. It was routine.

I was sitting on the right side of the front seat and B.J. was on the driver's side. We sat there awhile, watching the takeoffs and landings, when I suddenly kind of woke up, leaning against B.J. B.J. says, "What happened?" I say, "I don't know." I felt really sick. I vomited out the door, and some of it got on my boots.

We realized we were late. We were supposed to be back to check in a couple of hours earlier because the landing and takeoff practice was over. We didn't know what had happened, but knew we had to haul ass.

Our gear was scattered around. We picked up our boots and stuff and threw them in the truck. I remember that one of my shoes was off. My shirt was buttoned wrong and I was still feeling sick. Everything was kind of a mess. I don't think my pants were zipped or my belt buckled. There was a little blood from my nose.

B.J. was driving, fast. I remember I lit two cigarettes on the way in. . . . I was smoking one and had another one in my hand. I was shaking. I threw one of the cigarettes out the window.

When we got back and parked the truck, we went inside and that's when I noticed I was wearing B.J.'s shirt and he was wearing mine. I looked down and saw his name tag on my shirt. I swear I have no idea how that happened. He had my name tag on his shirt. We didn't even talk about it, we just switched shirts and went to bed. It was just too weird.

The next morning, I remember, I woke up and just sat on my bed and fucking cried. I didn't even go to roll call. They asked me to go to roll call and I said, I can't. I sat there and cried until about nine o'clock, well after our flight. . . . Our shift . . . had left. I don't know if they wrote that up or not, but I remember talking to . . . [the civilian] head of that shop . . . after that. He wanted to know if it was because of my wife leaving or what, and I said I wasn't sure.

That's when I started going to a psychologist. We took some kidding after that, from some of the guys . . . just because when we came in we were messed up and they saw we were wearing each other's shirts. Like B.J. and I had a thing going, but that was ridiculous. He started being a little cool towards me, I guess as a result of the kidding. The whole thing was just too weird and neither of us wanted to talk about it.

BH: *When did you first think this incident might have to do with UFO abductions?*

Dennis: Only during the last couple of years. It was partly because of some flashbacks I've had about that night. And because of some missing time experiences I've had since then, connected with UFO sightings.

Hypnotic regressions subsequently revealed what apparently happened that night to Dennis and B.J. As they sat in their truck out by the flight line, Dennis saw "a lot of light around us . . . coming straight down." When he stepped down from the truck to look up, he saw "something descending." He felt someone grasp his left hand, and then he was going up. The figure holding his hand was "a funny-looking person," like a "Pillsbury Doughboy melted . . . skinny . . . stretched out . . . distorted." He described being taken through a "clamshell-like" opening and then placed on a table. A series of very painful quasimedical procedures followed before he was returned to his truck, ill and disoriented.

Again, what is most important for our purposes is not the long, harrowing hypnotic account of his UFO experience but Dennis's consciously recalled memories from that night twenty-six years ago. Since Dennis mentioned the teasing that followed his and B.J.'s arrival back at their barracks wearing each other's shirt, we must consider the possibility that the "abduction" was actually nothing more than a sexual tryst. But a massive problem with that idea should be immediately obvious: Why, if it was only a sexual tryst, would Dennis ever have mentioned it to me in the first place?

Another debunking explanation would suggest the possibility that the two men were not sexually involved but instead were using drugs while they sat in their truck. But again, if that were so, the same problem arises: Why would Dennis have told me about the incident in the first place? And why would the men have taken off their shirts and exchanged them while doing drugs?

Dennis's account was, to me, heartfelt in its telling and moving to hear. His is the kind of strong, self-sufficient, macho personality that is hesitant to confess to intense emotional turmoil and grief. And yet, he told me that the morning after his experience, "I woke up and just sat on my bed and fucking cried. I didn't even go to roll call." In my dealings with Dennis I have seen no reason why he would have invented this story and admitted to such a reaction.

Once we accept his honesty, as I have, and recognize the similarities between his encounter and established abduction patterns, we must examine the setting of this incident, which is both unusual and extremely important. Dennis and, apparently, B.J. were abducted from an official military vehicle parked on the tarmac at a U.S. Air Force base! Obviously the personnel in the control tower that night would have been carefully monitoring all training flights, through radio and radar, while maintaining full visual contact. Anything unusual on or near the flight line would have been clearly visible from the tower. Any craft—Air Force trainer or UFO—approaching or leaving the airbase would have been tracked on radar. Any massive display of light shining down from a UFO onto a parked emergency vehicle would have immediately attracted attention. That is, of course, if the UFO, the light, and Dennis and B.J. were not somehow temporarily "unseeable."

If the three foregoing cases, from 1948, 1957, and 1974, are to be regarded as credible—and, given their similarities to the consistent patterns in thousands upon thousands of later UFO patterns, they are credible—then the idea of a "technology of invisibility" seems inevitable.

Chapter Three

UNCOVERING CLUES TO THE SCIENCE OF INVISIBILITY

B Y THE SPRING OF 1996, I'd been living for over six months in that initial state of "imaginative, muddled suspense" with regard to the UFO phenomenon. I felt I'd made a great deal of progress using traditional research methods: reading the field's body of literature, learning the subject's history (how the culture, the government, the media, and the scientific establishment dealt with UFOs over the past fifty years), as well as learning the various theories put forth to explain the phenomenon. I'd looked at both the skeptical and the pro-UFO sides of the question. In other words, I'd done my homework, as many people before me have. But at this point on my own path of discovery, it was convincing, mainstream scientific explanations of UFO reports that I wanted: *a conservative, logical hypothesis that allowed for an object that was 30 to 150 feet in diameter to be completely invisible.*

As I soon discovered, there are some major challenges for anyone looking for science to confirm the material existence of UFOs. Black-and-white analysis—as in "provable vs. unprovable"—is virtually impossible. Almost all UFO events reveal themselves in shades of gray. Some of the earliest reports of UFO visibility vs. invisibility on radar, for example, indicate conflicting conclusions. Sometimes radar responded to the mysterious flying object; sometimes the scopes showed nothing, even though there were multiple human witnesses to the same event. What could be believed here—the long, electromagnetic fingers of radar searching for shapes that *should* be there, but did not appear? Or was the human eye the more reliable instrument of detection?

Usually, when a person is in a situation that offers two or more choices of senses to trust, the selection is fairly clear. When I'm swimming off the Cape Cod shore and see a dark, angular fin slicing through the water nearby, the jolt of adrenaline tells me to head toward dry land, even though I can't actually observe the physical body of the shark. Whether from eyewitness testimony or articles or movies, over time I've come to *infer* that a fin gliding through the ocean waters is fairly good *evidence* of a shark's physical presence.

Radar, Yes—Eyeballs, No:
The Ghosts of Nansei-shoto

From the earliest UFO literature to the present, the "seeability" of the craft varies from case to case. In some reports, people see hard-edged, physical objects; in others, the moving aerial object is without structure—just a circular light. But what happens when we turn to technology to assist our senses? What about evidence of *radar visability?*

The answer is similarly ambiguous: Sometimes radarscopes capture the UFO seen by human observers, and sometimes they do not. During World War Two, a series of inexplicable radar sightings of large formations of UFOs stunned even the most skeptical military personnel. Retired Marine Corps major Donald Keyhoe, an aviation writer with an interest in UFOs, pushed the Air Force to reveal what it knew by publishing enigmatic cases like the following:

During the last year of the war, U.S. Navy officer James Dawson (a pseudonym) was a combat information officer patrolling Nansei-shoto, a group of Japanese islands. His aircraft carrier's mission was to prevent the Japanese from attacking the U.S. landing forces at Okinawa.[1]

It was a clear, bright day when Dawson and other officers aboard the carrier met the "ghosts of Nansei-shoto." They were below deck, monitoring the huge radarscope. Every thirty seconds, the radar plotters and operator reported changes within a hundred-mile radius. Suddenly a very large blip appeared on the screen. A plotter scrawled: "200–300 aircraft, unidentified." The huge blob moved directly toward the aircraft carrier, fanning out, extending two arms as if to cover the entire Navy task force.

All available American aircraft were immediately sent aloft at an altitude that would allow them to look down and spot the incoming enemy craft. Visibility was fifty miles in any direction. But, looking directly down, the trained pilots could not see the massive incursion that the radar so clearly showed. Nothing was there.

Stunned, Dawson and his men stared at the scope. The unknown force was just five miles away now and closing fast. Attack was imminent. They raced up to the flight deck and stared upward: nothing but bright blue sky overhead. *No sound, no fleet of enemy craft*.

After the war, the Navy officially confirmed the "ghosts of Nansei-shoto." But if there was a solid, definite explanation, none was ever made known to the public.

In such pragmatic life moments, we all use evidence and inference to decide what's known (or what's likely) and what to do about it. But in UFO research, "knowing" anything definitively, much less what action to take, presents an enormous problem for science as it is now practiced. In an ideal lab experiment, which is the basis for most scientific advancement, the researcher is the direct observer who has a theory she can test, measure, and retest until the theory either hits a dead end or repeatedly proves itself to be a valid explanation of some process of nature. Generally, other scientists in different labs then take up the challenge of that theory—conducting the same tests with the goal of either confirming or denying the initial results.

But the UFO investigator has a real problem in applying accepted scientific principles. She can't just order up a UFO or its occupants for testing and put them through their paces. Instead, she depends primarily on witness testimony and indirect observations. Essential databases are certainly being developed by groups such as the Fund for

UFO Research—records relating the time, place, electromagnetic effects, ground traces, etc., of UFO sightings. But even these data are primarily dependent on eyewitnesses. Nevertheless, as science historian Steven J. Dick points out in *Life on Other Worlds,* other major disciplines share the very same problems of evidence and inference:

> This is true whether we are dealing with the nearest planets of the solar system, the search for more distant planetary systems, or theories and experiments about the origin and evolution of life relevant to both. . . . At stake [is] not so much the difficulty of observations as the inability to make them, at least directly, resulting in heavy reliance on inferences drawn from experiments. . . . Beyond the solar system, with the exception of artificial radio signals that were the holy grail of SETI programs, all observations became indirect.
>
> . . . In the end, all arguments about the origin of life on Earth and its abundance in the universe remained presumptions. . . . [This] leads us to the conclusion that science has limits in its ability to resolve certain questions.[3]

An Early Case of Radar "Invisibility"

In this classic 1966 book, *UFOs and Anti-Gravity: Piece for a Jig-Saw,* engineer Leonard G. Cramp reports a fascinating case in which radar on the ground *did not register* what was happening overhead to a commerical DC-6 American Airlines flight and its thirty-five passengers and crew.[2]

On February 24, 1959, an evening flight from Newark Airport to Detroit was over Pennsylvania when Captain Peter Killian, a pilot with twenty years' experience and four million air miles to his credit, spotted three unusual lights in a line formation. The orbs changed colors at times and their speed varied, shooting ahead, then allowing the slower airliner to catch up to them. Since the DC-6 was flying a constant 300-degree course, the mystery object's movements were easily observed. Killian and other crew members testified that they could see both the Orion constellation *and* the moving lights. They also reported the night as cloudless, with a visibility of 100 miles.

Before long, the passengers also began to notice that they had company up here above the clouds. The obliging stewardesses turned out the cabin lights, and for the next forty minutes, astonished passengers watched what one man called an "out of this world," fantastic spectacle of glowing orbs dancing alongside their airliner.

Captain Killian, doubting his senses, radioed two other commerical planes in the area. Both planes' captains radioed back that they were also watching the objects. Later, people on the ground confirmed visual sightings. But, as Killian later testified: *"While the objects were in sight, I kept watch on the radar screen, but saw nothing on it."* [italics in original]

Three days later, the U.S. Air Force released an official comment to the public: Because the objects had not been tracked on radar, the conclusion was that three separate sets of civilian passengers and three experienced airline crews had mistaken the stars of Orion for UFOs.

In this case, neither ground nor flight radar was able to register aerial objects that were distinctly registering on many human retinas.

Here Dick is referring to such disciplines as cosmology and astronomy, among others. After all, no one has ever actually *seen* a distant planet outside our system, nor has anyone ever seen a black hole or dark matter. What astronomers see and can measure is only the repeated gravitational evidence of black holes' and dark matter's effects on their neighbors. But, at its best, UFO research works with the same set of problems that plague these other, more respected endeavors. Until we can design alternative accepted modes of applied science—and science that is *funded*—researchers in each of these fields are stuck with working at the very limits of early twenty-first-century science. What this means is that often the required scientific techniques and the handling of data are barely sufficient, which leads to shaky evidence. And inferences based on ambiguous or uncertain evidence, of course, are much less likely to be accepted by the rest of the scientific community. Lack of acceptance by the mainstream then disallows publication of research articles in peer-reviewed journals, which are essential both for the advancement of science and the scientist.

How, then, can we claim that the features of what we call "the UFO phenomeon" actually exist? The easy way out for anyone not willing to do the homework—and I mean *all* of the homework, not just the ivory-tower theorizing—is simply to say: "But they're *not* possible. That's what I've been trying to tell you. These events never happened. Impossible is impossible!" But although we're far from any clear understanding of alien technology, there doesn't seem to be anything magical going on in these cases—certainly nothing impossible, as our own technological development shows us. At face value, the reports of UFO phenomena are astonishing, but they don't seem to violate any of the known laws of physics.

However, it would be misleading to indicate that any kind of research has yet been able to definitively *explain* UFOs—their method of propulsion, their airborne abilities, or their apparent talent for invisibility. What science does offer at this point in time are human technologies capable of actions analogous to many of the seemingly "magical" feats of the UFO.

Anyone interested in UFOs or alien abductions may not want to bother with the heady theories of physics—and we certainly won't do more than touch the surface of such ideas. But in some of today's conceptual changes in physics, we can find intriguing new ways to think about ETs, or extraterrestrials. There always exists the possibility that UFOs and their occupants are not simply *extraterrestrials* traveling across the known universe from one planetary body to another to play with, or pillage, or study this fine emerald-and-blue marble we call Earth. We also need to include the possibility that the beings we call "aliens" or "visitors" might well be coming from other dimensions, other universes not yet seen, but whose probable existence is coming closer and closer to being accepted as reality—not only by mystics, but by our top physicists and cosmologists.

Even some of the most cautious and conservative of physicists are willing to entertain some version of this idea. In his book *Solid Clues*, physicist Gerald Feinberg offers a clue on how these beings might actually "get here from there":

At present this is no more than a science-fiction plot. However, if there are more dimensions than those we know, or four-dimensional space-times in addition to the one we inhabit, *then I think it very likely that there are physical phenomena that provide connections between them* [emphasis added].[4]

Given the enormous widening of our scientific horizons over the last quarter century, we might expect that the prime characteristics of a scientist would be humility and an endless exuberance of wonder. And for some, those are precisely the attitudes that allow them to acknowledge that so much is still not known, a concept that the most adventurous scientists find extremely invigorating. In 1998, for example, three postdoctoral colleagues at Stanford, led by Dr. Nima Arkani-Hamed, made the startling suggestion that what most of us think of as "the universe" (our known universe) may actually be part of something much grander: a three-dimensional island floating inside a fourth dimension just a millimeter wide. Think of this universe, if you will, as a sheet of paper, a two-dimensional "flatland" that is light-years in length and breadth—and it is floating inside a small sliver of space.[7]

What We Didn't Know a Few Short Years Ago

Early-twenty-first-century science has opened doors into realms of nature that may seem fanciful or just plain unbelievable to us. It has all evolved so fast. After all, in the short six years between 1995 and 2001, astronomers have discovered more than fifty single giant planets orbiting around distant stars, some of them with the potential to sustain life. If planets are not confined to Sun-like stars, astronomers are encouraged to think that other planetary systems may be more abundant than previously suspected. Probing deep into the far reaches of the cosmos where they'd previously seen only a handful of galaxies, astronomers have also recently unveiled 101 massive new clusters of galaxies.[5] And although it may sound like a throwback to the days of Christopher Columbus, scientists today have calculated that the universe is *flat*. By that they mean that the universe now seems that it won't continue to expand forever, as once thought. Instead, scientists now believe that the density of mass is just right and that gravity will cause the universal expansion to gradually slow to a stop after some finite amount of time. Twenty years ago, a poll of astronomers and physicists would have shown almost no support for the possibility of our living in a flat universe.

If that weren't strange enough, dark matter, the mysterious substance that may make up 90 percent of all matter in the universe, has astrophysicists' heads spinning. Is it truly possible that modern Western science knows *nothing* about 90 percent of the universe?

Then there's the oddness of quantum physics, where it's beginning to be seriously thought that this single reality we swear by may well be only one of countless dimensions—a bubble within a bubble touching another bubble within a bubble, and so on into infinity. And that's just one theory of the way the multiple dimensions would play out.[6] We'll look at several variations on that theme later on in this chapter.

The lesson of all this is that no one—skeptics, ufologists, theorists of all stripes—should ever assume that they have considered every possibility for how the world works. Speaking of his team's new theory, Dr. Nima Arkani-Hamed mused: "What it says to me is that you should never underestimate the feebleness of the human imagination. We're really struggling in the dark."

The Shadowy Realm Takes Shape

We know that human beings see and hear objects and events that occur within only a small fraction of the electromagnetic spectrum. Many physicists now propose that we similarly perceive only a tiny fraction of a *greater reality spectrum*. In other words, reality itself is much larger than it seems to our limited perception. We may only be seeing the tip of the iceberg—a shadowy, larger reality that is now being theorized and tested under the terms *supersymmetry* or *multiverse*. In February

2001, the Brookhaven National Laboratory in Upton, New York, announced results of a long-awaited experiment that measured the magnetic properties of subatomic particles. Their observations seem to be the best evidence yet that the Standard Model of physics—the current gold standard by which scientists define "reality"—is just a province within a larger realm called "supersymmetry."[8]

For David Deutsch, a physicist of unusual originality, quantum theory implies that there are many universes parallel to the one we see around us—that we actually exist in a "multiverse." Deutsch's revolutionary experiments showed how a particle's behavior in one universe effects its counterpart (or "shadow") in another. He theorizes that a huge number of parallel universes exist all around us, each similar to the one we see, and each obeying the same laws of physics. They differ from one another only in that the particles—each a shadow of the other—are in slightly different positions in each universe.[9]

> We do not need deep theories to tell us that parallel universes exist—single-particle interference phenomena tell us that. What we need deep theories for is to explain and predict such phenomena: to tell us what the other universes are like, what laws they obey, how they affect one another, and how this fits in with the theoretical foundations of other subjects. . . . The quantum theory of parallel universes is not the problem, it is the solution . . . It is the explanation—the only one that is tenable—of a remarkable and counter-intuitive reality.
>
> —David Deutsch,
> The Fabric of Reality[10]

Building further on quantum theory, Deutsch absolutely rules out the possibility that the tangible universe around us is all that exists. Although he is conducting research in an area fully recognized by most other scientists, David Deutsch struggles with the same problems UFO researchers have encountered for decades. Mainstream scientists simply don't want to consider ideas that will inevitably and radically alter their conception of reality. "After all," Deutsch says about multiverses, "It is such a large conclusion, and such a disturbing one on first hearing."[11]

For many people, the concept that we live in the midst of infinite universes might well be far more disturbing than the idea of extrater-restrials visiting our own little planet.

What Our Human Senses Can and Cannot Know

The first instruments that human beings ever used to measure and determine reality were the primary senses: sight, sound, touch, taste, and smell. For millions of years, people simply assumed that when they looked out at the world, the human eye gave them a fairly accurate view of their surroundings. But neurophysiologists have long been aware of the fact that the eye/brain is anything but a faithful camera. There are several reasons that we may not be seeing what is out there to be seen—that we humans actually are practically blind to much of our surround-ings. Of course, if this is true, that means that events go on all around us—big and small events, startling and mundane ones—and that many of them are literally invisible to our ordinary perceptions.

How Our Brains Edit What Our Eyes See

In his early vision studies, Yale's Dr. Karl Pribram discovered that when a monkey receives a visual impression through its optic nerves (just as we do), the information doesn't go directly to the visual cortex in the brain. Instead, the information is first filtered through other areas of the brain, where it is edited and modified by the monkey's temporal lobes before actually reaching its final destination.[12]

Since then, numerous studies of the human brain confirm that our own processing and editing of the "raw image" occurs in a similar way. In other words, what we see is not necessarily what we get. Some stud-ies suggest that 50 percent of what we "see" is not based on the infor-mation entering our eyes, but pieced together out of *our expectations of what the world should look like*. We're so used to responding to what we think is there that we don't always see what really is there. Although, moment by moment, we take in fresh evidence of our surroundings from our visual organs, it's really the *brain* that sees. I suspect that wives from time immemorial might take comfort in this fact. It suitably explains the extreme time delay in a husband's awareness of a change in his wife's hairstyle, hem length, or physique. Our brain's need to reinforce what it's used to seeing might also very well explain how someone might be able to look at a UFO that has landed in a field, for example, and see a round greenhouse. It has happened. (See Terry's case in Part II.)

Our Narrow Slice of the Electromagnetic Spectrum

There is an even more basic reason that we human beings are extremely limited in our ability to know what is really going on around us: unaided by technology, we subsist on such a tiny slice of the electromagnetic (EM) spectrum! If our position on the EM spectrum seems of passing insignificance to you, let's take a brief detour into that zippy, wavy, red-hot field of science.

We'll begin with the low-energy, long-wavelength end of the range: radio waves. To the great pleasure of one of our human senses—sound—radio waves emit their energy into the air, are captured by our stereo systems, and are turned into our favorite Mozart movement or Muddy Waters riff. Visible light waves—which let us see a yellow toy tractor, blue sneakers, or a red hound with black ear fringes—would seem, then, to be completely different physical objects from radio waves—and equally different from X rays, microwaves, or gamma rays. Actually, it's true that these waves of radiation are all produced in different ways and that we detect and utilize them in different ways. But they are all fundamentally the same thing: all part of the electromagnetic spectrum—a name scientists apply to many different types of radiation when they talk about them as a group.

Electromagnetic radiation is simply energy that travels, spreading out as it moves along in a stream of photons. *Microwaves* that cook your popcorn, *radio waves* that light up your television screen, and *visible light* from a flashlight—each occupies a different range along the EM spectrum. The major difference between them lies in the amount of energy found in their photons, massless particles that move at the speed of light and travel in wavelike patterns.[13] Extremely hot, high-energy objects and events create higher-energy radiation than cooler objects. The photons in radio waves, for example, have low energies, while microwaves radiate at a slightly higher level. The next level up, infrared, gives off still greater energy, followed in intensity by the visible spectrum, the one we're most familiar with. Continuing upward in ranges far above human sight and hearing, ultraviolet, X rays, and gamma rays radiate the highest energies of all.

Those Alien Eyes

Try asking an abductee what the commonly reported gray alien's most prominent feature is. What's the first characteristic that comes to mind? Nine times out of ten, it's safe to guess, the person won't even hesitate: "The eyes," he'll say. "Those huge black eyes."

In pop culture's extensive imagery of aliens, it's also the eyes that dominate—enormous, slanting, all-black eyes extending halfway around the head, like a street vendor's two-dollar wraparound shades. But rather than assuming that consumer culture itself was the creator of that alien with the iconic eyes, let's see if there's a possible scientific reason for a being to develop one of its senses in such a bizarre way.

All of the stars, including the Sun, shine at frequencies all across the electromagnetic spectrum. Fortunately for us on Earth, the Sun hits its peak brightness in the visible part of the spectrum. According to radio astronomer Michael Klein, a star's brightness will shift somewhat toward either the infrared or the ultraviolet end of the scale, depending on its size and age.[14] In the same way that senses evolving on any world would take their cue from the environment, human eyes have developed to match the intensity, or wavelength, of the Sun. But for life that has emerged on planets orbiting those older or larger stars, they would need to evolve a different form of "eyesight"—one capable of handling a wavelength that reaches a higher or much lower peak than ours. If the standard, big-black-eyed gray alien is designed for a solar system with far lower peaks of brightness than ours, it's possible that what the human abductee perceives as "alien eyes" really *are* two-bit, wraparound eye shields—a replaceable component part.

The Electromagnetic Spectrum[15]

Radio waves: TV and radio stations emit this kind of energy, which is then captured by consumer receivers. Radio waves, which we can't normally see or hear, are also emitted by other things, including stars and gases in space.

Microwaves: At home, they can cook a potato in minutes. In space, however, astronomers use microwaves, which are invisible to the human eye, to probe the makeup of nearby galaxies.

Infrared: Light radiating in the infrared (IR) range can warm up our skin, although it is invisible to our eyes. In space, IR light reveals the dust particles between stars.

Visible radiation: The extremely narrow portion of the EM spectrum that our eyes can see, visible radiation is given off by such objects as light bulbs, stars, fireflies, and fast-moving particles colliding with other particles.

Ultraviolet: Also called UV rays, ultraviolet radiation originates from the Sun, is invisible to us, and can burn our unprotected skin. Stars and other hot objects in space are also sources of UV radiation.

X rays: Used by doctors and dentists to look at our bones and teeth, X rays are emitted far out in the universe by hot gases. People cannot see or hear X rays without a technological interface that "translates."

Gamma rays: Primarily generated by the universe itself in a number of ways, powerful gamma radiation can also be produced by manmade sources such as nuclear power plants and big particle accelerators. Gamma rays are invisible to the naked eye.

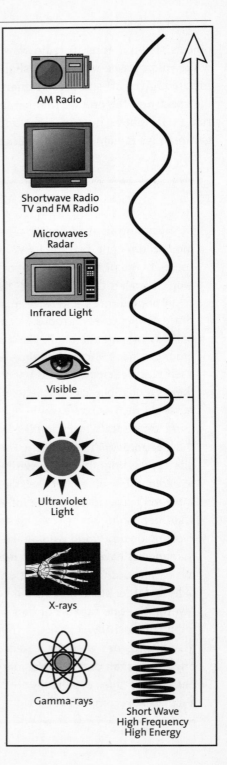

AM Radio

Shortwave Radio
TV and FM Radio

Microwaves
Radar

Infrared Light

Visible

Ultraviolet
Light

X-rays

Gamma-rays

Short Wave
High Frequency
High Energy

Looking at the graph, you'll see that the electromagnetic spectrum is also often described in terms of wavelengths and frequencies as well as energies. Long wavelength and low frequency are correlated with the lowest energy types of radiation.

It's humbling to realize that the largest portion of the electromagnetic spectrum falls on either side of the human range. Our comfort zone lies in a narrow middle range. Most of the events and objects in the world are therefore literally *invisible and inaudible* to us. To compensate, we've built countless instruments over the past century that can detect those invisible waves. Our stereo receivers, for example, detect radio waves and translate them into sounds we can hear. The television set, another comparatively recent and ubiquitous device, takes the same radio waves and translates them into both picture and sound. But without technological aides, we can neither see nor hear the high end (gamma rays) or the low end (radio waves). Nor are we aware of much of the light energy that's in between, either, such as microwaves, infrared, ultraviolet, or X rays.

One of the simplest ways, then, that a technologically adept intruder into our airspace might make an airborne object "invisible" to humans would be to work with the fact that we are oblivious to objects emitting radiation in either the low frequency, low energy or high frequency, high energy range.

Let's hypothesize that an unknown craft were to enter Earth's atmosphere; let's further assume that we will (later in these pages) scientifically establish enough about the UFO's propulsion system that we know it emits radiation while it is operating. Let's say the intelligently controlled UFO made use of those stealth abilities and dropped down to visit us on a dark night in Central Park. None of the runners or strollers would see the craft hovering over the meadows and ponds. Radiating energy at too low or too high a rate for the human spectrum, no eye or ear could detect it. The craft would exist just outside of our limited visual and auditory range. *But it would exist.*

Can Abductees Be Sent Messages by Aliens?

Just as with our visibility, the range of human hearing is also quite limited. Any sound within the human range tends to travel outward in all directions, scattering itself like a candle's beam. This unfocused property of the audible range has always made sound a public, shared phenomenon.

So, until now, we've had no explanation to offer for reports that abductees often hear a voice directing their actions just prior to an abduction. No one else around them hears the messages. Is this fantasy—or is there some way the abductee could actually be hearing sounds that others do not?

A radical technological development in acoustics is about to make us rethink what is possible and what is not. Its inventor, MIT graduate student F. Joseph Pompei, calls the device an "audio spotlight," referring to the way the device allows sound to behave like a focused beam of light. The audio spotlight emits a column of sound that is enveloped by silence, just as the beam of a spotlight is enclosed by darkness. From far away it can direct an audible sound or message to a specific listener. The person standing inside the beam that's emitted hears the sound or voice loud and clear. A person standing a few feet away, outside the beam, hears nothing. The device can also direct sound to bounce off walls to create a false impression of the sound source.[16]

Some engineers have called the audio spotlight the most radical technological development in acoustics since the coil loudspeaker was invented in 1925. But the revolutionary aspect of the acoustic beam is not that it's a new kind of circuit board. It is that sound can now be sent directly to the brain—a personal message meant only for you. And you wouldn't have to wear headphones or an ear jack. Nor would you necessarily be a voluntary recipient of the auditory information.

Abductees say they don't know where the voice comes from or even whether they are hearing specific words. They simply know that a communication has been sent by someone or something that is not necessarily in sight. A technology similar to our newly developed acoustic spotlight might be one way in which this "inner alien voice" can be heard—a remote and invisible form of human control.

A Recipe for Stealth Technology

Although the majority of mainstream scientists do not consider UFOs a serious topic of study—or are reluctant to say it is publicly—a small but significant cadre of physicists and other scientists have taken a hard look at the subject over the years. According to their databases of reported UFO activities, these scientists have inferred that the elusive flying objects have long been employing some sort of "invisibility technology." Let's take a brief look at what our own recently developed stealth technologies do and how they do it by way of comparison to the reported behavior of unknown aerial objects.

After World War Two, the high-tech Cold War between the United States and the Soviet Union was building slowly, chillingly to its moment of crisis. Both sides placed a premium on building the most *powerful* and the most *secret* weapons. From the 1960's through the 1980's, American aeronautical engineers set out to create secret, long-range, obliterative, and airborne technologies. In an urgent press to surpass the enemy, American scientists and military strategists began highly classified work on:

- reducing an aircraft's imprint on radar screens
- lowering the heat of its infrared picture to avoid heat detecting sensors
- improving aerodynamics (flexibility, speed, acceleration, maneuverability, etc.)
- making aircraft less visible to the human eye
- muffling the extraordinary noise of the jet engine.[17]

Looking back at the earliest UFO reports, one can only wonder if the engineers working for the great defense contractors, McDonnell Douglas or Lockheed, for example, had actually *already studied,* close up and in action, unconventional aircraft of nonhuman origin. Because, without a doubt, there are striking parallels between the aerodynamic "recipe" that American scientists urgently set out to achieve and the reports of UFOs' decidedly unearthly performances *made fifteen to twenty years earlier.*

Some of the most unbiased scientists, such as Paul Hill at NASA

(*Unconventional Flying Objects: A Scientific Analysis*, 1995) and engineer Leonard Cramp (*UFOs and Anti-Gravity: Piece for a Jig-Saw*, 1966) collected substantial databases of early UFO activity. According to their data, each UFO sighting confirmed aerodynamic performance that paralleled the United States' goals for its own aircraft, but was far advanced over what could be accomplished technically at that time. The following are some of their findings about observed UFO behavior:

- UFOs sometimes eluded radar detection but could be visually seen. At other times they showed up on radar, while remaining invisible to the human eye.

- Heat radiation, such as would be detected by infrared sensors, is missing from the surface and/or emissions of a UFO. A conventional aircraft's propulsion system would register as red-hot.

- A UFO's aerodynamic maneuvers are reported with amazement by human observers, including those who are military personnel: speeds at over 10,000 mph; sharp, right-angled turns; abrupt halts; hovering indefinitely close to the ground; acceleration that is so rapid (out of sight in one tenth of a second) that the human eye cannot follow, and the object literally seems to vanish; and many other exotic aerodynamic moves inconsistent with any known human technology of the time.

- Observers of both large and small UFOs most often report an atmosphere of total silence, even with the close overflight of a large craft. New Yorker Elliot Novak and his wife Debbie described a craft "as big as Shea Stadium," when telling the authors about their experience in upstate New York during the 1987 wave of black, deltoid craft sightings in that area. "It passed right over the open skylight of our car, so close that I could have thrown a rock and hit it," Novak added. "But the weird thing is that *it was totally, absolutely silent.*" Occasionally people report a whine, hum, or buzz, but they rarely report a UFO creating a roar or boom—even at supersonic speed. It's the *silence* of such large airborne craft that witnesses find stunning.

The B-2 offered a significant advance in the development of American stealth technology when it was unveiled in 1988 at Northrop Grumman's manufacturing plant in Palmdale, California. Although journalists were invited to watch, all guests were kept well away from the plane, which was built to slip through enemy radar defenses and drop up to sixteen nuclear bombs on its targets. The B-2 bomber was coated with radar-absorbent paint on each of its leading edges. Research had shown that the right-angled surfaces at the wing and tail roots were especially susceptible to reflecting radar signals. The materials covering the plane, soaking up radar, were so effective that the B-2 had the same radar cross section (RCS)—the profile that's visible to radar—as *a child's tricycle*. Another stealth craft, the F-117, had a different manufacturer and was deployed effectively in the Gulf War. Nearly invisible to radar, the F-117 had the RCS of a bird in flight. That's how effective we'd become at making early models of "invisible craft" by the late 1980's and early 1990's.

If we think back to the first major wave of UFO sightings in 1947, we recall that pilot Kenneth Arnold and other witnesses from the 1940's and 1950's were describing flat, pancakelike, circular "saucers" that almost disappeared to the eye when completely horizontal. One can only conjecture that the designers of the earliest reported UFOs understood—long before we earthlings did—the value of streamlining the craft's RCS to make it significantly less detectable. Both the earliest-known UFOs' makers and the American stealth designers were sharp enough to do away with right angles.

In the Plasma Zone

The few physicists and other scientists who have investigated the UFO phenomenon have long inferred from reports, photographs, and film that UFOs are surrounded by a zone of ionized, excited molecules—a plasma sheath. Depending on speed and environmental conditions, the plasma may either blur the solid outline of the craft or allow the observer a clear sighting of a hard-edged object. Witnesses often say: "I couldn't see a distinct shape, but I'm sure the object was solid."

In our own technology, we find other familiar applications of this principle. For example, when a space capsule reenters the earth's atmosphere, it is the plasma shield surrounding it at that point that causes a temporary but total communications blackout. Aeronautical research scientist Paul Hill used a small model experiment to reproduce UFOlike flight in a wind tunnel. The photo of the experiment shows a nearly invisible model of a craft traveling at high speed, sheathed in its excited, ionized plasma. It bears no small similarity to eyewitness reports of certain kinds of UFO sightings.

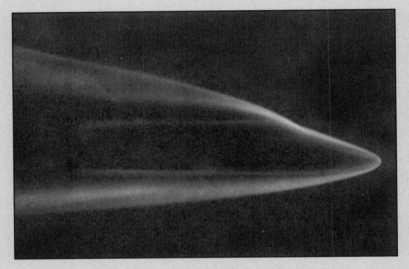

Graphic illustration of a supersonic wind-tunnel
model during test, photographed by N+2 plasma light.
(Courtesy of Hampton Roads Publishing)

Witnesses at night or twilight report that the ionized zone seems almost like a multicolored neon light. If the craft is in a low-power state (hovering or moving slowly), it will give off the colors red and orange, which take the least energy to excite. But when a UFO is either traveling or getting ready to head into high performance, we see the colors that take the most power to excite—blue and blue-white.[18]

For people having close-up night sightings, the plasma may blur the edges of the vehicle—at times even *completely concealing it.*

When the plasma zone is thick and intense, then we're looking at "invisibility." Why? Because there is a critical thickness or density beyond which a ray of light cannot penetrate. The excited molecules, in these instances, might absorb any rays of light radiated by the surface of the object. It reradiates that light in random directions that don't reach the eye or the camera lens.

And, just as UFOs so often reportedly do, the American stealth bombers were also designed to avoid radar by flying at very low levels. "Ground clutter," radar reflections given off by buildings or other objects, are useful to low-flying craft as a way of confusing radar. UFOs also seem to use a hovering, low-flying capability to avoid detection.

Adaptive Camouflage

Althought it's unclear how far along the project actually is, NASA's Jet Propulsion Laboratory has proposed a sensor-and-display system that would create an illusion of transparency around almost any object. Whether an aircraft, a tank, or perhaps a building, the objects would effectively be invisible. Called "adaptive camouflage," these systems generate displays that change in response to changing scenes and lighting conditions.[19]

This technological "magic" actually mimics nature's own camouflage adaptation in which an animal's exterior color gradually changes to blend in with the color and texture of its environment. In the Florida vacationland of the 1950's, for example, live lizards called anoles, or American chameleons, were often sold to tourists. As a small girl with a dollar and a love of all creatures, I'd buy one of the tiny lizards. With a noose and a pin, I'd harness it to my blouse and watch with amazement as the chameleon became a living, breathing, matching accessory. If I was wearing a pink blouse, the chameleon would gradually blush like a young girl. If I was wearing green, the chameleon became a twist of lime on my shirt.

But NASA is proposing something even trickier than what the lizard is doing by sympathetically altering its skin color: The agency's camouflage

Optical Tweezers

For decades, abductees have consistently reported being moved or lifted up by a beam of light shot down by a hovering UFO. Even objects as unwieldly as cars, cattle, and small airplanes have evidently been taken up a beam of light. Could these feats be anything other than magical thinking on the part of people experiencing extreme stress?

It seems now that there's nothing magical about it. At Keio University in Japan, researchers have developed a technology that uses laser light to manipulate and lift very small objects. The findings—explored in the journal *Physics World*—show how light, insubstantial as it seems, actually exerts pressure on any object that absorbs that light.[20] When researchers cause two pencil-thin laser beams to intersect, an extremely intense light field creates a type of pressurized trap at that juncture. By moving the intersection point of the lasers, the researchers can drag the object along inside the light trap. A set of "optical tweezers" has thus been created.

Since this discovery, the use of light pressure to move microscopic objects has become commonplace among scientists. In the laboratory, "optical tweezers," or beams of light, now grasp and move cells and even tie knots in DNA.

Scientists today are far from using laser beams to lift bawling cattle or hoist a Buick. In principle, however, a technology that begins at the microscopic level may eventually be developed for application at the macro- or human-sized scale.

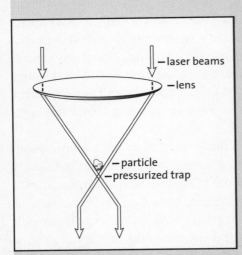

laser beams
lens
particle
pressurized trap

Illustration of dynamic optical tweezers (simplified).

system uses a sophisticated optoelectrical system to project the scene from the *far side* of an object onto the *near side* of the object (the side closest to the onlooker). The object's surface, then, would be akin to a movie screen, mirroring faithfully the ambient conditions through which the object travels—shifting clouds, foliage patterns, and lighting conditions.

NASA's Jet Propulsion Laboratory proposes developing this "adaptive camouflage" with a flexible network of electronic flat-panel display units, a bit like the flat, liquid-crystal, high-definition television sets now available to consumers. The display units are arrayed as a blanket that covers all visible surfaces of the object one desires to cloak. Each display panel contains an active pixel sensor (APS)—or another form of advanced image sensor—that peeks out of a small aperture, like an eye pressed to the peephole in a door. Behind each image sensor lies a complex network of fiber optics that transfer the image from each APS to a display panel on the opposite side of the cloaked object. The craft essentially becomes a big-screen projection of whatever environment it is flying through—in essence, invisible.

These lightweight optoelectronic systems are built to be readily operated on power provided by the vehicle's or object's electrical system. Using such a system, a UFO could hover in a bright sky fleeced with clouds and never be seen by the human eye.

UFO Invisibility Is Possible

Although we've only touched upon a few of the stealth technologies in use or under development by human military forces, it is clear that, to varying degrees, "invisibility" of large, flying aircraft is indeed possible. And it's possible today and using only human technologies. Whether UFOs are employing one or another of these methods, or combining some technologies we humans have just begun to hone—or utilizing systems we cannot at present conceive—we have no way of knowing.

So far, we've mainly looked to our own cutting-edge technologies as measures of whether UFO capabilities are "magical" or "fantastic"—or whether they might well be possible, either by extrapolation or by totally new forms of transportation. After reading the research of the scientists and aeronautical engineers who have studied UFO case reports, I have come to believe that the UFO is not just a zippier jet plane: It is a radically different form of airborne technology—one that could be far beyond our own in capabilities, especially in speed and maneuverability, as well as in the ability to shift shapes or to be visible one moment and invisible the next.

In fact, contemporary scientists and UFO researchers Dr. Bruce Maccabee and Stanton Friedman agree with the assessment of those earlier scientists, Paul Hill and Leonard Cramp, that all of our explanations of UFO propulsion and optical effects only partially explain the inner workings of the unidentified craft that have been overflying Earth for the past fifty years, if not more. They feel that the energy used by the UFOs is something extraordinary and far more technologically advanced than what we humans currently know how to build.

Chapter Four

THE CAMERA NEVER LIES?

S O FAR IN OUR EXAMINATION of the issue of invisibility in UFO abductions, we have been *inferring* its existence rather than presenting direct evidence in its support. We have made these inferences largely because no other theory is able to explain how abductions can regularly take place in crowded areas—the tarmac of a military airfield, for example—without being seen by hundreds or even thousands of witnesses. Skeptics, of course, will immediately assure us that this *proves* there are no such things as UFO abductions because the temporary invisibility of human beings, "aliens," and "UFOs" is a physical impossibility. However, in Carol Rainey's survey of radical new thinking about the issue of invisibility, we have already seen why both mainstream scientists and those who practice debunkery may soon be forced to change their minds about this issue.

There is nothing new about the debunkers' knee-jerk responses to reports of temporary UFO invisibility. From the beginning, in 1947, when UFOs were first widely reported over the United States, these committed skeptics also claimed that the amazing speeds and performance characteristics reported by UFO eyewitnesses were impossible; therefore UFOs as physical craft didn't exist, either. And even when trained radar operators reported tracking unidentified objects flying at extraordinary supersonic speeds and making right-angle turns without decelerating, the debunkers insisted that either the radar equipment was malfunctioning or the operators were incompetent.

Central to the failing of mainstream scientists to acknowledge the possibility of these UFO behaviors has been the use of traditional theories of physics to refute new data, no matter how authoritative, consistent, or objectively recorded it may be. According to mainstream science's blinkered frame of mind, if X is regarded as impossible, anyone actually observing X—even if he or she is offering supportive physical evidence—has to be mistaken. Or crazy. Or lying.

Unfortunately, ideology, training, tradition, and lack of curiosity afflict scientists just as they affect generals, politicians, business executives, and most of the rest of us. Science, as Dr. J. Allen Hynek once said, is not always what scientists do.*

My work in the field of UFO research has taken me virtually around the world, and in the fall of 1992 I visited Australia to deliver several lectures and to look into a few abduction cases. It was in the city of Brisbane when, for the first time, I came across some extremely interesting *physical* evidence with direct bearing on the issue of invisibility in UFO abductions. During a short break after my talk, I went to the lobby of the lecture hall, where I was approached rather cautiously by a middle-aged Brisbane couple whom I'll call the Washburns. They were accompanied by friends of theirs, an older American couple who, I later learned, had persuaded them to attend my lecture and to speak to me afterward. These two Americans, who had lived in Australia for a number of years, were very familiar with my two earlier books. And they were also aware of several incidents in the Washburn family that suggested that Sam, Jenny, and their two children might be UFO abductees.

Over the years I have become familiar with various types of people who approach me after lectures with different motives. Some, who come up to me smiling and eager to talk, are colleagues—UFO researchers and investigators with whom I may not be acquainted— who want to tell me about new cases they are working on or to hear an update on one of my cases. Others who approach me are just attentive, intelligent listeners who ask for clarification about some point I may not have explained clearly enough in my lecture. But the third and

---

*J. Allen Hynek was for twenty years the air force's scientific consultant on UFOs. He was chairman of the Department of Astronomy at Northwestern University, and made this statement during public lectures on the UFO phenomenon.

most important group consists of people who suspect that they, too, have had UFO abduction experiences and have come because they need to talk about them. Invariably these men and women approach me hesitantly, often waiting till no one is nearby before speaking to me almost apologetically, in lowered voices, about their suspected abductions. Even before I hear their accounts, I often recognize certain body language and quality of voice I've come to associate with abductees. This cluster of symptoms subtly conveys fear, self-doubt, and, unfortunately, an emotion not unlike shame.

The couple who approached me that day in Brisbane had these characteristics. They were solid, gentle, working people, the parents of two sons in their late teens and early twenties—John and Andy—and the kind of honest, unassuming folks one finds all over Australia. Nevertheless, they had been unnerved by certain things I said in my lecture. Sam Washburn, a man in his early forties, appeared quite nervous, though his wife, Jenny, was comparatively calm.

Among other things I had spoken about was the Linda Cortile *Witnessed* case, and one detail particularly disturbed them. I had described how, in the spring of 1992, Linda awakened, choking on blood from a serious nosebleed. Within a minute or two her husband, her two sons, and a young overnight guest of her older boy were all awake and had gathered in the living room. *All five* had serious nosebleeds, each in the right nostril, and further investigation of this incident suggested that the five had been the victims of nearly simultaneous alien quasimedical procedures in their nasal cavities. But because I do not do hypnosis with anyone under the age of twenty-one, and Linda's husband did not wish to undergo the process, I was unable to establish whether these nasal procedures had taken place in the apartment or inside a UFO.

A few days after the incident, to Linda's great surprise, the mother of the boy who was visiting that night called to tell her that she believed her son and Linda's family may have all had a shared UFO abduction experience that night. She went on to describe many strange, suggestive incidents her son had reported over the years, and even implied that she, too, had had a number of possible UFO experiences. I later met and interviewed this woman and found her to be highly credible and very possibly an abductee.

But for Sam and Jenny Washburn, this earlier incident of Linda's was disturbingly similar to an event that had occurred shortly before I met them. According to Jenny, five days before the couple heard me speak of the Cortile case in my lecture, they and their twenty-year-old son had awakened at the same time that night upon experiencing heavy nosebleeds. (John, their younger son was not home at the time.) Adding to their unease was the fact that all three were also bleeding from their right nostrils.

As interesting as this ostensible coincidence was, the Washburns had a more important story to tell. For most of his forty-two years, Sam had suffered from events that suggested classic abduction experiences. He was filled with a nearly constant anxiety and fear beginning in his childhood, when he lived on a farm. As he spoke to me, his expression, the tension in his face, his body language—everything—suggested a near panic state. He detailed a few incidents, but after a pause Jenny wished to tell me about something else. "Have you ever seen anything like this?" she inquired, giving me four photographs, obviously old and well handled. They were unexceptional snapshots, except for the fact that all were in various tones of red, as if a three-color printing process had only printed one color, omitting the blue and yellow.

The first of the red photographs showed a playground with a small boy, presumably Andy, peeking over the top of a slide near a second, unoccupied slide. The next two photos were similar views of the bay, a bit of sandy turf, and—off to the right of each—a tree; one could guess that the photographer had moved perhaps ten or twenty feet between shots. The fourth showed the same sandy turf and boatless bay behind, but since the tree was not visible, one can assume that the photographer had moved farther along the shore. These last three photos were extraordinarily bland, containing nothing of interest to engage the eye.

In answer to Jenny's question, I stated that I had never seen red-tinted photos like these and asked about the other images on the same film. She told me that all the other pictures on the same roll, before and after these, were in normal full color, and that the four red photos fell somewhere among the last ten or twelve exposures on the roll.

Not really understanding why Jenny had showed me these red snapshots, I was only mildly interested in them. But then she explained why she had handed them to me. "The thing about these pictures," she said, "is that we're supposed to be in them, and we're not. Sam took two of the boys and me, and I took one of him and the boys, and when we got the pictures back from the store, we weren't in them.* We were standing here in the middle with the water behind us, but we're not in the pictures. Have you ever heard of anything like that?"

My curiosity surged, but I replied as coolly as I could that I had never heard of this kind of problem. I asked the Washburns if anything else had happened that day at the playground that might have seemed strange. They recalled nothing unusual except the fact that they all wanted to go home shortly after they took the snapshots—an unusual reaction for the children. Sam remembered feeling agitated and his wife appearing tense, though their sons behaved normally, apart for wanting to leave the playground. It was only a ten-minute drive from their home and one of their favorite places, but after the day the photos were taken, neither of them ever wanted to go back. Though they lived in the area for another few years, this was their final visit. That, Sam and Jenny agreed, was strange.

I realized that potentially, these odd red photographs for which the Washburns posed—only to find themselves inexplicably missing— were of extraordinary importance, but I said nothing to either of them about my suspicions. I was also disappointed to learn that the Washburns did not know where the original negatives were. They had moved twice since the photos were taken fourteen years earlier, in 1978, and, like most of us, the couple had kept all their negatives loosely stored in various boxes and envelopes, which had become mixed up with other things. Jenny promised to search for the negatives but was not very optimistic about finding them.

Later that afternoon, at my invitation, Sam and Jenny and their friends came to my hotel room for a more extensive interview, and I was able to fill in a number of significant details. The playground where the photos were taken, Sam told me, was at a place called the esplanade in Wynnum, a residential area in Greater Brisbane. Wynnum is located about six kilometers from the center of the city, on

---

*This is a typical example of a witnesses' faulty memory of a small detail. Actually, Jenny took two pictures and Sam only one.

the coast and south of the Brisbane River. The film Sam remembers regularly using in his Pentax camera was Kodak ASA 100. He explained that when this incident occurred in 1978, relations between him and his wife had been strained for many weeks, and one of the purposes of their trip to the esplanade that day was to have a chance to talk while the children occupied themselves on the playground equipment.

Sam said that he had revisited the esplanade within the last year. "I went back to the spot, and . . . it was eerie. It was really eerie. It's . . . not scary, but myself, personally, I just wanted to walk fast past it and try to get away from it."

I asked if, in 1978, he had gone back to the esplanade after they first received their photographs and found they were not in them. His answer was quick and decisive: "No way!"

Jenny echoed Sam's impression of the esplanade that morning in 1978. "We just went there to relax, and have time to talk between ourselves while the children played on the equipment. But it was eerie."

Sam was more explicit about his feelings. "As far as I can remember, we sort of hung around—you know how you linger?—and I felt silent. It was as if I was lost. 'Cause we went back to the car and I remember thinking, *We need to go and get something to eat.* And I remember getting in the car and driving, but that's as far as I can remember.

"It's been on my mind so many times and I can't remember where we went. We didn't go home. To me, it was as if everything was in slow motion. That's the best way to describe it: as if everything had just slowed down. And even though I felt okay, I was feeling as if I wasn't there. That was my feeling: that I wasn't there."

It was obvious that, for both Sam and Jenny, the day was very unsettling, and since their sons never wanted to go back to their once favorite playground, one can assume that they were similarly affected. After a long conversation with the Washburns and their friends, I suggested the idea of hypnotic regression to try and recover the events of that day. Jenny immediately agreed, but Sam was extremely reluctant, even frightened at the prospect. Ultimately, I carried out a session with Jenny that afternoon while her husband waited downstairs in the hotel lobby with one of their American friends (the other stayed with us and witnessed Jenny's hypnosis).

After a long preliminary interview I began the induction. Going back fourteen years, we dealt with the Washburns' family car, their drive to the playground, and the first photo that Sam took of his son on the slide. The time was about 11:30 A.M. Jenny recalled a lunch of sandwiches as well as their various wanderings around the playground. Eventually the family moved over near the water, and Sam posed with the boys for the pictures Jenny took. In answer to my question, she remembered which son was to Sam's right and which was in front of him. While this was going on, she said she "felt funny," and things seemed "not right." I noticed that the pace of her recollections had slowed noticeably.

They strolled a bit and then Sam took the camera to photograph her with the boys. Jenny stopped speaking for several minutes. After a long pause I asked her what was happening. She seemed quietly agitated. "We're going up," she said. "There's something big up over us," and she felt she was surrounded by an intense light.

I asked who was going up. It was she and the boys.

"Where's Sam?" I asked.

"He's down there where he was . . . holding the camera." Jenny seemed frightened and confused, but not quite in a state of panic. "No one seems to see the big thing up over us. . . ."

What ensued was a standard UFO abduction. Jenny, John, and Andy apparently entered the craft through the bottom and, once inside, were approached by several small aliens. Suddenly, Jenny began to cry. She was becoming more upset by the second, and when I asked what was happening, she replied, "They're taking my boys away from me . . . and I can't move." I reassured her that her boys were fine, as she must know, because, I reminded her, soon after this experience they were all together with Sam down at the esplanade.

Next, Jenny described being moved into another room, where shortly after she found herself on a table, nude, being examined by several small gray creatures. Gynecological procedures followed, but she was still so upset that, rather than exploring them in depth, I moved her ahead to the moment she was reunited in the craft with her sons. Feeling immense relief, she next described their descent, all together, in the same bright light. Amazed, she saw her husband down below, his camera still raised, standing exactly where he had been before all of this began. As soon as they were back on the ground, he lowered the camera and normal—though subtly altered—reality resumed.

After the session ended, Jenny appeared to be shocked, relieved, and confused in about equal measure. I implored her not to tell Sam anything about what she had recalled, and she readily agreed. She, too, was eager for him to undergo hypnosis either to confirm or contradict what she had remembered. She found it almost impossible to accept her recollections as real, despite their vividness and coherence. The abduction experience, she realized, helped explain the strange photographs and the unusual reactions of the entire family to their trip to the esplanade. I decided, for the time being, not to spell out my own thoughts about these events.

The next morning I phoned Sam and we talked at length about the issue of hypnosis. Apparently because of our conversation the previous day and Jenny's reassuring description of the safety and ease of the procedure, Sam agreed to undergo hypnosis. However, when he and Jenny arrived at my hotel room later that afternoon, he was quite nervous and apprehensive. I spent some time explaining the process to him, reminding him that he would effectively be in charge and that he could end the session whenever he wished. We talked a bit about his conscious recollections of that visit to the playground, and then I began the induction.

As I always do at the outset of a regression, I set the scene, beginning with the Washburns' drive to the playground.

BH: *When you go to the esplanade, do you drive the car or does Jenny drive?*

Sam: I do.

BH: *Let's just see what happens. You get out of the car at some point and go over to the park. Let's just look for a few minutes. I want you to watch John and Andy and I want you to tell me what they're doing.*

Sam: Andy was going down the slide. John was climbing up.

BH: *John's climbing up? Do they look like they're having fun?*

Sam: No.

BH: *Now, at some point—incidentally, is this four o'clock in the after-noon? What time is it?* [This question, in which I mention a specific time, is an example of what I call a false lead, a basic technique that I will use again and again in this session as a test of Sam's degree of suggestibility.]

Sam: [Refusing to take my lead]: No, it's . . . don't know. . . . It's about midday.

BH: *Midday. Okay. Now the boys are having a good time, fooling around. You're with Jenny, I assume. Do you have a little chat, or are you watching them, or taking pictures? What happens now?*

Sam: Jenny and I are talking. . . . The boys go by. It's sort of . . . It's all sandy at the bottom of the slide.

BH: *It's sandy down there? They kind of land in the sand when they come down?*

Sam: Uh-huh.

BH: *Now, this is what I want you to do for me. Look into your feel-ings. . . . What are you feeling as this is happening?*

Sam: I was very concerned.

BH: *What are you concerned about?*

Sam: Don't know.

BH: *Just feeling a sense of concern?*

Sam: I don't want the boys to go high.

BH: *So you're keeping an eye on them?*

Sam: Yes.

BH: *What might happen to the boys? What are you so concerned about?*

Sam: [Responding quickly]: Don't know.

BH: *Now, at some point you go near the water and take some pictures.* [At this, Sam begins to tremble and moan softly. I put my hand on his shoulder to comfort him.] *Why are you afraid? It's an innocent thing, taking pictures.*

Sam: There's something there.

BH: *You see something?*

Sam: Yes—its there.

BH: *Tell me what you see.*

Sam: It's a ball.

BH: *Where do you see this ball? Is it on the sand?* [Another leading question, the first of several about the ball.]

Sam: No, it's floating.

BH: *It's on the water?*

Sam: No, it's floating in the air.

BH: *Is it black?*

Sam: No.

BH: *Is it yellow?*

Sam: No, it's silver. No, not silver, it's shiny.

BH: *Now, how big is it? Let's start with a football: Is it bigger than a football or smaller than a football?*

Sam: It's smaller. It's a bit bigger than a tennis ball.

BH: *How far away is it when you go over there?*

Sam: [Whispers, as if afraid "it" will hear him]: It's very close.

BH: *Meaning ten feet or more?*

Sam: It's watching us.

BH: *Now, does this thing move, or is it just staying there?*

Sam: It just moves around. . . . It's floating around. [Now Sam becomes very frightened and the tears flow down his cheeks.] *I don't know why other people can't see it.*

BH [Comforts Sam]: *Let's see what the boys and Jenny do. Do they see it also?*

Sam: No.

BH: *You're the only one who sees it?*

Sam: I think so.

BH: *Now, where is everybody when you see this? Are you all together in a little group? Is anyone separate from the others?*

Sam: I don't know. I tell them [his wife and sons] I want to take a photo . . . that I've got to take a photo.

BH: *Why do you have to take a photo? Something you want to do?*

Sam: Don't know.

BH: *Is it something you want to do? Supposed to do?*

Sam: Supposed to do.

BH: *How do you pose them? Do you tell them where to stand?*

Sam: They just stand there. I don't know why.

BH: *You aim the camera at them?*

Sam: Yes.

BH: *You get them in range and everything? You do all those things—*

Sam [Interrupting, very frightened]: They're not there!

BH:—*focus the camera?*

Sam: I don't think . . . I don't know. [Becomes very upset, cries]

BH: *Tell me what you're feeling.*

Sam: Panic.

BH [In a calming tactic, I move ahead for a moment]: *At the end of the day you all went home, didn't you? Andy is home right now, isn't he? He's fine, isn't he?* [I had earlier been told that his brother John was currently visiting a friend and so was not home.]

Sam: Yes.

BH: *And Jenny is here with us. And you're fine now?* [I reassure him that everyone is okay now.]

Sam: Yes.

BH: *When you look in the camera, what do you see?*

Sam: They're not there.

BH: *They're not there?*

Sam: The ball was moved and there's another one there. There's another ball.

BH: *When you say they're not there, where are they? Jenny and the boys?*

Sam: The ball's taken them.

BH: *Well, in what direction . . . out to sea, or back on the beach?*

Sam: They leave sort of up on an angle.

BH: *On an angle?*

Sam: The ball takes them . . . lifts them up.

BH: *Lifts them up?*

Sam: Yeah. They don't know. They don't even look surprised.

BH: *And where do they go?*

Sam: They're going up. The other people . . . they must help. They must help us.

BH: *Do you call out for help?*

Sam: I couldn't.

BH: *Tell me where the boys are standing in relation to Jenny. Who's on the left, who's on the right? What happens?*

Sam: John was just standing in front. Andy was sort of right beside John, and Jenny had her hands on their shoulders.

BH: *And it looks like they're not even noticing?*

Sam: Looks like they're just standing there, but they're floating upwards.

BH: *Can you look up to see where they're floating to?*

Sam: I don't know what it is. Just a thing. Don't want to look at it. [He becomes agitated again.]

BH: *Is it an airplane?*

Sam: No. Don't want to look at it.

BH: *Does it look big or small, or can you tell?*

Sam: Must be big.

BH: *Big as an automobile?*

Sam: Bigger, much bigger.

BH: *Can you see them approach it? You just tell me what you see.*

Sam: There's all these lights. It's so bright, you can't see. They just disappear in the brightness. It's like looking into a flashlight. They just disappear into it.

BH: *So, when that happens, what do you do? Do you put the camera down and walk away?*

Sam: No, I couldn't.

BH: *So, how are you posed?*

Sam: I'm just standing there. And this other ball is still there.

BH: *And where's the camera?*

Sam: In my hand.

BH: *Down at your side?*

Sam: No.

BH: *Where is it?*

Sam: Sort of like I was taking a photo.

BH: *At some point I want you to tell me what you feel. Before they come back, what do you do. Do you move around at all?*

Sam: No, I can't move.

BH: *Are you there for a short time or a long time?*

Sam: This ball, it's hidden me. It's got me hidden.

BH: *You mean hidden so people can't see you?*

Sam: No. It's got me hidden. It does this every time. [Very agitated]. It hides you.

BH: *Now, Sam, this is what I want you to do for me. At other times, perhaps you've never had a chance to speak to the balls, to say what you'd like to say. At this very moment we're all safe and all together here, let's just imagine you're looking at one. What would you really like to say to this ball? I want you to speak to it directly.*

Sam [Coldly, and speaking indirectly]: Just tell it to get out of here. Tell it to get away.

BH: *Do you think you have a right to be angry about this?*

Sam: You bet.

BH: *They did this without asking you permission, didn't they?*

Sam: You can't move.

BH: *That's not a way to treat somebody, is it?*

Sam: No.

BH: *If you had that power, you wouldn't do that to somebody, would you?*

Sam: I don't know why they do it. They've always done it.

BH: *The first time you saw the ball, how old were you? Were you a little boy?*

Sam: I thought it was to play with.

BH: *Where were you when you saw this? Indoors or out?*

Sam: Outdoors. I always knew the light, it was always there. It used to follow me. It never hurt me.

BH: *Did you ever see any people with these balls? Sometimes balls belong to people?*

Sam: They belong to that other thing.

BH: *What is the other thing?*

Sam: It's the thing that's up in the sky.

BH: *Let's move back to the beach again. Let's watch Jenny and the boys come back. Tell me what you see.*

Sam: They just appear. It's like as if this ball is back and just appears. I can't see. It's very bright.

BH: *And they're standing in front of you?*

Sam: No, away. They're just like as if they're not quite touching the ground.

BH: *How do they look? Look at their faces.*

Sam: Frozen. No expressions. It's like statues.

BH: *How do you feel now, to see them back?*

Sam: Better, but the ball's still watching.

BH: *Let's let the ball leave. Let's see how it leaves.*

Sam: No. It's staying there. The big thing's gone. It's still watching. There are all these voices. You can hear these things in your head.

BH: *What are the voices saying?*

Sam: They just tell me that its okay.

BH: *Everything's okay?*

Sam: Yes, that's it, but why do they do it?

BH: *We don't know why. Did you ask them why?*

Sam: They just keep babbling on.

BH: *What's the next moment when you begin to feel at ease with your family?*

Sam: That afternoon.

BH: *Where are you?*

Sam: I think we're at Jenny's mom's place.

BH: *You feel kind of relaxed now?*

Sam: Yeah—there's a lot of people around.

BH: *How are the boys doing?*

Sam: They seem to be okay. They're playing.

After a period of positive posthypnotic suggestions, I ended the session and brought Sam back to full consciousness. I asked him how he felt. "Like a bit of an idiot," he replied, and Jenny laughed. Then she expressed her astonishment at the corroboration of her own previous account. From their two separate perspectives, Jenny and Sam had described essentially the same bizarre incident.

From my perspective, my suspicions about their experience—which I had still not voiced to either of them—had been fully confirmed. Some time that morning—I do not know when—Sam, Jenny, Andy, and John had all four apparently become *invisible*, though they were not aware of that fact. Neither their bodies, their clothing, nor even their camera could be seen by the other families on the esplanade that warm Saturday.

At some point a small floating ball appeared, shiny, bigger than a tennis ball, and apparently visible only to Sam; Jenny was certain she had not seen it. After she photographed Sam and her sons—presumably just before the ball arrived—Sam involuntarily took a picture of his wife and sons. "I was supposed to" is the way he put it.

Just before she handed the camera to her husband, Jenny recalled, she clearly saw her family through the lens when she snapped their photos, and under hypnosis that memory remained firm. Initially, Sam remembered sighting Jenny and the boys through the lens when he photographed them, but under hypnosis he did *not* recall seeing them through the camera's eye. Perhaps when he snapped his picture, they had already levitated out of camera range, or possibly, when he was frozen in place and waiting involuntarily for their return, he snapped the shutter; we will probably never know.

Jenny's photos, taken along with her recollections of seeing her husband and sons through the camera's viewfinder, provide clear, though indirect, physical evidence of the phenomenon of invisibility. It seems plausible that Sam had to have been invisible in order to stand absolutely frozen, eye to the viewfinder, for perhaps an hour in a busy playground without attracting attention. Had he been visible, one can easily imagine at least some small child asking, "Daddy, why is that man standing over there looking through his camera and not moving for so long?"

Though it is bizarre to an extreme, the most logical explanation of the entire mystery is that at some point all four Washburn family members were literally invisible to everyone nearby, as was the UFO, its bright, levitating beam, and the small, floating balls. And to add more conceptual confusion, a temporarily invisible camera apparently was able to record the invisibility of the Washburns against a visible landscape—the images caught in tones of red on temporarily invisible Kodak film!

It seems to me that this case has only two possible explanations: Either it occurred more or less the way the Washburns said it did, or it is a hoax and Sam and Jenny are liars who invented the whole thing. I can think of no way in which this incident could be caused accidentally—and honestly—by either the joint misidentification of natural phenomena or the simultaneous occurrence of a shared psychotic episode. But those who practice debunkery, recognizing these problems and doggedly believing that such UFO events cannot happen, will insist that the Washburns fabricated both the photos and the entire abduction episode.

Such a complex and dishonest act on the part of the Washburns would require, first of all, a motive. They asked nothing of me, not money or attention or media exposure, and in fact firmly insisted upon anonymity. Rather than suggesting I buy the red photos from them, they gave them to me to take back to the United States for analysis. (As I write this, they are still in my possession.) So, what would be their motive for an orchestrated hoax? I can think of none.

Also, had there been a hoax, Jenny and Sam would have had to do several things: They would have had to carefully construct their esplanade account and orchestrate their stories so that they could be recounted from differing perspectives. Next, they would have had to teach each other how to fake hypnosis, to resist the induction, and, finally, to practice emotionally convincing acting to the point that they were able to effortlessly convince me they were experiencing genuine emotions. All of this work, all of this dishonesty, and for what?

No, all of the evidence suggests that this bizarre event occurred and that the Washburns' temporary state of invisibility was, in a way, recorded on film. These two utterly honest, sensitive people managed to present us with physical evidence that supports the reality of an alien technology of invisibility. For this, we are deeply in their debt.

Chapter Five

THE PERPETUAL PHOTOGRAPHER

Although there isn't any known science to back up this whimsical observation, there seems to be a universal parental imperative about picture-taking that children just don't get. Would they smile if we tried to explain it's a way to stop time, print the moment and hold it close? That it's a defense against loss that's sensed coming from just around the corner? I imagine that's what Sam and Jenny Washburn were trying to do for their family group in the Brisbane park in the summer of 1978. But the four red photos where the trees and lake are as they should be, while the Washburns themselves are completely missing from at least three of the four frames—what has happened here? Something they hadn't intended or wished for, certainly. These photos *are* a memento, but of what?

When it comes to exploring the issue of invisibility by applying scientific principles to a UFO report, the Australian Washburn case of the red photos is a particularly interesting one. It poses a number of problems beyond the issue of Jenny and her two boys being taken up into a UFO from a Brisbane playground in broad daylight while her husband Sam was evidently left standing below, frozen, a perpetual—and later, perplexed—photographer. We must ask:

- How did the many elements involved in this abduction—the four Washburns, the UFO, and the silver ball—all evidently achieve invisibility in the middle of an afternoon in a public park?

- If they were not invisible, how else might the event have occurred?

- Why were the four photos red, while those on the roll of film before and after them were normal? And why were the family members not in the last three red photographs?

- Did an invisible person manage to take photographs? If so, how was he apparently instructed to do so?

Several of the phenomena in these questions may be directly relevant to the UFO's propulsion system. Let's take a look at the way a handful of well-placed aeronautical engineers and physicists developed, over time, a speculative but also highly plausible theory for the internal workings of certain UFOs—a theory that includes the ability to shield themselves from human sight in several ways.

One Engineer's Explanation of UFO Propulsion

Published posthumously in 1995, Paul Hill's groundbreaking book, *Unconventional Flying Objects: A Scientific Analysis,* ferrets out the patterns of reported UFO performance from the 1950's through the 1970's. As chief scientist specializing in aeronautical engineering for NASA, Hill became an informal clearinghouse for UFO-related data passing through the agency. Officially, NASA wanted nothing to do with UFO reports, but as long as Hill kept a low profile, he was able to collect a substantial database necessary for a scientific analysis of the phenomena.

Hill took the reported observations of UFOs—including color, size, wakes, jitters, maneuvers, sound, clouds, landing traces, force fields, radiation, occupants, and interference with human technology—and compared those reports with all propulsion systems known to mankind. One by one, Hill systematically eliminated all known systems—mechanical, pressure, rocketry, high-speed particle propulsion, and friction—because their performance did not match the data for UFO behavior. But, sticking to accepted principles of flight dynamics and electricity, Hill concluded that UFOs "obey, not defy, the laws of physics."[1]

His conclusion, supported by other engineers and physicists familiar with the reports, suggests that UFOs most likely utilize an internally generated force similar to Earth's gravity, but one that *opposes* gravity and frees the UFO from many of the constraints of man-made aircraft. The field beam literally pushes down on the Earth's mass, which is thousands of times more dense than the atmosphere, and repels it.[2] That action and the exchange of quantum energy that occurs between craft and mass gives the UFO a solid scientific basis for the reports of amazing manueverability and speed.

In addition, UFOs have the ability to intensely focus their ionizing radiations downward. If we add this commonly observed phenomenon to the theoretical properties of UFO propulsion, we are coming closer to understanding what may have happened to the Washburns on a family outing in 1978.

Focusing the Energy Field

Saucer-type vehicles would be especially prone to emitting a field, or energy force, that undergoes a sequential focusing and demonstrates astonishing versatility. In *Unconventional Flying Objects*, Paul Hill cites several carefully observed cases of this occurring. One of the best cases he cites comes originally from Jacques and Janine Vallee's *Challenge to Science*, where the observer made sketches similar to those presented in the figure below.

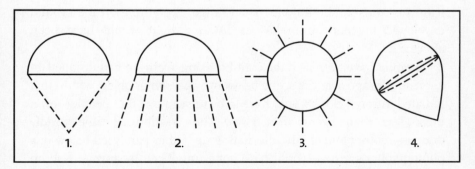

Illustration of an unidentified craft's focusing sequence—thought to be the basis of its extreme speed and maneuverability.

In this case, the witness saw first a luminous cone of light directed downward toward the ground (intense focus). As it hovered, the cone opened up under the object like an umbrella. The witness had the impression that there were "luminous flames" being projected toward the Earth, although we now believe that the craft was hovering above cold plasma, not flames. As the UFO rose and departed, it changed course by tilting and pointing the force field in the direction in which it wanted to proceed.[3]

Other researchers confirm Hill's findings. In Coral and James Lorenzen's *Flying Saucers: The Startling Evidence of the Invasion from Outer Space,* a series of photographs of a UFO taken in the Trinidad Islands is presented. In them, a swath of luminosity spreads out like a curtain between the UFO and the ground below. These photos are excellent evidence that the UFO is focusing energy in a downward directed beam.[4]

What might the "umbrella effect" mean in relation to the invisible Washburn family photos? Although there are many unknowns in this case, including atmospheric conditions and temperature, that would affect the craft's level of radiation, we can reasonably posit the following: At the point when both Jenny and Sam began to feel uneasy, right before the photographs were taken, the UFO was overhead, perhaps not yet seen, but sensed by the Washburns either by a change in the daylight or by the nearly inaudible humming sounds made by the power plant—even, perhaps, by the heat of infrared energy. It is quite likely that at that point the descending UFO was radiating—outward around itself and downward—an ionized plasma of excited molecules in the infrared or near-infrared range. As we know, that is in the spectrum just outside the human visual range. Everything on the ground enveloped in this "umbrella" of infrared light would have been affected.

It would have been as if the craft hovering overhead had dropped an enormous drape over the scene below. Any person or object within that radiated infrared cloak would have to be unseen by other people—even those less than twenty feet away. The Washburns' otherworldly drama—mother and children levitating up, father paralyzed below in a photographer's pose—would have gone unnoticed by anyone else on the playground.

Astonishing Einstein

The world of physics is a quirky, fickle field where very large ideas about the nature of time and space and our human place in it seem to be under constant reconsideration. But there was always one thing the harried physicist could depend on: the speed of light. Albert Einstein's theory of relativity declares that when light travels through a vacuum, *its speed never changes.* At 186,000 miles per hour, to be precise, light holds the top speed record for anything in the universe.

Recent experiments, though, suggest that not even the speed of light is sacred. In 1999 an American team of physicists slowed light to a comparatively tortoise-paced speed of thirty-eight miles per hour. Then, in the July 10, 2000, issue of *Nature,* other scientists reported having urged their light speed *forward,* speeding up the light pulse to exceed the cosmic limit. They accomplished this feat by encouraging pulses to travel in a bunch. This gave them a "group" velocity, making the whole greater than the sum of its parts. Together, the bunched pulses could go over the speed limit set by Einstein, even if none of the individual waves did so.

The major news implied in this finding is that when the speed of light is exceeded even by a factor of 1/300, the light appears to travel backward in time. We'll be looking at this idea later. But although Einstein's pickled brain may be twitching, the foundations of physics are not quaking: The experiments don't violate any of the established physical laws of nature, but they do show that it is possible to manipulate light—and possibly *time*—in ways that astonish scientists across the board.[5]

The Effect on the Film

So how did Jenny and/or Sam take those red photos under the UFO "cloak"? One clue would be to think of airports some years ago and the trepidation with which any photographer, filmmaker, or videographer approached the security gate. He or she would have known that the X-ray scanning devices used at that time were highly likely to fog, damage, or overexpose any film that passed through them.

We also know from our brief look at UFO propulsion that the UFO field engine—popularly known as a "force field"—like today's nuclear power plants, has an electromagnetic frequency range high enough to exhibit radioactive properties. In a case from the Korean War, Paul Hill tells of American pilots encountering two huge UFOs surrounded by a reddish glow. When the three planes prepared to shoot, the UFOs jammed the planes' radar on every frequency that was tried. As the unidentified objects circled above the planes, the six airmen experienced a warmth and a high-frequency vibration. After the flight, they found that all the gun camera film had been exposed or fogged. The red glow, strong enough to be seen in daylight, suggests that the radiation from the UFO was powerful enough to penetrate camera cases.[6]

Even Kodak warns that "X-rays can fog unprocessed film when the level of radiation is high."[7] However, the company has developed a special film in which infrared radiation and objects being photographed are captured in red tones on the film. Sam Washburn, however, had no such specialty film—just his Kodachrome and his automatic camera.

In the case of the Washburns' red photos, though, the radiation explanation doesn't fully explain the situation: There is no fogging or overall image blurring or distortion. In the background, although red-tinted, the trees stand straight and the land and water horizon lines extend from border to border in each shot. It's only the posed family that's missing.

Researcher Marc Davenport has suggested a possible time-warping field effect on the camera that would slow down or speed up the shutter.[8] That explanation would be consistent with some scientists' idea that the UFO has found a way to actually pull time-space along with its field. If that phenomenon affects the camera, it also would affect Sam Washburn, standing below the hovering UFO. If provable one day by mainstream science, the theory would also account for Sam's sense that everything had been slowed down—that he was, in effect, in a sort of time warp. And he's far from alone in expressing this odd sense of slow motion, as if his own body had been out of phase with the surrounding time-space. Many abductees report that, at the beginning of an abduction, they seemed to be moving in slow motion—that something didn't "feel right." Extreme stress, of course, is one obvious explanation for this sense of time distortion. It's also possible that the physical slowing down of light, or the altering of its energy, has something to do with what Budd has termed "missing time"—a consistent element of abductees' reports.

None of this offers any complete explanation for the Washburns' family photos. But one possibility remains: If the four people were indeed progressively enveloped in a near-infrared plasma, and then an infrared ionized beam that could be finely focused, it is logical that, in the photos, we would be able to see the background trees and the lake, but not the "cloaked" family. They would be hidden from the visible spectrum of light—the one that average consumer film was designed to capture.

Mission Control: Possible Alien Use of Infrared Technologies

NASA's "Observation Education Reference Model," available on-line, tells us that the infrared portion of the spectrum is one of the most useful tools for identifying what a surface is made of, because any surface both reflects energy and emits energy. For instance, a plant will reflect much more energy in the infrared range than in the visible range. An aerial explorer can learn a great deal about plants—and rocks, minerals, and human beings, for that matter—from their reflected energy. The occupants of a UFO, hovering low, sometimes shooting far out into space, would have ample opportunity to do an amazing amount of reconnaissance about the state of individuals, countries, and entire planets.

Color infrared films, originally designed for aerial photography and reconnaissance missions, are now being used to monitor pollution of air and water or surveying forests to determine their state of health.

It doesn't require much of a leap of imagination to suppose that visitors or explorers from other worlds would also find similar useful purposes for heavy investment in the infrared spectrum.

Paralysis and Direct Communication to the Brain

Two of the most common elements in abduction reports are the sense that the abductee is being told what to do by some "voice," and his or her temporary paralysis. The biggest questions here are whether that source of manipulation is coming from inside or outside the self—and how we might explain particular sensations and their actual, physical effects on the abductee. When Sam Washburn tells Budd that he's "supposed to" take the family photos, we don't know with any certainty whether that voice is coming from his superego, his wife's wishes, his own fear or guilt about their troubled marriage, or from the occupants of the craft vectoring in on them. What we can infer from the four red-tinted photos with landscapes but no family in three of them is that Sam evidently did as he had been "told," lining up the family and then snapping the photos just *after* his wife and children were levitated up into the UFO.

Of course "mind control," if that's what it is, isn't a new idea. From the beginning of recorded history, humans have heard gods commanding from on high and have obeyed. Research shows that governments have also long been interested in getting such a prompt and respectful response from their populace, when needed. There is documentation that throughout the Cold War, our own government has more than dipped a toe into the dark waters of "mind control." Type *acoustic psycho-correction* or "psychtronics" into your search engine and see what turns up:

1. At Walter Reed Hospital in 1973, Dr. Joseph Sharp participated in an experiment with pulsed microwave audiogram. Sharp sat in a soundproof room, while electronic signals were broadcast toward him in the frequency range of the electromagnetic spectrum (EM) that carries microwaves—ordinarily inaudible to humans. There was no receiver, no electronic translation device. Yet, in a direct transmission to his brain, Dr. Sharp clearly made out specific words.[9] How was that possible? The microwaves, causing microscopic thermal expansion of the brain tissue, had apparently directly stimulated the area of the brain that processes language. The human ear's

need for an audible pulse with a lower frequency and longer wavelength was entirely bypassed.

2. A 1993 article in *American Defense News* discusses a Russian mind-control technology, called "acoustic psycho-correction." Apparently demonstrated in laboratory experiments since the mid-seventies, the technology, say the magazine's sources, "could be used to suppress riots, control dissidents, demoralize or disable opposing forces and enhance the performance of friendly special operations teams."[10]

    In 1991, after the fall of the Soviet Union, Janet Morris, defense consultant to the U.S. Marine Corps and U.S. Army, was invited to Russia to assess possible commercial applications for the technologies. She and her team witnessed a demonstration of acoustic psycho-correction, (mind control technology) that Morris, an expert in the field of nonlethal weaponry, found quite intriguing. She described it as "infrasound, very low frequency-type transmission" in which the message "is transmitted via bone conduction. . . . An entire body protection system would be required to stop reception." The Russians stated that the message bypasses the person's conscious mind but is acted upon in less than a minute.

    (A frightening thought, but you do have to wonder about the validity of this report. With the godlike powers of mind control at their disposal, how is it that Russia is in its present state of dishevelment? Was it the fledgling capitalism or was it the technology that didn't pan out?)

3. The U.S. Defense Intelligence Agency (DIA) also appears to have been interested in the direct broadcasting of audible sound and voice to the human brain. In 1961, Allen Frey, a biophysicist working for the DIA, reportedly experimented with the concept that human beings are capable of hearing microwave broadcasts. He advocated the idea of learning to "stimulate the nervous system without the damage caused by electrodes." But, for UFO researchers, the most startling part of his report came next. It was almost a throwaway line. In

his experiments, Frey said, *subjects experienced the intercranial microwave transmissions as humming, buzzing or knocking sounds.*[11] As we will see in cases to follow, especially in the case of Anne-Marie, abductees often hear a humming or buzzing sound in their heads just prior to an abduction. We can speculate that they are either hearing the UFO's power plant as the craft approaches, or the craft's occupants are transmitting messages of some kind directly into the abductees' brains.

As to abductee paralysis, it could be caused by muscular contractions from electric shock—possibly a general by-product of the UFO power plants' electromagnetic effect that stalls vehicles and stops watches or by a more deliberately targeted and aimed form of shock to the human electrical impulses. We simply don't know. What we do know is that abductees regularly report paralysis before and during the abduction. In many reports, the person is temporarily paralyzed by a light beam or object held in the alien's hand. Richard M. Neal, Jr., M.D., hypothesizes that this effect is caused by "a selective type of microwave irradiation [unknown to us] . . . [that sets up] a chain reaction in the Central Nervous System to affect only certain areas and spare those that are essential to vital biological functions."[12]

Simulating Human Reality

Our alien visitors have earthly company in their interest in these technologies. Today's scientists are also experimenting with direct stimulation of the human sense organs. Often this work is done in conjunction with that of creating virtual reality systems, such as a flight simulator, where a pilot learns to fly a B-52 without ever leaving the ground. Many versions of such systems exist today, from simulated road race games to "war game" virtual reality projects sponsored by the Pentagon. This is not just television-watching with a new name. A true virtual reality system is one in which the participant actually "enters" into the system and touches objects, smells lavender or ocean air, and feels herself stride or float toward the sound of a rock concert just around the corner. The entire scenario would be achieved via artificial stimulation of her senses by electrodes worn on the body.

Physicist David Deutsch suggests that we might already be living in a massive virtual reality system without knowing it. He states that sight, sound, smell, taste, weightlessness, and all other senses can, in principle, be rendered artificially:

> Eventually it will become possible to bypass the sense organs altogether and directly stimulate the nerves that lead from them to the brain. . . . When we have understood the olfactory organs well enough to crack the code in which they send signals to the brain when they detect scents, a computer with suitable connections to the relevant nerves could sent the brain the same signals. Then the brain could experience the scents without the corresponding chemical ever having existed. Similarly, the brain could experience the authentic sensation of weightlessness even under normal gravity. And, of course, no televisions or headphones would be needed, either.[13]

In a limited way—and without even needing to delve into classified research—we can see that we already practice manipulation of the senses. Take the problem of how to get the highest fidelity of sound—the most faithful reproduction of what our auditory senses would experience if we were *there* in the concert hall or recording studio. With the compact digital disc and the high quality of sound reproduction equipment, humans have already come quite close to the necessary delicate techniques for stimulating our auditory nerves into becoming "believers."

Screen Memory

Knowing that comparison doesn't imply proof of any kind—just possibility—let's look at the idea that Budd calls "screen memory." In case after case of reported UFO abductions, the aliens appear to directly control the sights and sounds that the abductees perceive. One woman with a history of paranormal experiences, "Margaret," recalls that as a girl, she would sometimes feel herself unexpectedly paralyzed. At the same time she could see a raccoon sitting on the ledge of her window. The only logical problem with this memory is that the "raccoon" was sitting in a second-story apartment window in Queens, New York, with no trees around to climb up and it was on the *inside* casement of the window ledge. Budd's earlier hypnosis sessions with the same woman were connected to totally different incidents, where she did recall alien abduction experiences. It was only some time later that she casually mentioned to us that she recalled the practically impossible animal on her ledge. Budd has felt for many years that the UFO occupants in some way control what the abductee sees, usually substituting a more benign, common image (the raccoon) for something that might be more truly disturbing and anomalous (the alien).

Neurologists tell us that our brains actually run on microelectric signals. We can hypothesize, then, that an advanced alien technology that is actively giving off electromagnetic energy on many levels of the spectrum may be using one or more of those spectrums in a very targeted way—to broadcast directly to the human brain. Depending on how widely or narrowly the target beam was focused, anywhere from one to unknown numbers of people could be affected. Perhaps only one abductee "hears" or receives a brain signal to sit alone in the park for a convenient rendezvous with a UFO. On some very different occasion, might ETs or UFO occupants broadcast a command to large numbers of inhabitants of a large city? In *Witnessed,* Budd reports that that is exactly what seems to have happened to a crowd of dazed New Yorkers.[14]

A Hybrid Implant for Your Brain

Let's flip the scenario and suppose that, rather than *remote manipulation* of the human brain, aliens are able to discern the thoughts and feelings of their involuntary human participants in this study or experiment they have under way. If you find this idea to be entirely too sci-fi, consider some of our most severely handicapped citizens. The severely disabled have adapted quite easily to the idea that their brains are able to both artificially receive and transmit some form of communication. With miniature wireless electronic gadgets invading their bodies, these disabled pioneers don't bother to quibble about whether they are more or less human than before. For years they've been collaborating with scientists in an intimate way, using body or brain implants to interact with and communicate with the world.[15]

A pioneering group of neurobiologists affiliated with Atlanta's Emory University have created a device that would acquire a signal from *inside* the brain—a signal hardy enough to travel through wires and manipulate objects in the outside world. The brain in question belongs to a sixty-three-year-old contractor and musician, Johnny Ray, who suffered a brain-stem stroke in 1997 so massive that it produced what doctors call "locked-in syndrome." Ray has virtually no moving parts; he is trapped inside his body, with no way to interact with anyone else. But his intellect and human desires continue, maddeningly, to exist.[16]

One of the original team's members, Roy Bakay, is now at Rush–Presbyterian–St. Luke's Medical Center in Chicago and devotes his work to creating alternative brain-body interfaces. Although Bakay describes his achievements modestly, the scenario sounds to me like something from a posthuman, postmodern fiction: "We simply made a hole in the skull right next to the ear, near the back end of the motor cortex, secured our electrodes and other hardware to the bone so they don't migrate, and waited for a signal," Bakay says. A signal, that is, generated from *inside* Johnny Ray's locked-in brain.

This particular implant development is a significant improvement over a taped-on electrode such as those used in EEGs to monitor brain waves. Ray's implant, an intriguing hybrid of electronics and biology, actually physically melds with his own brain tissue. Gold wires carry signals back out, where they're amplified so that others can access them. Gradually doctors were able to codify a simple thought coming from Ray—such as up or down, hot or cold—into electrical patterns that changed as Ray's thoughts changed. That signal from inside the brain could then be turned by the doctors into a corresponding signal that programmed a computer cursor. Eventually, Ray was able to reproduce his brain patterns so reliably that he could use the cursor to spell and even generate musical tones.

But it gets better. Drs. Bakay and Kennedy had hoped that Ray's focused mental activity might cause some neurological changes. But even they were surprised when Ray's facial muscles and eyes began to move as he entertained different thoughts. It wasn't a magical cure; it didn't mean his paralysis had receded. But it did mean that Ray's thoughts about motion were now triggering clusters of motor neurons into firing and new action. Even a devastatingly "locked-in" man could reach out and be understood, just by having a thought.

If you're an abductee or a researcher, the fact that this is technically possible probably won't surprise you. Let's just hope it gains your report of such communiqués a little more respect from the scientific community.

The Little Ball That Spied on Sam

In many of Budd's cases, I have heard abductees mention the fact that occasionally, prior to an abduction, they would see a small, tennis-ball-like object floating around their room or in an outdoor situation. Often the ball seems to be glowing from inside without emitting any light in an outward pattern, as a candle does. One person recalls the ball moving up and down her body, as if checking out her overall condition. In Sam Washburn's case, under hypnosis, the small floating orb felt quite familiar to him. It seems to be something like a "smart ball," a programmed or intelligently controlled object related to the much larger craft hovering above.

We can theorize that these are miniature scout craft, sent out to reconnoiter the situation and the people. Quite possibly, as we've discussed earlier, these devices may also perform some direct communications with the abductees-to-be. Sam seemed to have an idea that the ball always hid him, making him invisible in some way we don't understand.

In an article from *New Scientist,* I ran across a piece of current research that raises some interesting possibilities. Entitled " '*Smart dust' could soon be spying on you,*" the article reports that a development team at the University of California, Berkeley, is designing tiny "motes" capable of communicating with each other. Only five millimeters long, each mote is invisible to the eye but is large enough to hold a number of microelectromechanical systems. Packed full of lasers, sensors, and communications transceivers, the "smart dust" particles are wired up to form a simple computer. The Berkeley team made the choice of this optical communications system because optics require much less energy than radio communications.[7]

If we may mix the benign with the more ominous uses, their range of applications could be anything from weather monitoring to indus- trial espionage to spying on individuals—to whatever it was that Sam's ball did to him.

But where this new technology will really pay off is when these tiny computers can be made even smaller. They will literally become dust— small enough to stay suspended in air, buoyed by currents, sensing and communicating with each other and home base for hours. The base station will be a hand-held unit, the size of a pair of binoculars. In addi- tion to making the computers smaller, the team plans to produce "swarm behavior" by building distributed intelligence into the motes.

We've just explored some of mankind's most recent and quite star- tling achievements: intelligent nanotechnology; virtual reality; remote stimulation of human senses; a hybrid implant that melds electronics with human brain tissue; direct transmission of messages to the brain via microwaves; and more. When we compare these discoveries with abductees' reports of their experiences, it's valid to speculate that some of our own technologies are only a few steps behind that of the UFO occupants.

Chapter 6

THE STRANGE CASE OF
THE RELUCTANT FAUCETS

KATHARINA WILSON IS AN INTELLIGENT, sensitive, rather shy, but thoroughly credible woman whom I have known for nearly fifteen years. She has had numerous UFO abduction experiences, some of which I helped her to explore and others that she has apparently recalled without the aid of hypnosis. Despite her personal avoidance of the spotlight, in 1993 she wrote a book, *The Alien Jigsaw,* documenting her experiences and illustrating them with many of her own drawings.[1] I contributed an introduction to her book, describing our initial meeting through a letter she had written to me in 1987 in which she explained why she felt she was having abduction experiences. I went on to write about our ensuing friendship and my early investigation of her suspected UFO encounters.

Katharina and I have met several times since then at various UFO conferences, and in a casual way we still keep in touch. It was at one of these gatherings that she told me about the following unusual experience, and though I volunteered to carry out a hypnotic regression on the incident, she declined. She said that for some reason she found this particular experience to be unusually exhausting and emotional to deal with, but said that perhaps one day she would change her mind and want to explore it further.

It began on October 5, 1995, when Katharina departed from

Portland, Oregon, where she and her husband then lived, to fly to Chicago, where she had been invited to speak at a local UFO conference. She told me that she began to "feel funny" on the plane, shortly before it landed:

> I remember there was a lady sitting in front of me, and she was reading a book on Scientology. It wasn't a book book, it was like a little study book, and I remember peeking between the two seats and trying to read what she was reading, but I couldn't quite make it out. But I know the topic was Scientology and for some reason I immediately started thinking about the aliens. I can't explain why. I don't know anything about Scientology except that it's a cult [laughs]. But there was just something about it that I connected with the ETs. And that's when everything started getting weird. My state was agitated and confused. Whatever happened later that day, I think it began on the plane.
>
> I saw the Scientology woman first from the side. She seemed like an attractive, elegant older woman with pretty gray hair, and she looked like she'd be really nice. I just felt that I'd like to get to know her. Something about her made me think she would be nice and loving, and so afterwards it seemed strange that I connected her with the experiences in the airport. I don't know what that part of it all means. The whole thing was bizarre, like nothing I'd ever do.
>
> We arrived at O'Hare a few minutes early, because I remember looking at my watch and seeing that it was 2:10 Portland time. The hostess of the conference, Mary Kerfoot, and her assistant "Judy Williams" were supposed to meet me in the United Airlines luggage claim, so I was kind of in a hurry. I left the plane and walked straight up to the women's rest room near the gate. After I came out of one of the stalls I looped the handle of my briefcase around my wrist and walked over to the sink to wash my hands. I put soap on them, but when I put my hands under the automatic water faucet, nothing happened. The water wouldn't come on. I tried the next sink and the same thing happened.
>
> There were other women around me and I noticed that when they tried to use the sinks the water came on fine. I tried using the same sinks the women had used, and several times I quickly placed

my hands under a faucet just after someone left it, when the water was still running, but then it suddenly shut off.

I was beginning to feel somewhat panicked. I started thinking to myself, *I'm not registering. I'm not registering on the sensors.* I started thinking about Mary and how she was waiting for me at the baggage claim, and how I couldn't go down there with soap on my hands. It was all very strange. Feeling helpless and even more panicked, I stood in the middle of the rest room and looked at a young woman who had light brown-blond hair, and I asked her, "Am I invisible or something?" She looked in my direction but didn't respond. I know she must have heard me. You'd think she would have said something back.

She walked right past me and left the rest room. She didn't run into me, and I wouldn't walk into her. Just when I became most angry and panicked, I walked around her and went around the corner and I saw this baby-changing station. It was a little cubbyhole and it had three sides. Only the back was open. And when I went in there and saw the sink had a faucet with a regular hot and cold handle, everything was better. I turned on the water, washed my hands, and left the rest room.

I asked Katharina if, when she was standing at the row of sinks, she had looked at herself in the mirror.

Uh, yes, I think so. They have so many mirrors I must have seen myself. I remember seeing another lady at my left, in the mirror. She had dark hair. But all I wanted then was to get the soap off my hands. I know I didn't comb my hair or anything because then I had soap all over me and I was really in a panic. Things didn't feel right, none of the sinks would work, and I was in a hurry.

After I left the rest room I saw some pay phones and remembered that I promised to call my husband after the plane landed. Usually, I don't call him till I get to my hotel room, but this time I called him right away. I was extremely agitated, and the first thing he said was, "I see your plane was late getting to Chicago." I looked at my watch and it read about 3:20 Portland time. I didn't really want to think about the fact that when we landed it was 2:10, and now, just after my short trip to the ladies' room, it was 3:20. I felt really disoriented and afraid. I didn't know what to say. I began complaining to my husband that you can never fly into or out of Chicago and be on time. We only talked two or three minutes, and I remember feeling a little guilty because I was so frustrated and confused during our conversation.

After I said good-bye I decided to walk to the baggage claim area, but I don't remember much of anything about getting there until I was about ten yards from Mary and Judy. I remember being on a second level. Everything was all yellowish tan. I don't think it took very long at all to get to there. I vaguely remember an escalator, but I might just say that because there are two levels.

What I really remember after the phone call and being in the bathroom is being in the luggage claim area and walking up behind them and seeing my bags. I had a big red suitcase and a box of books. It was really heavy. I was carrying my purse and my briefcase with my slides in it: If everything gets lost, at least you have your presentation. But there weren't any people standing around the carousel, and there were just my bags.

The police person had just taken them off the carousel, and I got a little nervous 'cause there were no other bags around and she was getting ready to take my things away. At that time they were worried about bombs. I walked up to the security officer right at that moment and said, "These are mine," and then I walked up behind Mary and Judy and they seemed to be staring out the window. I thought I'd been gone fifteen minutes at the most after we landed, and I was rushing to let them know I was there. I remember both of them turning around and being totally surprised that I was there. That's when Mary said, "It's like you just appeared. Where did you come from?"

She said they had been waiting a long time, but I didn't believe her. I really felt bad because I was late, but I was kinda bothered because I *wasn't* late. Mary said she and Judy thought I had missed the plane and were wondering what happened to me. I fudged and told her that our plane had been vectored all over the place. "You can never be on time at O'Hare." I didn't want her to know that I had been in the rest room, trying to wash my hands. I looked at my watch again and remember reading the time as 3:20 P.M. and experiencing a great amount of confusion. It was about the same time as when I was talking to my husband on the phone.

Sometime later, when I talked to Mary by phone to try to get the facts straight about what might have happened, she said that the first thing I started talking about when we saw each other at the baggage claim was that I had experienced a missing-time event while I was in the women's rest room. I don't remember saying this to Mary, but she is absolutely certain that I did. I find it unbelievable that I can't remember talking about a missing-time event. Mary said she thought, *Well, Katharina is an abductee, so I guess it's possible.*

During this same phone call, she was quick to tell me that she and Judy do not believe I walked up to them as they sat on the bench looking for me. She told me at least twice that to Judy and her, [I] "appeared out of nowhere." She said, "At first I refused to believe that you were standing there behind us, because it seemed as if you appeared out of nowhere."

When I came back to O'Hare after the conference, I realized there wasn't anything familiar about the United Airlines terminal area. Nothing was yellow-tan like I remembered: Everything was blue, green, a totally different color scheme. I thought I was in a totally different airport. I thought, *I don't remember this at all.*

I think that something really bizarre happened that day, because there is missing time, and the way it came. It felt the same as other times, other UFO experiences I've had. Something happens and I don't remember it, and then all of a sudden there's a trigger and it all comes back. A lot of times I just remember a lot right afterward, but other times there's a trigger and then I remember. And then, like this time, there's a trigger but the memories don't come back, and you think, *Oh, I know what this is. I've done this before.* And in the rest room that day I thought, *What is this? I'm not afraid of faucets,* and that's when it all clicked.

Mary Kerfoot, Katharina's host for the conference, is a woman I have recently come to know and respect for her intelligence and great personal warmth. Two years ago Carol and I were privileged to be her weekend guests when we traveled to Chicago to research another abduction case. Recently, however, through a long telephone call, Mary described to me the scene in the United Airlines baggage claim area when Katharina suddenly appeared:

> Judy and I were sitting on a bench. There was room for about three people, but there weren't any individual seats. The carousel for her flight was near the end of the long room, and the escalator was on the left. Katharina would have had to come from that direction. But she came up behind us and was standing next to the carousel. Neither Judy nor I commented to her about how really shocked we were by the way that she just appeared. We just pretended that everything was okay. We didn't want to say anything upsetting. What was more interesting is that Katharina seemed to be making a major effort to find a rational explanation for being so late. She apologized and said, "Well maybe it's because I stopped to call Eric," and then she seemed confused because she said they only talked for about two or three minutes.
>
> I wanted to say something about how this doesn't make any sense, but it seemed rude. I didn't know her really well. We weren't intimate friends, but we were good enough friends that I could have mentioned something, but I just didn't want to upset her.
>
> Judy and I were sitting right near the carousel and about twenty feet or so from the back wall. Maybe not that far. There were no more suitcases going around. We had been watching for her, and there weren't very many people at all in that part of the baggage claim. I don't know how she got there behind us without our seeing her. It seemed impossible. And I don't know why she didn't call to us first or wave or something. She just came up behind us directly. It was just very odd, popping up behind someone and saying hello. Judy and I commented that we both thought she just popped out of the conveyor belt somehow. [Laughs]
>
> She mentioned, too, about feeling like she was invisible or something in the bathroom, people treating her that way, and she couldn't get the faucets to operate. We knew immediately it was strange. When I heard her behind me my first thought was, *Oh, she was teleported here.* [Laughs] I didn't think of being invisible as suddenly popping up.

Listening to Mary's and Katharina's accounts, I realized that together they raised almost as many questions as they answered. But the first issue to be considered is the period of about an hour of missing time that Katharina experienced immediately after landing at O'Hare. The flight apparently arrived on time at around 2:10 P.M., according to Katharina's watch. She walked into the ladies' room, experienced difficulties with all the faucets, and then only a few minutes later called her husband. At that point it was about 3:20, *an hour and ten minutes later.* Since her perception was that only four or five minutes had passed between the two readings, it should have been only about 2:15 when she phoned her husband.

Next, she has virtually no clear memories of the confusing trek from her gate, through a very large terminal building, to the baggage claim area and Mary and Judy. In answer to my question, she did not recall having to look for and follow the signs which lead passengers through a maze of hallways to the baggage claim. She recalls looking at her watch when she arrived, and, remarkably, it still read about 3:20 P.M., as if she had hung up the phone and arrived almost instantaneously at the baggage claim area. For anyone who has faced the layout of O'Hare Airport, that is an impossible feat.

Katharina's attempt to explain her tardiness to her friends by claiming the plane was late made no sense. Had that been so, the other passengers would still be arriving at the carousel when she did. Mary and Judy had no doubt that the plane had arrived on time—they had called to inquire about its estimated arrival time before they left for the airport—but they also had watched everyone arriving at the carousel at the proper time and picking up their luggage. They are certain they had waited for an hour or so for Katharina, concluding finally that she had missed the plane. Mary told me that she was so concerned, she checked with United Airlines, and a clerk assured her Katharina had been on the plane and had disembarked along with the other passengers.

And so, if Katharina Wilson, an abductee with a lifetime of UFO encounters, was abducted during that hour-long period of missing time, how did the aliens remove her unseen from a crowded airport terminal? The answer, by now, should be obvious. At some moment shortly before or after she deplaned, she must have been rendered "unseeable," and yet so far as she was concerned, nothing was different—other than her deepening sense of panic. It was probably just after her trip to the restroom (2:10 P.M.) that the aliens took her from the building, and the abduction itself must have ended just before she made her phone call to her husband (3:20 P.M.). Yet, it would seem that her state of invisibility was still in effect, along with alien control, until she was quickly transported to a nearly vacant part of the baggage claim area, behind Mary and Judy, where she suddenly became fully visible again.

As I have said, there are many unanswered questions about the precise qualities of her state of invisibility. First, when I asked if she recalled seeing herself in the mirror as she went from sink to sink, she said she thought she would have seen herself because there were so many mirrors around the room. However, Katharina mentioned seeing only the reflection of a dark-haired woman using the sink to her left. I found this response interesting but inconclusive. And then, if she did see her own reflection, would the other women have also seen it—the reflection in the mirror of an invisible person in their midst? That seems highly unlikely. And if Katharina herself did not notice her own reflection, should we regard the mirror as being like the situation of the Washburns' camera, in which the film was unable to register their images?

Also, there is the matter of sound. Katharina said that when she asked a young woman, "Am I invisible or something?" the woman was looking in her direction but didn't respond. "I know she must have heard me," Katharina said. "You'd think she would have said something back." Did the young woman hear a detached, sourceless voice only a few feet away? It would seem that if she had heard the question asked in a disembodied voice undeniably close by, she would have paused nervously and looked all around her. The fact that Katharina said she glanced in her direction but didn't respond is interesting but possibly coincidental. Had the young woman seemed suddenly frightened, glancing frantically around the room, it would have been a much clearer indication that she had indeed heard Katharina's question.

At the heart of Katharina's experience is the fact that she did not "register" on any of the automatic sensors controlling the water faucets. It was this vivid and unexpected mass malfunction in the world of electromagnetic devices that led her to think for the first time that she was no longer physically visible. However, if she was indeed invisible, her body worked properly, efficiently affecting its surroundings. She used the toilet, opened and shut doors, carried her briefcase, worked the soap dispenser, and finally was able to turn a faucet in the baby-changing area to clean the soap off of her hands. And yet, during all this, she was apparently unable to register as a physical presence before an entire row of otherwise normally functioning sensors.

This presents the same kind of enigmatic "contradiction" we found in Sam Washburn's ability to work a camera and actually take pictures while he himself was in a similar state of invisibility. Washburn looked through the camera lens and saw his wife and sons, but they did not show up on the developed film. As we have seen, their absence from the pictures reinforces the idea that while he was photographing his family, Sam, his wife, and his sons were all presumably invisible to every other person at the playground. Could it be, then, that in the airport rest room Katharina saw her reflection in the mirror just as Sam Washburn saw his family, but, like the playground visitors, the women standing at nearby sinks could not see her image in the mirror? Does the bathroom mirror, like the Kodak film, demonstrate the mind-numbing, almost impossible complexity of the invisibility process?

At this point in our examination of this phenomenon, I confess that these issues are beyond my understanding. I leave to Carol the seemingly insurmountable task of sorting out these intertwined philosophical, neurological and physical-science problems.

But a few more mundane observations about the psychological reactions the women have described are definitely in order. First, it seems to me that Mary and Judy's reluctance to question Katharina very closely when she first appeared makes a great deal of sense. They were undoubtedly aware that she was extremely nervous and uneasy and had no explanation for her hour-long delay. She was, after all, their guest, a speaker at their conference, and polite consideration of her feelings would dictate that they would not press her on the reasons she had made them wait for an hour, then startled them by turning up so suddenly.

Likewise, Katharina's desire to come up with a plausible explanation obviously coexisted with her need to vent a little of her shock and confusion to her friends. And so she did both: She said she was late because the plane was late, and then, amazingly, she said she had seemed to be invisible in the ladies' room. Her helplessness and her edge of panic would have led Mary and Judy to calmly go about getting her luggage together—Mary rented a cart—and then leaving the building as soon as possible to drive to the hotel. Questions about what really happened could come later.

All of this behavior seems, in retrospect, to be what one might have expected if Katharina's experiences were as she described. All of the details of the womens' accounts seem inherently truthful and far less gaudy and sensational than they would almost inevitably have been in an invented tale. For example, the important detail of the bothersome soap on Katharina's hands is nevertheless as dull—and as realistic—a detail as one can conceive.

And so once again we are left with a situation in which all of the evidence supports the "impossible" idea that UFO occupants can at least temporarily control the physical visibility of themselves, their craft, and their abductees. With this extraordinary technology, the covert daytime abduction of Katharina Wilson from America's busiest airport was as problem-free an operation as the abduction of Betty and Barney Hill from a car on a lonely mountain highway in the dead of night.

Chapter 7

HOW TO EXPLAIN KATHARINA?

A T THIS POINT IN OUR SCIENTIFIC PARADIGM, it would be absurd for me to make any attempt at a definitive statement about Katharina Wilson's experience *in the world as we know it*. As we see so often with the UFO phenomenon, our current scientific understanding of the universe is totally incapable of explaining certain areas of human experience. Without any ready tools with which to examine these experiences, mainstream science tends to ignore paranormal and anomalous experiences such as telepathy, precognition, and any form of mystical experience—including near-death experiences or a feeling of oneness with the universe—no matter how often reported. Michael Talbot, in his influential book *The Holographic Universe,* quotes Willis Harman, former senior social scientist at Stanford Research Institute International:

Why don't we assume that any class of experiences or phenomena that have been reported, through ages and across cultures, has a face validity that cannot be denied?[1]

Harman feels this acceptance is crucial not only to the development of science but, more importantly, to the ultimate survival of humankind. Throughout Talbot's work, as well as that of many respected scientists such as physicist Hal Puthoff and former astronaut Edgar Mitchell, there is the dawning urgency that scientific materialism—"What you see is what you get"—has blinded us to the fact that the physical world is only a small part of the greater reality around us. By our social and academic insistence on clinging so tightly to this current model of the world, we leave claw marks on the familiar, even as it slips away. By this clinging, we are willing ourselves into a static poverty of the mind and spirit.

Many physicists believe there are subtle energies still unknown to science, perhaps at a subquantum level beyond the atom. David Bohm, a protégé of Einstein's and one of the world's most respected physicists, is one of them. Using the holographic, 3-D image as a metaphor, Bohm suggests that what we think of as "reality"—the tangible aspects of our everyday lives—is actually a kind of illusion. Underneath this appearance is a deeper order of existence, a primary level of reality that is the source of all of our being, the originator of all of the objects of our reality—just as a snippet of holographic film gives rise to the realistic 3-D hologram. Bohm refers to this ground under all reality as the implicate, or enfolded, order. He states: "The implicate order has many levels of subtlety. If our attention can go to those levels of subtlety, then we should be able to see more than we ordinarily see."[2]

In looking at Katharina Wilson's troubling, confusing experience at O'Hare Airport, we may speculate about an abduction, or a changeable human energy field, even the possibility of teleportation, although we currently possess a limited knowledge of such subjects. Her experience that day appears to bear some relevance to one or more of these somewhat disparate ideas. But attempting to explain the incident definitively with these tentative concepts would be like a child struggling to build a toy cabin with the major beams of the Lincoln Log set missing.

In an attempt to locate the "major beams," we will look at several leading-edge technologies and draw some analogies to the physicality problems presented by Budd's "Strange Case of the Reluctant Faucets."

How Smart Are Those Sensors, Anyway?

A first rule of research is to eliminate the mundane by finding the most ordinary resolution to the problem. If that explanation is unsatisfactory, move on to the next reasonable cause and explore that, and so on. It wouldn't be logical or true to the principles of scientific discovery to bypass those nuts-and-bolts possibilities before reaching for the more exotic explanation.

So, in this case, I started with the faucets in the O'Hare Airport bathroom that wouldn't respond to Katharina's need to wash the soap off her hands. Unfortunately, I wasn't able to discover the manufacturer of the equipment in that particular women's room on that date. But by exploring the wide variety and types of equipment, we know what issues would be relevant to "reluctant" faucets.

I began by studying a diagram from a troubleshooting guide for automatic faucets: It's support material from one of dozens of American manufacturers of automatic sanitation equipment, which we've all used in public facilities countless times. When you stand at the sink, the infrared sensors at the base of the faucet go to work, quickly, invisibly, and usually reliably. Some sensors are designed to detect movement; some to detect heat. The most effective ones, heat sensors, measure the radiation temperature of your body to determine whether you're a human candidate ready for spritzing. Any object that generates heat also generates radiation, including the human body. Our skin is nearly an ideal radiator in the infrared range, which makes it relatively easy to set up a rest room's automatic sensor to do its job. When the human range of radiation temperature is sensed, the sensor turns the water on; the sensors turn the water off after the body (heat) moves away. Using timed sensors keeps the water from running too long when people linger in front of the sink and mirror.

There are a number of obvious technical problems that could explain the faucet's nonreaction to Katharina. Some automatic faucets are battery-powered; perhaps the batteries were low. But Katharina said she stepped right up behind other women using running water, indicating operative equipment. When *she* stood before the sensors, the water stopped. Nor is it likely that batteries for *all* the sinks ran down, simultaneously, in that brief interim. Katharina had tried different sinks, each time with the same result.

Other sanitation equipment is run off direct electrical current. If we posit that the electrical system was broken, we're left with the same logical problem as above. If the faucets worked for other physically present women, why not for Katharina, just seconds behind them? This same question applies to all the other troubleshooting suggestions given to me by a manufacturer—cleaning the diaphragm, stretching the solenoid spring, etc.

Now let's add to that problem with the faucets the fact that the woman Katharina spoke to directly did not respond to her in any way. On one hand, that might not be a significant detail. The encounter happened in an airport rest room, after all. Perhaps the other woman was an international traveler and didn't speak English. But complete disregard of a troubled question directed at one in close quarters isn't the way most people, no matter the language barrier, normally respond. There would be a look, a headshake, an *"Excusez-moi, je ne comprends pas,"* at the very least. From the entire set of circumstances, we can infer that Katharina was, for all practical purposes, invisible and inaudible in that ladies' room.

Budd and Katharina both suspect an abduction experience happened to her that day, beginning with her feeling of unease on the plane itself and her attraction to a woman reading an L. Ron Hubbard paperback—a pleasant, gray-haired woman Katharina was thinking she'd like to know. The missing hour is another indicator that Katharina's day had not proceeded along the same time line as the other travelers. What we don't know is whether Katharina was in the rest room *before* or *after* the abduction experience: This might be crucial in attempting to tie any invisibility technology to this incident.

If Katharina was abducted and then deposited back in the women's rest room in O'Hare, perhaps she was temporarily "stalled" in the state of invisibility, or cloaking that made her abduction from a crowded airport possible in the first place. Based on this premise, consider this possibility: Katharina was invisible to both the infrared sensor and the human eye because, during those few minutes between the rest room and the luggage terminal, she was not a light-absorbing body at all—neither in the visible human range nor infrared (the range for which the sensor was set). She might have been invisible like glass: Light passed right through her. An exotic explanation, to be sure, but one that is theoretically possible according to modern-day physics.

New Experiments with Transparency

It's certainly possible that Katharina's "invisibility" in the airport rest room had some ordinary explanation that we haven't considered. But it is also conceivable that her physical transparency was analogous to actions of quantum physics that even astrophysicists had not imagined until a few years ago.

Researchers have recently reported in the journal *Nature* that certain opaque substances can be made transparent—essentially invisible—when specially treated. Their experiments relate to two new phenomena in physics: the slowing down of light under laboratory conditions, and a complex phenomenon in certain gases called electromagnetically induced transparency (EIT).[3]

A team of physicists at the Harvard Smithsonian Center for Astrophysics have built on experiments in 1999 that slowed light down from its normal speed of 186,000 miles a second to 38 miles an hour. The next round of experiments slowed light in a gas called rubidium, which is opaque because it naturally absorbs the dark-red laser light used by the team. But when they shined a second laser with a different frequency through the gas, the scientists rendered it transparent. This is due to "the EIT effect," a quantum property in which the two lasers create a "beat frequency"—similar to what happens to two tuning forks that simultaneously sound slightly different notes.

The atoms of the rubidium gas don't easily absorb that new frequency (or light wave), so it lets the light pass right through. In other words, the gas becomes transparent. The light has actually been brought to a stop and stored completely in the atoms of the gas. "Essentially, the light becomes stuck in the medium, and it can't get out until the experimenters say so," said one of the researchers.[4]

We know that if something happens on a subatomic level, it is conceivable that a similar process can occur in the world visible to our senses. We can only wonder if Katharina might have been impacted by EIT in some way that we simply cannot yet understand.

Blackbodies

Another possible, related explanation for Katharina's frustration with the inert sensors involves a main principle of quantum physics: blackbody radiation. In 1800 an English astronomer, Sir William Herschel, noticed something surprising as he was using a prism to spread sunlight into a swath of colors. When he moved a blackened thermometer across the color spectrum, he found that the temperature heated up as he moved toward the red end of the spectrum. Maximum heating occurred far beyond the red end of the visible light spectrum—in the invisible spectrum we now call "infrared." Eventually, Herschel's discovery would lead to another relevant discovery: that all objects radiate infrared energy—all, that is, except objects with a temperature of absolute zero.

So where does the idea of a "blackbody" enter into the picture? Let's back up a moment and consider how different materials absorb radiation. This is important to our discussion, because how much energy is radiated, and at which wavelengths, depends on the surface of an object—its temperature and how effectively it radiates energy. Some materials, like glass, hardly absorb any light: Light goes right through, making such a material effectively *invisible*. On a shiny metallic surface, light isn't absorbed, either, but that doesn't cause transparency. The light is simply reflected, or reradiated. But in the case of totally black material like soot, heat and light are almost totally absorbed and the material becomes quite warm as it transfers energy from the light into heat. Max Planck was the first scientist to develop an equation to model the existence of a blackbody as an object that absorbs almost all incoming light and then emits any energy from that exchange *at all wavelengths*. His discovery, one of the most important in the field of physics, also established that blackbodies, as good absorbers of radiation, are also good emitters of radiation.[5]

Evidence gathered over the past fifty years clearly indicates that the aliens employ technologies more advanced than our own. Let's hypothesize that, in Katharina's case, they had the ability to manipulate the very particles of her human body, altering their normal ability to radiate energy. In effect, Katharina's alien abductors would have temporarily changed her into a being with a radiation frequency similar to a blackbody's—almost completely absorbing light and then reemitting it.

Wouldn't she then be setting off the automatic infrared sensors all over the airport rest room? No, and for a rather simple reason: Our theoretical blackbody gives off its energy at *all* wavelengths.[6] Consider how confusing that would be for the mass-produced, inexpensive sensors used in public facilities. They come preset to detect the normal human body's radiation level, energy, and wavelength. Any blackbody object— emitting levels traveling all over, from left to right of the senors' simple task—would most likely elicit confusion from the sensors and an inability to respond with a flow of water.

Blackbody theory as a form of invisibility can only be laid out as a possibility, one that we don't yet know how to manage, technically speaking. The next concept involves a human technology that is only a little further along in development than the theory of blackbodies. However, it has been realized in several limited applications, much to the astonishment of the scientific world.

Teleportation: Extra-Aerial Transport at O'Hare?

"We are not stuff that abides, but patterns that perpetuate themselves," said Norbert Wiener, a major figure in the history of molecular biology. The most crucial aspect about any organism isn't whether it dressed in vintage clothing, made a lovely mousse, or loved pug dogs. To Wiener, the most important aspect was the memory of an organism's *form,* the information about its structure and process. This *memory of form,* he believed, was what continued on in the organism's transmittal of genes and during cell division. Wiener was quite sure that scientists would one day be able to transmit a human being from one place to another simply by transmitting his or her informational *pattern.* Keep in mind that this was an idea from the 1950's, long before *Star Trek* began "beaming up" the crew of the starship *Enterprise.*[7]

Wiener and his colleagues went on to explore the idea that, metaphorically and actually, we humans are nothing but manifestations of information—like heaven and earth and everything in between. Later writers, like Michael Talbot, would concur: "The body is an energy construct and ultimately may be no more substantive than the energy field in which it is embedded."[8]

That was the idea that would influence so many creative thinkers, both in the arts and the sciences. *Teleportation* was the name that science fiction writers gave to the concept that a person or object could be made to disintegrate in one place, while a perfect replica appeared somewhere else. Think fax machine when you think of a teleportation machine, but one that would work on 3-D objects as well as documents—one that would produce an exact copy of the original but would destroy the original in the process of scanning and teleporting it to another place.

Until recently the idea of teleportation wasn't taken seriously by most scientists, mainly because it appeared to violate the uncertainty principle of quantum mechanics. This principle states that you can never precisely measure both where something is and how fast it is moving—not at the same time, that is. And without this precise description of the object you want to teleport, fashioning a replica of it seems impossible.

Then, just as a science problem appears bleakly impenetrable, our old mantra kicks in again: *Science is always a work in progress.* And, thankfully, the scientific playing field is positioned with some unorthodox thinkers looking for an end run around accepted principles. As recently as a month before this writing, a discovery about *quantum entanglement* was made that changed many people's ideas about the validity of "Beam me up, Scotty."

"From One Quantum State to Another, It's Shades of *Star Trek*" and "Teleporting Larger Objects Becomes Real Possibility"[9] read some very recent newspaper headlines. For the first time, the fantasy of teleporting molecules and atoms—and also larger objects—has entered the realm of the possible. Physicists have developed a method that in theory could be used to "entangle" absolutely any kind of particle. One day this could allow the teleportation of objects by transferring their properties instantly from one place to another.[10]

A bizarre property of physics, quantum entanglement, allows two particles to behave as one, no matter how far apart they are. Changes that occur to one particle instantly alter the other. For example, physicists can entangle two photons—particles of light—so that the measurable electric fields of each will point in the same direction. Measuring the whereabouts and state of one photon gives the orientation of the other: The photons appear to instantly communicate with each other, and the moment they are observed or measured in any way, they suddenly collapse into one reality, behaving as one photon. This phenomenon defies common sense and makes some scientists very uneasy. Even Albert Einstein, the father of quantum mechanics, wasn't comfortable with the idea. He called it "spooky action at a distance."[11]

Entanglement of atoms in a gas called cesium is the most recent experiment—and the first time that a quantum connection had been created between between two such tiny objects. A group of scientists at the University of Aarhus in Denmark reported that they had entangled trillions of cesium atoms, divided into two clouds. They shot a laser beam through the first cloud, causing a measurable tilt in the oscillating electric field of the atoms. When the laser then passed through the second cloud, the electric fields tilted some more.[12]

What happened next was a "trick" that the scientists pulled on nature, since they're not allowed by quantum mechanics to look at the clouds without destroying their separateness. The scientists *measured* the final tilt in the second cloud, which instantly entangled the atoms of Cloud One with those of Cloud Two.

The first two clouds then became a pair of secret encoder and decoder rings for finding and revealing—in a different place—a message carried by a third cesium cloud. Cloud Three—and its message— became entangled with Cloud One by a second laser beam, thus mangling the message, which essentially disappeared. But when one scientist transmitted information *about the laser* to a recipient, a beam identical to the second one could be constructed. And when the sender shot that duplicate beam back through the entangled cloud, there was a match from both sides between lasers and clouds. Suddenly the message reappeared in yet another cloud. A cluster of atoms containing information had just been "teleported" from one place to another.

These new findings have caused some knitted brows and quiet reconsideration of the teleportation issue. If teleportation actually exists in some form, it would entail transporting not matter (your body, say) but the complete set of information about you, every molecule of you, in such a way that the original information in the first location is destroyed.

But science fiction fans will have to be quite patient. None of the scientists working on this problem expect to be able to teleport people in the foreseeable future—mainly for engineering reasons, not because it would violate any fundamental laws of nature to do so. The comparatively mundane applications being discussed at this point revolve around developing unbreakable encryption techniques and building quantum computers.

But what if a visiting alien civilization has overcome the engineering problems of teleporting matter? After all, if something is possible on the subatomic level (which it now is), there isn't too big a jump of logic to believe that, given the right technologies and knowledge, it would be possible for a much larger object to exhibit the same behavior.

In other words, perhaps Mary Kerfoot, Katharina's host for the talk, was more correct than she knew when she laughingly told Budd about Katharina's appearance in the luggage area of the airport: "It was just very odd, [her] popping up behind someone and saying hello. Faith and I commented that we both thought she just popped out of the conveyor belt somehow. [Laughs] When I heard her behind me my first thought was 'Oh, she was teleported here.' "

It's worth considering. The mind boggles at the potential implications and applications of such a technology—military, of course; sexual trysts, without doubt; spying and espionage of all sorts; getting the business drop on competition; popping in from Istanbul for your mother's birthday in Brooklyn; or being abducted by a UFO in broad daylight out of a major American airport.

Chapter 8

THE RIPPLING WINDOW

JUST BEFORE CHRISTMAS in the year 2000, Carol and I made a multi-
purpose trip to the Chicago area to visit her family, to spend some
time basking at the Chicago Art Institute among the Cézannes and
Matisses, and to investigate several interconnected UFO abduction
reports. With regard to the subject matter of this book, we had been
quite reticent about discussing it with anyone, and at the time of our
Chicago trip the manuscript only existed in skeletal form. But, as often
happens, valuable new information about a subject we are currently
researching suddenly appears serendipitously. And so it did during our
Chicago stay. Entirely by accident, valuable new information about the
issue of UFO and abductee invisibility came to light from a reliable
source.

While looking into a complex multiple abduction case that involved
a former military officer and several other people, we met "Maggie."
Maggie is a married, middle-aged businesswoman who, rather than
making exaggerated claims, struck me as being somewhat hesitant,
even self-effacing when she described her UFO experiences. One of
these was a joint abduction with the Army officer whose various
accounts we were primarily investigating.

When I first interview possible abductees, I employ a series of subtle, covert tests designed to measure their credibility, and both Maggie
and the officer passed without the slightest problem. There is no need
here to go into the details of their recollections beyond saying that,

throughout our work together, I found absolutely no reason to doubt the veracity of either person. In fact, I judged them to be people of great natural integrity.

Carol and I ultimately spent several days looking into their shared and individual UFO experiences, conducting interviews and hypnotic regression sessions, and examining the sites of certain of their encounters. But then one evening lightning struck. As several of us were driving to a local restaurant for dinner, I asked Maggie if she recalled any odd childhood experiences that she thought, in retrospect, might be imperfectly recalled UFO abduction encounters. Somewhere amidst the things she said in reply was an offhand remark that riveted our attention.

"I have a friend named Joyce," she said, "who told me that when we were teenagers she watched me disappear, right before her eyes. And then she saw me return, but I don't remember anything about what might have happened to me that day. She didn't even tell me until years later that she'd once watched me disappear."

As coolly as I could, despite my immediate and intense curiosity, I asked for more details.

"At that time," she replied, "when I was in high school, I was having these experiences of feeling that I'd been taken at night from my room by somebody, and I was often pretty frightened. But I didn't connect any of it with UFOs—not till years later."

Other than Joyce's statement that it happened during their teenage years, Maggie could not pinpoint the time of her apparently sudden disappearance, a problem that, for me, was most unfortunate. It is almost always useless, I believe, to employ hypnosis with a subject who recalls no date, no time, or no specific conscious memories of an event allegedly witnessed by another party. But, luckily for us, Joyce, the first-hand witness, also lived in the Chicago area, and she and Maggie had remained close friends for perhaps thirty years, speaking frequently on the telephone.

In answer to my questions, Maggie described her friend as sensible, grounded, and not given to any special interest in the UFO phenomenon. I learned that Joyce was married and a mother, and although she was not highly educated, she was emotionally stable and economically comfortable. Throughout the interview I had with her a day or so later, I found nothing to suggest that she was particularly imaginative or given to wide-ranging speculation. What she saw the day when her friend vanished before her eyes had apparently been so startling that from that time forward she more or less willed herself to forget all about it, stowing it away on some shelf in the back of her mind.

Surprisingly, that "burying" reaction is more common than one might think. When a bizarre, previously unthinkable event is witnessed by someone like Joyce who is neither intellectually curious nor well read, and whose self-esteem is not very strong, that person will often keep the experience to herself rather than report it and run the risk of invoking ridicule and disbelief. There was no doubt to me that what Joyce witnessed that day had frightened her: She did not understand how it could have happened and seemed not to have the words to describe it in a way that would make it plausible. It was safer, she must have felt, to keep it to herself.

A day or so after Maggie informed me of what her friend had seen, Joyce and I talked by telephone. The following is a slightly edited version of the transcript of the conversation:

Joyce: You know, I never told anybody about this before I told Maggie, because I thought I was losing my mind. We were the same age at the time, about fifteen or sixteen, sophomores or juniors in high school. It was the summer because I remember it was green out, and we were at Maggie's house, upstairs in her bedroom. It was daytime.

Well, Maggie was out on this little sundeck she had off her bedroom, and I was inside looking out at her and she just disappeared! It looked so strange. It's hard to describe how she looked. Do you remember years ago when they first came out with plastic windows? You know how thick that plastic was? Well, when she disappeared, it was like somebody was wiggling that heavy plastic in front of her. She just vanished. And I thought, okay, *what's this?*—you know? And I blinked my eyes and rubbed my eyes and turned away and when I turned around she was back! I don't know if I turned around right away, but I did at some point, and she was back. The closest I can come to how she looked when she disappeared is how things look if you hold that heavy plastic up and kind of ripple it a little, wiggle it a little bit.

BH: *When she was back again, what did you say to her?*

Joyce: Well, when she came back in the bedroom—I wasn't out on the porch with her—she didn't say anything and I didn't say anything because I thought I was nuts! And I'm not even sure if she knew she did it.

BH: *Apart from thinking you're losing your mind or losing your eyesight or something, what were your feelings at the time you watched her disappear?*

Joyce: I don't know . . . just the feeling that you would have if something just disappeared and then popped up in front of you. We weren't that far apart. She was right outside the window and I was inside, in her bedroom. You know, I closed my eyes and rubbed them and turned my back to the window and then, when I turned back, she was there. I don't know what I felt, actually. I was kind of scared.

BH: *Did she seem to do this disappearing all at once or did one part of her disappear first and . . .*

Joyce: Well, I guess . . . I guess it would be all at once because she kind of like rippled, but that's not a good word. It's the only one I can think of. It looked a little like when you're driving along a highway and seeing the heat rippling on the road.

BH: *When you saw her on the sun porch in the daytime and she disappeared, was there anyplace she could have gone?*

Joyce: No, not unless she jumped off. It was the second floor. And then she'd have to fly back up.

BH: *Do you have any idea of how much time might have passed between the time you saw her disappear and the time you turned back around and saw her again?*

Joyce: No, not really. Because, like I told you first of all, I was a kid and I thought I was losing my mind.

Anyway, I'm going to guess that it was not a short time, but not a long time, either. Maybe a couple of minutes, because I didn't believe my eyes. That's why I turned around. And then I turned back again, and there she was.

BH: *Do you think that when you saw her disappear, you might have called out to her, like "Where did you go, Maggie?" or something like that?*

Joyce: I don't remember doing it. But I don't think she would have heard me anyway.

BH: *So you're facing her direction, but when she disappears, you turn away, and then you turn back to face where she'd been, and she's there again. Now, it seems to me that often, when you see something very strange, you may intensify your gaze. You might squint and stare, but why would you turn away? When you think back on the fact that you turned away, does it seem like the sort of thing you would have done under the circumstances?*

Joyce: It sounds like something I might do because I'd do it today. I'd turn away and then look back, you know.

BH: *At the time it happened, that day, did you tell anybody, like your mother or another friend, about this weird thing that happened to Maggie?*

Joyce: I only told my sister, but she was younger—three years younger than me—and she just didn't pay any attention.

BH: *Did you ever see anything else strange happening involving Maggie when you were younger?*

Joyce: Well, no, not really, except that she used to talk about how she felt—she used to talk to Sandra, too, that was her other friend—about how she would feel. Sometimes she would say she had the strangest feeling that somebody came and got her the night before.

BH: *Did you or Maggie ever discuss UFOs at the time?*

Joyce: No. But a few years ago, when she first talked about her UFO experiences, I got to thinking: Maggie's not one to make up stories. We don't drink or do drugs, and I got to wondering about it and you go back and think, *Maybe that's what it was about . . . UFOs . . . the time she disappeared.*

Much more can be said about this incident, and much more needs to be investigated. Joyce is not eager to try hypnosis, and so this case is currently at something of a dead end. But when we examine what she was able to recall, and when we consider her emotions and reactions at the time of the incident, there are valuable insights to be gained.

First, and most immediately significant, is the credibility of Joyce's testimony. She made no attempt to change or embellish her account, even though I asked the same questions in slightly different form at various points in an interview (which was longer and more repetitive than the edited version above). There is also something convincingly modest and "everyday" in the way she described the way Maggie looked as she disappeared, "rippling" as if she were being viewed through thick plastic window covers. Had Joyce been making things up and seeking to attract attention, she surely could have invented a simile a little more interesting or exotic than plastic window covers. Special effects in sci-fi films and television would provide many possible prototypes far more wondrous than thick commercial plastic.

Also, there is the way Joyce presents herself in her account. Rather than giving herself a dramatic or even central role, she appears to be not only passive and marginal but frightened and confused. "I was a kid," she said, "and I thought I was losing my mind." When I asked if she had said anything to Maggie when she reappeared, if she been making things up, she could have used my question as an opportunity to invent an interesting dialogue. Instead, she portrayed herself as silent, shy, and uncertain, saying nothing about what she had observed.

And when she later told her little sister about it, the younger girl "didn't pay any attention." This is hardly the way one glamorizes one's role in reporting a dramatic incident, yet it has the ring of truth when one imagines a twelve-year-old hearing such a bizarre and unbelievable statement from her fifteen-year-old sister.

If we speculate as to what actually happened that day to Maggie and Joyce, it is easy to imagine that just prior to her abduction, Maggie had been rendered "unseeable" while her friend watched. (An alien slip-up? A deliberate demonstration?) Then, a moment or so later, Joyce was switched off until the abduction was over and Maggie was returned. Since it is clear that Joyce has no firm idea of how much time passed between her friend's disappearance and reappearance, there could have been a minute between the two, or an hour, or any other period of time. People recovering from a switched-off state generally perceive no time loss at all—unless they check a watch or clock, or it is suddenly dark out—and so naturally they assume that events were continuous. It is surely plausible, then, that Joyce may have stood for quite some time in Maggie's bedroom before she turned around and once more saw her friend. We will undoubtedly never know.

To summarize: Here, in Joyce's testimony, we have a third kind of evidence for an alien technology of invisibility: eyewitness testimony from an independent, outside observer. I began the argument for the presence of the invisibility technology by citing three examples from among thousands of relevant abduction cases that establish *by implication* the functional necessity for temporary alien-UFO-abductee invisibility;

1. Molly and her brother floating *unseen* from their bedroom window into a huge UFO hovering over their building in a busy neighborhood in broad daylight, and then being returned to the ground outside their house, again unseen.

2. Marianne and Angie being taken *unseen* from their suburban Queens house up into a UFO, again in daylight, and being returned, still *unseen*, as police, neighbors and Angie's mother searched for them.

3. And finally Air Force noncoms Dennis and B.J. being abducted *unseen* from their firetruck parked on the tarmac at an Air Force base, in full view of the control tower and other Air Force personnel.

These three cases are excellent examples of why researchers have come to believe that the only way abductions could take place under these circumstances is if the entire operation, craft, crew, and abductees were somehow unseeable. This is the argument for invisibility based on implication.

But then we have gone on to support this implication by outlining three more abduction cases, each of which presents a more direct kind of evidence:

1. First, there are the Washburn photographs, taken while the four family members were apparently invisible, which show the settings in which they were posing in a busy playground on a Saturday afternoon, but which also demonstrate the fact that they themselves did not register on the film.

2. This bizarre physical evidence is followed by the Katharina Wilson case, in which she became aware, in a women's rest room at O'Hare International Airport, of her own invisibility because of the behavior of other women who were apparently unable to see or hear her, and because of her inability to affect the sensors on any of the water taps at the lavatory sinks. Her sudden appearance before her friends, who should have seen her approach, indicates her instant return to a visible state.

3. Finally, with Joyce, we have the eyewitness testimony of an independent outside party who watched the process of invisibility occur when her friend Maggie vanished before her eyes.

I present these six cases, not with the idea that I have thereby *proved* the existence of an alien technology of invisibility, but in the belief that cumulatively these cases provide enough credible, coherent, and mutually supportive evidence to demand the attention of UFO researchers, scientists, military leaders and open-minded citizens everywhere. The possibility that aliens possess this kind of technology should leave all of us profoundly uneasy. We should demand nothing less than a thorough scientific investigation of the UFO abduction phenomenon and all that it implies.

Chapter 9

MAGGIE'S HOLOGRAPHIC BODY?

R ECENTLY, BUDD AND I HAD A VISIT from a friend we'll call Anne-Marie, whose story will be told more fully in a later chapter. But I mention her now because she's the abductee who has most recently talked to us about her childhood memories of an intense *humming* sound. "It wasn't just that I heard it," Anne-Marie said. "I would actually *feel it vibrating* through my whole body. And that's when I'd start to get scared. Somehow, I knew something was going to happen to me. . . ." Over the several years that Budd worked with Anne-Marie's conscious and hypnotically retrieved memories, it became clear that this humming sound was a definite indicator that an abduction was soon to follow.

In Budd's case files, many abductees report both hearing and feeling a vibrational kind of sound just prior to an abduction experience. But is their humming connected to Joyce's rippling in the last case? Let's take a look at several cases reported by former NASA engineer Paul Hill:

- The general manager and chief engineer of a St. Louis broadcast station went fishing on Lake of the Ozarks. On a foggy day, four hundred yards from shore, their outboard motor died. The men heard a humming noise, and when the fog parted, they saw a disc hovering right above the water, about one hundred feet away.

Directly under the craft, the water was agitated into in thousands of sharp-pointed waves. Hill comments: *"The force field was vibrating the water."* [emphasis added.]

- In the Lorenzens' *UFOs Over America*, the authors cite a case of two Swedish men who investigated a light coming from the woods. They discovered a saucer-shaped object on the ground and encountered several small beings. After major cultural shock on both sides, the saucer took off. One of the witnesses said that the most remarkable thing was "the high, intense sound you felt rather than heard. When the object left we were shaken by powerful, extremely rapid vibrations that quite paralyzed us." A medical team that examined the men concluded that the men "had actually encountered a field force [or "force field"] of enormous strength."[2]

Hill devotes a substantial segment of his book to this phenomenon, saying that the "feeling" of the noise indicates that a vibrational force of precisely the same frequency as the sound is at work.[3] Putting this evidence together with other reports of people seeing UFOs that cause stationary objects like street signs to vibrate violently and set smooth water roiling (the sharp-pointed waves in the earlier example), Hill and his colleague Dr. Robert Wood concluded that a UFO's force field is cyclic. In other words, the energy put out by a UFO isn't just a static field but is made up of a large number of waves that are sent out repeatedly from the craft, in much the same way that water ripples out from a pebble dropped into it.

Proceeding with calculations in physics to show the validity of his theory, Hill further investigates what might happen right below a hovering UFO. He shows in some detail what effect that sound pressure could have on an ordinary flexible body that was under the cyclic field:

Energy is transported across space by the cyclic field, and sound, at cyclic field frequency, is generated *at the body surfacess* . . . at the interface between two mediums having different stiffness . . . i.e., a different ability to resist the accelerations of the cyclic field. In the human body, *that interface is the skin.* [emphasis added][4]

In other words, the humming sound that abductees often report could also be felt. The cyclic force field would cause an object below it to ripple or express vibrations and waves on its surface. Think back to the "window" effect Joyce described: The rippling may have been vibrations on her friend Maggie's skin—an effect caused by the wavelike vibrations sent out by the cycling field of a UFO that was either just arriving or just departing.

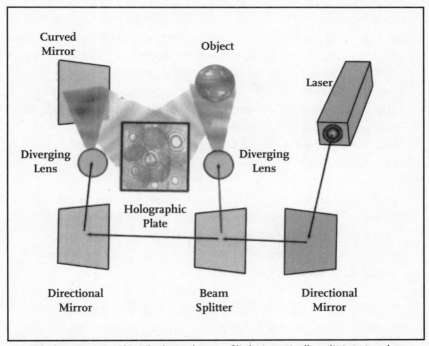

A 3-D hologram is produced when a beam of light is optically split into two beams. One, the object beam, is bounced off the subject of the hologram. The second, a reference beam, is directed to circle back and collide with the reflected light of the object beam. The interference pattern is recorded on film. (Graphic by Charles Foltz)

If this incident, which coincided with a period of abductionlike experiences in Maggie's young life, was actually a precursor to an abduction, it's possible to speculate that some characteristic of the engulfing, wavelike force sent out by the craft itself may contribute to making individuals temporarily invisible.

Clues From the Hologram?

You might recall that in the first *Star Wars* movie, Luke Skywalker's journey begins when a beam of light shoots out from a robot and projects a small, three-dimensional image of Princess Leia. Mesmerized by the ghostly figure pleading for help, Luke is hooked forever. The Princess Leia that Luke sees is a hologram, a 3-D image made with the aid of laser lights and a phenomenon known as interference patterns. Luke would be able to walk around the hologram and see the entire princess from every angle. She would turn, speak, and actually seem to *be there*. But if Luke reached out to touch her, his hand would pass right through the lovely lady.

Another way to consider Maggie's disappearance and reappearance is in the context of the theory of the holographic universe. Based on the work of David Bohm and Karl Pribram, the theory suggests that what we think of as concrete reality is not so solid at all. As Michael Talbot explains:

> *Our brains mathematically construct objective reality by interpreting [wave or energy] frequencies that are ultimately projections from another dimension, a deeper order of existence that is beyond both space and time: The brain is a hologram enfolded in a holographic universe.*[5]

Technically, what makes a hologram possible is the phenomenon of *interference*. This refers to the rippling pattern that occurs when two waves cross paths. If, for example, you dropped two rocks into a pond, each one would send off a series of concentric waves expanding outward. When the two sets of expanding waves cross one another, it's in the crests and troughs of these waves that the interference pattern occurs. Waves of water, waves of sound—any wavelike phenomena—can create interference patterns. In creating a visual image, scientists have found that laser light, being pure and coherent, is especially good at recording interference patterns on film. But all you see by looking directly at the film is a jumble of crisscrossing wavelike images. It's only when the film is illuminated later with another laser that a 3-D image of the original object reappears in front of your eyes.

The hologram can also be useful as a metaphor for conceptualizing the design of the universe:

> *We have very different aspects to our reality. We can view ourselves as physical bodies moving through space. Or we can view ourselves as a blur of interference patterns [within] the cosmic hologram.*[6]

Perhaps it was this blur of "interference patterns"—or the ripple effect—that Joyce caught a glimpse of at the moment her friend Maggie entered into a different state of reality or a spectrum that we rarely see into.

Chapter 10

A NOTE ON UFO RESEARCH

BEFORE WE LEAVE THE TOPIC of the unseen to take up an even more controversial pattern within UFO abduction accounts, a bit of historical clarification is called for. Beginning sometime in the early 1980's, a few abduction researchers were forced by the data to hypothesize that the aliens possessed an "invisibility technology" that enabled them to carry out abductions in daylight in densely populated areas without being seen. The subject was, however, talked about only in private. I recall a conversation I had with my colleague David Jacobs around 1983, in which we discussed the aliens' capability of operating so that neither they, their craft, nor their abductees were visible to the naked eye. Both of us felt that there was no way that abductions could be carried out on the scale the evidence implied unless total visual cloaking was possible.

But in 1983 the idea that UFO abductions were extraordinarily frequent and widespread was, in itself, highly controversial, even among those who took the UFO phenomenon seriously. Therefore, to suggest in published articles or even in public lectures that the UFO occupants possessed a technology of invisibility was to court disbelief and rejection even among our colleagues. And so abduction researchers kept silent on the issue, confining our public statements to other aspects of the phenomenon for which abundant evidence exists.

Finally, it was David Jacobs, perhaps the bravest and most forthcoming researcher in the field, who broke the ice. At a UFO conference in

Santa Barbara, California, in 1990, he presented the first carefully researched paper on the subject, arguing that the abduction reports themselves *required* a condition of temporary UFO and abductee invisibility. Several years later I presented a paper on the subject at a conference in Virginia, but these venues were intimate enough that the general public was unaware such a radical idea was being taken seriously.

This is the historical background for the subject we have been considering. The second section of our book deals with a different subject that is, if anything, even more radical than the issue of invisibility. But then, the thought of intelligent nonhuman beings coming here and interacting with planet Earth—that widely accepted idea itself—is so revolutionary that it undermines many of the most cherished tenets of traditional science and, like much cutting-edge scientific thought, forces us to consider a virtually infinite array of new possibilities.

PART II

SEEN

Chapter 11

ALIENS HERE AND NOW

I F WE ACCEPT THAT THOUSANDS of well-investigated UFO abduction cases provide authoritative evidence that nonhuman alien beings are visiting our planet, we must now consider the unsettling possibility that they are also living on Earth. They may be only temporary residents, but they are operating unnoticed among humans, helping to facilitate an as yet undisclosed agenda. If this is true—if some aliens can survive or even flourish here—then what might their coexistence eventually mean to us, to our children, to our planet? What might the future hold for our civilization as we know it?

Xenophobia—the fear of foreigners or strangers—is unfortunately basic to man's essentially territorial nature. To show how deeply this xenophobic fear of the unknown infects all of us, let me use myself as an example. In 1964, I had a daytime UFO sighting on Cape Cod, an incident which led to my subsequent research into the UFO phenomenon.[1] At the time, I remember regarding the circular, hovering, dull-aluminum-colored object as a *thing*, an artifical craft of some sort, but I did not for a moment think there might be intelligent nonhuman beings inside. That was too exotic a thought to entertain even for a moment—and on some unconscious, primitive level, far too disturbing.

My reaction exactly echoed the attitude of many of the early UFO researchers, men and women who took the UFO phenomenon seriously, virtually assuming its extraterrestrial origin, but remained dubious about the authenticity of any UFO *occupant* reports. If these alien craft existed, the idea that there might be intelligent life forms inside, controlling the craft, was eminently plausible but—for us nervous, irrational humans—too much to accept. In rereading some of the early books and articles on the subject of UFOs, I was amazed, again and again, at how *unadventurous* the thinking of some of these researchers—myself included—actually was. Our hypotheses were as parsimonious as we could make them, a situation as much due to the unnerving nature of the subject as it was an attempt to adhere to the demands of the scientific method.

My past ideas about the subject include yet another embarrassing example of narrow, hypercautious thinking. Having seen, on Cape Cod in 1964, along with two other witnesses, the hovering and maneuvering UFO—and having subsequently read what I could find about the phenomenon—I bought the 1966 issue of *Look* magazine in which John Fuller presented a condensed version of his book on the Betty and Barney Hill abduction account.[2] I simply could not believe it. I had no solid reason to reject their story, and within a year or so changed my mind, but in 1966 this first publicized abduction account was just too wild, too disturbing, to accept. In some illogical way I viewed the Hills' abduction account as an affront to reason.

UFOs were supposed to be *out there* somewhere, looking down maybe and flying around, but essentially leaving us alone. The closer the phenomenon seemed to come, the more my natural self-protective, xenophobic objections manifested themselves. Speculation about UFO propulsion systems was fine. Thoughts about antigravity, aliens' study of Earth's natural resources, and the various places they may have come from—all of this was easier to handle than the idea of the UFO occupants temporarily borrowing us against our wills and treating *us* as specimens. Technology—even advanced, alien technology—is always a more neutral subject for speculation than potential alien interactions with us and our planet. When that subject is broached, muscles tense, nerves go on full alert, and we glance warily over our shoulders.

And so we come to the way this homely truth has directly affected the structure of our book. After years of examination of the data, researchers such as myself have absorbed a great deal of information about the appearance and interests of both the UFO occupants and what seem to be their hybrid creations. Based upon that mass of eye-witness testimony and various kinds of physical evidence, our anthropocentric logic suggests that from time to time these beings want to explore our environment, unobtrusively mixing with us and experiencing something of the quality and complexity of human life. There are many credible eyewitness accounts supporting such alien explorations, as we will learn. And yet, the idea of such coexistence, even if temporary, is so unsettling that it is likely to be rejected out of hand by many of those who nevertheless accept the existence of UFOs and their alien occupants.

To avoid such a knee-jerk reaction, Carol and I decided not to open this book with witness accounts of alien life forms interacting with us, at least temporarily, in somewhat quotidian ways: visits to stores, to playgrounds, and to offices. Instead, we began our book by examining a technological issue: the apparent alien mastery of tactical invisibility. But which is really the more outrageous concept: that one has the ability to render oneself, one's craft, and one's captive humans invisible, or the possibility that UFO occupants might wish to leave their craft temporarily to visit us and learn from our day-to-day environment? Ironically, the idea of alien sight-seeing visitations draws more natural resistance than the concept of a highly developed technology of invisibility. It is all, I believe, a matter of emotional distance. We can contemplate the UFO occupants' ability to render matter temporarily invisible, but we don't want alien "hybrids" in our schools and bookstores.

The next portion of this book takes up these accounts of alien-human interactions and the science that deals with advanced transgenics and issues of hybridization. Please stay with us, no matter how incredible the reports, no matter how uncomfortably close the UFO phenomenon seems to be coming. You have plenty of company in your unease—Carol and me included.

We have seen that most early researchers were loath to deal with reports of UFO occupants until the sheer mass of data forced them to swallow that bitter pill, and that they were then even more hesitant to accept abduction accounts. Too close, much too close. But after that emotional barrier was also forced aside by the weight of credible witness accounts, most researchers—and I was one—erected yet another roadblock against a new kind of data: We did not want to consider the many reports of alien reproductive procedures apparently carried out upon abductees during their encounters. That was *really* too close!

But these kinds of disturbing data were present in the very earliest abduction reports. In the seminal Betty and Barney Hill case in 1961, Betty described the painful insertion of a long needle into her navel, a procedure the aliens described to her as a "pregnancy test." Another important and somewhat similar detail from that 1961 abduction was not included in John Fuller's classic account of the Hill case because it was regarded as too unseemly: The UFO occupants also extracted a sperm sample from Barney Hill.[3] Researchers somehow managed to set aside such intimate and uncomfortable details—particularly the so-called pregnancy test—partly because in the 1960's the idea of insert-ing a needle in the navel to determine pregnancy seemed ludicrous. That, of course, was well before amniocentesis—a procedure in which a needle is inserted in the navel to extract a sample of the woman's amniotic fluid—became a commonly used test of the health and viabil-ity of the fetus. In other words, a kind of "test of the pregnancy."

Later abduction accounts and the analysis of many case studies sug-gest that the aliens' "needle-in-the-navel" procedures were not tests to determine if a woman is pregnant but might actually have been ova-retrieval operations and thus exactly analogous to commonly reported sperm-sampling operations such as the one Barney Hill underwent.[4] I believe that the deeper reason few researchers in the sixties wanted to pay much attention to such details was that they were too disturbingly intimate.

In 1965, a small-circulation British UFO magazine published an important and shocking article that alerted UFO researchers to yet another apparent reproductive procedure.[5] It was an account of the 1957 abduction in Brazil of a very credible witness, Antonio Villas-Boas, in which he described being taken into a landed UFO and made to perform two acts of sexual intercourse in quick succession with a small female. He described her as not entirely earthly in appearance, with whitish-blond hair, a wide face with prominent cheekbones, and a pointed chin.[6] She had "big blue eyes, rather longer than round, for they slanted outward, like those pencil-drawn girls made to look like Arabian princesses."

After the second act of intercourse with Villas-Boas, this odd-looking woman spooned from the side of his penis a small sample of his sperm and placed it in a vial. Then, just before she left the area in which he was was being held, she pointed first to her belly and then to the sky, an ambiguous gesture that can easily be interpreted as implying a hoped-for pregnancy. Again, most serious UFO researchers put such an unsettling account on a mental back burner and proceeded with the decades-long investigation of craft sightings.

My own hesitant attitude toward data suggesting an alien reproductive agenda—sperm and ova retrievals and, theoretically, the systematic creation of beings who share human and alien genetic qualities—changed dramatically in 1983. The turning point was my investigation of the "Kathie Davis" abduction case, which I presented to the public in my 1987 book *Intruders: The Incredible Visitations at Copley Woods*. Kathie's was the first of hundreds of similar cases I subsequently investigated in which women reported being abducted and apparently artificially inseminated, after which they found themselves pregnant. Then, equally mysteriously, about the end of the first trimester but often weeks or months later, the pregnancies disappeared, with no trace of fetal tissue. In one case, an abductee who is by profession an obstetrical nurse had her fetus disappear in the fifth month, and though she passed the fetal sac and experienced some bleeding, she was disturbed to find that there was no actual fetal tissue. I have investigated two remarkable cases in which the pregnancies disappeared overnight in the seventh month, without any of the serious, even dangerous symptoms that usually accompany such late miscarriages.[7]

In investigating missing-fetus cases, I have often encountered both difficult emotional issues and nearly insuperable problems in locating old medical records. For example, in 1988, I was contacted by a Massachusetts woman concerned about a series of UFO sightings and missing-time experiences that had always puzzled her. In the course of an interview she mentioned that well over twenty years earlier, at the age of nineteen, she had become pregnant, and the fetus had mysteriously disappeared in its *seventh* month. Her mother, whom I also interviewed at length, had regularly accompanied her daughter, a young and inexperienced bride, to her obstetrician. The pregnancy was developing normally, until one morning when the mother-to-be awoke with some odd, fragmented memories and knew that she was no longer pregnant. Though her belly was not as distended as it had been, she was not bleeding. Her mother immediately took her to the obstetrician, who examined her and found that the fetal heartbeat he had regularly heard was no longer detectable. After further examination he performed a dilation and curettage, or D & C, a cleansing procedure often performed after a miscarriage or the death of a fetus; though he located the placenta, he found no trace of the fetus itself. He also had no explanation as to what had happened to it.

The mother of this saddened and mystified young woman confided to me during our 1988 interview that she had never liked her daughter's husband, the father of the vanished baby. In fact, she said, she distrusted him—and his family as well. Then, when her daughter was out of earshot, she described to me the evil plot that she thought lay behind the disappearance. Speaking in a near whisper, she said:

> I believe her husband and his family plotted with the doctor to drug my daughter and steal her baby. I think they drugged her when she was sleeping and took her to the doctor's office, and then he delivered it so they could keep it. Then they brought my daughter home when she was still drugged and put her back in bed. That's why she doesn't remember what happened to it. They stole her baby. That's what I've always believed.

This was, of course, an explanation every bit as bizarre as the widely reported alien reproductive program, though the mother was unable to offer even a shred of evidence for her theory.

As to the problem of locating the medical records, the fetal disappearance had occurred over a quarter of a century before I was told about it. The obstetrician, I learned from both mother and daughter, was probably no longer living, as he had been quite elderly at the time. And since he had been in private practice in a midwestern city and was probably long since deceased, I was not even certain that his medical records still existed, even if his bygone office was traceable. Also, because obstetricians are the medical specialists most often sued for malpractice, one might well imagine that he would not wish to keep scrupulous notes about such a potentially damaging mystery.

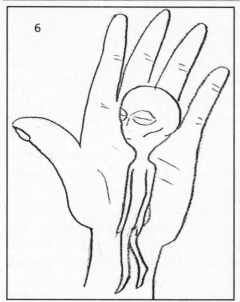

Drawing of a tiny transgenic fetus with closed eyes, drawn by male abductee A.M.

Drawing of a tiny transgenic fetus in a female abductee's hand. (B.C.)

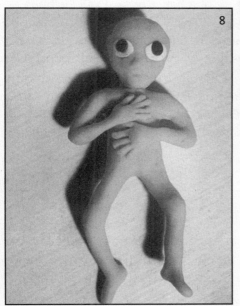

Clay model of a transgenic baby as presented to female abductee L.C.

Even today, few obstetricians are willing to state in their notes that the disappearance of a patient's fetus after the third month presents a medical mystery—or that it is even unusual—lest they become targets of malpractice suits. Instead, they offer many different theories to explain away such uncomfortable problems: missed abortion, fetal "absorption," unreported miscarriage, and so on. If nature abhors a vacuum, medicine abhors a mystery.

Though the phenomenon of a vanished fetus is a fascinating part of the alien reproduction program, for our purposes here its most important aspect is the "baby presentation" scene which I described at length in *Intruders*.[8] In scores of cases I have investigated, female abductees recall being reabducted months or even years after their missing fetus experiences and are then shown a small baby or even a toddler that they are made to feel is their own. During these reabductions the aliens usually want the putative mother to hold the baby and to bond with it. After a short time the infant is taken away and the abductee, often grieving at the separation, is returned to the place from which she was abducted.

These children—who, for want of a better term, I call "hybrids"— are described by the abductees as showing a mix of alien and human characteristics. Often the eyes are quite large and either blue or almost entirely black. They usually have thin, wispy, white-blond hair that does not seem to evenly cover their scalp. Their noses are small or nearly nonexistent, their lips are thin, and their heads often overly large. Though they have not often been naked when they were presented, on those exceptional occasions abductees have said that the children seemed to lack navels.

Interestingly, the description Antonio Villas-Boas gave of the "not entirely earthly-looking female" he encountered during his 1957 abduction—whitish-blond hair, a wide face with prominent cheekbones, large, slanted blue eyes—sounds like an adult version of the typical hybrid child or baby reported in hundreds of later baby-presentation accounts. It should also be pointed out that sometimes men are shown small hybrids in these scenes and made to feel that in some way they are the children's fathers. Perhaps even more important, the emotions reported by abductees during these presentation scenes vary—from intense love and acceptance of "their" children, all the way to revulsion and the impulse to physically drop the children rather than accept them as their own. To me, this range of reaction seems psychologically appropriate if these baby presentations are actual events, rather than some new type of parental fantasy.

Carol Rainey will discuss the thorny but immensely interesting questions of how these creatures are actually produced—and what methods of "genetic engineering" might be utilized—in forthcoming chapters, but there is one final detail that warrants mentioning here. When Betty Hill was abducted in 1961, she described an alien "doctor" scraping her arm with a kind of dull knife, apparently taking skin samples. Hundreds of later abductees have described the same puzzling operation, and Linda Cortile, the subject of my book *Witnessed,* said that the instrument used to scrape her arm was "like a kind of butterknife," inflicting no pain and drawing no blood.

Similarly, hundreds of abductees recall a small scooplike instrument being used on their bodies—most often on their lower legs—to dip down and remove a sample of flesh. This procedure often draws at least some blood and usually leaves a distinctive scar—a round or oval depression sometimes as large as the size of a dime. Medical observers who have examined these scoop marks describe them as resembling the marks left by punch biopsy procedures, though we do not yet know the purpose of this alien skin-sampling program.

It is only in the last few years of human genetic research that skin-sampling procedures have become common as an efficient way of collecting useful genetic material. Is it possible that the decades-old scoop marks and skin scrapings were signs of an advanced alien technology preceding our own, in the way that Betty Hill's "pregnancy test" was a precursor of amniocentesis?

Since 1987, when the alien transgenic program was first described in *Intruders,* researchers have amassed a great deal of new data on this aspect of the abduction phenomenon from similar cases around the world. One would expect that this new case material would tend either to confirm or contradict what had previously been hypothesized. In every related report I have seen, and in my conversations with the other experienced abduction researchers in the field (our numbers are, unfortunately, small), I have seen, over and over again, striking confirmation of the accounts I presented in 1987 and virtually nothing to discredit those findings.

Chapter 12

NEW LIFE-FORMS

B Y THE WINTER OF 1999, Budd and I had married and the UFO strangeness had become an integral part of my life. Letters, calls, and E-mails from abductees poured into our Manhattan home. Budd was often occupied with face-to-face interviews or hypnotic regressions in our living room, kitchen, and studio, and I often videotaped those sessions. As I got to know the abductees, I saw for myself that they were, on the whole, quite credible individuals and that their independent stories formed a chain of anecdotal evidence. Whether these experiences were occurring "in outer space or in inner space," as Carl Sagan had once famously declaimed, I was profoundly intrigued by the inexplicable nature of the phenomenon.

Yet, there were many times in those first few years when I was shaken with great doubts—and in no area more than that of the abductees' reports of mysterious reproductive procedures and "hybrid babies." At first glance, these accounts—implying human-alien interbreeding—seemed too illogical, too implausible, and too disturbing to be true. Most of us, after all, had been taught in high school and college biology classes that nature has erected barriers between species that make interbreeding an extraordinarily rare event. Abductees telling us of their human-alien offspring simply overstretched the limit of my credulity.

Yet, as I continued my research in the burgeoning new fields of genetic engineering, cloning, and transgenics, it struck me that many of the most recent accomplishments of our own science were nearly as strange and unacceptable in some visceral way as is the abduction phenomenon. Here are a few examples of our current capabilities in reproductive science:

- Children born with genes from *three* parents, which permanently, and with no one's permission, have altered the human genome. Long-term results: unknown.

- Humanized mice and pigs—animals with human genes inserted into their genetic code. Purpose: to make pigs more human so that their organs can be transplanted into humans without being rejected (a process called xenotransplantation).

- A transgenic rabbit that glows green under fluorescent light, the result of an artist's conceptual piece. The rabbit was custom-designed by hiring scientists to insert a permanent new gene from a jellyfish into the bunny genome.

- Recent creation of a sheep-goat chimera at the University of California at Davis—a cross-species breeding previously thought impossible.

- The cloning of herds of genetically identical, genetically engineered goats and cows that carry human genes and are designed to produce drugs in their milk for human use. Pharmaceutical factories on four legs.

- Biologists who have transplanted a specific *behavior* from the brain stem of one species of bird into another—resulting in young chickens with the head-bobbing movements and song of a quail.

This is all major news from the far edges of science. How each person may feel about these accomplishments and their possible future applications varies widely. One common reaction is very like the seemingly intrinsic repulsion people feel upon first hearing of the possibility

A technician checks on future transgenic peach and apple orchards. Each dish holds tiny experimental trees grown from lab-cultured cells to which researchers have given new genes. (Photo courtesy of the Agricultural Research Service, U.S. Department of Agriculture)

that extraterrestrials or nonhumans from not-Earth are blending our genomes with their own. There's a shock, a kind of moral disapproval, a sense that science (like the aliens) is playing a God-like role in altering what was originally created. Fear, I suspect, is also part of the emotion—the feeling that we're moving into a world where nothing seems

We are now able to transcend the limitations of particular species and combine the virtues (and vices) of different species and indeed program into species ... attributes never before a feature of any species. ... We can, or eventually will be able to, create new "transgenic" creatures of unprecedented nature and qualities. It would not be an exaggeration to say that humanity now stands at a crossroads.

—John Harris,
Wonderwoman and
Superman: The Ethics of
Human Biotechnology

set and determined, where everything in nature can be tweaked, twisted, altered, and changed beyond anything we know. Including our own human selves.

And that is why the new research above has distinct implications for our speculation on the alien-human hybrids so often reported. It is clear that the borders that have always prevented cross-species breeding from occurring are collapsing. Most of us—the public, scientists, and philosophers alike—have always thought of species as unchanging and sharply distinct entities, with each defined by its own genome. This idea explains, for example, much of the "confirmation jolt" felt by both scientists and the lay public when the final sequencing of the human genome in 2000 showed that humans and chimpanzees differ genetically by a mere 1.3 percent. In fact, nearly all life on Earth is genetically quite close. It's not only primates that have a great deal in common with humans. Mice and humans have a great deal in common, as do yeast and humans. If we persist in holding on to the concept that nature has put up firewalls between different species, sharply delineating them according to their genes, we are in for even greater shocks. In the following chapters, we'll see how those firewalls are quickly becoming permeable boundaries—and how the life-forms that are being newly created, by both humans and aliens, are born into and exist in a no-man's-land on a map we have yet to locate.

Chapter 13

EYEWITNESS TESTIMONY AND
A COMMAND PERFORMANCE

THE RADICAL NATURE OF THE MATERIAL I am about to present requires some discussion of the issues of personal credibility and eyewitness testimony. The validity of the following accounts—in which apparently nonhuman beings are seen operating, at least temporarily, within our quotidian reality—is almost completely dependent upon two factors: the believability of the individual eyewitnesses, and the extent to which these reports form distinct, mutually corroborating patterns. Unlike UFO sightings and typical abduction cases, these are not the kinds of reports in which the gathering of supportive physical evidence is sometimes possible. Here, so far as I know, there are no photographs, videotapes, radar returns, ground traces, medical anomalies, scars, lesions, or X rays of any sort. Nevertheless, I have done what I could to investigate all of the following cases, relying upon such techniques as probing interviews, subtle credibility testing, and extensive hypnosis, and have found no reason to doubt their validity.

The reliability of eyewitness testimony has often been challenged—it is challenged in courtrooms every day of every week—but recently it has become the subject of extensive study and argument by psychologists and social scientists. Personal testimony has become a contentious issue. At the fringe of this discussion, there are some who characterize eyewitness testimony as ranging from thoroughly unreliable to absolutely worthless. However, in the light of our normal, every-day activities, this rejection of eyewitness testimony is not only a grotesque brand of ultraskepticism but an unnecessary obstacle to the search for truth.

To help us understand the importance of eyewitness testimony in UFO cases, let us consider a parallel situation—its role in the criminal court system. Apart from cases in which the accused confesses to the crime or pleads guilty, a jury in a criminal trial would never convict anyone of a crime without hearing and believing eyewitness testimony of some sort. Even if only documentary or laboratory "circumstantial evidence" bearing on the crime is presented in court, someone—a police officer, a lab technician, a scientist, whoever—must testify to his or her personal, eyewitness examination of fingerprints, DNA, blood samples, handwriting, photographs, or other types of physical evidence. A jury must accept this kind of personal testimony, often in the form of an ostensibly objective lab report, in order to convict. Thus, somewhere along the line, the validity of so-called circumstantial evidence has to be attested to in court by the words of a (possibly fallible) human being. In short, an eyewitness.

To illustrate this point, let us consider a hypothetical homicide case. The murder weapon, a pistol found on the accused, is placed in evidence, along with a bullet taken from the victim's body. A forensic expert presents scientific evidence that the bullet that caused the death shows patterns consistent with the bore of the weapon taken from the accused. All of this is objective, scientific evidence, we assume—a far cry from eyewitness testimony. But is that true? Who says this pistol was actually taken from the accused? An "eyewitness" police officer who *claims* he seized it during a search. Who says that the bullet offered in testimony actually came from the victim's body? Another "eyewitness," a doctor who *claims* he removed it during an autopsy. And photographs of the match between the marks on the pistol's bore and the bullet: who says that they are genuine, and the ballistic tests legitimate? Another forensic scientist makes that claim. Whom do we believe? Everyone involved—every expert witness—is giving personal, eyewitness testimony that the jury can believe or disbelieve.

One need go back no further than the infamous first O.J. Simpson trial to recall an example of jury members questioning the objectivity, competence, and credibility of various forensic scientists, laboratory technicians, and police officers who testified about so-called circumstantial evidence. The jury members acquitted Simpson because they disbelieved *personal* testimony—not that of eyewitnesses to the crime (apparently there were none), but the testimony of eyewitness participants in laboratory procedures, DNA testing, evidence collection, and so on. These varieties of eyewitness testimony were deemed by the jury to be insufficiently credible, and Simpson was freed.

If this logic is followed to the next step, one can argue that every convicted criminal was judged guilty because of some form of eyewitness account. Whether the testifying witness was present when the crime was committed, or arrived later at the crime scene—or, later still, was in the laboratory, observing, analyzing, and conducting tests—personal eyewitness testimony of some type must be believed by jurors who neither saw the crime committed nor were present when the laboratory and police work was done. These partially informed men and women must decide the accused's innocence or guilt—sometimes even ordaining his execution—by the degree of their faith in the personal testimony of strangers.

The importance—the centrality—of eyewitness testimony manifests itself not only in the courtroom but in most of life's judgments, large and small, day in and day out. A thousand factors, both rational and irrational, enter into one's judgment of the credibility of eyewitness testimony. To take another example, the latest report of a primatologist studying gorillas in the field is accepted—believed—on the basis of that scientist's earlier work, on his or her support by colleagues, and on the cogency and thoroughness of the report itself. Most of the primatologist's assertions are not replicable under controlled laboratory conditions, just as thousands of other kinds of observations in other fields of science, from astronomy to geology, cannot be replicated at will.

And it is in this kind of situation—the primatologist's—that UFO investigators find themselves. It is here that we must begin to consider the criteria by which we can make judgments about the validity of eyewitness reports. There are many factors, from the most obvious to the most ephemeral. For example, the validity of a single individual's account is obviously affected by the status, experience, and general credibility of the witness. Thus, a UFO sighting report handed on by a well-trained astronaut like Gordon Cooper or an astronomer such as Clyde Tombaugh (the discoverer of Pluto), automatically carries more weight than a sighting report by a teenage boy at an outdoor beer party. Next, and very important, is the nature of the account. Does it fit little-known patterns of UFO reports, or is it radically different from case reports accumulated over time, by multiple witnesses and investigators?

Also, does the account seem psychologically true—do the individual's emotional reactions seem plausible—or is there something false or even self-serving about the way the incident is described? An example of the former: "At first we thought it might be an airplane, but it didn't seem to have any wings. Then we thought it might be a helicopter, but there was no sound. And then it moved suddenly, coming down silently at tree-top height, and we were very frightened." Compare that kind of testimony with this: "A glowing figure in a long robe approached me and said he wanted to impart wisdom to me, and that I had been selected to spread the word. He told me his name was Zadac and that he was from a planet called Xenos. I felt calm and serene and godly in his presence, and the wisdom he imparted is the most profound I have ever known. I will present this wisdom at a public lecture this evening."

The first account seems natural in its "escalation of hypothesis" (a useful term coined by the late Dr. J. Allen Hynek), moving from the most mundane explanation of the sighting to, finally and reluctantly, the judgment that the object is truly *unknown* and, moreover, frightening. The second statement—admittedly a caricature—seems calculated to cast glory upon the witness, to render him special, even cosmically significant, with possible financial rewards.

One need not spell out more of the many clues we instinctively use every day to decide the credibility of eyewitnesses to every kind of incident and experience. Reading these credibility clues accurately is a survival skill all of us must learn if we are to avoid becoming victims of con men, salesmen, telemarketers, pie-in-the-sky politicians, and would-be seducers, to name just a few of the dishonest types we meet all too often. Of course, none of us is a perfect judge of personal, eyewitness accounts. All of us can be misled, as P. T. Barnum implied, at least some of the time. And so I leave it you, the reader, to judge as best you can the credibility of the participants in the following cases.

The Strange Children at a Cape Cod Playground

"Tom and Ann" live year-round in a town on Cape Cod with their four young children and a variety of pets. Their small, comfortable home is situated in a pine woods and is somewhat isolated from their immediate neighbors. Originally, Ann had contacted me in 1988 about several UFO experiences she recalled. Preliminary interviews strongly suggested that over the years, not only Ann but also her husband and all four of their children had apparently been undergoing UFO abduction experiences. The two older daughters were quite frightened by what they had experienced, though "Jen," the youngest, was calm and even professed to like the strange, hairless, large-eyed "little man" who she said sometimes came into her bedroom at night.

Early in 1991, Ann called me in New York to relate what Jen had just told her about as she was having breakfast that morning and getting ready for school. She was so startled by what her little five-year-old daughter was telling her that she excused herself and brought back to the table a small tape recorder to get the account down in Jen's own voice. The child insisted that this was not a dream, that she was wide-awake, and that "it was real."

Sometime during the night she had awakened and the room "was filled with pretty sparkles." The little man with the big black eyes was standing near her bed, but this time he was not alone. "There was a little girl with him," Jen said, but "she didn't look like him and she didn't look like us, either." After a few questions, Ann was able to get a clearer description of this little girl. "Her hair was white," Jen said—very light blond, apparently—"and she didn't even smile or say anything." Eventually, Ann learned that she was wearing what seemed to be a snug-fitting one-piece garment.

As Jen lay in bed, the little man held a "beautiful flower" in front of her, but when she reached for it, it disappeared. He then told her that she must come with them for a while, because there were people waiting for them. Still hoping to be given the flower, she got out of bed, and then she, the little man, and the white-haired child "went right through the wall—and we didn't even get splinters."

Jen told her mother that they went to the town playground—an actual place a few miles away that apparently looked to Jen exactly as it

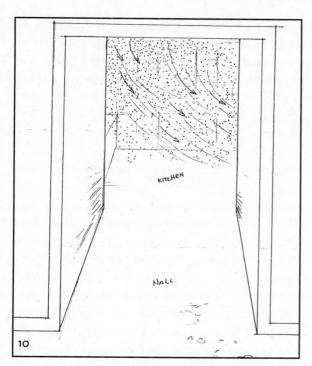

Drawing of "sparkles" sweeping into the room—drawn by abductee witness V.E.

Second drawing of "sparkles" as they began to surround sleeping abductee.

does in reality—where, she said, "some boys must have been playing baseball because all the lights were on." Since this playground has no nighttime floodlights, the source of these elevated bright lights may have been a well-lit, hovering UFO. At the playground Jen saw a group of other children sitting there. "They were all twins," she said, from which her mother deduced that they all resembled one another and were dressed alike. Jen didn't like these other children because "they just looked at me and they didn't smile and they didn't say hi."

Through a series of questions, Ann was able to estimate that there were about seven or eight of these unfriendly, virtually identical children, all apparently close to her daughter's size and age. The little man then told Jen that she must play on the swings and slides and "show the children how to play." As Jen dutifully climbed on the playground equipment, all of the "twins" apparently watched her intently. After a time she asked the little man if the other children could play with her, because she didn't like playing by herself. He answered that they could not play with her, she was to play alone, and the other children were there to watch and to learn from her. This was very disappointing to Jen, since she didn't like playing alone. She wanted to go home. She didn't understand why the strange children would not play with her or why they didn't talk to her. One child, she told her mother, was sitting on the ground, lifting up little handfuls of sand and letting it sift down on one of her feet. Jen thought this was silly.

Soon the episode at the playground was over. The little man brought her back to her house and put her in bed. Jen never saw the children again, was never given the beautiful flower she was offered, and never understood why she had to go to the playground. All of this she related to her mother that morning—though obviously not in the linear, chronological way I have outlined it here—and all of it was tape-recorded.

What is one to make of such an account? There are, of course, three basic possibilities: that the little girl simply made up the story; that it was a dream she mistook for reality; or that it happened more or less as she recalled. To take the first possibility, there is, I feel, little reason to think that Jen deliberately invented this story as a fanciful series of lies. Ann insisted that her five-year-old was a truthful and not particularly imaginative child. I generally trust mothers' perceptions about their children's habits of lying or truth-telling and their imaginative story-telling abilities, especially when the mothers are not only credible themselves but have also called me to voluntarily relate their child's account. Knowing Ann and her family as I did, I could think of no reason to doubt her assessment of her daughter's usual truthfulness and lack of an inventive imagination.

Consider also the fact that Jen's account does not contain the obvious melodramatic or fairy-tale qualities that often color children's fantasies. From a child's perspective this highly detailed account is a non-story. More important, perhaps, is the fact that a number of the unusual details that Jen relates have turned up in other UFO abduction reports. The "sparkles" that she said seemed to fill the room have been reported in at least three other abduction cases I have investigated. In fact, in one of these cases the witness V.E. made drawings showing what looked like glowing raindrops or snowflakes suspended in the air—sparkles that seemed palpable even though the witnesses could not feel anything when they tried to touch them. Needless to say, we have no idea of the nature of these glowing sparkles, or their function, or why they seem to be reported so rarely by researchers. This present description is, to my knowledge, the first time the sparkle phenomenon has been discussed in print, so I am certain that five-year-old Jen had never heard of such a thing.

Next, she spoke of passing through the wall without getting splinters. At the time of her report, the idea of abductees being moved through closed doors, windows, and walls was known to UFO researchers but was not part of general popular knowledge. And in 1991, only four years after the publication of *Intruders,* the appearance of apparent hybrid or genetically engineered children was also not familiar to the general public. And yet, Jen described the "twins" in the same way Kathy Davis and many other abductees have described what they believe to be part human, part alien offspring: unsmiling, with thin, very pale blond hair and wearing one-piece garments. "She didn't look like him and she didn't look like us, either," Jen said, a child's unwittingly succinct description of these apparent hybrids.

Even more damaging to the idea that all of this was just a five-year-old's invention is the fact that Jen's account made no sense to her at all—though it clearly resonates with those of us familiar with the abduction phenomenon. From a child's point of view, although the events of that night were not normal, they were not meaningful, either. The odd children neither threatened Jen nor were friendly to her. If this was either a dream or a fabrication, it contained no monsters, no saviors, no obviously meaningful events. Throughout, the main participants—the odd children—were merely neutral observers, and for Jen, what they were observing—her play on the swings and slides—was stupid and incomprehensible. Hardly the colorful subject matter of a child's imagination or dream.

Finally, Jen reported one other detail that, in its very triviality, shows every sign of a real observation and carries absolutely no flavor of the kind of detail a child might invent or dredge up in a dream. The image is that of one of the "twins" sitting on the ground, watching Jen at play on a swing while idly lifting up handfuls of sand and letting the grains run down over her foot. It seems to me that this utterly inconsequential detail—a throwaway visual image if ever there was one—is exactly the kind of thing a child might notice in the real world but that would never turn up in her fantasies, dreams, or made-up stories. Details like this are sometimes invented by a clever adult, particularly if that adult is a novelist or a cinematographer, but not by an unimaginative five-year-old. To me, the image of a strange little girl idly dripping sand across her foot sounds far more like something Jen actually saw.

So now, if we accept the validity of Jen's account, what are we to make of it? The answer involves a look into abduction patterns discovered in earlier research. When I first came upon the aliens' apparent interest in creating hybrids, I became particularly interested in the "baby presentation" scenes I described previously. Central to these presentation scenes were the abductees' perceptions that their instinctive, human reactions to these strange children were being intensely perceived and absorbed by the UFO occupants. One woman described a rush of emotions so sudden and confusing that she was uncertain if she or one of the aliens was the source of this flood of feeling. She believes, as do many other abductees, that the UFO occupants can telepathically "read" human emotions just as easily as human thoughts. Perhaps such artificially contrived situations as baby presentations facilitate the aliens' understanding of the human psyche and the way in which we might one day accept actual alien infants in our midst. And perhaps the UFO occupants can only achieve this kind of immediate emotional understanding by face-to-face observation of human beings in such confrontations. If little five-year-old Jen was being unwittingly used to instruct hybrids in the correct feelings of human play, one can hardly avoid the thought that at some future date these nonhuman children will be used to infiltrate our conventional world of swing sets, jungle gyms, and play groups.

But now we must face another disturbing but eminently logical extension of this idea: If the UFO occupants' agenda includes preparation for *eventual* coexistence with us humans, is there any evidence that right now, at this very moment, beings allied with them are already here, living covertly among us? To answer this question, we must first define which of the various types of beings described by abduction experiencers could actually be living among us and still "pass" as sufficiently human-looking. Clearly, the ubiquitous small, hairless, huge-eyed gray creatures would hardly be acceptable. Nor would the tall, insectlike "praying mantis" type of creature, or anything scaly-skinned and reptilian, to name two of the rarer, more exotic alien types that have been reported from time to time.

Part-alien, part-human hybrids similar to the children Jen encountered are often described by abductees as appearing acceptably human-looking, and, despite the occasional presence of overlarge eyes, larger-than-usual heads, and other odd features, apparently many could blend successfully into normal society. But there is still another category altogether: individuals who appear to be fully human and with virtually no alien characteristics except, sometimes, extraordinary telepathic gifts. This type of individual seems to exist cooperatively right along with the more typical hairless, gray-skinned UFO occupants, sharing their aims, values and manipulative skills. These genetically complex creatures—the "normals"—will occupy our attention in the following chapters.

All of this, of course, is not only highly speculative but also unpleasantly tinged with paranoia. But might it be true nevertheless? Might there actually be, living among us, aliens who look like us but who have the dazzling psychic skills and unnerving manipulative abilities of their small, gray, black-eyed allies?

Chapter 14

THE BREAKDOWN OF THE BARRIERS BETWEEN SPECIES

LAWRENCE KRAUSS, CHAIRMAN of the physics department at Case Western Reserve University, would likely have no disagreement with the assertion that sexual reproduction between aliens and humans would "obviously" be impossible. In his 1997 book, *Beyond Star Trek*, Krauss stated that producing viable offspring as an outcome of two different species mating was as unlikely as "running a Macintosh code on a Windows 95 system."[1] In the course of my own research, I've come to much the same conclusion. You'd think, then, that I could simply wash my hands of the most disturbing aspect of the abduction scenario—the hybrid baby-presentation scenes and some abductees' accounts of meeting such hybrids as adults, right here in daily life on Earth. If science says interspecies hybridization is impossible, why not accept that as one of nature's givens?

For decades, it has been a well-accepted biological fact that even species with almost the same genetic codes are biologically incompatible when it comes to reproduction. One of the most striking aspects of nature's barriers was highlighted in 2000, after scientists completed the human genome sequencing project. Although biologists had long estimated a very high correlation between our genetic material and that of the great apes, nearly everyone was startled to find how small the differences actually are between the species—for example, only 1.3 percent difference in the genomic sequencing (or lineup and matching of chromosomes) between ourselves and the chimpanzee. Yet, as far as is known in the public literature, there have never been any ape-man hybrids—not even any chimpanzee-gorilla hybrids.

Tracking Down the Stolen Genes

In a case of genetic thievery of astonishing proportions, researchers have described how a hot-springs bacterium snatched at least a quarter of its genes from another species. Scientists have conventionally believed that every type of organism sat on its own distinct branch on the tree of life—that new species evolved, slowly, gradually, as their genetic structures mutated or recombined in unusual ways through sexual reproduction.

But now evidence is mounting that *lateral gene transfer*—the wholesale exchanges of genetic material from one species to another—can quickly create an entirely new species. A team of researchers at The Institute for Genomic Research (TIGR) in Rockville, Maryland, says: "The tree of life has become a weird, inter-mixing bush."[2]

Doing their initial detective work with a hot-springs strain of bacterium, the team mapped the complete two-million-gene sequence of *Thermotoga maritima*. They then compared that complete sequence with others in a comprehensive database that contained all twenty known microbial genetic sequences on file. A strikingly close match was found in an organism called *Archaea* that lacks a nucleus. Because the hot-springs bacteria and *Archaea* come from such separate domains, the researchers speculated that the genes were somehow transferred in large bundles between the two species. It is a phenomenon that is highly unlikely to happen in the natural process of a species changing over time, i.e., through adaptive evolution. "This is the strongest evidence to date for lateral gene transfer," says molecular evolutionist Ford Doolittle of the Canadian Institute for Advanced Research.[3]

Like minuscule football players, bacteria hold the world record for completing these lateral passes of the genetic ball. Animals, on the other hand, are generally thought to be at the other extreme: Their overall complexity—of DNA sequencing, and mating rituals, among others—generally keeps the genetic ball within the species' boundaries. But even in animals, interspecies transfers can sometimes be forced. What we still don't know, though, is how or why *any* organism is able to seize such a fortune in raw genetic material from another species and get away with it. Nor is anyone certain how often the heist is pulled off—and in how many species.

There are a host of reasons why Krauss and others like him who disdain the idea of alien-human hybrids cannot be easily dismissed. As you probably learned in Biology 101, a hybrid offspring—like any other offspring of sexual reproduction—would receive half of its genetic information from the male sperm of one species and the other half from a female egg of another species. Applying this basic science to what was

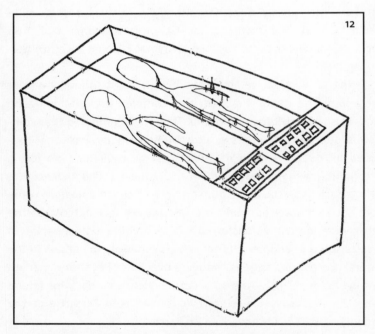

A pair of fetuses in a double nursery tank, drawn by
a female abductee. (from Budd Hopkins's archives)

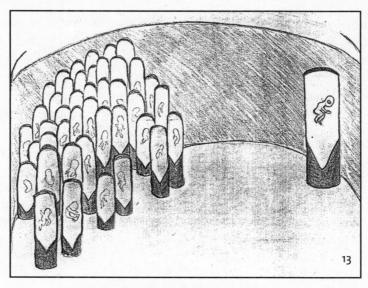

A forty-year-old abductee's sketch of an alien
"baby factory" she recalled during a hypnosis session
in 1994. (Courtesy of David M. Jacobs)

being reported in abduction cases, UFO researchers speculated that the frail, half-alien, half-human-looking children reported by abductees were the hybrid products of human gametes (sex cells) fused with an alien equivalent. After fertilization—most often in vitro, although sometimes through coerced sexual intercourse—these hybrids were then implanted in a female abductee for a short time, days or weeks. Usually in the first trimester—or even sooner, before she even realized she was pregnant—the woman would be reabducted and find herself in a "medical" setting aboard an alien craft. With the small gray beings going about their business with robotic efficiency, the woman would often see or sense that a fetus was removed from her. It would then be left to mature in a sort of baby laboratory/factory on the alien craft. In the work of abduction researchers like Budd Hopkins, David Jacobs, John Mack, and John Carpenter, the fetus factory reported by abductees aboard UFOs became a standard pattern of the field.

But there's one big problem with this scenario, as espoused by UFO researchers. It describes a process that evolutionary biology tells us is highly unlikely. According to earthly biologists, there are specific ways that nature maintains its formidable system of barriers between inter-species breeding:

- **Different courtship signals between species.** Let's imagine a male firefly urgently courting a female beetle. He'd do what his genes tell him to do: send her a specific pattern of blinking lights. But, to his disappointment, he'd find his signal totally lost on his lady-love. She, perhaps, never looks up from the leaf mulch—just keeps her head cocked, alert for a certain scent or pheromone from the underbrush. It is the beetle wooing signal she recognizes. Besides, given their circumstances—him flying about up there, her down here—she just knows it wouldn't work out. An insect's *Casablanca.*

- **Anatomical incompatibility.** Male dragonflies, for example, use a pair of special appendages to clasp the female during copulation. When the male mounts a female of a different species, he is unsuccessful because his clasping appendages don't fit the stranger-female's form well enough to get a firm grip. Some species' genitalia form a lock-and-key pattern, preventing mismatches.

- **Species-specific chemical signals.** These are sent out from both sperm and eggs of many animals; the signals zero in on similarities and allow only the correct sex cells to fuse. Even if your child's guinea pig did have a little fling with the family's pet rat, the guinea pig's eggs would not recognize the rat sperm, and no zygote or (pre-embryo) would be formed.

- **Different species pack their genes in diverse ways.** For this reason, the honeymoon luggage would be wildly mismatched. The egg from one species and the sperm from another aren't likely to go anywhere together. They carry enormously different amounts of DNA, and each one stacks its genes into chromosomal structures that the other can't even recognize. Human cells, for example, have 46 chromosomes (the genetic material from combined sperm and egg) made up into 23 pairs. But other animals can have anywhere from 2 to 200 such structures. In order for any fertilized egg to develop, *identical structures,* one from each parent, must find each other and pair up. If the amounts of DNA, the sequence of chromosomes, or the chemical coding are different in any way, so that the pairing isn't perfect, there will be no hybrid baby.

In the normal, same-species dance of mating, the male and female sex cells of each organism would blow chemical signal "kisses" to each another and then, as the band played on, the organisms' chromosomes would touch and come together at just the right places and time. Eventually, in beautiful, preordained harmony, the proteins and DNA of male and female would meld together into the makings of their future offspring. But if the male and female partners are drastically mismatched—out of sync—and don't even speak the same chemical language, their baby-making potential is doomed. Even on the odd chance that the egg is fertilized, it is destined to spontaneously abort. That's why a test-tube mating of mice and humans doesn't produce offspring, even though there's 90 to 95 percent sameness in the DNA and proteins between the two species—a piece of trivia that should be humbling, if not thought-provoking.[4]

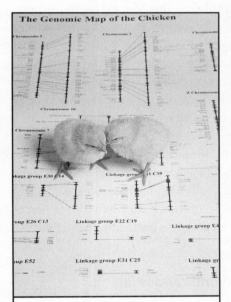

The Genomic Map of the Chicken

Chicks atop a picture of a genetic map of a chicken. The chicken genome has thirty-nine pairs of chromosomes, while the human genome contains twenty-three pairs. (Photo courtesy of the Agricultural Research Service, U.S. Department of Agriculture)

The One-of-a-Kind Mule

There are very few exceptions to the strict boundaries that nature has erected between species interbreeding. Any country person, of course, knows that mules are one of the few exceptions. As the granddaughter of a turn-of-the-century Oklahoma farmer, I have a passing interest in mules: One of those powerful draft animals permanently crippled my maternal grandfather with one swift kick. A cross between a horse and donkey, the mule is intentionally bred and highly valued by farmers as a sturdy work animal. But an unfortunate outcome of most hybridization (cross-species breeding) is sterility. The exceptions mostly occur in plants: Researchers have found it is quite likely and common for certain segments of DNA to be transferred between plants and inherited as a permanent genetic change. Modified crops that resist insects are a bioengineered example of this principle. But in higher mammals the transfer of entire genomes between species is much more complex, leaving the hardworking mule stranded, unable to produce *fertile* sex cells (gametes). Therefore he can't reproduce himself in future generations. He's just one of a kind, not the beginnings of a new species.

In the rare instance where a hybrid does reproduce a second generation, biologists use the term *hybrid breakdown* to indicate the almost inevitable downhill slide of the new hybrid species. While the original hybrid (F1) may be fertile, by the second generation (F2) the animals are deformed, frail, and sterile. Researchers believe that the benefits that might be gained by an organism inheriting the genes of another species are balanced out by costs to the organism which we don't yet recognize.

These are only some of the interspecies genetic-transfer issues that might well be complicating the lives of our alien visitors and their purposes, because, as far as we know, the aliens are not magical or impervious to mistakes and misunderstandings about their human subjects. During abductions, they've been reported to be absolutely flummoxed by a pair of false teeth, a tampon, or how to put an abductee back into a pair of jeans.

Rethinking the Alien-Human Hybridization Plan

Given such complex natural barriers between species, it seems that we must seriously question accounts like those of the child describing the hybrid-seeming group of "twins" on Cape Cod, or many women's (and some men's) reports of aliens handing them the strange, listless babies they somehow know are their own—the children that look a bit like us and a bit like "them." Yet, credible abduction researchers such as Budd

Hopkins, David Jacobs, John Mack, Richard Hall, Raymond Fowler, John Carpenter, claim that there is a strong alien interest in collecting human sperm and ova in various ways and that they are engaged in a cross-breeding program with earthlings. As most mainstream scientists would say, since such a thing doesn't exist in the natural world, it is *obviously* an impossible and silly scenario.

The issue here is that, technically, hybridization, a process of sexual reproduction, *isn't* biologically feasible between two such unlike species as aliens and humans. But even without the science to back them up, abduction researchers stubbornly persist in reporting what witnesses tell them.

Time, though, has an odd way of justifying the iconoclast, the dissenter from the norm. And time has led to some interesting developments that may lead us to hesitate in dismissing these experiencers' reports of hybrid infants. Within the last five years, human science has developed to the point where the technology of gene transfer (transgenics) gives the abductees' stories scientific credibility, even by human standards. *We, in fact, are just beginning to learn the techniques of breaking down the barrier between species*—something the aliens appear to have mastered many generations ago. So forget sex. It's not about sexual reproduction. It's about a much more refined and targeted way of intermingling genetic material between species.

Even those who have long contributed to UFO research, such as natural scientist Dr. Michael Swords of Western Michigan University, have been critical of abduction researchers' insistence that the primary purpose of abductions is an ongoing program of interspecies mingling. In a 1988 article, "Extraterrestrial Hybridization Unlikely," Swords laid out some of the well-accepted biological facts about the firewall that stands between species. At that time he concluded:

> If ET is not an incredible molecular architect, it can't make the independently evolved sperm and egg genetically compatible; if ET is such an incredible molecular architect, it has many more sensible ways of pursuing such experimental programs (or whatever they are). . . . In fact, sperm and eggs would be the stupidest cells to harvest as they contain only half the genes [of each parent]. It would be far simpler and less traumatic to take simple surface somatic cells and use the genome they contain.[7]

Humanized Mice

In May 1997, a Japanese pharmaceutical research laboratory made history. In a landmark achievement, they transplanted an entire human chromosome and its complete genetic code into a mouse. That's fifty times the amount of DNA that earlier techniques had allowed them to transfer between species! But just as dramatic was the news that the tagged human genes actually functioned normally in their new mouse host. For years scientists have been able to transfer isolated human genes into the mouse genome. But they'd never before been able to insert both the gene and the instructions for where they wanted it to be deployed in the mouse's body—not to mention what it was to do once it got there.

The newborn "humanized" mice surprised even the researcher, Isao Ishida, a geneticist at the Kirin brewing company in Japan. For the first time, Ishida said, the transgenic mice were properly expressing a group of human immune genes in their own major organs, such as human liver genes in the mouse liver and human heart muscle genes in their mousy little hearts.[5]

The current trend in labs all over the world is to insert more and more human DNA into an animal of another species. In pigs, for example, the technique is being used to breed pigs with "humanized" organs that won't be rejected when transplanted into a human recipient.[6] Although gene transfer, in this case, makes the pig organs more human only in the limited sense of altering certain surface proteins, all of these developments are being hailed as major advancements in the creation of animal models to study human genetic diseases and how complex gene families work together. They are also due to become major issues of social concern, related to ethics and human values.

What the successful transfer of genes does for our present discussion of the problems inherent in alien-human hybridization is to offer us another way to think about how that goal might be accomplished.

As anyone familiar with the abduction literature knows, researchers have reported over the past twenty years that experiencers consistently discover a large scoop-mark-type scar someplace on their skin, a finding often directly associated with a consciously recalled UFO abduction. Swords's comment about alien harvesting of human skin cells would support the hypothesis that ET is indeed interested in obtaining a complete genome from an abductee, rather than—or in addition to—the individual's gametes or sex cells, which only contain *half* the person's DNA.

According to Dr. John Altshuler, the Denver pathologist who has extensively studied cattle mutilations, soft skin tissue of the type associated with abductee scoop marks is the most rapidly reproducing form of mammalian cells, outside of ova and sperm. Altshuler also sees certain universal aspects of the genetic code: At the molecular level, the production of specific structural proteins is identical across species.[8] At this point we can only speculate that a species more advanced than ours might well find a way to use the human skin cell and/or sex cell as basic source material for reproduction or regeneration of their own genetic material. The stuff of which we're made is not as special as we'd like to think.

When it comes to the subject of alien-human cross-breeding, there are at least three major assumptions being made by Krauss, science writer Clifford Pickover, and Swords in his 1988 argument. Those assumptions are: (1) that ETs (or aliens) have evolved independently from humans (meaning it is likely that they are less related to us than a cockroach would be); (2) that aliens *must* have different subcellular chemical and structural characteristics, which would make hybridization impossible; and (3) that if aliens are sophisticated enough to arrive on Earth, they are most likely superb molecular bioengineers—knowing all about human physiology and able to redesign or intermix genetic material within this new species the moment their bipedal limbs hit terra firma.

For some people, assuming that ETs are independently evolved, technically sophisticated beings with knowledge that dwarfs our human abilities imbues those creatures with a nearly godlike mystique and power. But isn't it more likely that we're simply talking about other intelligent beings—intergalactic anthropologists or travelers, if you will—who fly over and occasionally land on this strange planet called Earth that is simply crawling, striding, bouncing, rolling, and floating with billions of life forms they may never have seen before? Why assume that they enter the earthly fray omniscient and all-knowing? In order to manipulate life on Earth, some types of aliens would most likely face a learning curve. They'd have to learn how to control and reshape the most basic elements of human life—our molecular structures, our DNA code, and the complexities of timing when certain developments

Versatile Skin

Until recently, most scientists believed that adult cells, such as the surface somatic cells that make up the skin, had made irreversible decisions about what type of tissue they were and what their function was. A cell skimmed from the external layers of skin, for example, could only make more skin cells, but not kidney or heart cells. But some preliminary studies suggest that may not be true.

Neurobiologist Freda Miller of McGill University in Montreal says that skin would be "a dream source" for her work with neural cells. Miller says skin is "easily accessible, and there would be no danger of the immune system rejecting cell transplants derived from a patient's own skin."[9]

In another study at the University of Wisconsin at Madison, skin cells were taken from sheep, pigs, monkeys, and rats. The skin cell's nuclei, an inner mass containing each animal's full genome, were stripped from each cell and successfully fused into cow eggs that had been emptied of their own nuclei. The cow cells had effectively become containers—support systems—for the other animals' genetic material. Although the study ended before any pregnancies were carried to term, the fusion clearly worked. The fibroblasts from monkey, pig, rats, and sheep all began to develop and grow inside a cow cell.[10]

Given these recent developments in somatic (skin) cell techology, we're forced to consider its possible use by extraterrestrials who regularly leave distinctive scoop marks on the skin of people reporting abduction experiences.

occur. It's a prodigiously time-intensive, complex, and experimental process that we ourselves know comparatively little about. *Any* foreign scientist or explorer would have to go through a process of learning the complexities of an unknown intelligent organism's physiology, neurology, psychology, and reproductive system, the subtle interactions of all those elements, and more.

But Michael Swords argues, hypothetically, that ETs *have* had plenty of ramp-up time: They might well have been visiting Earth for several hundred years, at the low end, and up to three billion years for a full-blown project called "human development":

> The entire Earth ecology hangs together genetically and structurally, from bacteria to humans, and therefore certainly from the beginning of Earth-life, 3¹⁄₂ billion years ago till today. The alien zookeepers must have seeded the Earth's pre-biotic oceans aeons ago, and kept regularly managed development experiments going throughout evolutionary history to correctly order gene and chromosome structures until we . . . finally arrived, ready for cross-breeding. An extremely patient project, but one which allows eggs-and-sperm hybridization, if you wish.[11]

That's certainly one scenario—one that's impossible to prove at this point, but a good hypothesis that would explain the modern-day abductees' reports of ongoing medical manipulation. But even if we're not willing to take that three-billion-year leap of faith, there are more prosaic reasons for reabduction of the same human individuals over and over. Even if the aliens—over a much more limited period of time— have been able to develop a substantial body of knowledge about our species, the experimentation and tinkering, the educated trial-and-error method, would likely apply *each time a new procedure was undertaken* by our extraterrestrial visitors upon our hapless selves. At the National Institutes for Health, this periodic, formalized exploration of human responses to new stimuli is called a clinical trial: Take an individual, infuse her with a new drug or put him into a novel setting, and study what happens. There's not just one clinical trial where human scientists study their fellow humans and learn all that they can discover: There are literally thousands of such scientific trials going on simultaneously around the world. Is it too foolhardy to speculate that scientists from non-Earth also have use of human subjects for multiple trials?

The analogy, of course, is to that of human scientists in white lab coats, holding in cages a wide range of "inferior" species—mice, dogs, rabbits, monkeys, and apes. The researchers—and our society—regard these animals as fair game for use as medical models. The animals repeatedly undergo tests of all kinds involving physical, neurological, surgical, genetic, and other procedures that are of interest to human beings. It certainly would be a shock to our system to think that the tables could be turned—that we humans are the wildlife being studied in our natural environs by beings so technologically advanced that they seem magical or godlike to us.

Unless, of course, the visitors *are* the source of our origin—which brings us back to the most essential human questions that are regularly stirred up by the UFO phenomenon: Where do we come from? Who are we? Where are we going? Many people can't help but wonder how the alien visitors are tied in to these questions—if perhaps their role has been, over millions of years, to play some part in our human past, present, and future. Some scientists speculate that we are an originally "seeded" species, engineered to be genetically similar to the aliens.[12]

Transgenics versus Hybridization

Since most of the witnesses' experiences, both consciously recalled and hypnotically retrieved, point back again and again to some procedure that relates to blending aliens and humans, let's assume there's something there to be explored. We've already established that hybridization, as in a blending of egg and sperm in sexual reproduction between different species, is not the most likely candidate, so let's look at one of the most revolutionary fields of science today, transgenics, or the splicing of a gene from one species into the genetic material (genome) of a totally different species. Think of a tomato bearing the genes of a salmon, enabling it to ripen despite the chilly autumn. Imagine corn genetically fused with an insect-repelling bacterium, or a pig born with multiple human genes in its liver, heart, and kidneys.

These oddities are not science fiction. They are actual examples of bioengineered organisms that are, or can become, part of our daily lives. It's even possible to imagine news stories like these in the not-too-distant future:

- A large grocery chain is sued after it was discovered to be selling strawberries grown in December. The problem was that they hadn't disclosed that the berries were implanted with specific genes from a fish that can swim comfortably in the icy Atlantic Ocean.

- A couple's agent announces a prebirth, multimillion-dollar contract for the future services of their custom-designed embryo that will grow to be eight feet tall and gifted with superior athletic abilities.

- A conceptual artist at the Art Institute of Chicago releases 250 normal-looking toddlers, each born with a spliced gene from a jellyfish, into an exhibition space. Before worldwide cameras, the babies turn on their charm: When the fluorescent light switch is thrown, they all glow a greenish-blue.

What Does Transgenics Have to Do with Alien Abductions?

It's a new millennium, one in which engineered biology could well change the course of the world or the universe—for better or for worse. Nobody's offering any guarantees. But, given our new insight into bio-engineering of earthly organisms, we can only speculate that this technique of gene transfer in larger and larger quantities between species may offer some new clues about what is really going on with the so-called human-alien hybrids. In its most basic form, transgenics refers to genetic modification, usually in a single gene. The genome is changed by injecting a small segment of foreign (another species') DNA into a developing egg or embryo. (This usually requires a "bus" of some kind to carry the gene into the host genome; usually a harmless virus is used as the vehicle.) If the foreign DNA becomes fully integrat-

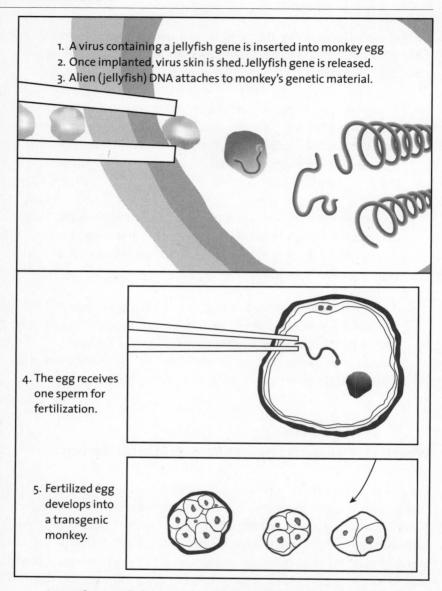

1. A virus containing a jellyfish gene is inserted into monkey egg
2. Once implanted, virus skin is shed. Jellyfish gene is released.
3. Alien (jellyfish) DNA attaches to monkey's genetic material.

4. The egg receives one sperm for fertilization.

5. Fertilized egg develops into a transgenic monkey.

A gene from a jellyfish is implanted into the egg of a monkey. A virus is used as the foreign gene's vector, or carrier, into the egg. After fertilization, the egg is transferred to the womb of a host mother. She later gives birth to a genetically modified young primate, whose DNA carries a fluorescent marker gene. If the foreign or alien gene is expressed outwardly and if the lighting is correct, the infant monkey will glow bright green.

ed into the host's genetic structure (genome), the "transgene" can be fully operative in the transgenic animal and will be inherited by its offspring, which will pass the altered gene along to all future generations.[13]

I'm suggesting now that what the ETs may be creating are not hybrids at all but *transgenic human beings*. It is both biologically possible and would best fit the profile of a secretive, invasive force that might be intent on conquering us from within—or, equally possible, healing or altering the genes that no longer work for us in our present environment. The change could happen one genetic code word at a time—or an entire chromosome at a time. Either way, if the genes to be modified were carefully selected, it could take thousands of years before any significant outward physical change would be noticed. The cultural devastation and massive destruction of the movie *Independence Day* would never have to be played out, Hollywood-style—not if the human race was becoming, one gene at a time, more like the aliens. Or they more like us.

Biologists open to the reality of the UFO phenomenon have indicated as early as 1988 that partial hybridization between humans and aliens would be the only reasonable scientific possibility—if there is any truth to abductions at all.[14] Yet there is still an insistence that the "sperm and egg routine" reported by abductees isn't a very likely route for such blending of interspecies traits.

Looking at the most recent studies on transgenic animals, however, I'd prefer to leave human sex cells in the running as likely candidates for alien harvesting. According to a citation in *PubMed*, the respected on-line site for juried scientific research, the journal *Environmental Health Perspectives* reported:

Transgenic mice are a unique tool for understanding how interactions between individual genes and the environment affect human health. . . . Most transgenic mice are made by injecting a transgene into fertilized eggs. The eggs are removed from the oviduct, and an ultrafine glass pipet is used to inject a solution containing a few hundred copies of the transgene DNA into the nucleus. The injected eggs are put into the oviduct of a surrogate mother, and the pups are born 19 days later. Some of these mice will have the transgene incorporated into their genome and their descendents for generations to follow will also carry the transgene.[15]

In other words, when attempting to modify a species, our own scientists insert the gene of the "alien" or other species into an egg that has already *known* (in the best biblical sense of the word) a sperm. The researchers in animal science at University of California at Davis also state:

> Transgenic animals carry a genetic modification, usually a single gene, that was introduced by injecting a small piece of foreign DNA into a developing embryo. If the foreign DNA is stably integrated into the host genome, the "transgene" can be expressed by the transgenic animal and passed in the gametes to future generations.[16]

These are difficult issues to take in, both emotionally and intellectually. The subtle but inexorable alteration of the human species? Who wants to deal with navigating the complex technological and scientific issues of that idea? Even if we think of bioengineering dilemmas as strictly human, earthly technologies, it's likely to take a series of highly emotional or outrageous incidents to bring society face-to-face with the implications of transgenics. When it does, don't be surprised if you hear loud rumblings and find skid marks on the pavement surrounding the subject. Because if hybridization is a calico alley cat, transgenics is a glossy, cybernetic cheetah. It's as invisible as it wants to be—a high-tech, easy-to-conceal kind of genetic manipulation. And it can change the genome of an entire species in a condensed amount of time—*without being visible in the exterior traits of the animal.*

This last point is a significant one to keep in mind as we explore further what might be happening to abductees. If there is genetic manipulation or gene transfer going on, it would be a very subtle process of change. Biologists tell us that an entire species can do most of its changing internally, with new species traits only gradually manifesting themselves in outward appearance and behavior.

Remember the imagined uproar caused by consumers who bought strawberries in December and later discovered that a salmon gene had been covertly inserted into their fruit, allowing it to survive a frost? The current biotech industry shows that we can already harness and reroute the basic elements of life by inserting specific genes from one species into another. A perfect example of this is the general conversion, worldwide, to genetically modified foods—often unlabeled as such—which have become the most widely adopted products in the history of cultured crops. According to Michael Specter, writing in *The New Yorker,* an estimated thirty thousand products are now made from genetically modified crops. Have you eaten corn or corn products lately? What about tomatoes, soybeans, squash, pasta, breads, ice cream, candy, or processed meats? If you have, you've almost certainly consumed genetically modified foods.[17]

The First Bioengineered Monkey Born

Scientists in Portland, Oregon, announced in mid-January, 2001, the birth of the first monkey with genetically engineered cells. Molecular tests prove that the foreign gene from another species is definitely in the newborn's cells, the scientists say, making him a genuine transgenic monkey. But it's still too early to tell whether the gene's function will express itself in the monkey's physical appearance (phenotype) or be permanently passed along in his sperm.[18]

But if and when the foreigner's gene does turn on, it will literally light up the monkey. The gene that was inserted was a "marker gene" from a jellyfish—a visible way for the scientists to track the gene's progress. It causes the monkey cells to make a protein that glows under a fluorescent light. Among the group of researchers at Oregon Health Sciences University, this is seen as only a first step in the ultimate goal of creating colonies of monkeys that have been genetically modified to develop human diseases. Lucky them. And they didn't even have to sign an informed-consent form.

Still, it's a step that other scientists consider controversial. "Once you start attempting genetic engineering in monkeys, humans can't be far behind," says Professor Lori Andrews of the Chicago-Kent College of Law.

Actually, UFO researchers have been suggesting for some time that this is exactly what is going on with millions of adults living in the United States alone. And, just as in the monkey's case, the abductee does not go willingly and never has to consent.

But a simple, stark fact that most scientists agree on is that when you move DNA from one species to another, there's no telling how the new combination of genes will interact or what possibly lethal effects might result.[19] For those of us interested in the impact upon our species of ostensible ET genetic manipulation, the opponents of bioengineered foods make a major relevant point: that the action of any gene can depend upon the species in which it is placed. Abductees, instead of having nightmares about possible creations of "superweed," might substitute the term *supervirus*—a highly possible by-product of DNA transfer between species that could be unleashed on the human race, either unknowingly or intentionally. In a somewhat different problem of biology, scientists know that although transplanted organs from primates to humans would provide the best chance of "taking," the idea is rejected for fear of transmitting retroviruses into the human population.[20]

With virtually no informed public consent, science has taken the human species to the very outposts of a new frontier in understanding how life can be created, altered, manipulated, and changed. Whether all these things should be done or not is a different question—one that we all need to seriously consider. Just because science can make something happen doesn't always mean that it should, according to the distinguished philosopher of science Philip Kitchner. There is, he says, no definitive right to pursue knowledge for its own sake, with no regard for consequences.[21]

It may very well be that a culture several million years in advance of our own culture has already confronted the technology of bioengineering. The basic building blocks of life—proteins, amino acids, sugars, etc.—appear to be the same throughout the universe. The question is: How different are the issues and problems of altering the life-forms on Earth from those of other planets or in other dimensions? On Earth, as most biologists will tell you, the process is complex, intertwined with other systems, and not yet well enough understood to be predictable and safe for human use. With no federal or institutional support at all, abductees can only hope and pray that the extraterrestrials know what they are doing—that we are not just the experimental-lab "wet-brains," those mushy and unstable biological organisms who might well be candidates for upgrading to posthumanist level, at the very least.

Disturbing thoughts, I'll admit. Who wants to feel this helplessly ignorant and in the hands of an unknown force that most people are still embarrassed to acknowledge as an intermittent presence on Earth? Our little lives are difficult and complex enough without the oblique shadow of alien intruders or anthropologists hovering over our heads. The predicament we're in brings to mind one of Budd's many stories, an anecdote about one of his first New York art dealers, a tiny Jewish woman named Tirca. Taking some paintings up to her Madison Avenue gallery one day, Budd, a politically involved young artist, launched into a passionate monologue on a particular issue of the day. As he pressed on, enumerating the intricacies of the problem, Tirca put up a weary hand: "Stop! Stop! Just tell me this," she said. "Is it *good* for the Jews, or is it *bad* for the Jews?"

The Sweet Spot in the Asteroid Belt

Even the phrase *It came from outer space!* almost needs to be accompanied by a theremin, that quirky electronic instrument—a slightly ominous, tongue-in-cheek sound—that accompanied so many 1950's science-fiction movies. But in December 2001, scientists from the NSA's Ames Research Center reported in the journal *Nature* that their most recent findings led them to a startling conclusion: Sugars from space may have nourished the first life on Earth. This source of life *did* come from outer space, with no theremin accompainment.

A pair of meteorites, carbon-rich asteroid fragments that fell to Earth have been well studied, mainly because one of them is loaded with organic compounds, including amino acids and sugars, the building blocks of proteins. The NASA team says this implies that life on Earth might have originally been "seeded" by organic compounds falling from the skies. An alternative theory suggests that all Earth's life would have had to start from scratch, forming its own life-giving compounds here on the young planet.

Now the team has discovered a sugar molecule in the same meteorites—another essential building block of life—that might have landed here from outer space. Sugars, life's main energy store, form part of the backbone of the DNA and RNA molecules, found in all living organisms.[22]

So, like Tirca, let's jump to the bottom line: There's a daily unfolding drama over what's safe and what's still unknown about bioengineered plants, animals, and humans. How can we know if what seems to be substantial alien intervention in our population is good for the humans—or bad for the humans? The best we can do at this point is stay tuned to the cutting-edge work in our own biotechnologies, hoping for some parallel insights into alien activity.

A First Step: Creation of a Sheep-Goat

In the 1980's, dramatic advances in gene transfer technology began toppling the presumed solid barrier between species in laboratories around the world. For example, in the Department of Animal Sciences at the University of California at Davis, researchers are working with a variety of transgenic technologies using domestic livestock. The group's emphasis is on establishing cows and other large animals as producers of pharmaceutical drugs, such as blood-clotting factors for humans that would be expressed in the cows' milk.[23]

By combining cells from goats and sheep, The Embryo Transfer Lab at UC Davis has also made an end run around the natural barriers that generally put an end to interspecies pregnancy through miscarriage. In the usual scenario involving interspecies fertilization, the fetus is experienced as a foreign body within the mother and she expels it from her body. The UC Davis team transferred cells between the species to produce fertile, healthy sheep-goat chimeras, i.e., a goat or sheep that produces both sheep and goat blood cells. By using certain embryo manipulation techniques with a chimeric female, the researchers have created an interspecies pregnancy in which the pregnant nanny goat is able to tolerate the foreign sheep fetus without aborting it. The sheep genes flowing in the nanny's blood recognize the fetus as hers, preventing her from rejecting the fetus as a hostile takeover attempt.

The Cloning of a Sheep Named Dolly

Why does the whole world know the name of a curly-haired barnyard beauty named Dolly? Since she burst upon the science scene in 1997, Dolly, the Scottish sheep who was cloned from another sheep's adult cell, has been mentioned in over four thousand news articles in major U.S. magazines and newspapers alone, as well as in countless other print outlets and radio and television broadcasts around the world. She's also the subject of at least fourteen books for the layperson. Intercut on television with footage from *Frankenstein, Brave New World,* and *The Boys from Brazil,* Dolly's fame emerged instantly, not from what she really is, but from what she represents. To the billions of people who took note of Dolly's creation, she's the living proof that genetic cloning of adult human beings is no longer in the realm of the impossible. This innocent-looking white ewe has become a metaphor for the seemingly godlike power that scientists now have to both create and control life.[24]

Dolly's creators, biologists Ian Wilmut and Keith Campbell of Scotland's Roslin Institute, are a bit startled at the public's fascination with Dolly, who has become the world's first famous cloned large animal. What the researchers wish that we understand is that Dolly should matter to ordinary people for reasons other than because she was successfully cloned from a single adult cell of another sheep or that she is that sheep's genetic replica, in some spooky imitation of science fiction.

In their book *The Second Creation: The Age of Biological Control by the Scientists Who Cloned Dolly,* Campbell and Wilmut are clear that popular media has misrepresented what Dolly represents *to them,* at least. Her true significance, they say, is in the fact that Dolly's creation laid the groundwork for making the best use of transgenic animals—those expressing a specific transplanted gene from another species. The transplanted trait might involve the production of leaner meat, for example, or spider-silk strands and pharmaceutical drugs that can be expressed in animals' milk. Dolly isn't significant only because she was a clone from a mammary or skin cell, but because once the ideal transgenic sheep is created, the refined craft of cloning gives scientists the power to multiply that ideal animal almost indefinitely.

Cloning, or the making of multiple copies of an organism, the biologists believe, is just the beginning of the many benefits that humankind will derive from engineering all types of organisms, both plant and animal. Human and environmental needs, after all, are always changing, never constant. The bioengineer's goal is to discover ways to genetically alter the life-forms around us—including us—to better meet those new conditions.

To many people, this Promethean power has been wrongly wrested from God or nature by scientists whose work they don't understood and therefore fear. Only mankind, they say, would have the hubris to play with the very ingredients of life itself, rearranging molecules and matter like sesame seeds shaken up and oven-browned to suit our own liking. What this objection doesn't take into consideration, as biologist Michael Swords points out, is that people have been genetically modifying stock and plants for hundreds of years—by selective breeding, grafting, cross-pollination, and many other means.

But UFO researchers and abductees might well argue that there's another player or two in this game—that extraterrestrials (or ultradimensional beings; take your choice) have long been engaged in a similar manipulation of our genetic material, just as we have with Dolly's. The evidence provided by hundreds of well-researched cases suggests that this is the case.

What we don't know is how "alien," exactly, are their motives from our own? Is it as simple as drawing an analogy between human experiments and what appear to be similar alien experiments? It would be comforting if we even knew that for a certainty, no matter what the implications. But my hunch is that, the way things go with this strange phenomenon, nothing is likely to be simple—or even simply analogous.

As Budd nears the end of a hypnosis session, he often asks the abductee if he or she would like to ask a question of the alien "doctors." More times than I care to remember, they usually whisper or cry out: "What do you want from me? What are you doing this for?" That's more than Dolly had a chance to ask.

"My Blue Heaven": It Just Isn't the Same Anymore

In the popular 1927 song "My Blue Heaven," Americans responded to the ideal image of family: a man, a woman, "and baby makes three."

And so it has gone, for the billions of years that homo sapiens have been pairing off and reproducing. It's long been considered an inviolate law of nature that every child would be the result of two sets of parental genes coming together, one from Mom and one from Dad. But in yet another disruption of nature's "laws," researchers have announced that babies born from a new method of treating infertility have genes from *three different people* in their cells. In this case, "Molly and the donor and me and baby make four." The fact that an old tune doesn't roll off the tongue quite so trippingly is the least of the complexities here.

In dealing with certain rare forms of infertility in women, doctors at the Institute for Reproductive Medicine and Science at St. Barnabas Medical Center in Livingston, New Jersey, began to suspect that the problems stemmed from some defect in the women's own cytoplasm, the material that surrounds the nucleus of the egg and directs its development after fertilization. So, in recent experiments, Dr. Jacques Cohen of St. Barnabas began injecting cytoplasm from fertile women into the eggs of the infertile women. The eggs were then fertilized with the sperm of the women's partners.

Out of thirty women treated with this technique, fifteen gave birth. Using a "genetic fingerprinting" method on the infants, Dr. Cohen and his colleagues revealed in the British journal *Human Reproduction,* that genes from the donor cytoplasm are definitely present in some of the babies, along with those of the moms and dads. But the researchers are emphatic that the additional genes of the third-party donors are inconsequential and won't have any effect on the children's characteristics.[25]

Not so fast, say ethicists writing in the journal *Science.* The donated cytoplasm of these eggs contains more than just proteins to help the egg grow. It also holds mitochondria, the tiny structures that manufacture energy for the cells out of oxygen and nutrients. And mitochondria contain their own genetic material. The ethicists suggest that these "experiments" would never have been approved by the federal committee that oversees genetic work. But, because the work was privately funded, the researchers weren't required to get anyone's permission except the parents—all three of them.[26]

In short, no one knows what effect these third-party genes will have on the new babies—except for the fact that these children have now been permanently genetically altered. Which means that these changes, whatever they are, will be passed down to their own children and their children's children. In an environment where desperation for a child and commercial enterprise jointly conjure up the power to force nature's hand, who on Earth is looking out for the future of the species?

If we Americans aren't doing it—and we clearly aren't moving as quickly as our science and technologies are—it's easy to see why many people might be hopeful that the alien visitors to our planet *are* overseeing our future—that they *are* the benign outside force that ensures we'll be able to survive whatever catastrophic event comes our way, as such things inevitably do.

The more optimistic branch of ufologists likes to say that such benign oversight is precisely what the aliens are doing each time they swoop down and take people off to their mysterious laboratories. But we have no way presently to confirm that belief—or to flat-out refute it. We don't know what the aliens are up to any more than scientific oversight committees know the inner workings of the thousands of privately funded fertility clinics around the world.

In fact, you might fairly state that the UFO occupants are operating without federal oversight (none that we know of, at least) *or* informed consent. And, according to the 1991 Roper Poll on "Unusual Personal Experiences," there are an estimated 2 percent of adult Americans (approximately four million people) who have had experiences consistent with those of the abduction phenomenon. The scope of the aliens' apparent genetic mission is staggering.

And here we sit, in the dark about their ultimate purpose. Unfortunately, unless we can get the human race to focus on this problem—or until the aliens tell us what they're up to—we're likely to remain in that state of darkness for a long time.

My own concern is not that we are being altered, because that is an ongoing natural process, the slow, evolutionary morphing of the Earth and all the organisms in and on it. For centuries, people have believed that a power larger than themselves—whether they define that as God or the laws of nature—has been the unseen force determining their collective futures. While the religious trusted their respective gods, the scientists put just as much faith in the laws of nature as the ultimate shapers of our destinies. There was a certainty, an order, inherent in either belief system.

But then who are these little gray humanoids popping in and out of our world, taking our sperm and ova and skin samples, only to present us later with what they say are our offspring—wan, listless, big-eyed infants whom some people have cradled in the palm of one hand? They are, to borrow a famous phrase, "neither fish nor fowl." The aliens don't fit anybody's conception of a being made in God's image—certainly not the God of the Christians, Muslims, Jews, or Hindus. And, according to most scientists, UFOs and their occupants are not possible (or acceptable) in the realms of science, either.

The UFO occupants' ambiguity, their elusiveness in being categorized, and their profound secretiveness are strokes of genius, it seems to me. In this way, they have all the control in terms of our relationship to them. These same qualities offer our alien visitors the perfect opportunity to slip between the two mighty cultural rocks of human religion and secular science. They slide right through our nets, evade both our old and new systems, pass by our understanding, and go quickly, efficiently, about their business—without full disclosure, without our permission, and without official public acknowledgment that something significant is happening to us as a species.

In comparison, my thoughts turn back to the fertility clinic in New Jersey. What if it was suspected that some such institute was covertly, experimentally manipulating the genetic structure of not thirty human embryos but *five million* embryos? Would anyone in high places take it seriously? Would renowned scientists speak up? With the threat of a public uprising, would the government offer immediate resources to uncover the facts? Or, because the idea is so inconceivable, so overwhelming, would we simply turn away and laugh it off?

Chapter 15

THE MAN WHO KNEW TOO MUCH

I N ITS DECEMBER 1987 ISSUE, *Omni* magazine published "Missing Time: A New Look at Alien Abductions," a long and generally favorable cover story with extensive coverage of my work with abductees. Accompanying the article was a page-long, twenty-five-item questionaire entitled—by the editors—"Hidden Memories: Are You an Abductee?" that I had been asked to prepare for the magazine. Those readers who suspected they might indeed be abductees and who also wished to be contacted by an investigator were encouraged to write to me in care of *Omni*. As one might have expected, there were a surprisingly large number of cogent, intelligently written responses.

"Terry Winthrop," a resident of New Jersey, was one of those who wrote to me about her intriguing, not-so-hidden memories. What follows is the text of her original letter, which was neatly handwritten on notebook paper:

Dear Mr. Hopkins (or Associate)

I have rewritten this letter a hundred times in my head and on paper, it just never sounds right. I've just concluded it's the topic that is the problem, not the way I write it, so here it goes.

Approximately 14 years ago my first husband (now ex) and I were driving home from the Jersey shore in the late afternoon. The next thing we both knew we were sitting in the parked car and it was dark, and we were in a place we'd never seen. There were 2–3 hours unaccounted for. We had suddenly "wakened up" in a barren sort of field—not on a road—with nothing at all in sight. But neither of us had a "last memory" about how we got there. It was very frightening, there was no explanation. It took a while to find our way out of there as it was pretty remote and because we weren't on a road we didn't know which way to go. Even when we did get onto a road, it was one that we had never been on before. But since we couldn't figure out what happened we just pushed it off as something strange and never talked or thought about it again. Neither one of us had ever heard of missing time "events." It wasn't until a few weeks after I had read the December issue of OMNI that the memory hit me in a flash. Even as I read it, nothing. Since then I've been wracking my brain to try to remember more, but as hard [as] I do I can't. I still don't think that something like that could have happened. But I do feel almost obsessed with remembering. It's disturbing my life.

I have to tell you about something even I'm not sure of.

I'll try to be as accurate as I can. Last summer on a very warm, clear beautiful night, after the kids were in bed, I decided to go outside to look at the stars. I took a couch pillow and went to lie down on the picnic table. I had never done that before. After a while of looking up and relaxing I watched a star that seemed to be throbbing, pulsating as if it were going forward and backward. Not twinkling like other stars do. I was feeling so comfortable and relaxed. After a while something made me look to my right above the next road. And there (I think soundless) was a very large vehicle. It was just hovering perfectly still in mid-air about 20–30 ft up. I was in awe and completely unafraid. Fear was the furthest thing from my mind. I sat up on the picnic table to get a clearer view, as my house is surrounded by woods. Now even as I was looking at it, I was questioning my imagination. I was thinking "this can't possibly be real," yet I wasn't afraid. I was truly wondering if it was my imagination. I guess I looked at it for about 3–4 minutes, then it slowly moved forward and went up in a gradual incline, then suddenly it took off *real* quick, and it was gone before I knew it. It was then that I got scared. I couldn't get into the house quick enough. I can't account for any missing time here because I didn't look at my watch when I went out, but I did when I came in and it was much later than I thought it was. I just didn't realize that I had been out as long as I was. The vehicle itself was different than I've ever heard of. It wasn't round or flat or cigar shaped, it was more like a pentagon shape. Maybe this is proof that it was my imagination. There were lights on the sides and I think they were red, blue-green, and white. I guess it was about 100' from me. After feeling as scared as I did (and having a cigarette) I went back out on the *front* porch because I felt safer there, closer to the road. After I was there a while another or the same vehicle came overhead again. It was a little higher up and didn't stop. It just (I think silently) flew straight over at a slow speed, and then like the other one zipped off.

I can't help thinking that you think I am a crackpot as you read this. That is my greatest fear. But sometimes I think the same thing. I told my husband about this the next day and he just kind of humored me. That's when I remembered the other incident [with my ex-husband]. I didn't tell him. He doesn't know I'm writing to you, either. He would think I've gone off the deep end, and sometimes I feel I have.

There are some other things I would write about but I'm afraid they don't mean anything and you'll just think I'm crazy. It's nothing. So, if my letter warrants a response please deal only with me for now. Then I'll tell my husband. But there's no need for me to talk about this right now.

I do hope you will and can help me. I'm really on the verge of questioning my entire life, constantly.

Before I end my letter I'll just tell you a little about myself. My name is [Terry Winthrop]. I'm 32 years old, mother of three children, a very happy housewife. Here is my address and phone number [deleted] in case you can help.

Thank you for taking the time to read this. I'll be waiting and hoping for a response.

Sincerely,
[Terry Winthrop]

Having received and read literally thousands of similar letters from people reporting similar anomalous incidents, I noticed a number of features in Terry's letter that point to a high degree of personal credibility. First, as with most witnesses whose accounts turn out upon investigation to be reliable, Terry does not claim that she is an abductee. Quite the contrary. Over and over she states that perhaps there is nothing to her account. After vividly describing one incident, she goes on to minimize it by saying it is "something even I'm not sure of." Even while she was looking at what she calls a "vehicle" with red, blue-green, and white lights at its corners, hovering one hundred feet away and only twenty to thirty feet above the ground, she says she "was questioning my imagination" and thinking, "this can't possibly be real." Rather than trying to ingratiate herself to me, she says, "I can't help thinking that you think I am a crackpot as you read this. . . . [And] sometimes I think the same thing."

Equally indicative of Terry's reluctance to accept the evidence of her eyes is her description of the vehicle she saw as having five sides—a pentagon in shape—which she terms "different than I've ever heard of. It wasn't round or flat or cigar shaped . . . Maybe this is proof that it was my imagination."

Collectively, these remarks lend credence to Terry's account for several reasons. First, anyone inventing a UFO encounter will virtually always cite familiar mainstream images so as not to raise suspicions at the outset by describing an "anomalous anomaly." Second, anyone eager to fool an investigator will deliberately avoid raising even more doubts by admitting that maybe the reported image was a product of her imagination. And third, though Terry did not know it, rectilinear UFOs of the type she describes—five-sided, six-sided, and so on—have occasionally been reported, the Travis Walton UFO being a prime example.[1]

But there is another, even more important aspect of Terry's letter that caught my attention: the presence of a number of clues that suggest that both of the incidents she reports are unremembered, and unclaimed, abductions. Her account of "waking up" with her first husband in their parked car, in the middle of a field, at night, with no idea where they were, is a classic missing-time experience. As Terry so aptly put it, "neither of us had a 'last memory' about how we got there. . . . [T]here was no explanation." Obviously, *something* happened to the two of them during the missing two to three hours, and *something* caused them both to forget what it was.

Those who practice debunkery like to offer tortured conventional explanations of how such a missing-time experience might happen to one person—an epileptic seizure, an alcoholic blackout, "highway hypnosis," and so on—but these experiences do not happen simultaneously to two people. That fact creates a real problem for the committed skeptic, though this kind of simultaneous missing-time period, involving two, three, four, or even more people, has been reported in hundreds of similar reports gathered by UFO investigators.[2]

Yet another indication that this bizarre experience was UFO-connected has to do with something Terry mentioned in her letter about her backyard sighting of the five-sided craft, fourteen years after her first UFO experience: "I told my husband about this [UFO sighting] the next day and he just kind of humored me. That's when I remembered the other incident." Terry had never associated that fourteen-year-old incident with UFOs; now, however, after her sighting in the backyard, she connected the two episodes. One is tempted to suggest that she did so because, subconsciously, she knew the two incidents were related.

Terry's backyard UFO encounter, while lacking a clearly measurable sense of missing time, still offers many subtle clues that point to an unremembered abduction. In one well-established series of reports, abductees reported finding themselves doing something new or unusual immediately before their abductions, as if the UFO occupants were somehow able to compel behavior that facilitated the abductees' capture. Thus, an individual might suddenly decide to get dressed and go outside to take a walk at three A.M. or, while driving home, might turn down a completely unfamiliar road and stop in the middle of a field.

With this pattern in mind, it is interesting to note that Terry begins her discussion of her pentagon-shaped-craft encounter with: ". . . on a very warm, clear beautiful summer night, after the kids were in bed, I decided to go outside to look at the stars. I took a couch pillow and went to lie down on the picnic table. I had never done that before." Thus, the UFO's arrival coincided with Terry's doing something that to her seemed unusual. "Coincidences" like this are far too common in abduction cases to deserve the label *coincidence*.

Another pattern present in thousands of UFO abduction cases is an improbable sense of calm and lack of fear, notable at some point in the basic sequence of events. This near tranquility usually comes after the initial—and usually frightening—encounter between the abductee and the UFO occupants, as if it were the result of a psychically induced anesthetic or sedative of some kind. Then, very often when this effect is no longer needed to render an abductee tractable, it fades and fear returns, sometimes suddenly. In her case, Terry says that when she first saw the UFO hovering nearby she felt awe and was completely unafraid. "Fear was the furthest thing from my mind," she reports, in itself an unusual reaction to a large, unearthly-looking craft hovering nearby only twenty or thirty feet off the ground. But a few moments later, after the object zoomed away, she suddenly felt very frightened: "I couldn't get into the house quick enough." These sharp emotional fluctuations, though typical of different stages in a UFO abduction, are rarely reported in UFO *sightings.* In this latter type of encounter, witnesses more commonly describe simultaneous but contradictory emotions—curiosity *and* an edge of fear; a sense of awe *and* a cautious wariness.

Terry's emotions, as she recalled them, seemed to be a consecutive series of intense highs and lows, switching from awe and a sense of safety at one point to a later sense of dread and real danger. One can speculate that if she was consciously recalling only certain isolated moments from a long, mostly unremembered abduction, her recollections of the emotions she felt would be equally fragmented, as indeed they seem to be.

A final clue pointing to the possibility of unremembered abduction experiences has to do with the way Terry says these experiences have disturbed her life. Sometimes, she says, she feels she's "gone off the deep end." "I'm on the verge of questioning my whole life," she writes. "I feel almost obsessed with remembering." She does not say she is obsessed with wanting to know what UFOs are or where they come from, two obvious and objective scientific, even philosophical questions. Instead, she is obsessed with remembering what actually happened *to her,* a deeply subjective personal question concerning her own life experiences. The fuel for her unease is the knowledge that something possibly traumatic and as yet unremembered had happened to her.

Shortly after I read Terry's letter, and knowing that she lived close to

New York City, I contacted her by telephone for a short interview. She came to my studio for the first time in early 1988. As her letter had led me to expect, I found her to be a gentle, rather shy, and intelligent young woman who radiated integrity. She was delicately pretty, with a becoming modesty and humorous, self-deprecating skepticism.

Over the next year I met with Terry a number of times, conducting extensive interviews and hypnotic regression sessions dealing with the experiences detailed in her letter as well as a few other UFO abductions she had omitted. Together, we uncovered what happened to Terry and her first husband during the earlier missing-time experience when the two found themselves in their car, parked in the middle of a field, and we also explored her memories of a later abduction from her own backyard the night she lay on the picnic table looking up at the stars.

Terry recalled under hypnosis that the earlier missing-time experience began when her husband abruptly turned the car off the main highway and drove down a side road, making a few more turns along the way as if he knew where he was headed. Terry did not question him about this sudden change of direction—they had been heading home from a weekend at the shore—and he said nothing about it to her; they simply drove on in silence, as if it were the most natural thing in the world. When they reached a level farm field, her husband swung the car off the small side road, drove up into the middle of the field, and switched off the engine. They sat for a while in silence, obviously in an altered state of some kind, until several small gray aliens took them out of their car and walked them a short distance to a landed UFO. They were led up a ramp, taken inside, and then separated. Terry was led into an examination room, stripped, and placed upon a table. At this time she was about three months into her first pregnancy, and she felt that her developing fetus was the focus of the aliens' interest.

After the aliens ended their various procedures, they returned Terry to the ramp of the craft, reunited her with her husband, and the two were led back to their automobile. By this time it had grown dark, and the next thing Terry knew, they were both suddenly alert, awake, and dumfounded to find themselves in the middle of a field, after dark, no longer on the highway headed home. As her husband started the car and drove over the rough ground, searching for a road and an explanation, Terry tried to question him. "Where are we? How did we get here?

What happened?" Her frightened queries only made him angry and even more disoriented. He refused to answer her, saying that he had no idea what had happened, and then in effect told her to shut up. Obviously, as a driver so utterly lost that he was no longer even on a road, and as the supposed protector of his pregnant young wife, her panicky questions must have underlined his sense of impotence while adding to his own fear and confusion.

In the weeks and months after this event, Terry said that her husband began to exhibit a new and disturbing pattern of behavior. At first he seemed unusually concerned about the security of their apartment, checking and rechecking windows and locks on the doors, but once their baby was born his actions became bizarre. One morning Terry realized that he was in the hallway outside their apartment door, and she could hear sounds of tools being used as well as the metallic rustle of a chain. Her husband had installed several sturdy eyebolts in the door and door frame and, after running a chain through them, fastened the chain with a heavy padlock. He told Terry she would not be able to leave the apartment with the baby until he returned from work and unfastened the chain. He had done it just to protect them, he said.

Since they lived on the second floor, and because there was the possibility of a fire or a medical emergency with their infant, Terry and her husband fought over this extreme security measure. Eventually, she told me, it contributed to the dissolution of their marriage, but it wasn't until years later that she connected her husband's growing security panic with the incident when they found themselves parked in the middle of a farmer's field.

The details of Terry's other abduction experiences need not concern us here, because along the way we accidentally uncovered an even more significant and unusual event. As should be clear by now from earlier cases, once an abductee like Terry has begun the process of exploring specific incidents that have always bothered her, such as the two she wrote about, certain other odd experiences that may have seemed too marginal to bring up will begin to float into view. This is exactly what happened with her recollection of "the man who knew too much."

Initially, Terry mentioned the incident almost casually, as if it probably had no connection with the various UFO abductions we had been exploring. But in fact the experience had always been deeply disturbing to her, for reasons that will become clear. It began innocently enough when Terry, then only sixteen years old, was sitting in a pizza parlor with a group of high school friends. A man came over to their table and asked her if she would like to be interviewed for a summer job at his company. She immediately accepted, and the man said he would pick her up the next day at her house. She gave him her address, and he left. Terry said that he looked as if he were in his late fifties or sixties, with salt-and-pepper hair, and was well dressed in a suit and tie. She did not get his name or any details about his company or the job he was offering.

The next day Terry's mother wished her well, expressing no reservations at all about her daughter's going off with a stranger for a job interview. When the man stopped in front of the house, Terry walked out and got into his car. Uncharacteristically, her mother made no effort to meet the stranger or find out where he was taking her daughter.

Terry recalled that once she was sitting on the front seat beside him, a mood of eeriness immediately ensued. As the man began to talk to her, she said, he seemed to know everything about her, especially certain personal things that no one knew. The job interview took place in a virtually empty office space, and from then on things became even more unnerving, and at one moment Terry feared for her life. Many details of her account suggested a complex paranormal event of some sort, and so, after a long and detailed conversation concerning all of her conscious memories of that day, the decision was made to explore the experience through hypnosis.

On March 2, 1989, Terry came to my studio and we began the session, not knowing what her memories would reveal. After completing the relaxation procedures which induce the hypnotic trance, I take Terry back to the moment she first meets the man who conducted the job "interview":

Terry [Speaking slowly, softly, with many long pauses between sentences]: It's in a pizza parlor. I'm with my friends. He came over and introduced himself to the table. He knew my first name. He said he had a company in Flemington and wondered if I would be interested in working for his company. I said I would. Sometime after, I told him where I lived. He said he'd pick me up the next day at two o'clock. Then he left. Everybody that I was with was happy for me.

And then, the next day . . . I got ready. And he pulled up in front of the house but he didn't get out. I saw his car. I had been waiting, so I went out.

BH: *What kind of car was it?*

Terry: I'm not sure. It was a late-model car.

BH: *Does your mother feel okay about your going out with him?*

Terry: Yes. She thought it would be a great opportunity for me.

BH: *Does the man explain what the job is?*

Terry: He says it's just office work. I get in the car. Hmm. [Long pause; then, with emphasis]: I feel tiny. What are we talking about? That doesn't make sense. I feel like the size of . . . the point of a needle. My body is huge.

BH: *What do you feel is small, like the point of a needle?*

Terry: The inside of me. [Pause] He says, "How are you today?" "I'm fine, thank you. How are you?" He says, "Very well. Are you looking forward to this?" I said yes. He asks, "What does your mother feel about what you are doing, going out on an interview?" I tell him she's happy for me if it works out. He asks me, "Are you happy?" I said yes. He said, "You haven't always been happy." I didn't say anything. Then he told me . . . "Do you remember when your father left?" I said, "No. How do you know about that?" He said, "Well, I knew. You weren't very happy then." I said, "I don't remember," and then he told me . . . "You liked living with your grandparents." I thought it was impossible, because I didn't think he knew my whole family. I asked if he knew my family. He said, "No, I just know you." And then he tells me, "That was a terrible thing that your stepfather did to you."

I got very upset. I asked how did he know that? He said, "I just know." And then he said things about my brother and my boyfriend. He told me that . . . [long pause] "Did you have a good time yesterday?" I said it was all right. Then he told me that he knew everything I did. He said, "I know all about your day yesterday." I asked, "How do you know?" "I just know," he said. "At twelve o'clock you went to Jimmy's house." That's my boyfriend. Nobody was home then. And we made out. [In fact, it was then that Terry lost her virginity.] He told me about that. But he couldn't have known that. There was only one window, but it was covered. So I asked him how he knew. He said, "Oh, I just know."

And then we got to Flemington. He parks on the street in front of an old office building. And he says, "This is it." We get out and I follow him in and we go upstairs. And it's dark on the stairs. He opens the door. It's a big old empty room. Two rooms, one right next to the other one. Very big, long windows. In one room there's a desk and a chair and that's all, and in the other room there's a map on the wall. But I don't know what's on it.

And he says, "Well, this is it." He says he likes me, and the company will open in about two weeks, and he takes me over to the desk and tells me this will be my desk. "You'll answer the telephone and take messages and keep in touch with where the people are."

BH: *Does he explain the nature of the business?*

Terry: He says, like, trucks and people. Just says trucks and people. My stepfather was a truck driver, and I don't know all the terms, but I think it's dispatching, but he didn't say that. And he tells me that this is a wonderful opportunity, and I'll be in charge of the office, and all I have to do to get the job is to do what I did with my boyfriend.

I didn't know what to say. I was surprised. And then I said, "No, no, I can't do that. This has a very wrong purpose, this interview."

BH: *Tell me about your emotions at this point. Did you feel anger, fear, disappointment, or what?*

Terry: I felt nervous at first. But then he started telling me everything was all right. Even in that building I wasn't scared. I should have been scared, but I wasn't. I was just adamant. I said no. It was like I knew he wouldn't hurt me, but I shouldn't have known that, because he might have. Then I was standing at the desk and he came up from behind me and pulled me . . . but I just moved his hand that was wrapped around me and I stepped back. He didn't do this with strength, to force me. But now I stepped back and I said, "I can't." And he said, "Oh, why not? Come on. You can. It's a wonderful job." And he sat down on the floor and told me to sit next to him. I said no and walked right up next to the door and said, "I have to go. I don't want the job." He got up and he said, "All right, but you are the one I want." We just walked out and he locked the door.

We got in the car and he didn't say anything to me then. He was quiet and I was quiet. We started to go home, but then he took some turns that I didn't know. I didn't know where we were going, and then, after the second turn, I said, "Where are we going? He said he had to stop to see a friend for a minute. It would not take more than a minute. But then I was getting very scared. I felt more confident in the office that he wouldn't hurt me, but now we were in the middle of nowhere, woods and fields everywhere. But I just sat there. And I thought if I jumped out of the car I'd probably get hurt, so I didn't do it. Then we came up to a little house on the left with a dirt driveway and we pulled in. Hmm. [Long pause] He asked me to sit in the car. [Long pause] I wonder why that house was there. [Sighs. Another long pause] It's hard to see it. It's like . . . field grass covers it. Higher than grass . . . like straw . . . hay. Hmm. I didn't get out but he goes in, and I slump down in the car. He goes in a door. It's like an overhang over it.

BH: *Is it a two-story house?*

Terry: No, it's like one level. I keep seeing the roof like a smooth stone roof. No peaks. And I don't look at it because I'm too scared. I don't want whoever is in the house to see me. I knew that when he went in they were probably talking about me. So I slumped down on the seat so they wouldn't see me. I feel so shaky. . . .

BH: *Do you hide under the dashboard or lie down on the floor?*

Terry: No. Slumped. My head's on the back of the seat. [Long pause] It seems to be taking a long time. I'm all shaky. [BH assures her everything will eventually be all right.] I'm afraid I'm going to be killed. That's what I think.

BH: *Do you think of trying to escape?*

Terry: No. I don't know where I am. I don't see anything on the road.

BH: *Are there cars going by?*

Terry: No. I don't know where I'd go. I'm thinking, If he comes out with somebody else, I don't know what I'll do. I was afraid of him. He came out then. [Long pause] Hmm. And he got in the car. I felt confused for a minute.

BH: *What confuses you?*

Terry: I don't know. I can't . . . I just feel funny.

BH: *Let's go back to when he comes out. See which door he comes out of, and how he approaches the car. How he approaches you. Do you feel relief? Or fear? Or what?*

Terry: I don't know what it is. [Long pause] I don't know. . . .

BH [Setting the stage for a different visualizing technique]: *We're going to picture a movie being made of this scene. You and I will sit atop a tall hydraulic camera boom, and we'll be lifted up about thirty or forty feet to look down and film the scene below: the car with a young girl, an actress playing you, sitting slumped in the front seat. We will be able to clearly see the house, the field grass, the dirt road, and whatever else is around. You will be safe with me on the camera boom. We will only be observers.*

Terry [Sighs deeply]: I see him! [Very alarmed] Oh! Oh!

BH: *What are we seeing?*

Terry: Him and them. Lots of the other ones. A lot . . . six or seven.

BH: *People like him from the company?*

Terry: No! They're smaller. All the same. No hair. Same color all over.

BH: *Does he look different?*

Terry: No. He looks the same. But he looks like a giant.

BH: *We can see the house too.*

Terry: It looks funny, the house. Oh. It keeps going back and forth. It looks like a house and then it looks like not a house. It looks all metal. Little windows, along the bottom. The door is like . . . it's like an awning, but it's not an awning. Something over it.

BH: *Let's look down at that girl in the car. What exactly is taking place?*

Terry [Speaking very slowly, as if observing]: She's . . . alone . . . in the car. Hmm. I'm scared. He comes out. Oh! He comes out and just stands in front of the car, but these other things come out to the side and just look at me. Oh! [Very frightened] I close my eyes and slip down lower, to the floor, and then I look, and I . . . and I stay down there and start crying. . . .

BH: *Are the doors to the car locked?*

Terry: No. But they didn't try to get in. They just looked. I look up. I don't see them. I climb up again and then I'm fine. It was so scary. I wonder what he's doing with them. [Sighs deeply] I don't know. I think one comes to my door and I'm just sitting there, and it opens the door and I get out, but now I'm feeling funny. [Sighs] I'm feeling scared but I'm not doing anything. I'm not hiding. [Sighs] I don't know what happens. I just get back in the car.

BH: *Just keep your eyes closed. I don't want you to look at anything. You are standing outside the car. Tell me what your body is feeling, what you're doing. You may be getting ready to run. . . .*

Terry: I feel panic. I don't know why I'm not running away. I wonder why he took me here. I walk [long pause] a little bit.

BH: *What direction do you walk?*

Terry: Two of these things are on each side of me. I don't know. It doesn't make sense.

BH: *Now, looking down again from our position on the camera boom, we see a girl, and two of them on either side. . . . What are they doing?*

Terry: They just walk. I feel like, at the time, I'm . . . I feel like a mother hen and her chicks. Everybody walks, everybody turns. . . .

BH: *Is there a goal to this walk?*

Terry: No, just a stroll. Down the road, a dirt road, and then I turn around and I walk back. . . .

BH: *What do you see at the turn in the road? Do you see the house or any obstacle?*

Terry: No. I don't know how they determined where to turn. I'm thinking . . . I have to be out of the car I don't know why. I just had to be out of the car for a while. And then they went back in their house. And then he came back.

Once Terry and the man were back in the car, nothing else seemed to be happening. She was driven home and the bizarre adventure was over. In the remaining minutes of the hypnosis, I tried to find out the job interviewer's name, but Terry could not recall it. I asked if perhaps the name sounded English or Italian or Jewish or Irish or some other identifiable nationality, and after a long pause she concluded that it did not seem to have any ethnic coloration. "Maybe it was something like Nelson," she said, not because she thought that might be the name but because *Nelson* suggested its bland neutrality.

After some minutes of positive, ego-strengthening posthypnotic suggestion, I counted back from five to one and brought Terry out of her relaxed trance state. It had been an extraordinary session for her, but perhaps even more extraordinary for me, as I will explain shortly. In our debriefing conversation immediately after the hypnosis ended, Terry made a remark that aptly demonstrated how innocent and naive she was in 1971, the year this incident occurred: "Once it was over and he was taking me home," she said, "the only thing I was worried about was that he would tell my mother what I had done with Jimmy the day before, and I would get into trouble." For sixteen-year-old Terry, the very real perils she had endured with "Mr. Nelson" were over—she had survived them—and since she had no conscious recollection of the UFO occupants and their "metal house with windows all around it," her only fear was that she might be grounded by her mother. As she told me this, she smiled at her ingenuousness.

As I later reviewed the session, listening to the tape and making a transcript, I was able to delineate many different stages in the encounter, as well as moments of what seemed to be firm alien control of external circumstances. The first example of possible alien management occurred when Terry's mother immediately gave the sixteen-year-old permission to get into a stranger's car and go to a job interview—with no request for information about the interviewer or the destination, and no cautionary remarks of any sort. Terry said that even at the time this seemed totally unlike her usually protective mother. If the interviewer (or the aliens) had somehow arranged her mother's surprising indifference, one wonders if he was not secretly gloating when he asked, "What does your mother feel about what you are doing, going out on an interview?" and Terry replied that her mother was happy for her.

But the first clear indication that something was wrong occurs almost as soon as Terry settles down in the front seat of the car. After a long pause she makes what is for her a very cryptic observation: "I feel *tiny.*" Then she seems confused by what is being said, presumably by the man: "What are we talking about? That doesn't make sense." And

then: "I feel like the size of . . . the point of a needle. My body is huge."
I ask, "What do you feel is small, like the point of a needle?" and she
answers, again cryptically, "The inside of me."

Terry is not the kind of woman given to making enigmatic
metaphorical observations about her body image, but something made
her feel extremely strange—physically and emotionally—as soon as
she took her seat in the car, and she expressed this strangeness as best
she could. In a much later conversation she told me that what she
meant by "the inside of me" was her "self," her soul, her ego, which
had become tiny, shrunken, inoperative, while by comparison her body,
her physical self, had become "huge."

I wondered, without mentioning it to her, if these reactions had anything to do with the fact that the interviewer was beginning to direct
the conversation to Terry's recent sexual experiences with her
boyfriend, because it was his "impossible" knowledge of her most intimate feelings and experiences that most disturbed her. She told me
that the interviewer had described in rather graphic detail exactly what
she and Jimmy had done the day before, something she knew that
Jimmy would never have told anyone.

Even more disturbing, the man said, "That was a terrible thing that
your stepfather did to you." Terry told me that when she was only six
years old she had been sexually molested by her stepfather, a traumatic
experience she had never reported to anyone, not even her mother. One
can safely assume that her stepfather had never told anyone about it,
either. So how did this stranger, the interviewer, know about all of these
things?

It would seem that he knew in the same way that abductees report
the UFO occupants often demonstrate intimate knowledge of the people they regularly abduct. Whether the aliens somehow observe these
incidents or are able to access them from the memory banks of the
abductees who experience them is a question we cannot answer. Still,
the phenomenon is one that is frequently reported.

Another factor to be added to the mix is that, once in the empty
office, the interviewer not only coldly propositioned Terry but put his
arm around her in a strange, easily resisted physical attempt. Two
things strike me about this scene that make it seem something other
than a sordid and unsuccessful attempt by an aging roué to seduce a

pretty young sixteen-year-old. First, there is the self-defeating coarse-nesss of the man's sexual proposition, followed by the weakness of his physical move. One assumes that any man of his age who was at all experienced in enticing young girls would have understood that such a cynical proposition—unaccompanied by either a compliment or even a seductive word or two—would be regarded as insulting by a shy, reserved girl like Terry. What could he have been thinking? Then his unwelcome physical attempt to hold her was easily rejected because, in Terry's words, it was not "forceful." The man's behavior in this exchange seems not only inept and immature but also evidence of a complete lack of understanding of a young girl's basic psychology.

But the other bizarre element in this scene has to do with Terry's reaction. Why didn't she immediately flee the desolate, empty office space after "Mr. Nelson's" unappetizing, even frightening behavior? Why would she get into his car once more, knowing what he had tried to do to her and fully aware that his intimate knowledge of her life was extremely disturbing? Any illusion she might have had about the won-derful job offer would have long since evaporated, so that explanation of her behavior makes no sense. Surely she could have walked into a store or found a telephone nearby and called home, asking her mother to come and pick her up. It seems inescapable that to some extent she was still under the control of Mr. Nelson, whoever or whatever he was, and that she really had no choice in the matter.

And then we have the short, almost silent drive to the countryside and the small metal house with glass windows around the bottom. "Mr. Nelson" has his rendezvous with what can only be interpreted as a group of UFO occupants, and there are more examples of Terry's illog-ical behavior, clear signs of her inability to act freely and independently. She is sure she is going to be killed, but she sits in the car, apparently unable to try to escape or even lock the car doors. The events that ensue, including her regimented walk with the small aliens, is indis-tinct and probably incompletely remembered. All of this later part of her misadventure was only recalled under hypnosis, and since the ses-sion had been long and difficult for Terry, I decided not to continue it, hoping to discover at some other time what else may have happened. And so, as I often do, I ended the hypnosis rather than stumble into another, perhaps even more disturbing series of events.

But for our purposes here, the focus must remain on "Mr. Nelson." What do Terry's recollections tell us about him?

First, that his physical appearance was unexceptional. He had approached a table in a pizza parlor occupied by young teenage girls and apparently did not strike any of them as looking other than like a normal older man. Most emphatically, "Mr. Nelson" did not resemble a small, ageless, gray-skinned, huge-eyed alien. He seemed to Terry to be in his late fifties or sixties, with salt-and-pepper hair and wearing a conventional suit and tie.

Second, "Mr. Nelson" was able to operate in the real world like a normal man. He was able to drive a car, walk into a food shop, speak somewhat conventionally, and find his way around the local New Jersey roads. And, if one wishes to, one can add that he seemed to have the sexual desires of a normal man.

But his conventional aspects end here. His extraordinary abilities and connections mark him as being far different from the rest of us. First, there is the issue of his "impossible" knowledge of Terry's intimate life—in particular her sexual life. This knowledge seems paranormal, as does the effect the man had on her from the moment she stepped into the car, when she felt as if her "self," her soul, had shrunk and her body had become "huge."

Second, there is the matter of "Mr. Nelson's" intermittent control of Terry's behavior, though this control apparently did not extend to her sexuality. And here we must also remember how clumsy and ineffective his own sexual approaches were.

Third, and perhaps most astounding, is his rendezvous with the UFO occupants to whom he delivered the helpless, deeply frightened young girl.

So, putting these odd pieces together, who—or what—was "Mr. Nelson"? An apparently normal-looking man with alien gifts? Some sort of hybrid creature, the product of an exotic genetic process? Whatever he was, he was a true anomaly here on earth, neither completely familiar with, nor effective in, the world of normal humans.

But perhaps "Mr. Nelson," Terry's very strange job interviewer, was not unique. There are other, similar, cases to be discussed.

Chapter 16

THE CASE OF THE MISSING LADIES' ROOM

"L ISA," A HIGHLY INTELLIGENT, articulate young woman in her middle thirties and, like Terry, a New Jersey resident, wrote to me in 1986 about her odd experiences and disturbing UFO recollections. For example, she recalled a puzzling missing-time incident that occurred when she was only about seven years old. She and her mother had driven out one evening to pick up a pizza for dinner. Consciously, Lisa recalled their buying the pizza and starting back home, when they encountered some kind of roadblock, intense lights, and an indistinct group of men. In her next bit of conscious recollection, she and her mother were continuing their drive, feeling confused and shaken. When they arrived at home, Lisa's father was at the door, extremely worried, because the short trip had taken an inordinately long time. Worse, neither Lisa nor her mother could explain what had happened or why they were more than an hour late, and were shocked to realize that the pizza they had bought was missing.

Lisa and I explored this incident, among a number of others, with the aid of hypnosis, and what emerged was a full-scale abduction of mother and child. Among the harrowing images she recalled was that of her mother, naked and in some kind of trance state, being placed on an examination table by several alien beings. It was the first time Lisa recalled having seen her mother naked and helpless, a traumatic memory that had remained deeply etched within her subconscious mind.

She had had other, equally disturbing UFO encounters, which we explored over a period of a year or so, but one day she happened to mention an apparently unconnected incident that had always puzzled her. As we have seen in the case of Terry Winthrop, once an abductee begins to explore partially recalled UFO and missing-time memories, other highly unusual but on their surface non-UFO-connected occurrences begin to float back into conscious memory. Lisa described a newly recalled incident this way:

I was about twenty years old. I discovered an ad in the paper, and the job description was a . . . like a security job. I want to say private-eye kind of thing, but it wasn't private-eye. . . . It was like an inside security job, something like that. It was very appealing because they mentioned what great pay it was. I was going to college at the time and the hours were good for me. Evening hours.

They must have given me instructions on the phone when I called from a number in the ad. This part is hard to remember, but I remember it was near Woodbridge, New Jersey. A woman told how to get there. It's sketchy in my memory. I drove over to this office building, but it wasn't like a huge office complex. It wasn't a high-rise building. It had an elevator and was about three to five stories. I don't remember a sign on the door or anything like that, or the name of the company. It was, like, "Go to this address and we're on the third floor."

I got to the place and it was very austere . . . not very nice office space. It was really shabby. There was a woman sitting at a desk. And I remember there was a phone on the desk and a wastebasket, and that was it. No pictures on the wall, no typewriter, no files, nothing. There wasn't even anything in the wastepaper basket. And I had to go to the bathroom and I asked the woman where the ladies' room was, and she was totally confused. It seemed she didn't know where it was. She never gave a yes or a no, or even "I don't know." That would have been okay, but she never said a word. She just looked stricken. There was no one else to ask, and it was really awkward. She got flustered and left the room. She had this very timid, frightened look, and it made me frightened, too.

There was nobody else there getting interviewed. Just me. If I remember correctly, there was only one chair. I thought, *What is this room for?* It didn't look like a meeting room or a reception area particularly. It looked like someone just put a desk there and a wastebasket and a phone. Now that I think about it, I'm not even sure there was a place for me to sit. But I was pretty quickly ushered into the next room, and I met this black gentleman. Not real light-skinned, but just kind of a fair black. He had a nice-looking, well-presented suit and tie and he came off kind of stiff-backed, like a military type. But it was a security job, so that makes sense. His office was a pretty small place with a window, and there was a water cooler. No files, no typewriter or anything like that. It seemed they must be only using this space to interview people. I remember filling out something on a clipboard, basic information, and then . . . he poured me a cup of water, which I didn't really want, since I had to go to the bathroom. It was the last thing I needed.

And then he did all the talking. I was twenty years old and I didn't know any better. He went on about this position, a position where you would be watching employees as they did their day-to-day work, to make sure they weren't stealing anything, to make sure they were on the up-and-up, and he said not everyone can do this. My impression was that this was some kind of warehouse job where you'd have to squeal on your fellow employees. He didn't specify what kind of place it would be. It was general. He really wanted to impress on me, rather than the particulars of the site, this position, that not everyone can do this kind of work: "Could you do this? Is it something you could handle . . . psychologically . . . rat on your fellow employees?"

I said it would depend on what kind of place it would be: "I don't really know what you need. Will this be a warehouse, or what?" He went on and on. "We're really concerned if you'll be able to do this. . . . You'll get to know these people. . . ." He was doing all the talking, droning on and on. It put me to sleep. I remember having to lift my head up and having the distinct impression that *Oh my God, this is really bad,* that I had fallen asleep at a job interview. I was extremely self-conscious and embarrassed. I thought, *Oh my God, I hope he didn't notice I was asleep.* And what happened immediately after that is, he ushered me out of the room.

I don't remember that he had ever specifically mentioned a salary or any money amount. He was impressing on me that I would be paid very well, but again, the whole thing was "not everyone can do this." It was the evening hours that I was interested in, that met my needs. Something else that was odd about this interview was that he never asked about my experience, or really anything else. Normally at a job interview you're the one on the spot, you're the one who talks. He did all the talking. He didn't seem interested in what I had to say about anything.

I don't know how long it lasted, but then I kind of lost track, because I just remember his droning on and on and I fell asleep, so I didn't know how long he'd been droning on about the whole thing. As soon as I woke up, he said, "Okay, thanks for your time, we'll definitely get together," and then kind of bum's-rushed me out the door.

I felt the interview couldn't have gone well. I'd fallen asleep on the guy. When I left the room, the receptionist had gone. Nobody was around. The building was empty. It just seemed weird. It seems very weird, the whole thing. And I left without any particular impression. Usually you get a handshake. I kind of felt this was all too strange. I'm not sure what it was all about, and after his long droning on, I thought maybe I don't even want a job like this. It was almost like he's trying to talk me out of it: "It's a difficult job, not many people can do it," and so on. I was happy to get out of there.

And there was something else. When I stood up, I felt that my pantyhose didn't feel right: The crotch wasn't in the right place. My pantyhose weren't exactly down around my knees, but they were not fitting right . . . it was uncomfortable. I remember feeling very self-conscious when I woke up.

BH: *When the interviewer offered you the cup of water, did you drink it?*

Lisa: Yes. I believe I did. He had a command of the room. He handed it to me and I drank. He had a kind of military command and he gave it to me and I drank it down. He was in control. And I didn't think he gave a damn about what I thought, one way or the other.

It was weird. It was very weird. You know when something very weird happens, and then years later when you look back it still looks weird. It stood the test of time.

BH: *If the ad said the pay was good and the hours were good, isn't it odd that no one else was there applying for the job?*

Lisa: There was nobody else there, I can assure you. There wasn't even anyone in the lobby. This happened at a time when a lot of strangeness was going on in my life: missing-time episodes, turning up in places and not knowing how I got there. But this was different. It was a distinct thing. I know I drove there. But the whole thing of falling asleep at a job interview was really peculiar. The whole nature of the interview was really peculiar. I have an image of him sitting on the edge of the desk, one cheek of his bottom up and one leg up, casual, like. And I just remember the droning ya-da-da, ya-da-da, ya-da-da, and my just nodding off. At least that's how it seemed to me.

My feeling was, if he's going on like this, I should just sit there politely and listen, and that's what I did. I felt awful about falling asleep. How could I have done that? At a job interview you're usually hypervigiliant. Strange interview. Strange interview.

BH: *Usually, if you fall asleep sitting down, your head drops and then snaps back up, and the shock of that wakes you up. Did that happen to you?*

Lisa: I don't remember that, but I guess my head had been drooping. I was really shocked that he didn't catch it. If I was giving a job interview and somebody fell asleep, I'd say, "Are you okay?" I would be concerned.

Unfortunately, I was never able to carry out a hypnotic session with Lisa about this bizarre incident. Essentially we were concentrating on her more obviously UFO-connected recollections, but she also seemed somewhat reluctant to explore this experience. I sensed that this so-called job interview made her particularly uneasy, since it took place in what we might euphemistically call the real world and apparently involved normal human beings. But the similarities to Terry's experience were too great to ignore. (It should be pointed out that at the time each told me about her experience, they had never met or communicated, though eventually I introduced them.)

Considered in chronological order, the similarities are striking:

1. Both women were quite young at the time—sixteen and twenty—and both were undergoing a series of UFO abduction experiences.

2. Both were "interviewed" in empty, unfurnished spaces, rooms that suggested impoverished, even amateurish stage sets rather than locations for serious businesses. In Lisa's case, the flustered inability of the blond receptionist to steer her to the ladies' room suggests an unprepared actress as well.

3. Neither "interviewer" spelled out any details about the job for which the woman was applying. Neither mentioned specific hours, pay, or requisite skills—surely basic issues in any serious job interview.

4. Neither woman was questioned about her past employment record, training, schooling, availability, home address or telephone number. (Although Terry was not asked to fill out an application, Lisa vaguely remembers a clipboard and a form she filled out.) These facts alone show that these experiences were not actual job interviews but pretexts for something else.

5. Both Terry (directly) and Lisa (by implication) were aware of the sexual aspect of their experiences. Terry reported that her interviewer's behavior stressed his interest in her sexuality, but Lisa's account of falling asleep at the droning, hypnotic voice of her interviewer and then awakening to find her pantyhose disarranged is even more ominous.

6. Neither woman was given the specific name and address of the company to which they were ostensibly applying for work, and neither left the interview with even so much as a business card or a piece of paper.

7. In both instances, Terry and Lisa were the sole applicants for these alleged jobs—in Lisa's case at least, a highly unlikely situation.

8. Another simularity has to do with an important but subtle aspect of their experiences. Terry originally heard about her job from a stranger who approached her in a pizza parlor. She left home the next day, getting into his car with virtually no knowledge of who he was, what the job entailed, or where they were going. Lisa told me that she could not remember where she first heard about her job offer—she thinks she might have read about it in a newspaper—and she is very unclear about how she knew where to drive for the interview: "They must have given me instructions on the phone from a number in the ad. This part is hard to remember." She does not recall writing anything down, clipping out an ad, or keeping any kind of notes about how to get to the office. Thus, there is no evidence to suggest that she herself initiated the visit to the office, which leaves me with the suspicion that Lisa, like Terry, was summoned by her mysterious interviewer for some kind of encounter which is not fully recalled.

9. Another similarity, though less clear-cut, has to do with the interviewers themselves. The interviewer in Terry's case, "Mr. Nelson," was apparently gifted—if that term can be stretched a bit—with truly surprising psychic power, in addition to possessing obvious connections with UFO occupants. By contrast, the only odd thing about Lisa's black interviewer was his droning voice and what we must suspect was his ability to put his interviewee into a hypnotic trance. These are hardly the basic skills of run-of-the-mill personnel managers.

So, what are we to make of these young female abductees' bizarre experiences with normal-looking men of unusual abilities, who meet with them for unknown reasons in real-world empty offices in crowded, real-world New Jersey? Who are these men? Are they human, or alien, or something in between?

Chapter 17

A VERY SPECIAL PERFUME

THERE IS YET ANOTHER of these peculiar job interview cases, which I will mention only briefly. This incident involves "Sally," a highly credible young woman whose abduction experiences I had been looking into since she first wrote to me in 1987, and whom we will meet again in a later chapter. At the time she told me about her bizarre job interview, Sally had never met either Terry or Lisa and was unaware of their similar experiences. Her so-called interview encounter is the only one of the three that, under hypnosis, was thoroughly explored to its unpleasant conclusion on the aliens' examination table. Earlier, I had been reluctant to press Terry for many details in the final section of her hypnosis, and Lisa had declined to undergo any hypnosis to reveal what remained in her memory as an extremely disturbing experience from early youth. I should also mention that, unlike Terry and Lisa, Sally is a resident of Ohio, where her "job interview" took place, thus sparing the state of New Jersey further embarrassment.

On October 2, 1993, during a visit to New York, Sally agreed to undergo hypnosis in order to recount this recent experience. After the induction I set the scene, based on details that she had consciously recalled, beginning with a phone call.

Sally: It's a lady. . . . She tells me I have to go to this interview.

BH: *She asks you?*

Sally: She tells me I have to.

BH: *Do you ask about the job?*

Sally: No.

BH: *Does she tell you where you have to go for the interview?*

Sally: Yes. Very complicated instructions. I write it down. I think I better start early, because I don't want to get lost. I want to make it before three-thirty. I leave the house early. She told me to be on time. I don't get lost at all.

[Beginning to seem frightened] There are trees . . . and men behind the trees. There is equipment out. I go up to look for the second floor. There's a lady in the middle of the hallway, and she tells me about the men I saw.

BH: *Was there anything unusual about these men?*

Sally: They all have the same suits on.

BH: *Are they wearing neckties?*

Sally: No.

BH: *White shirts?*

Sally: Yes. I thought it was odd that they all had the same suits on. Also, they didn't have the right shoes to go with the suits. They had loafers on. They didn't match.

A man came in . . . and he took me to another guy.

BH: *Did he introduce you?*

Sally: No. It's an office, and it's empty. Nothing. Not even chairs. None. I don't like it . . . this office. There's nothing in it. Nothing like anyone ever worked here. The desk is empty. He starts talking to me, and there's one chair and I sit down in it. [Long pause] I think I saw a flash of light in the corner of the office. . . . There are no windows in this office. He tells me about my salary, how high it is, and I think it's a joke. He says they sell perfumes, and shows me a little bottle. He says, 'Would you like to try it on?' and I say no. He put it underneath my nose The chair begins to spin and I fall . . . and I keep looking at this light. [Long pause] I'm standing up and he's shaking my hand and telling me the interview was very good. And I go home.

BH: *Let's go back to the perfume. Does he ask you to smell it?*

Sally: It has a strong smell.

BH: *How does your body feel?*

Sally: I don't remember.

BH: *Yes you do. You can feel the sensation of the chair spinning. But now you are in a safe situation here and you can talk about it. You're okay.*

Sally: I tell myself not to remember. . . . The chair's spinning. . . . I just don't want to . . . I feel really sick.

BH: *Do you vomit?*

Sally: No. The light's getting brighter. They're telling me everything's all right and I tell myself, *Not again. This isn't going to happen again in this room . . . what happened before.* . . . He's in control after I smelled that stuff. He tells me I'm okay, I'm not going to fall. Keep smelling the stuff. He has it right under my nose. . . . The light's getting brighter. He goes around to my back and he says, "I'm glad you were able to come." When I open my eyes I'm on a table. . . .

What follows is a series of physical procedures such as those Sally has experienced many times before during alien abductions. But this scene, which apparently takes place in an empty Ohio office, includes several normal, human-looking men as well as small gray aliens.

For our purposes it is more useful to briefly concentrate on the beginning of this experience, so I will not go into the later stages of another harrowing alien abduction complete with invasive gynecological procedures. Over and over during the hypnotic session, Sally pleaded with her captors: "Leave me alone. Leave me alone. I feel like screaming. . . ."

Eventually she was returned, shaken but silent, to her car. She drove home, unable to remember the interview itself, the details of the so-called job, the presence of the aliens, or any of the physical procedures carried out upon her.

Obviously, there are many striking similarities between Sally's experience and those of Terry and Lisa, beginning with the promise—or pretext—of a job interview. Then there are the shadowy, ambiguous ways in which each of the three young women first heard about the job opening and the implausible ways in which they were led to the scene. Lisa and Sally both had phone conversations with "ladies" who directed them to the respective interview sites. The three empty offices were quite alike in their absence of furnishings or any semblance of workplace paraphernalia. In Terry's and Sally's accounts, there were female "receptionists" who seemed, again, as if they were living props in a bargain-basement stage set. Sally's inhaling of some kind of anesthetic is analagous to Lisa's listening to a hypnotically droning voice and drinking a cup of water; both led to a state of semiconsciousness. Terry's and Sally's experiences both ended in encounters with small gray aliens, but since hypnosis was not employed with Lisa, one cannot be sure what occurred during her period of induced "sleep."

But the salient point of all three accounts is the presence in earthly locations of apparently normal-looking beings who interacted cooperatively with UFO occupants and who also seemed to possess distinctly nonhuman characteristics. Do these people live here among us, renting rooms and apartments, holding down jobs, driving cars, eating in restaurants, and having romantic and even sexual relationships with unwary human beings? The evidence thus far suggests that some of them do. How extensive is this bizarre underground society?

Chapter 18

VULNERABLE IN A THOUSAND WAYS

JOB INTERVIEWS FOR AMERICAN teenagers are almost always stressful but usually necessary life experiences. In the latest set of incidents that Budd related, three young women—strangers to each other, in different decades, and from different parts of the country—went through strikingly similar and bizarre "job interviews." That all three had a history of abduction experiences and were young, white females were the only significant points they had in common.

It would be easy to toss these accounts aside as hysteria, stress, fabrication, or faulty memory. But consider this: How many of you, as young job applicants, were ever personally invited to apply for a vaguely specified job, interviewed in a deserted building with minimal furniture and no signs of an ongoing business, and were distinctly aware of sexual overtones in your interview with a "boss" who seemed to have paranormal abilities—one who knew your intimate secrets from early childhood up until the day before?

Personally, I don't know anyone else besides these three women whose interview experiences combined these circumstances—which, of course, doesn't prove that they happened as told. Anecdotal testimonies such as these are vulnerable, offering no solid proof. Any one of the girls' reports might have functioned to shield her from a possible rape scenario. But together, with the background of the girls as UFO experiencers, the rarity and oddness of these encounters make it hard to explain away the actions of their interviewers as either desperate employers finding ingenious ways to fill difficult jobs, or human sexual predators who lured young women into vulnerable positions with the potential of paying jobs.

In order to understand who these men—these "potential employers"—were, one must appreciate the fact that the women were abductees and the men, who respectively apparently drugged one girl, put another in a trance state, and delivered a third girl to the occupants of a UFO, did not seem engaged in "normal" business activities. The interview was a pretext for something else. Furthermore, these men were not brilliant or forceful seducers, if that was their game. So who were they and what does their interaction with these young women signify?

As we begin this scientific exploration of yet another new pattern in the UFO phenomenon, you, the reader, shouldn't expect smooth sailing—not in these uncharted waters. We're in a situation similar to that of physicist Philip Morrison as he first approached the question of extraterrestrial intelligence:

> Unlike most of science, this topic extends beyond the test of a well-framed hypothesis; here we try to test an entire view of the world, incomplete and vulnerable in a thousand ways. That has a proud name in the history of thought as well; it is called exploration.[1]

Where we'll go in the following segment, what we'll speculate on, and what we can tentatively posit as theories about these three men is also "incomplete and vulnerable in a thousand ways." In our attempt to link rapidly evolving earthly sciences with the UFO phenomenon, Budd and I are not suggesting these are explanations or proofs of any kind. We are simply trying to take the "magic" out of some very advanced technologies related to the UFO occupants. We do this by showing how such seemingly impossible UFO aspects as telepathy, mind control, and cross-species breeding are within the human realm of possibility today.

Big-Headed Babies

It might be possible that the UFO occupants far surpass human beings in raw IQ, just as we surpass caterpillars and mice. The difference between us and any intergalactic space travelers may well be that they have outstripped us in more than technology. Human history suggests that the power of their intellect would be far in advance of our own. Brains in humans, after all, developed quite quickly—and then stalled out at a limited size. One of our pint-sized ancestors, *Australopithecus africanus*, laid claim to only a pound of gray matter. In the cosmic scheme of things, this ancestor's two million years of roaming across the veldt gained him only a paltry tripling in the size of his brain, which is the housing of his essential neural interconnections—his computing power.

Why haven't we advanced further in this crucial trait? The simplest answer is that big-headed babies can't be born to human females. The dimensions of the human female pelvis, the bony structure that surrounds the birth canal, limit the size of a baby's head and brain.[2] Perhaps ET had found a way to compact and reduce the size of his neurons while increasing the number. A small change in neural numbers would make a huge difference in performance.

Abductees' standard alien drawing shows a big-headed, sloe-eyed biped with a puny body—obviously a species whose environment requires cranial space and neuronal capacity far more than physical prowess. As scientists Josef Shklovskii and Carl Sagan noted years ago, there's possibly no limit to the extraterrestrial's intelligence.[3]

At the same time, we know this material is very risky business to discuss—risky because the only supporting material for the presence of aliens among us is anecdotal. We can offer multiple, overlapping, highly specific and detailed anecdotes, but that's it—no DNA, no fingerprints, no sperm samples, no landing traces. We explore this material despite the risk that much of what we'll discuss seems improbable at best, and too frightening to examine at worst.

Silent Speech

In February 1999, during the First International UFO Symposium of Turkey, Budd and Dr. John Mack worked together to explore the troubled memories of Fusan, a young woman from Istanbul. Her conscious recollections of small gray beings in her home led to a hypnosis session. During the course of a very emotional hour, Fusan relived the abduction in which alien beings presented her with a child they said was her own.

At one point during the session, Mack asked Fusan how the aliens communicated with her. Could she hear spoken words? What did they sound like? But Fusan shook her head. "No, I don't hear them speak," she said. Budd probed further: "But you think they're communicating with you?" "There's something, maybe a phone wire between their heads," Fusan replied, apparently an attempt to describe telepathy.

But a group of NASA scientists are exploring a somewhat different means of producing "silent speech." The research involves gesture-based, or bioelectric, control in which electrodes would transmit signals to a computer from muscle movements in the tongue as words are formed silently in the mouth—but not actually spoken. The computer would then translate the sender's signals into digitized speech for the listener. Dr. Charles Jorgensen, lead scientist on the project, said: "The idea would be to get away from having people talking on their cell phones. You could more or less sit there and communicate and have it be translated electronically."[4]

Three Faux Employers

Among ethicists and biologists around the world, debates rage over whether the human species should be reengineered. Notice, the question is not *if* or *when*: We already have the capability to carry out some fundamental changes to the human genome through various modes of gene manipulation and transfer. More quickly than society is ready for, science is also coming to understand and bypass many of the biological and technical barriers that stand in the way of redesigning our species. In fact, the pro argument goes, in order to ensure our survival, we may soon need to make alterations to the human genome to repair ongoing genetic damage.[5]

There are, after all, a growing number of human genetic abnormalities, many believed to be a result of environmental damage: low sperm count and abnormal, slowed-up sperm in human males; four times more infants born with genetic diseases today than one hundred years ago; and burgeoning rates of cancer and heart disease, among others. It isn't yet known how many of these disorders are related to damage at the genome level, meaning they would be passed along to any offspring. But the individual suffering from such problems is enormous, and science and medicine are paying attention. Perhaps genetic tinkering will become inevitable, but not without a great outcry from both the public and many scientists. Other than bioengineered foods, no controversy—not abortion, or nuclear power, or global warming—looms larger in the public arena where science, social values, and commerce collide. Reengineering the human being may be possible in the lab today, but it's not, as they say on television talk shows, a "total makeover" that's likely to be celebrated on the networks anytime soon.

But what if another species, such as ET, already has the drop on us? What if they have dealt with all the ethical and technical issues that we still face? What if they have mastered both the chemical coding and insertion (or deletion) of minute segments of foreign code into the human genome—gradually, systematically? No one who is knowledgeable about the UFO phenomenon would be surprised to discover that ETs are more technically skilled and highly adaptive to environmental change than humans are—and that they'd like to stay here on Earth, in some form that wouldn't send the natives shrieking to the hills and pushing buttons to launch bombs. Fifty solid years of UFO buzz-overs and landings and abductions could mean they've been studying a place where it would be nice to leave behind a sizable presence, even as their intergalactic travels continue—a bit like Americans stationed in Japan and Cuba's Guantanamo Bay. Only in this case the transgenic "normals" would—at least physically—blend right into the rest of the population.

Gene Therapy

Genetic disorders—specific types of breast cancer, hemophilia, or Huntington's disease—run in families, and genetic testing can show which family members are quite likely to be unfortunate inheritors of a disease. Although still novel and highly experimental, scientists hope that gene therapy will eventually be an extremely effective treatment for diseases that may be inherited through a single gene. Its promise is based on correcting disease at the level of the DNA molecules.

Essentially, there are two forms of gene therapy: One form is *somatic gene therapy,* which involves manipulation of the cells' DNA in a way that makes it corrective for the patient, but the engineered trait will not be passed along to future offspring. The other form is called *germ-line gene therapy,* which modifies an individual's germ (reproductive) cells, thus permanently altering his genome so that the bioengineered DNA changes will be inherited by the patient's descendants. Because of the major technical and ethical challenges of germ-line therapy, this intervention is currently limited to experimentation in animal models.

The first human gene therapy trials began in 1990, with limited success in treating children with inherited immunodeficiency disorders. Since then, advances in understanding genetics and the causes of disease have led to the development of many research centers, such as The Institute for Human Gene Therapy at the University of Pennsylvania. High-tech companies with names like Nature Technology Corporation: A DNA Development Company have also sprung up to custom-build DNA and to develop "vectors," often modified viruses that encapsulate the therapeutic gene and carry it into the disease cell.[6]

According to Dr. David Jacobs in *The Threat,* his work over the years with hundreds of abductees has convinced him that the creation of a new species—or what researchers earlier referred to as "hybridization"—proceeds in stages. The first stage, which geneticists call "F1," the first generation, seems to resemble the "half us, half 'them' " children who didn't know how to play on the slide with young Jen from Cape Cod. Abductees have regularly been shown these F1 children as babies and then again at various points during the children's development. These youngsters, tiny, big-eyed, with so little hair it doesn't cover their bulbous foreheads, do not look enough like us; they couldn't pass in human society. Based on abductees' reports, Jacobs suggests the possibility that this F1 transgenic being is later "crossed" with an older, second- or third-generation hybrid.

However, given our new understanding of trangenics, it's more likely that F1, the first transgenic generation, would have their gametes, or sex cells, *genetically manipulated* again once they reach sexual maturity. The aliens would add or subtract or move around fragments of the human genome in the gametes of the maturing F1 offspring, tinkering, experimenting, in order to improve the standout "defects"—or their more overt nonhuman appearance—in the next generation. Two sets of modified F1 gametes might be combined in vitro to form F2, the next new and improved transgenic generation. Other techniques for this modification will be discussed later in this chapter. Possibly by the fifth generation, Jacobs estimates, the "resulting late-stage hybrids are so close to human that they could easily 'pass' without notice":

> Although it is unknown precisely how many stages of hybrid development exist, the evidence points inexorably to the development of an increasingly human-looking and human-behaving hybrid armed with the aliens' ability to manipulate humans. . . . Once the hybrids are born, the aliens funnel them into specific types of service. For example, [abductee] Kathleen Morrison was told that some hybrids are for acquiring knowledge, some are for "assisting," and some are for both. She also understood that the later hybrid "models" have greater "power" than the earlier ones. Clearly, hybrids are not all alike in ability and behavior. [7]

The work of other researchers, working with unrelated abductees in other parts of the world, suggests that such a "late-model" hybrid has already been created. The testimony of independent abductees indicates that there is a growing subpopulation on Earth made up of individuals like the three strange job interviewers. This is also a revolution that will not be televised. It has happened—and continues to happen—invisibly, off-camera, and off the radar screens of nearly every scientific discipline.

Tinkering with the Human Genome

In a recent telephone conversation with scientist Michael Swords, I asked if the recent advances in gene-transfer technology or DNA manipulation had caused him to rethink his cogently written 1988 article "Extraterrestrial Hybridization Unlikely."[8]

"Not really," Swords said. "Nothing in the new technology has made it any more likely that a crude mushing together of DNA from different species would form a hybrid." However, Swords does concede willingly that aliens might well be able to "tinker" with the human genome, just as scientific researchers worldwide are now doing in the field of transgenics. That's now possible for us, Swords says, because we know so much more about the basic *chemical codes* of human genes, including how they're read, translated into amino acids, sequenced, duplicated, etc. That's really the easier part to learn to manipulate, according to Swords, because the chemical code is static: Its atoms are stable across generations, just waiting to be read and decoded. A cinch for a brainy team of extraterrestrials.

Many scientists agree that a high-tech alien culture would know the code to building our DNA, just as we are starting to do. Whatever human traits they wanted us (or themselves) to have, they could construct in the lab, molecule by molecule. Or they could minutely adjust DNA already present. But what makes gene transfer so difficult, so unpredictable and frustrating, are the *dynamic* aspects of the genome—the precision of geometric stacking, timing differences, the unknown interactions between the many moving parts of each species' chromosomes, etc.

Scientists concede that we're far from ready to tinker safely with the elements of human life. But that it doesn't stop us from ongoing, not-very-pleasant experiments on animals. We use monkeys, mice, and cows to work out the glitches in our theories. Consider this: Why should humans expect any different treatment at the hands of a higher intelligence? After all, they could just be working out the glitches. . . .

The suggestion here is that these human-looking men reported in Budd's cases—the ones with ostensible paranormal abilities and links to the aliens—are members of a recently bioengineered species. It's possible that over time—whether it's decades or millions of years, we don't know—the UFO visitors have systematically designed a transgenic species that combines human appearance and the ability to "pass" in our culture along with certain alien abilities: telepathy or mind-reading, remote control over one or more human subjects, and even an ability to step in and out of this material reality as needed. This subpopulation of "normals" (as in resembling normal human beings) also exhibits possibly the most significant trait of all: a willingness to be intermediaries to the aliens—delivering the human goods on command, so to speak.

For the pleasure of friendly debate, let's presume these normals are the equivalent of an alien Special Operations team—a highly bioengineered and specialized group of beings like the three "businessmen." But, as with any creature bringing new skill sets into new environments, the "normals" don't walk on set ready to perform perfectly. We don't have any indication that these transgenic beings grow up as we do, in a wide variety of relationships and situations where one learns to improvise interaction. Actual socialization is needed for that.

But just as in gene transfer, human behavior is, in part, easy to grasp and in other ways more subtle and nuanced. "Normals" would have to learn behavior that can only come from interaction with a living, unpredictable human (unless, of course, they've developed virtual-reality training programs that are *really* good!). At the start of Lisa's job interview, for example, she threw the "receptionist" a simple, unexpected question that landed on her like a grenade: "Where's the ladies' room?" The woman—whether alien, "normal," or some sort of human helper—simply "looked stricken," Lisa said, and practically ran from the room without answering. Even aliens and trangenics get stage fright, it seems. So no matter how quickly their brains process new information, they need some practice, a few tryouts before they can be expected to pull off a believable human performance. After all, as many researchers have mentioned, the aliens themselves—to whom we tend to impart such superiority—make mistakes. They put a swaddled infant on the floor instead of in the crib; they return abductees with their legs jammed into someone else's pajama top; their craft break down and sometimes, apparently, they crash.

From the few reports of "normals" that researchers have gathered, we can tentatively conclude that, while these beings often look and speak as we do, they could certainly use some practice in the behavioral- and emotional-skills departments. Recall "Mr. Nelson's" crude sexual approaches to sixteen-year-old Terry, and Lisa's interviewer droning on, never giving her a chance to speak, then rushing her out of the building? In a case to be discussed later, Budd tells of a farmer's friendship with a "normal" who one day allows him to see his nude wife surrounded by aliens inserting a needle into her abdomen. The "normal" is positively baffled at the farmer's rage and fear. He said: "We wanted you to see, but we didn't think you would be angry." As human as he looked, this being had no insight at all into human psychology or love.

Understanding this emotional-psychological blind spot in the transgenic "normals" might give us another way to speculate on what the so-called job interviews were all about. Conceivably these prearranged contacts might have been pretexts for the real intent: to give the "normals" practice interacting with human beings. But they certainly wouldn't want to practice on a hefty male, firefighter type of human being. From the aliens' point of view, a transgenic, male "normal" practicing human behavioral and sexual skills would be best paired up with—whom? A vulnerable teenage girl, of course. Another purpose for their Special Ops job interviews might have been to test the "normals" readiness for integration and their suppleness in handling what the ETs might well have earmarked as the most emotional and unpredictable population within the human species. You guessed it: vulnerable teenage girls.

But such accounts as Terry's, Lisa's, and Sally's suggest to us that the alien program, whatever its purpose, has advanced to another stage. It's taking place, ostensibly, on the ground, in everyday life, in situations that *compel* abductees to take on a new alien task—that of interacting in real-life situations, in cars, apartments, and offices, with the "normals."

They're Here for Whose Benefit?

But what is the point of these hidden agendas? Secret meetings, half remembered; nothing adding up; and all of it happening in what seems like real time to the experiencers, and in actual, material buildings they can and do locate again later. It's not like a patchy memory of lying paralyzed on a table in a bright white room, not knowing how you got there, while small creatures work on your body. This is terrestrial contact, paradoxically both firmly grounded in our accepted reality and also disturbingly askew from what we consider "normal." Terry, Lisa, and Sally took phone calls from their interviewers and rode in cars to their encounters. Each girl located an actual address in her community, went into an odd but distinctly material office, and had a face-to-face meeting with a normal-looking man who had murky physical intentions.

Where is this new abduction pattern leading us? UFO researchers who haven't taken doctrinal stands on the issue—are they here to save us or coolly utilize us as a resource?—will tell you that the aliens' purpose here is as much a mystery now as it always was. We know more about their methodology, but that's all; we still don't know the meaning of the acts. Since neither the aliens nor the "normals" are explaining themselves, the best we can do is to arrive at what I hopefully refer to as "informed speculation." Over the next few chapters we'll explore a limited number of scenarios that seem especially intriguing in light of the almost exponential growth in human information, science, and technologies in the last decade.

Every day I scroll through a set of on-line research journals chock full of new discoveries: Our universe is now believed to have ten dimensions—the ordinary three dimensions of height, width, breadth, plus a fourth one for time—but we don't comprehend it because most of the other six are curled into infinitesimally small balls that we'll never see. Some mad scientist reprogrammed baby chick genes, hatching a batch of them with two beaks apiece. A research institute has just bio-engineered goats to produce valuable spiderlike silk strands in their milk; the animals essentially become organic factories for human products. I am, by turns, shocked, amused, and amazed at the wonder and nerve of it all. I stay glued to the chair in front of my computer, trolling, really, for some more of those rich bare little facts that might shed some light on this baffling UFO phenomenon.

One day, for instance, I was reading a paper on-line that had been presented at a scientific conference in October 1998. The author presented a well-documented case that addressed the high rate of failure in most large animal cloning experiments. In one such experiment, 277 nuclei from skin cells of adult sheep were transferred into the eggs of other sheep from which the nucleus had been removed. The "outer shells" of the sheep eggs reset the clock on the adult cells they cradled. Embryonic clones of the adult sheep began to form, and these were transplanted into surrogate mothers to be carried to term. However, often not more than 1 percent of the embryos resulted in live births. And the few cloned offspring that lived were often deformed and frail; they failed to thrive and eventually died or were destroyed.[9] Something ineffably delicate about the rubbly process of life has eluded us so far.

As I read the material, my mind was immediately flooded with the images, words, emotions, and drawings from abductees describing the listless cross-species infants they're asked to hold on board an alien craft. Often the infant lies limp, completely contained in the palm of the person's hand. It's alive, even sensed sometimes to be "wise," but has none of the reflexes or sounds or movements of normal human infants. Here, too, an attempt to manipulate nature's boundaries is not quite working. Our own scientists who are tinkering with the basic building blocks of life are certainly familiar with such frustrating outcomes. It's possible that some groups of alien scientists are experiencing many of the same problems that we are.

The Zoo Hypothesis

How might the aliens' focus on reproduction or genetic manipulation relate to their ultimate purpose? The first and most consoling thought is that these visitors—from a civilization that has billions of years of superior neural development, computing brain power, and technology on us—have come to help save us from ourselves. It's likely that long ago their own civilization went through the same stages we're going through now, from the discovery of controlled fire through the creation of nuclear bombs or some other means of mass extinction. In this scenario, the aliens know that some cataclysmic event is likely—or even imminent—in the near future on Earth. Their "global monitoring system," like ours, reports back on the decimation of vegetation, the daily extinction of species, the clouds of pollution shadowing the land, the dead zones in the oceans where nothing lives, and the sad, slowed-up waggle of the human sperm.

In 1973, John A. Ball proposed the "zoo hypothesis" in *Icarus,* an international journal for solar system studies. Then a radio astronomer at the Harvard-Smithsonian Center for Astrophysics, he seriously proposed that Earth was a zoo and that extraterrestrials were here, already observing us. Ball added: "The perfect zoo (or wilderness area or sanctuary) would be one in which the fauna do not interact with, and are unaware of, their zookeepers."[10] Of course, Ball was derided by many scientists for his theory, especially since it implied that ETs were purposely avoiding human contact. For some reason, that particular assumption raised many a scholarly eyebrow and occasioned much underlining and exclamation marks in writing about the "zoo theory." Even today it doesn't sit well with scholars and skeptics—the thought that aliens from another civilization, past, present, or future, would not, first and foremost, establish a formal connection with the White House, Congress, and scientists, preferably in inverse order. It seems obvious to theoretical physicists, especially, that such beings would want to deal initially with intellectual power (the scientists). Later, satiated after a meeting with equals, they would descend on the political and economic earthly powers-that-be.

The elite of the scientific world seem to find it side-splittingly absurd that an intelligent species that *could* "get here from there" would actually prefer to interact with ordinary, anti-intellectual civilians without any political or economic clout. Here's the renowned physicist Stephen Hawking, speaking on a 2001 *Nova* television program about time travel. He's addressing the fact that he has no faith whatsoever in the concept that beings from unknown worlds are already here:

> I think that if people from the future were going to show themselves, they would do so in a more obvious way. What would be the point of revealing themselves only to cranks and weirdos who wouldn't be believed?[11]

Cloning an Endangered Species

In the fall of 2000, Lulu, an ordinary cow on a midwestern farm, was heavy with calf. But she wasn't having a cow. Inside her uterus was an endangered mammal, the gaur, a sturdily built, oxlike animal native to the bamboo jungles of Burma and India. A group of Massachusetts scientists at Advanced Cell Technology (ACT) are making plans to clone a series of endangered species such as the gaur, the giant panda, and the bucardo, a Spanish mountain goat. As each species neared extinction, scientists perserved some of their cells. These cells now sit frozen in liquid nitrogen.

Noah, the embryonic gaur, was the first endangered species ever to be cloned and the first cloned creature to come to full gestation in the womb of another species. "One hundred species are lost every day, and these mass extinctions are mostly our own doing," a spokesman at ACT said. "Now that we have the technology to reverse it, we have the responsibility to try."

Scientists at Advanced Cell Technology produced Noah by fusing a gaur's skin cells with cow eggs from which the nuclei had been removed. The forty-four resulting embryos were then implanted into thirty-two surrogate mother cows. Out of these, only eight pregnancies developed, and five of them ended in miscarriages—a common failure rate in cloning procedures. Two more fetuses were removed for tissue culture, leaving only one calf left gestating: Lulu's Noah.

Although many cloned animals are born with serious defects, health problems, or abnormally large birth weight, Noah was born on January 8, 2001, with a clean bill of health. He was strong and not oversize. But a day later Noah contracted a fatal bacterial infection that's common among calves. He died two days after his birth. However, scientists at ATC say they're ready to try again, possibly by cloning the bucardo with cells taken from the last living member of the species.[12]

In other words, if aliens or time-travelers actually were here, they would be abducting the crème de la crème, humans as close to the frail-bodied, bulbous-headed, pure *brain* that they are—not the likes of you and me. *If aliens were here, they would definitely be talking to Stephen Hawking.* If they aren't conferring with him, it's a given: aliens are not here.

A more moderate and modest "zoo proposal" comes from science writer Clifford Pickover:

> Maybe there are signs of alien life all around us that we have not looked for or have not understood. Imagine that our civilization is quarantined by a galactic cartel as a kind of zoo, not to be touched, only to be observed, either because aliens don't want to contaminate our world with alien ideas or be contaminated by us. They could have no desire to interfere with us anymore than we want to go out and buy a net to catch butterflies or seahorses.[13]

So if the UFO occupants are our caretakers and zookeepers, they might well answer to a higher authority. The gray guys do the menial work while a higher intelligence, the bosses, orders a certain set of genes in a population to be manipulated and maintained over time as a way to help us adapt to our changing environment. Perhaps, like Monsanto's corn, we would be bred by aliens to have genetic resistance to toxins in the air, soil, and water around us. Or perhaps they're focused on altering the gene sequences for violent behavior that inevitably develop in a competitive environment.

Why would the alien zookeepers go to the trouble of doing this? Maybe for the same reason we attempt to save vanishing pandas and black-footed ferrets. We're cute, we're smarter than most, and we bring a lot to the table. The planet wouldn't be quite as interesting without us, they think. Besides, a civilization that's as truly enlightened as these aliens may well be would understand this: that as humans go, so goes the planet, if not the universe. Any major-impact species in danger of going extinct or blowing itself up doesn't take itself out alone and without repercussions that could spread throughout the known (and unknown) universe. The ETs will help us to help themselves too.

Tracking Gorillas and Grannies

In the UFO abduction literature, one pattern is quite clear: Abductees are taken early and often. Piecing together the experiencers' unaided recall with their families' accounts and sometimes also with hynoti-cally retrieved memories, we know that the abductee is generally taken aboard an alien craft as an infant or young child and is subsequently followed or reabducted throughout his or her life. If abductions are related to an ongoing study or manipulation of the human race in some way, this recurring exam aboard a craft is the "longitudinal" part of the study, and in scientific terms there's a good reason for doing it that way.

During my filmmaking work at a New England research institute known for its studies of health trends in society, I became familiar with the way epidemiologists designed the protocols, or the approved guidelines, for many long-term, longitudinal studies. One of the basic principles of this sort of study is to keep track of and collect data from the same group of people over a several-year period—sometimes even from several generations of the same families. A good example of this is the Framingham Heart Study, which was initiated by the National Heart Institute in 1948. Over a fifty-year period, a large group of healthy Framingham, Massachusetts, residents were followed and studied in their natural habitat, so to speak. At regular intervals they were visited at home by field-workers for the study, all of whom fol-lowed identical protocols in collecting and recording the health, ill-nesses, and living habits of the individuals. Every two to four years, study participants were brought into a medical center for extensive medical exams and testing, including blood tests, DNA sampling, bone scans, eye exams, and echocardiograms. (To any reader who is an abductee, these procedures will sound much too familiar for comfort!)

At various points during the study, the data were crunched, ana-lyzed, and studied for factors that were the most likely contributors to heart disease and other disorders. But another component was crucial to the scientists managing the study: the children.

In 1971, the study recruited 5,124 children (and their spouses) of the original cohort [participants] for another study, called "The Offspring

Study." With two generations worth of data, the Framingham Heart Study acquired an unmatched base of scientific riches.[14]

One further detail from the Framingham Heart Study will hold speculative interest for people concerned with the UFO phenomenon: The researchers have amassed a DNA library of blood samples from two generations of participants—approximately five thousand individuals. The samples will be used to help researchers track down what diseases run in families and identify what genes might be responsible. The data bank is also a way to retain *a genetic fingerprint* of each individual in the study.

(As an aside: It's interesting to note how much these longitudinal studies depend to some extent on self-reported, anecdotal evidence that UFO researchers are critized for: such lifestyle information as caloric intake, exercise, types of foods eaten, stress level, and alchohol and drug use. Without a doubt, though, adding the quantifiable lab tests and medical exams to the self-reported material is a scientific methodology that ufology can only hope to match one day.)

I mention the heart study to show how similar its methods and intent are to the aliens' program: tracking selected human beings over a lifetime and regularly returning to abduct them and bring them into a laboratory setting; then medical procedures are performed that suggest both long-term health monitoring and interest in reproductive issues. For instance, we know that abductees often return from their "field visit" with fresh scoop marks—similar to punch biopsies—taken from their skin, or sometimes their skin is scraped and the exterior cells collected. Sometimes they are made to drink a particular viscous liquid and told it's a supplement they need. For women, a long needle may be inserted in the navel area, while the men may be artificially stimulated to give a sperm sample.

If the UFO occupants are indeed tracking and studying certain people and their children and their children's children—in other words, an alien version of the "Offspring Study"—how might this be accomplished? Certainly not with a clipboard-wielding, bulbous-headed, bug-eyed alien field-worker knocking on doors in Framingham, Massachusetts. Our alien scientists would need a much more effective way to track such a restless and mobile species as human beings. After all, they aren't even voluntary participants in this apparent study. Given the large number of reported abduction experiences (an estimated 2 percent of adult Americans), the UFO occupants are looking at human population management on an enormous scale—because abductions do not happen only to Americans. Similar reports come to researchers from areas as diverse as Brazil, the Congo, Canada, Turkey, Belgium, Venezuela, France, and England.

If this is the aliens' version of a long-range, longitudinal study of Earth and its human beings, the scope of such a study is breathtaking but definitely possible. We humans already have certain pieces of the technology to do something like it ourselves. What follows are two interesting examples: a unique residential setting for human elders, and a tracking system for monitoring the endangered mountain gorilla.

Rowdy Elders Opt for High Tech

In September 2000, Oatfield Estates, the first high-tech communal residence for elders opened in the shadow of majestic Mount Hood in a suburb south of Portland, Oregon. Oatfield's founder, entrepreneur Bill Reed, was thinking ahead to his own aging needs as well as those of the burgeoning number of geriatric baby boomers. He was dismayed by his research and visits to nursing homes. According to government figures, Reed learned, two-thirds of American nursing homes are understaffed, and the staff is generally undertrained and underpaid. Often the health care aides don't speak English, adding to an elder's confusion and the managers' stress. Staff turnover is relentless, leading to inferior care. A report from the General Accounting Office informed Reed that one in four of these facilities actually harms patients. Due to the usual age-related disabilities, our elders in these nursing homes are often placed at risk of death or serious injury. Most can't move about freely without being accompanied by already overburdened aides. Some, like Alzheimer's patients, are confined to lock-in units.[15] In a "zoo" situation like this, sedation of patients and tying them into wheelchairs are sometimes the "keepers' " only options.

Reed also believes it's a safe guess that boomers will live longer than previous generations and aren't likely to age placidly, nodding off in wheelchairs. They're more likely to totally reject the traditional nursing-home option for themselves. Baby boomers are going to demand a more productive old age by keeping alert, active, *and safe* with technology-assisted devices.

In Oatfield, Bill Reed has designed the country's first wired, totally monitored, remote-controlled facility for frail, fumbling grannies and grandpas. Here the precise location, activity, and even memory lapse of every resident—caregivers, family members, and patients alike—is monitored and recorded twenty-four hours a day. A small badge attached to each person's clothing contains infrared and radio-frequency locator chips and an emergency call button. These emit tracking signals, which are constantly transmitted to the local-area network. When a resident falls, she can press a button on the badge, which promptly displays her name and location on computers throughout the facility. If the alarm (a human voice continuously muttering, "Uh-oh") isn't answered within five minutes, the system floods the e-mail boxes on supervisors' cell phones. Inside and outside of Oatfield the patients are monitored on video cameras, and tripped-beam sen-

The sensing unit that a technician is attaching to this steer records motion and other physiological data that enable scientists to determine how much time the animal spends grazing each day. (Photo courtesy of the Agricultural Research Service, U.S. Department of Agriculture)

sors alarm the staff if a patient wanders off the grounds. By 2003 the Matshita company plans to offer these facilities toilet seats that detect and transmit vital signs. Such monitors are already in every Oatfield senior's bedroom, a technological component of the bed itself. At this point, let's draw the curtain and move on. There are probably some things you and I don't mind waiting to know about.

Ironically, these residents have, in effect, retained their freedom by surrendering it to Oatfield's tracking system. Unlike most nursing homes, the Oatfield residents can walk outside unassisted, cook their own meals in the kitchen, maintain private living units, and entertain guests with dignity. Their touch-screen computers can even save them from the embarrassment of short-term memory loss by reminding them of a visiting grandchild's name or, on a certain date, display a memo to "Call Steve." Uh, who's Steve? The programmable computer will show the elder a photo of Steve and information that will fill in the blanks: who, where, and why Steve is to be called.[16]

Tracking Gorillas on Your Desktop

If wandering, forgetful elders can be tracked so thoroughly, monitoring mountain gorillas in central African jungles might seem like an unsolvable nightmare for the scientist: there is malaria, the snipers, and the snakes. A typical trek into Rwanda, home to about half of the remaining six hundred mountain gorillas, requires a small army of local guides, machete-carrying trackers, and armed soldiers. But a newly developed technology is just beginning to allow scientists to study the endangered species from desktops rather than treetops.

Primatologists at Georgia Tech and software engineers have teamed up with the Dian Fossey Gorilla Fund to develop a geographic information system (GIS). From Rwanda, GIS data is sent to Georgia Tech by e-mail and CD-ROM. There, other layers of information are added by satellite tracking systems (GPS) and remote-sensing software that produce high-resolution, 3-D images of the area being "explored." The next stage of the project will go wireless—a technology tracking system very similar to the one that keeps tabs on the elders at Oatfield Estates. A limited number of trackers in the field will instantly send satellite tracking system coordinates (the animal's location) over a local cellular network to a Web-linked database. The satellite data can not only determine the number and condition of gorillas in a certain area but also relay information about the vegetation in that habitat and assess the gorillas' food sources.[7]

Georgia Tech primatologists monitor African gorillas from afar, mapping their every move. The Oregon senior residents have the very rhythm of their lives tracked inside and out, floor to ceiling, morning through evening. Isn't it therefore conceivable that a technologically superior civilization—one that is able to reach our planet and dip in and out of our habitat while generally avoiding detection—would be able to do the same?

Chapter 19

FIRST YOU SEE THEM, THEN YOU DON'T

IN WHAT I EUPHEMISTICALLY CHOOSE to call "the real world," there is yet another bizarre but frequently reported type of encounter with what seem, again, to be nonhuman beings existing among us. These experiences are quite different from those we have been examining, and though they disturb, they are not so much traumatic as deeply puzzling. There is nothing covert about the way these entities show themselves; in fact, in their often outrageous manner of dress and behavior they are apparently deliberately calling attention to themselves. "Look at us," they seem to be saying. "We're here; we really exist!"

The witnesses who report these encounters are often UFO abductees or researchers in the field, but so far as I know there is no definitive evidence of missing time or traditional abduction scenarios associated with this kind of incident. For that reason this particular sort of report has largely escaped the attention of the UFO community, with the prominent exception of the thorough and conscientious researcher Jerome Clark.[1] To remedy that situation, I will present several examples of these "first you see them, then you don't" cases—the sudden appearances, disappearances, and impossible reappearances of weirdly costumed entities.

In 1952 two young men, recently graduated from high school, set out on a cross-country drive to the West Coast in a 1941 Oldsmobile. One of those boys, "Arthur," would eventually become a lawyer and involve himself deeply in UFO research. As he told me in March of 1982, the two friends had had a pleasant and fairly uneventful drive halfway across the country, and when the incident occurred, they were passing through the endless wheat fields of Iowa. The highway stretched for miles without an intersection. It was straight as an arrow, with only an occasional narrow side road leading to an isolated farmhouse. There were often slight undulations in the flat landscape, so from time to time their car would pass over a gentle rise, dip into a shallow declivity, and then rise once more, as if they were in a boat gliding across low, regular swells. But as they drove over a slight rise and then descended, they came upon an eerie sight: a little old man on a bicycle, wearing lederhosen and sporting a long white beard, like something one might see rendered in wood in a Bavarian souvenir shop. The two young men stared in amazement as they passed the energetically pedaling little man. They drove on, trying to imagine who this odd person might be, and, since the farms were so far apart, they speculated on how long he must have to travel on his bicycle to visit even his closest neighbor.

But soon the boredom of the unchanging landscape took over and they dropped the subject of the strange bicyclist. Until, that is, about a half hour later, when they drove over another gentle rise and encountered the same little bearded man in lederhosen, pedaling happily along in the same direction, many miles ahead of the place they had first come upon him. They passed by in complete amazement, not believing what they were seeing. Was there some kind of shortcut the old man had taken, a cutoff that eliminated many miles of pedaling? They realized that the highway had not changed direction, and there were no side roads other than an occasional long dirt road to someone's distant farm. They concluded that there was no way that they could have possibly passed this man twice. There was very little traffic, they were driving at or above the speed limit, and they did not recall having been passed by a faster car or truck that might conceivably have picked up the little man, bike and all, driven ahead of the young men, and then deposited him farther along the highway.

For a few minutes they debated turning around and driving back to this lone figure and asking him how he did it, but eventually they decided against it. As Arthur told me years later, the experience was so eerie that they felt better just driving on and forgetting about it. It was the outrageous appearance of the bearded little man in leather shorts that remained in their minds as the most disturbing and inexplicable part of the experience. In the middle of Iowa, on a long, lonely highway with few intersections, what elderly man, dressed like a beer garden Bavarian, would ride a bicycle? Where was he going? Where was he coming from?

The legendary radio comedians Bob and Ray once presented an improvised skit in which they interviewed people in the studio audience to find who had the strangest profession. The studio audience was, of course, nonexistent, and the two comedians supplied a wide variety of voices for the characters they pretended to interview. The winner, they announced, the man with the strangest job, turned out to be the only lighthouse keeper in the state of Kansas. "It's a terribly lonely, even useless job," he complained in a peculiar nasal voice. Bob and Ray commiserated with the poor man and awarded him first prize, a nested set of aqua-colored mixing bowls. To me, the little bearded man in lederhosen, energetically bicycling across Iowa and able to magically pass autombiles, is no less implausible—whoever, or whatever he was—than the Kansas lighthouse keeper.

But as we shall see, some of these cases have a more ominous overtone. In *Intruders,* I wrote about an Indianapolis family, the "Davises," whose various ongoing abduction experiences were the focus of the book. "Kathy Davis," her sister "Laura," and their children received the most attention, and though I knew a great deal about the encounters of their youngest sister, "Sarah," I decided against including her in an already overburdened family saga.

One of the strange experiences Sarah recounted to me in 1983, when I was in Indianapolis doing research for *Intruders,* bears retelling in this current context. In July 2001, I telephoned her to refresh my memory as to what she had told me years before. Her account was exactly as I had remembered it, attesting to the profound effect the experience had had upon her.

In 1981, Sarah was in her early twenties and living alone in a suburban apartment complex in Indianapolis. She described the incident— really a series of incidents—this way:

I came out of my apartment one morning, and on the sidewalk right in front of my door was this guy who looked just like [cult mass murderer] Charles Manson. He looked really scraggly. He was tall and real skinny, with brown, long, hippy hair and a scraggly beard. He looked up at me and I thought, *Ugh!* I remember thinking, *This guy is going to rob my apartment.* But I thought, *Oh well, I haven't got anything worth stealing.* I'd never seen this guy before in my life.

So I just walked out to my car, got in, and drove about eight blocks down the street and I saw him *again*, walking along in front of me. He could not have beaten me to that destination even if he'd been in a car! I went further down the street, about eight more blocks, to the gas station, and I got out to put air in my tire. I bent down and turned around and there he was again, walking up behind me, maybe twelve feet away. It freaked me out again because he couldn't have gotten to that point even with a ride.

And he went inside the convenience store, a Village Market they had at the gas station. I finished putting air in my tire and got back in my car and proceeded to go back home, and I saw this guy *again* in the exact same spot I saw him the second time, when I was driving to the gas station. But this time when I went by him he stopped walking and turned and looked up at me and just stared. He scared me to death.

I had seen him four times altogether, the first time when he was walking along right in front of my apartment. The instant I opened the door he was right there. He glanced up at me and that's when I thought, *Ugh, he's probably going to rob my apartment.* That was seventeen or eighteen years ago and I remember exactly what he looked like, and that's kinda weird, 'cause I don't usually remember people's appearance like that very well. Each of the other three times I saw him that day he looked right at me too. It was so weird. It was like he was following me, but he couldn't have got to those points before me even if he'd gotten a ride. Even if he'd had his own car.

I remember that he was wearing old, faded jeans, really scraggly. His long brown hair was parted on the side: I remember that too. When he looked at me it kinda gave me the creeps 'cause it startled me so much. When we had eye contact, I freaked and then I looked away.

All of this happened in about ten minutes or so. It was weird, too, that when I saw him the second time he wasn't walking towards the gas station: He was walking back towards my apartment. Instead of going to the gas station where he ended up, he was going the wrong way. The first time I saw him, when I came out of my apartment, it startled me because he looked like Charles Manson and he was right there, about ten feet away. The second time I saw him a minute or so later it kinda flipped me out but not too much, but when I bent down to put air in my tire and he walked up behind me I really started freaking out. He gave me a major rush. And when I saw him for the *fourth* time about a minute or so later, I was almost a basket case.

Another thing that was unusual was that after something like that I'd usually call my mom. I didn't tell Mom for several weeks after it happened. I didn't tell anybody, which was odd. I don't know why I didn't. It wasn't because they wouldn't believe me: In our family, with all the weird stuff that was going on, we always talked about it. I don't know why I didn't tell anybody.

That last time I saw him, he was walking back towards my apartment and I came driving up behind him. As I approached him he stopped and turned all the way around. It was weird. I don't know how he could have known I was coming up behind him. He stopped walking and stared at me. And I remember as I passed him I looked in the rearview mirror and thought, *Damn, he's still stopped and still staring. . . .* It was one of the weirdest things that's ever happened to me.

Strange as these reports seem to be, there are many like them. One of the most bizarre was recounted to me by "Joseph," a college professor who describes himself as interested in the UFO phenomenon, even though he remains skeptical. Ironically, he has himself experienced several UFO sightings, one of which included a dramatic episode of missing time while driving his car down a steep mountain road, so there is a clear possibility that he—as well as Sarah and even possibly Arthur—may have had as yet unexplored UFO abductions.

At the time of the encounter I'm about to describe, Joseph was a young physics student in graduate school and on vacation, making a backpack solo trek through rural Spain. He said that he hiked into a small village one afternoon and found a place to stay in a tavern that had a few modest rooms for rent.

After making himself comfortable and having a meal, he decided to stroll outside the village and have a look at the local farms and landscape. As he passed a plowed but barren field, he suddenly observed a totally incongruous sight: Hurrying across the dusty field was a man in immaculate white tie and tails, dressed as if he were about to attend an important diplomatic reception. Joseph was stunned at the sight, and began immediately to hypothesize: The man was going to a fancy rural wedding. He was a magician heading for a theater to perform. But neither theory seemed at all plausible in this sparsely populated, rather poverty-stricken part of Spain.

Joseph said he glanced away for a moment, and when he looked back the elegantly attired individual had completely vanished. There was no foliage in the field behind which the man could have hidden, no deep crevasses, nothing. He had just disappeared into thin air.

Joseph told me that he immediately turned around and hurried back to the village, completely confused and a little frightened by what he had seen—and then not seen. The bizarre figure had been no more than twenty yards or so away from him, and it was still daylight. There was no mistake about what the man was wearing, the fact of his physical presence in the field, or his instantaneous disappearance.

Here again we can see several characteristics that tie these three examples together. First, and probably most important, all three witnesses I knew to be either possible UFO abductees or deeply interested in the subject. Considering the presence of screen memories in so many abduction cases—images of owls or deer or cats or gorillas or whatever being used to replace images of small gray aliens in the memories of abductees—the possibility exists that any or all of these cases might have been concealed abduction experiences that so far have not been recalled consciously. I have investigated a number of cases in which screen memories of apparent *human beings* were imposed upon abductees: A child may see slightly incorrect images of his parents standing at his bedside, or an adult might see a deceased relative. In a few cases abductees have even been made to see comforting but oddly staring religious personages such as Jesus or the Virgin Mary.

But if the bizarre figures in the foregoing cases were screen memories, why would the UFO occupants want to leave an abductee with such an outlandishly vivid memory, a reminder that might suggest an abduction had taken place? After all, abductions are carried out with a great deal of secrecy, so why would the aliens willfully leave a tantalizing memory image and not black out the event altogether?

This is a very logical question to ask, and it is exactly analogous to a related enigma that has dogged researchers for decades: If UFOs have the capacity to operate invisibly, why are they *ever* seen? Sometimes, instead of operating covertly, they seem to be deliberately attracting attention to themselves by striking arrays of colored lights. Also, if they can be invisible to radar, why are they so often tracked? These queries about the craft themselves are just as difficult to answer as the analogous question about vivid screen memories in abduction cases.

To reiterate: My best guess is that each of the incidents involving a weirdly costumed figure is actually an unremembered abduction. Perhaps, in some perverse way, to impose an "impossible" screen memory, such as a disappearing man in white tie and tails in an arid Spanish field, would be almost to guarantee that anyone reporting such a sight would be ridiculed or at least disbelieved. For that matter, the witness may also doubt his own sanity, thus placing the memory itself into a kind of personal gray basket where it may languish for years.

One thing is certain, however: The evanescent beings in these three cases are inherently different from those I choose to call the "normals": Terry's "Mr. Nelson," the two other "job interviewers," as well as a number of other strange individuals we will soon examine in depth.

Chapter 20

THE PHANTOM SUPPORT GROUP, STEWART, AND OTHER MYSTERIES

IN THE MANY YEARS I've worked with UFO abductees there has been no shortage of bizarre accounts involving beings who, like the fraudulent "job interviewers," appear to be human but possess what we have come to regard as alien characteristics. Metaphorically if not literally they are hybrids of some sort, able, at least some of the time, to function autonomously in our world while remaining somewhat independent of the alien UFO occupants.

As has been pointed out before, forensic evidence of the sort we so often find in abduction cases is hard to come by in these reports. We find ourselves having to depend largely on the integrity of the witnesses and the presence of distinct patterns across a variety of cases in order to evaluate the credibility of any given account. What follows are a few more "hybrid" reports that I admit sound fantastic, even unbelievable at first, but that I have investigated and have found to be credible.

The Phantom Support Group

Despite its peculiarities, the case of the "phantom support group" is supported by the testimony of *four* credible witnesses: two married couples, the "Johnsons" and the "Mehlmans," who are friends both socially and professionally. I was able to interview each of the men separately and at length, but because of time considerations I interviewed the two women together.

"Dennis Johnson," a tall, courteous southerner, was an abductee I had known and respected for perhaps fifteen years, but I was saddened to hear that he passed away a year ago from complications from diabetes. By training and career he was an investigative reporter and newsman, and nothing I have ever seen in his life, in his psychological makeup, or in his immediate circumstances would suggest for a moment that he was not being truthful about this incident.

"Don Mehlman," the second man in the case, is also an abductee, but I have been acqauainted with him for a much shorter time than I had known Dennis. I am aware that he is a onetime law enforcement officer, but my only contacts with him were two interviews lasting for several hours in which he discussed his various UFO experiences. Most important, however, is the fact that his version of the peculiar "support group" experience matched Dennis's account in virtually every detail, though presented from his own perspective.

In their joint interview, the two men's wives, "Janice" and "Betsy" independently corroborated their husbands' accounts. I was able to discuss the incident with them only that one time, but I saw nothing in their demeanor suggesting they were not fully as believable as their husbands—or as disturbed by what they observed that night.

I can think of no motive for this group of four respectable citizens to risk their reputations by inventing and carrying out a four-person hoax. None of the four asked anything from me in the way of publicity or financial remuneration, and in fact, to my knowledge, this is the first time the incident has ever been made public. I heard the details first about ten years ago, from my reporter friend Dennis, and shortly thereafter went to the other three to ask for their recollections. Adding to my sense of their personal credibility, I was aware that all four seemed genuinely unnerved by what had happened the night of the incident.

One final reason I take this report seriously is that it conforms in many respects to the patterns we have been examining in these pages. It seems to me that the "phantom support group meeting" is not so much a one-of-a-kind anomalous anomaly as it is yet another strange example of alien or part-alien beings living and operating among us and displaying the kind of intermittent awkwardness we have seen before—behavior one might expect of creatures who do not share the subtleties of our culture, our mores, and our languages.

This is how the incident came about. Dennis and Don had collaborated on producing a videotape of their investigation into a UFO abduction case in their area, and together they presented it at a small public meeting of about fifteen or twenty UFO investigators and interested laypersons, some of whom they knew and some of whom were strangers. Both men spoke briefly, showed their tape, sold a few copies, and that was that.

One week later Don received a phone call from a man who said he had been present at that gathering and was calling to invite Don to an abductee support group he conducted. At their presention of their tape, Don had, of course, identified himself as an abductee, so he was not at all surprised by the phone call, even though he had never heard of an abductee support group in his somewhat sparsely settled part of the country. As the anonymous caller began to arrange an evening when Don would be available, he said something about having to make sure his "husband" would be there. Don was taken aback because the caller definitely had a male voice. He later told me that he assumed the anonymous man was gay and was referring to his partner as his husband—an odd thing to do, since this was not an area where gay liberation had had even the slightest impact.

A date was agreed upon and an address provided. Don promptly called Dennis to tell him about the strange call, and the more the men thought about it and discussed it with their wives, the more intrigued the four of them became. There were two reasons for their curiosity. The first was the presence of a UFO abduction support group right in a neighboring town, an association neither of them had ever heard about. The second was the inviter's odd remark about his "husband"— a genuine enigma for all of them. Dennis and Don in particular wondered who would be attending this support group and who had organized it, because at this time, the early 1990's, abductee support groups were a rarity outside of a few of the larger cities. Don had another, more personal reason to attend: Perhaps he and Dennis could sell a few more of the videotapes in which they had invested so much time, effort, and money.

When the appointed evening arrived, the two couples drove to a neighboring town and, following the instructions they had been given, came to a group of newly constructed condominium apartments, not all of which were occupied. They climbed the stairs to the designated apartment on the second floor and knocked on the door. Since Don had been the one who had received the phone call, he led the group, with Dennis and their wives standing behind him. The door was opened by what they later described as a very strange, "blank-looking," rather short man who appeared to be as startled as they were.

"Who is *he*?" the man immediately asked Don, indicating Dennis.

"Why, he's my partner on the videotape. Don't you remember? You said you were at the meeting when we presented it. We both talked about it."

"Oh, yes," the man responded unconvincingly. Both Don and Dennis later told me that since there had been at most only twenty people at the meeting where they were the central attraction two weeks before, if the host had been there it would have been virtually impossible for him not to have recognized Dennis. Beyond that, both men said that since the man was memorably odd-looking, they thought they would certainly have remembered *him*, even if he had forgotten Dennis.

But before he would let them enter the apartment, this unusual host had another question.

"Who are they?" he asked, indicating the two women.

"They are our wives, Betsy and Janice," Dennis said, confused by the direction things were taking.

After pausing further to consider, the unfriendly host stood aside and reluctantly let them in. Becoming more uneasy by the second, the four visitors entered the new, sparsely furnished apartment that was free of pictures on the wall, books, magazines, or any of the more casual amenities. They were ushered into the living room, where four or five equally blank-looking people sat stiffly on chairs and a sofa, staring at the new arrivals. These so-called support group members seemed to have no social skills whatsoever—no body language, no expression of interest or curiosity or even anger in their faces—and it was this total lack of affect that Dennis and his party later described as "spooky" or "zombie-like." However, both Dennis and Don mentioned to me that one member of this group was an extremely beautiful but rather severe-looking woman.

None of the seated support group members spoke, and no introductions were offered. Since I have conducted abductee support group meetings for years and have attended many others in various parts of the country, I am quite familiar with the way such gatherings are usually conducted. Upon entering, participants generally either introduce themselves or are introduced by the host, using first names only. There is usually an "ice-breaking" table of refreshments—coffee, tea, soft drinks, and the like—and veterans of these meetings often initially make small talk with the newer attendees in order to lessen the inevitable tension.

In this case, as all four of the witnesses reported, there were no introductions, no refreshments, and no small talk. In fact, no one ever spoke except the host-leader. Dennis, Don, and their wives took their seats and the host suddenly began to berate Don for having made the videotape about a local UFO abduction investigation. "It was wrong," he said, "to make money on this," and Don should not do it again. It was very bad to do things like that and to try to sell the videos, he said, without giving any reason why he felt so strongly about it. The other participants sat in silence, staring vacantly, while their leader continued rebuking Don.

Finally Dennis, feeling anger on top of his unease, interrupted. "Is this support group connected with MUFON?" he asked, naming the largest UFO research organization in the United States.[1] The question was not answered or even acknowledged, but he persevered, turning to the other strangers in the room as if to pull them into the conversation.

"Are you connected in some way with Budd Hopkins?" Dennis asked, knowing that I had had a hand in setting up a number of support groups and had written and lectured widely on the subject of UFO abductions.

"Who is Budd Hopkins?" the leader asked.

Surprised but undaunted, Dennis made another query: "Are you connected with David Jacobs?" naming my friend and colleague whose work in the field is equally well known. Jacobs had also organized an active support group in his home in a suburb of Philadelphia.

"Who is David Jacobs?" the man replied.

By this time Don, Dennis, and their wives were eager to leave what they had come to regard, in the later words of Don's wife, as "the weirdest group of people I've ever seen in my life." As Dennis thought to himself that whatever this was, it surely was not an abductee support group, an incident occurred that brought the four to their feet and into a somewhat hasty, ungraceful exit from the apartment. Both Don and Dennis later told me that one of the silent, staring members of this group, the mannequinlike female whom they regarded as almost unnaturally beautiful, suddenly stood up. As she did so, both men said that she seemed to metamorphose into an incredibly ugly, inhuman-looking creature with large eyes and sparse hair. It was this sudden metamorphosis that triggered their speedy exit from the apartment. They hurried down the stairs and piled into their car, not feeling safe until they were on the highway and getting close to home.

As the four witnesses related it to me, this is the complete story of their very short evening at the "support group," or whatever it was. The first thing that must be said about the "spooky" attendees and their leader is that their affectless demeanor prevented their guests from easily accepting them as normal humans, despite their somewhat unexceptional physical appearance. Though all of them at least had eyes, ears, a nose and a mouth, none of these vacant-seeming individuals "looked right" and none behaved as normal humans would under such circumstances.

Though members of this unusual group were obviously able to rent a condo, assemble furniture, use the telephone, and sit still for the so-called support group meeting, this was apparently the extent of their ability to mimic human behavior. In this context the leader's reference to his "husband" might have been just another glaring confusion about normal earthly usage, a phenomenon that is often reported.[2]

The larger question is simple: Why did they arrange this transparently fraudulent abductee support group in the first place? No one shared any UFO experience or asked about Don's or Dennis's encounters. No one was offering any kind of *support* to anyone. No one had apparently ever heard of MUFON, or David Jacobs, or myself. How was Don supposed to be taken in by this awkward subterfuge? And since the leader also seemed completely surprised that Don did not come alone, what was the group planning for him had he shown up unaccompanied? What was their objection to the men's videotape?

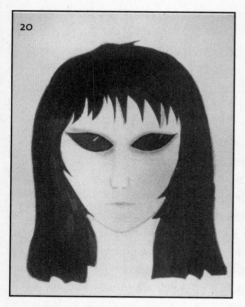

Adult transgenic female being wearing a wig, as drawn by M.C., a female abductee.

Adult transgenic female wearing a wig, as described by Linda Cortile.

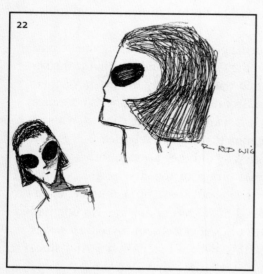

Adult transgenic female being wearing a red wig, as drawn by L.R., a female abductee.

Transgenic female child, as drawn by C.D., a female abductee.

There are a multitude of secondary questions too. When the beautiful woman stood up and changed before their eyes, was that some type of signal? Was it an accident? Was it a threat of some kind? Was her initial appearance a kind of imposed screen image that faded when Don, Dennis, and their wives resolved to leave? Is there possibly a period of unnoticed missing time associated with the event? Were the aliens' telepathic abilities not functioning for some reason, leading to the host's surprise at the presence of Don's friend and their wives?

Questions, questions, questions . . . and few answers that make coherent sense.

Stewart

We have met Sally, the young abductee who was summoned to a bogus job interview where she was made to inhale what her interviewer referred to as perfume, a substance that caused her to lose consciousness. This interview pretext, the reader will recall, preceded a UFO abduction in which small gray aliens took over from the more human-appearing "interviewer" whose supporting role was somewhat like that of Terry's all-knowing "Mr. Nelson."

I first met Sally in 1987 when she wrote to me about a puzzling missing-time experience that had occurred a few years earlier on a bitterly cold afternoon when she left home to ride on her snowmobile. Her parents became alarmed when their teenage daughter hadn't returned after several hours, and set out to look for her. A neighbor found her standing alongside the snowmobile, which was lying on its side in the middle of a field. Sally appeared dazed but unhurt and was not wearing either her coat or her gloves: They were neatly folded on the snow-covered ground next to her. She had no idea what had happened to her. She was extremely frightened of something, however, and initially fled the neighbor who was coming to her rescue, even though she knew him well.

Inspection of the ground a few days later showed that the field where she was found was dead level, so the upsetting of the snowmobile was itself a mystery. Sally's stepfather, a physician, was alarmed by her lack of memory of the accident and ordered a series of neurological tests, all of which were negative. Meanwhile, Sally was having vivid dreams and flashbacks of small, huge-eyed, frightening beings and of the snowmobile's being lifted off the ground.

When we finally met after I received her letter, hypnosis revealed that the accident was actually a UFO abduction, at the end of which Sally was returned to her overturned snowmobile without her coat and gloves. They were simply put on the ground next to her, neatly folded— a not uncommon type of alien error at the end of an abduction.[3] As I worked with Sally off and on over the next few years, a number of other, similar unexplained incidents came to light. Most important for our purposes here are her bizarre adventures with a man she referred to as "Stewart."

Sally described Stewart as a tall man with a long, thin face, curly blond hair, and oddly shaped eyeglasses. He seemed to be in his middle thirties, and though Sally consciously recalls seeing him first when she was a child and encountering him again and again over the next twenty-five years, he never seemed to age. While his appearance was not very unusual, his behavior was decidedly abnormal. As we explored her later partially recalled abduction experiences, Stewart turned up frequently, sometimes playing the role of facilitator in the "Mr. Nelson" mode, arriving in her apartment first before turning her over to the gray aliens, and a few times as a more violent sexual abuser.[4]

Sally recalled a number of conversations she had had with Stewart, and over many years she had come to regard him ambivalently as dangerous and yet in some way also as a caretaker, a pairing of responses not uncommon in such cases. Now, I am aware that all of this sounds utterly subjective, even delusional, and that would be that if it were not for the presence of independent witnesses and the familiar patterns of her account. In one case, Sally was living in a suburb of Washington, D.C., where she held a secretarial job in a government bureau and was sharing an apartment with another young woman, "Hannah."

One night Sally awoke, startled to find Stewart standing next to her bed. Despite the fact that her apartment was on an upper floor, the windows were locked, and the door was securely bolted on the inside, there was Stewart, next to her bed. Frightened, Sally nevertheless felt herself compelled to get up and go with him into the living room. There she served both Stewart and herself a drink, and the two sat together on the couch talking audibly, not telepathically, as was sometimes the case. Stewart was, as usual, interested in her daily routine and questioned her about the mundane details of her life and secretarial job.

At one point, Sally told me, she gathered her courage and decided to ask him a rather basic question: "Are you real?" she wanted to know. "Are you a human being? What are you?" Stewart smiled and ignored the question.

Determined to find out something about him, she noticed that his shirt had fallen open a bit, so she suddenly reached inside, took hold of a long, curly chest hair, and pulled it out. He winced and gave her an angry look, but she was pleased to realize that on some physical level he was real and not a phantasm. A few moments later three small gray aliens approached and she was taken out the window and into a hovering UFO for a more typical abduction experience.

Sally phoned me within the week to tell me about her partial memories of this incident. The morning after Stewart's visit, she awakened and remembered both his sudden appearance beside her bed and the later image of the two of them sitting on the sofa in the living room. She even recalled pulling out one of his chest hairs and was pleased, I thought, to have caused him even a little pain. She had immediately determined that all the locks on the doors and windows were still intact and the main bolt on the inside of the front door was in place.

Though there was no way he could have entered her apartment, there were two things, Sally said, that made her accept this as a real event instead of a disturbingly vivid dream. First, she said, when she went into the kitchen that morning to make coffee, she noticed that there were two glasses containing half-finished drinks on the counter, which then caused her to remember having served the drinks as they talked.

Second, and more disturbing, was her conversation with Hannah. I interviewed her roommate by telephone later that day, and she repeated to me what she had told Sally:

I woke up sometime during the night and there was a roaring sound in my head. I was very scared because I didn't know what it was and then I found that I couldn't move. Something was going on. I heard voices coming from the living room. Sally was talking and there was a man's voice. It was the middle of the night and I couldn't move, and I had no idea who was out there or what was happening. I guess I just must have gone back to sleep, which doesn't make much sense when I think about it. The whole thing was very scary, because there really was a strange man in the apartment and I couldn't even move.

A few years later, in a another Washington-area apartment that she shared with a different roommate, Sally was entertaining a woman friend from New York. She had met "Molly," an artist and abductee, through my support group, and though they were not close friends, Molly had been eager to visit Washington and had asked if she could stay with Sally.

One night, while sleeping in Sally's bedroom, they awoke simultaneously to find the room filled with light and themselves paralyzed. Then they assumed they had just gone back to sleep.[5] However, when they compared notes the next morning, the two young women found that they consciously recalled many details of a shared, traumatic abduction experience that began with their paralysis and the appearance of several small alien figures in the bedroom. The most significant detail for our purposes here is Molly's description of having seen a tall, curly-haired blond man with oddly shaped glasses operating inside the UFO along with the small gray aliens.

Sally, who also remembered Stewart's presence inside the UFO, asked her artist friend to make a drawing of the man she had seen without telling her about Stewart's appearance. When her friend completed her drawing, Sally recognized it as an even better likeness of Stewart than the drawing of him she had once made for me.

So, after all of this, what can we say about Stewart's attributes? First, he appeared to be fully human in appearance and seemed to possess at least one common frailty, poor eyesight, though both women vividly described his piercing, electric blue eyes. Sally commented that he did not seem to age normally, but apart from those recollections he would seem to have no trouble passing in human society. And he even has chest hair, something never before, to my knowledge, described as an alien feature.

Stewart clearly seemed gifted in the paranormal sphere, apparently being able to pass through closed doors or windows alien-fashion, able to communicate telepathically, and able to impose paralysis on human abductees and possible witnesses such as Hannah. Despite all of this, he apparently also had to visit an optometrist to see well—a stunning contradiction, as if Superman could fly but only at an altitude of twenty feet.

One final experience of Sally's bears mentioning, but one in which the mysterious Stewart did not appear. During her stay in Washington in the early 1990's, Sally was abducted and examined inside a UFO and recalled being taken into a small room where a gray alien presented her with a very tall, affectless being who was dressed in a dark, tight, conservative business suit. To Sally, he seemed superficially human but, like those at the phantom support group, awkwardly robotic in his lack of reactions. The small gray alien telepathically asked Sally a rapid-fire series of questions about her typical day at the office, and said that she was to answer them to help the tall man "understand."

"What do you say to your fellow workers when you come into the office in the morning?" he asked. "How do you operate a copy machine? How do you punctuate sentences? What do you say to the other employees when you leave in the evening? How do you operate a computer?" And so on: a series of bewildering questions, each of which might take weeks, months, or years to answer fully. Sally was almost in tears at this mass of challenges, which she could barely begin to answer because they came quickly, tumbling into her mind, one after another, from her telepathic captor. The entire process seemed ludicrous to her. She wasn't sure whether she was being asked to instruct or was in some way being tested herself as to what she knew and how she could express herself. Ultimately she was just as frustrated and angry as little Jen, when the child was asked in the Cape Cod playground in the middle of the night to "teach the children how to play."

Chapter 21

THE OUTBACK STEAK HOUSE INCIDENT

B RAND-NAME THEME RESTAURANTS, popular because they offer reli-able, uninteresting food at affordable, unsurprising prices, are ubiquitous in the suburban American landscape. Outback is one exam-ple of many, a chain of pseudo-Australian steak houses with at least one branch in the Chicago area. On a Saturday night in December 1999, however, inside Outback's orderly, unexciting dining room, "Edward," his wife, and a friend had an unsettling encounter with a strange entity who, to put it conservatively, did not look like your nor-mal Outback customer.

Ed is a quiet, highly intelligent man in his late fifties who teaches physics at a Chicago-area institution. He was originally trained as an engineer, a field in which he had a distinguished career after a stint as an Air Force officer during the late 1960's. We first met in the early 1980's in the office of Dr. J. Allen Hynek, the Northwestern University astronomer who had been, for some twenty years, scientific consultant to the Air Force on UFOs. At that time Dr. Hynek had retired from his Air Force work and was heading the center for UFO Research, a civil-ian investigative organization that Ed Reynolds had contacted for help in understanding his unusual experiences.

After a long preliminary interview with Ed, I had enough informa-tion to theorize that since childhood he had been undergoing a series of frequent UFO abductions, and that it would be helpful for him, with Dr. Hynek sitting in, to explore his memories under hypnosis. Though time constraints limited us to a single hypnosis session, we learned a great deal about one of Ed's childhood experiences. Subsequently we kept in touch by letter and telephone, and though we met a few times, I was not able to carry out any more hypnosis until the spring of 2000. It was just prior to one of these hypnotic sessions that Ed's Outback experience came to light, and I pressed him to describe it to me in detail.

Early one Saturday evening, shortly after the restaurant opened, Ed, his wife "Doris," and a visitor from out of town, "Doug," parked their car in the parking lot in front and went into the restaurant. Ed explained that he has known Doug, one of his closest friends and the CEO of a large and very successful manufacturing company, for about thirty years. This particular night at Outback was Doug's treat. The three friends finished dinner and stood up to leave while Doug took care of the check with a credit card.

At this point Ed glanced to his left and saw a strange-looking man and one or two companions standing by a table about two or three yards away. The man was staring intently at him. He was dressed in a rather odd coat of a bright plaid pattern with large leather elbow patches, and was wearing a brown fedora. He also had a distinctive beard and an unusual bronze flesh tone, "like a Native American," Ed said.

The stranger continued to stare so intently that Ed finally smiled back at him, assuming either that he had met this man somewhere before or that he was pulling some kind of bizarre joke. This was not surprising, since, to Ed, his clothes and beard suggested a costume rather than normal casual wear, as if he were a clown from a circus or an actor of some sort.

Ed's friend Doug glanced at the stranger and then slipped on his coat and returned his wallet to his pocket. Doris apparently had not noticed him when she, Ed, and Doug turned and walked twenty feet or so to the restaurant's front door, leaving the strange bronze-skinned man and his party behind them, still beside their table.

For Ed, the staring man in the restaurant had been unsettling, but what happened next left him astonished. A few seconds later, as Doris, Doug, and Ed passed through the front door of Outback, he was stunned to see, standing by a red sports car about two hundred feet *ahead* of them, the same bearded figure and his companion whom they had left behind them in the restaurant less than half a minute before. Once again the man was staring intently at Ed, who was frightened by the impossibility of what he was seeing. There was literally no way this unusual-looking person could have gotten through the restaurant door ahead of them, let alone walked two hundred feet into the parking lot and then positioned himself so that he was facing Ed when he and his party emerged from the restaurant. The fact that he was still staring fixedly lent a deliberate, unnervingly personal quality to the bizarre encounter.

But it was not just Ed who witnessed this impossible scene. When Doug saw the staring figures in the parking lot, he muttered something to Ed to the effect that this was certainly strange, as if "we've entered the Twilight Zone."

One of my first projects in the ensuing investigation was to speak to Doug by telephone about his recollections of the incident, which at the time of my call had occurred about four months earlier. After establishing who I was and why I wanted to speak with him, I asked how he knew that the odd man he saw in the parking lot was the same person he had just seen in the restaurant.

Doug: Well, first of all, there were only the two parties in the restaurant, ourselves and his, who were paying our bills and getting ready to leave at that time. Number two, it was a very large parking lot because I think it was adjacent to a mall or some other large lot that was right there, but at the particular time that we were there, there wasn't anybody else out there. So it was not a situation where there were ten or fifteen people coming and going. Fact of the matter is, I think we had gotten there just as the Outback opened.

BH: *Was there anything about the man's appearance that let you know for sure that these were not two different people? Supposing you saw him in the restaurant and then you go outside but you see somebody different out there who happens to resemble him.*

Doug: It wouldn't have happened that way. I didn't pay a whole lot of attention to who he was and what his clothes were. However, at that particular time, what he was wearing was identical to the person inside. And I say that somewhat euphemistically. He was wearing a brown fedora with a plaid jacket with leather elbow patches, you know, something like that. It couldn't have been mistaken.

BH: *How about his face? What did he look like?*

Doug: I think he was around fifty and I saw him somewhat obliquely when we went outside. I thought he had a beard. He was walking away from me, but Ed had a better recollection of what his face was. But he was the same guy, there was no mistake.

BH: *So you were going more with the clothing rather than the . . .*

Doug: The clothing and the stature, the age, and there wasn't anybody else there.

BH: *Is there any way he could have somehow gone out another door and gotten out there before you?*

Doug: There's only one [front] door in and out. I looked up and saw this guy some distance ahead of me and I thought, *That is funny. How did he get up there?*

BH: *And I take it this was after dark, since it was December.*

Doug: No, it wasn't. I don't think it was after dark. It was near dark. . . .

BH: *Was the parking lot lit, do you think, or not?*

Doug: Well, it was not dark as I recall. I think it was just late in the afternoon. But then, you know how Chicago is in the wintertime. But it was not dark.

BH: *Right. One more question. If you were heading to the door and they were still behind you in the restaurant, how long do you think it was after you left them behind in the restaurant until you saw them out front?*

Doug: Twenty seconds. I mean, there wasn't any lapse of time here. If there had been, I would have passed it off as something else. I just thought it kind of odd.

BH: *Yeah, well, it certainly is. I guess that since Ed had more contact in the restaurant than you, the man's appearance was more impressive to him.*

Doug: Well, sure. He would have consequently paid more attention to something like that than I would have because I was concerned with paying the bill. I recall I had a jacket I was putting on—I forget what the hell it was. I had a jacket behind me and it fell down the back of the bench or something like that and I wound up putting it on backwards or something. I *do* know how to dress myself, but there was something odd about that. I wear a hat and I was putting that on and I put my jacket on and then I was going to pay the bill, so Ed was not doing those things.

· Budd: *Right, so he had time to have a longer look.*

Doug: So he would have consequently been more aware of those things that were going on around him.

This phone conversation with Doug served to confirm Ed's account of the strange events at Outback, so I was now more interested than ever to try hypnosis to find out whatever else there was to learn about that unusual night. But there were several things Doug said that puzzled me. First, there was his assertion that it was not dark when they left Outback. On Saturday nights Outback restaurant does not open until 5:30 P.M., the time Ed remembers they arrived. If one assumes that drinks—which Ed recalled were served first—and then a relaxed dinner would have taken at least an hour, it is certain that in early December, when the days are shortest, it was dark by 6:30 or 7:00, probably the earliest they could have left. And yet, Doug insisted that it was not dark.

And then there was his cryptic remark about his coat problem as they were leaving: "I wound up putting [my jacket] on backwards or something. I *do* know how to dress myself, but there was something odd about that." Struggling with one's winter coat is not unusual for anyone, so I found it curious that Doug described it as seeming "odd." In my experience of investigating UFO cases, I have learned that often, when a witness describes as "odd" such a completely minor thing as a struggle with one's coat, the remark can suggest that, to him, it seemed more peculiar than it should have.

So my phone call with Doug raised two new issues that remained to be resolved: his struggle with his coat, and the time and amount of daylight that remained when Ed's party left Outback. The latter issue became even more confusing when Ed mentioned that it was quite dark when he drove home and required the use of his headlights.

A few hours after my phone call with Doug, I began a hypnotic session with Ed in the home of one of his friends. I began the induction and set the scene:

BH: *You're feeling comfortable and relaxed. I want you to see yourself now on that particular night back in December when you and Doug and Doris are on the way, driving to the restaurant—the Outback in River Oaks—driving along. You're at the wheel; Doris is with you in the front. It's late afternoon, and I want you to see yourself pulling up to the restaurant. It's going to be a nice night; it's going to be fun for the three of you to have a nice dinner. Going into the restaurant; I want you to see yourself being seated, the three of you, at a table. I'm going to ask you some questions and you can speak whenever you like. This table that you sit at, is this a round table as they have in restaurants sometimes, or is this a rectangular table?*

Ed: It's square.

BH: *Is Doris to your left or to your right or in front of you?*

Ed: She's to my left.

BH: *To your left, okay. And is this dinner an enjoyable dinner? Is it relaxed and fun or is it . . . How do you feel when you're having dinner there?*

Ed: It's fun.

BH: *Now, Ed, this is the night you see something odd that we've been talking about earlier. So I want us to move to when you get ready to leave, when you're finished and you stand up. I believe Doug drops his coat or something, he has to pick up his coat. You stand up and as you're standing up, I'm going to count to three. At the count of three, you're going to notice somebody at a nearby table. So you're standing up. One . . . getting ready to notice somebody at a nearby table. Two . . . you're just about to look at this person. Three. Tell me a little bit about this person. Allow yourself to look at him, time to look.*

Ed: I see the person. I see the person and I see . . . The funny thing about it is, I don't see the legs. The legs seem to . . .

BH: *You don't have to see the legs. Tell me what parts you do see.*

Ed: I see the upper part; I see the face.

BH: *Does this person seem to notice you?*

Ed: Yes, immediately there's . . . As soon as I stand up we seem to just look at each other. It's like he wants to get my attention.

BH: *How is he dressed? You said you can see the upper part of him.*

Ed: He's dressed in . . . it's a funny-looking outfit. It has a circular round collar that goes about his neck and it's sort of, there's an opening and underneath the collar there's like an undergarment or an undercoat. I don't see his arms; the arms are not apparent. . . . There are different colors. There's a pattern to the undergarment, and there's brown and I think it's purple and very dark red. It doesn't appear to be cloth. It has another texture to it. . . . I don't see any buttons.

BH: *Now I want you to look past him, to one side or the other, and see if he's alone, or does he seem to be one of a party?*

Ed: No, there's . . . wow. There's another person that's standing very close. The other person is very hard to describe because the person's standing very close and the body of the other person seems to blend, sort of blend into the scene, so to speak.

BH: *Is it possible to tell whether this other person is a male or a female?*

Ed: I would say it's a female. It appears to be more female than male, although when I look closely, very close—and I'm looking very close at this other person—it's a little difficult to say, but because of the expression on the face—and I'm getting a closer look . . . the expression is sort of more female than male.

BH: *Can you see anything about the hair, the length of the hair of that person?*

Ed: The hair is rather short but I'm not really sure if it's hair. It could be a covering over the head, covering most of the upper portion of the head, including the forehead, but the eyes and a portion of the forehead is very clear and part of the person's face is clear.

BH: *Now, does this person look at you in the same way that the man . . .*

Ed: No, although it does look at me. It does look at me.

BH: *It does look at you. Well, let's examine that look. Is there anything you can tell about that look? For instance, are these people people that you know? Perhaps the reason they're looking at you—or the man is— is that they've met you before and they're friends or they've seen you somewhere. Did somebody attend a class of yours or something at one time?*

Ed: No.

BH: *Never seen either one of them before?*

Ed: The smaller one, no.

BH: *But the taller one you think you may have seen before?*

Ed: Perhaps.

So far in this session, a number of potentially important details have come to light. First, his various reactions to the man in the round-necked jacket: "I don't see the legs. . . . I don't see his arms; the arms are not apparent." And yet, Ed can describe his bizarre clothing, its various layers and colors. The focus on his face seems intense. But even more potentially significant is the fact that the man seems familiar.

Ed's comments about the figure standing next to the man are also interesting. He says he can't describe it too well because its body "seems to . . . sort of blend into the scene . . ." Is he implying that the body is partially transparent? That it lacks definition? He feels it is female because of its facial expression, but he is not certain that whatever is concealing most of its head is actually hair. It could be "covering most of the upper portion of the head, including the forehead," though the eyes are quite clear. All of this at least suggests that what we have here is not a middle-aged Chicago couple having a Saturday night steak dinner at the Outback.

At this point in the hypnosis, I decided to move on to Ed and his party leaving the restaurant and heading through the door to the parking lot, with the odd pair remaining behind them.

BH: *You move away from these people and go towards the door. Is there some kind of inner door, a vestibule, that you see there in front of you?*

Ed: There's only one door. Only one door that opens to the outside. It opens into a receiving area for people who are waiting for dinner, and then there's another door that exits to the outside. So there are two doors to go out of before you reach the outside and the parking lot.

BH: *Now, Ed, I want you to understand that with any kind of story, memory, experience, whatever, there is always a sequence of events. Something happens and then something happens after that and then something happens after that. So, just very slowly and gradually, things unfold. And when I count to three, I want you to get the feeling of finally going through the outside door, out towards where the cars are, and I want you, as I count to three, to feel yourself stepping outside. One . . . you're getting ready to go through that last door, out to the reception area. Two . . . the door is opening, you're going out. Three. [At this point Ed begins to tremble, and I put my hand on his shoulder to comfort him.] Tell me what's happening, Ed. I just want you to tell me what you're feeling and experiencing as you go through that door and step outside.*

Ed: I step outside but I'm alone. I'm not with . . . [pause] It's dark and . . . but it's . . . I don't believe I see this. I'm looking into the backseat of the car and [Doug and Doris] are both asleep in the backseat there. At least they appear to be asleep. Doug and Doris. I'm looking down and they're . . . it's dark and they're . . .

BH: *When you say you're looking down, do you mean you're standing up beside the car, looking down?*

Ed: No, I'm somehow looking down into the backseat of the car from the rear window and they're both asleep.

BH: *When you say looking down, I don't understand what the distance is that you're looking down. Are you five feet from them or ten feet or . . .*

Ed: Maybe ten feet and I'm looking. And they seem to be asleep. . . . It's very hard to describe: It's like I'm there but I'm not there. It's like I look back and I don't see the people that should be there and yet I know that they should be. It's like I'm sort of not part of it, not part of what should be happening. It's like I'm sort of blended into something else that's not there.

For various pressing reasons we had to end the session at this point, with Ed in what seemed to be a type of altered state. From past experience I was aware that when a subject recalls an altered state of consciousness *within* a hypnotic trance state, the combination can be very disorienting, and so I was not surprised by Ed's confusion. Our plan was to resume hypnosis a bit later, so I felt things would eventually become clearer.

But from what had occurred so far, I had begun to suspect that something dramatic—possibly even an abduction—had taken place between the moment Ed and his party left the restaurant and the time that they remembered seeing the oddly dressed man and his friend standing in the parking lot. Thus the problem might be one of missing time, rather than an alleged example of the "teleportation" of the mysterious strangers.

A few hours later we resumed the hypnosis. Retracing our steps, I began at the beginning, inside the restaurant, when Ed first notices the strange man.

Ed: I look at him and he smiles and I think he's smiling because he thinks that since he's so funny-looking, I'm amused.

BH: *Are you amused?*

Ed: No. There's a person or something or someone that's standing directly to his left—to my right—and it's smaller. It has, well, it's sort of dark and I can't see the legs. . . . I can't even see the arms, but I do see the face. It isn't moving, it's standing, staring at me.

BH: *When you say* it, *that's the way one might refer to a child. Why are you saying it? Is this a man or a woman?*

Ed: I thought at first it was a woman but now I'm not sure. It has . . . I can't see the whole face, part of it is covered, but the skin has high cheekbones, very high, and I see eyes. The rest of the face seems to be covered. The skin is sort of ruddy red but more of a darker red than . . . The eyes are black; at least they appear to be. There's a covering over the head. If I look at it very closely, it isn't hair. That's all I see.

BH: *Now, Ed, obviously these two are unusual-looking in a restaurant. Let's just look and see. Are the waiters and other customers noticing them too?*

Ed: No. Only one waiter does and he seemed to walk past and look back but the other waiters, no. They walk. It's the waiter that waited on us, on our table. He's standing too. Oh! Hmm. .,. . He's stand-ing and he's watching too.

Ed's descriptions further suggest that these two figures are not visi-ble to the other people in the restaurant—except, for some inexplicable reason, they were at least glimpsed by Doug and, apparently, the waiter who had served their table. As the hypnosis continues, I move the action ahead. After dealing with Ed's actual exit from the restaurant, we return to his earlier memory of seeing Doris and Doug through the back window of the car, asleep.

Ed: I sense fear and I look around and I'm, like, floating. I don't see Doug, I don't see Doris. This is happening so fast. [A long pause] Now I can see. I'm looking down and I see they're in the backseat of the car and it's like they're asleep. I'm sort of going up, further, fur-ther away.

BH: *Okay, let's go back to when you feel that you are moving away from them, from Doris and Doug. You can see them through the car [window], but let's go back to your feeling of movement. How were you moving? Down the street or moving back towards the Outback? Which direction are you moving in?*

Ed: Up. It [the car] is getting further away and I see something.

BH: *What do you see?*

Ed: I see something metallic and it's shaped like a . . . looks like a shovel. Well, the head part is shaped like . . . no, it's more like a . . . it's hard to describe. Like a giant arrow.

BH: *Sort of pointed more on one end?*

Ed: Yes, but the shaft is very thick.

All of Ed's descriptions begin to suggest that he had apparently been abducted that night either from the front reception room of the

Outback restaurant or the area immediately outside, and that Doug and Doris were switched off in some way and placed in the backseat of his car.

I move on to the next change in Ed's posture and circumstances.

Ed: It's like I'm lying down. . . . I'm lying on a . . . it seems like lying on my back. But I don't feel anything. My thoughts are strange.

BH: *What are those thoughts?*

Ed: That . . . why is this happening to me again?

What happened to Ed as he lay on what he felt was a metallic table inside this arrow- or shovel-shaped craft need not concern us here. The UFO occupants carried out one highly unusual procedure that was familiar to me from several earlier cases. Since it is reported rarely and has never been made public by any investigator, I prefer to keep it confidential as a way to help test the credibility of people who describe UFO abductions, and for this I beg the reader's indulgence.

As I was winding up the hypnosis session, I returned Ed to the moment he found himself back on the ground. I asked if he could see Doris and Doug, and if they appeared to be smiling, happy, and talking.

Ed: Yeah, I guess, sort of.

BH: *Is there anything about their behavior that seems different than what you expect it to be at that time, or are they acting as people do after they've left a nice meal in a restaurant?*

Ed: Well, Doris looks to be in a hurry to get to the car.

BH: *Is that the way she usually is?*

Ed: Not always.

BH: *How about Doug? How does he look?*

Ed: Stumbly.

BH: *He looks stumbly?*

Ed: Yeah, he stumbles a lot.

BH: *Is that the way he usually walks, or is he more stumbly than usual?*

Ed: He's more stumbly now than normal.

BH: *Does he say anything to you?*

Ed: No, I do all the talking.

BH: *But you mentioned to him something about the odd-looking man?*

Ed: Yeah, I was curious if he had noticed him in the restaurant and he said, "Yeah, that's strange. I did, I saw him."

BH: *Is it easy to see? I assume there's plenty of daylight and you can see everybody. Maybe the lights are on in the parking lot? Describe the lighting conditions for me.*

Ed: It's really bright.

BH: *Really bright? So you can see very clearly?*

Ed: Oh, yes, very clearly.

BH: *Do you see the other cars in the parking lot?*

Ed: No, I don't see the other cars but I see a white Mercedes. It's to the left of my car and next to that is a red . . . oh yes, it's a red BMW, the small sports model, yes.

BH: *Well, how about the other cars? I assume that this is a parking area for the restaurant.*

Ed: Yes. But I don't see any other cars. Just the three cars.

BH: *Well, let's look around and see if we see people and the usual Saturday night activity.*

Ed: No, no people.

BH: *Do you hear traffic? I'm sure you hear car doors slamming and coming and going.*

Ed: No, no, nothing.

I asked these leading questions—false leads, all of them—for two reasons: to further test Ed's suggestibility, and also to direct his attention to the scene around him. It was clear to me from what he had said that wherever he was in these last moments, he was no longer in the parking lot of a popular restaurant on a Saturday night at about 7:00 P.M. Also, the fact that he described the lighting as "really bright" suggests that it was neither the evening sun nor the mall's street lamps that illuminated everything so clearly. And what he says in answer to my next question strongly implies a fixed source of intense artificial light that seems focused on him:

BH: *So you get in your car at this point or . . . ?*

Ed: No, I look at the red car because it's so bright and it is so red and I can see this bright . . . well, it looks like an image of the sun that's coming from it and it's glaring right in my face. It's sort of blinding but it's so pretty, and Doug noticed it too. He said, "Wow, that's really pretty."

BH: *So what time is it? Around three or four in the afternoon? Do you have an idea of the time?*

Ed: I don't know what time it is. The sun is out so . . .

BH: *The sun is out? It must be early.*

Ed: I don't know what time it is. I never thought about the time. Oh! The sky is blue. Or—wait . . . I think . . . no, I don't see the sky. I thought I did but I don't.

BH: *Now let's see how you get in your car and what happens to the odd man who's been looking at you.*

Ed: I don't see him anymore. He's gone.

BH: *Did you see him leave?*

Ed: No, no.

BH: *But you can still see the white Mercedes?*

Ed: No, I don't see the white Mercedes now.

BH: *Do you see the red car?*

Ed: I see the red car.

BH: *But the Mercedes is gone?*

The next exchange indicates that the abduction and the distorted circumstances around it have ended and normal memory resumes for Ed, Doug, and Doris:

Ed: The Mercedes is gone. Well, I get in my car and now I remember. I back up and I'm backing to my right.

BH: *Who's next to you in the front seat?*

Ed: Doug. Doris is in the back. Now there are other cars. I back up, then I pull out to my . . . I back up to my left, not the right, to my left.

BH: *I guess it's an easy job to back up if it's so brightly lit and you can see since the sun is out.*

Ed: Well, now it's . . . dark. I see the lights in the parking lot and I see other cars. And I back to my left, then I pull forward, then I turn to my right to go out of the parking lot, and there's another car that's also coming out, and I stop and I wait for the car to pull out and it pulls out, in front of me and it goes ahead. It makes the right turn, to the exit to the parking lot, and I follow it out, and then I go out and I go back to the street and I wait for the light to turn green.

BH: *As you're doing that, I assume there's enough light that you don't need your headlights.*

Ed: Oh, no, I need the headlights because it's dark. And then I drive home.

Shortly thereafter I ended the session, and I felt we had uncovered the explanation of the original mystery—how the strange man had seemed to travel magically from inside the restaurant, behind Ed and his party, to the parking lot, ahead of them, in mere seconds. But now several new mysteries loomed on the horizon. Ed felt that this strange-looking person he had seen in the restaurant was the same man he saw later inside the shovel-shaped UFO during his abduction. This possibility creates a different kind of mystery. How did a not-wholly-human figure, wearing a beard and an outrageous costume, appear *inside a popular restaurant* on a busy Saturday night and be seen, apparently, only by Ed, Doug, and possibly their waiter, the latter two independent and presumably uninvolved witnesses? Who was this strange being, and what manner of "man" was he?

And what was Doug's role in all of this? He not only saw the strange man and his companion inside the restaurant but he also described the parking lot under what seemed to him daylight conditions, even though the sun had set some time ago. And Ed, after returning from his abduction, described Doug as "stumbly,"—as if he had not quite recovered from whatever altered state he had been placed in during the encounter.

I have no reason to think that Doug himself was abducted that night—or at any other time, for that matter. Not only did Ed not see him in the craft, he saw him "asleep"—switched off?—in the backseat of the car as Ed was taken up. Most perplexing is the fact that if Ed, during his abduction, was in a world or physical state halfway between that of the aliens and that of his fellow humans, why was Doug able to see some but not all of its peculiar manifestations?

Did anyone but Doug and Ed see the strange man and his companions in the restaurant? Were they actually visible to other diners, including Ed's wife, Doris, who later claimed to remember very little of the evening? As in the perplexing matter of Sam Washburn's photographs in which the Australian landscape shows up but the Washburns themselves do not, the events in the Outback restaurant and parking lot that December night seem greatly confused both philosophically and scientifically.

Once again, in the Outback incident, we have a case of what seems to be a weirdly costumed and therefore deliberately *memorable* nonhuman in an everyday setting, a theme restaurant in the suburbs of Chicago. Where do these strange beings actually live?

Ted Bloecher, a friend of mine and a pioneer UFO investigator, spent many years as an actor in the musical theater. Someone once asked him where UFOs or their occupants go when they are not being seen, and he replied simply, "They go behind the scenery." As good an answer, perhaps, as any other.

Chapter 22

BEHIND THE SCENERY

I MUST ADMIT A PARTICULAR fondness for the sorts of inexplicable, things-that-go-bump-in-broad-daylight stories that Budd started off with in the last chapter—the Spanish dandy, the old bicycle-peddling Bavarian, and the Charles Manson clone. There's absolutely no mundane explanation for them, unless you're willing to write them off as the aftereffects of bad food, cheap wine, or a certain slant of light in the eyes. It's the kind of thing people say when no life experience *they* have had confirms that such anomalous events do happen. Perhaps I like the fact that there's no obvious UFO connection and that sets my mind free to wander in the tall grasses of a more mystical, less nuts-and-bolts field. Maybe it's the frisson, the almost shuddering glimpse into some other reality separated from this one by nothing more than a semi-opaque, living membrane in which at unexpected moments, a flap parts and one of "the Others" slips through on a brief expedition.

Partly, too, I confess to the pleasure of privilege: These accounts are so paranormal in tone, so inconclusive as anecdotes, that Budd passes them along to very few people. In his investigations of UFO events, reports in the "high strangeness" category are handled with caution. So when Budd suggested including this last grouping of bizarre reports in our proposed book, it took me aback.

It simply didn't seem possible to pursue an investigative inquiry of any substance into these decades-old events. None of the usual UFO physical evidence had trailed down behind them through the years—no photos of landing traces or documented electromagnetic effects, no lab-tested artifacts or body scars. What was there to say about these elliptical stories that would be concrete without destroying their most intriguing quality—the fragmentary and very fragile essence of a possibly otherworldly mystery?

We might begin by considering these elusive human experiences from a metaphysical or psychological perspective. It's possible, in that light, that the primary value of the first three experiences—brief cameo appearances by oddly costumed characters—is simply to open our awareness that reality (or consciousness) exists on a broad spectrum, as philosopher and psychologist William James understood:

> Our waking consciousness is but one special state of consciousness, whilst all about it, parted by the filmiest of screens, there lie potential forms of consciousness entirely different. . . . No account of the universe in its totality can be final which leaves these other forms of consciousness quite disregarded.[1]

And perhaps we should leave it at that for moments like these—a simple acknowledgment of their existence as fleeting human experiences, and an acceptance that not everything can be known.

Besides, what sort of material science could begin to explain these theatrical characters, the "non-story-ness" of the stories, and the strange people's seeming ability to be in two places at once, both "back there" behind the witnesses who have passed them and, in an impossible glint of time, "right there" in front of them, too? Is it possible there's a science—yet to be invented—that would allow for these flamboyant characters who call marked attention to themselves and then perform vanishing acts? Is there any way to discover who or what they are, what their purpose is, and where they go when they leave? Maybe the best we can do is accept ufologist and actor Ted Bloecher's wry, intuitive remark: "They go behind the scenery."

But perhaps we could push that metaphor a bit further when it comes to the more developed cases that follow. Science, physics in particular, is always trying to discover what's behind the scenery. What is the underlying order of the universe, if any? Or might there be many universes operating parallel to one another, so that, at any given moment of choice—marrying or not marrying, studying medicine or writing novels, choosing to be a parent or not to be one—all of those alternative possibilities could be occurring, one in each universe? Is human consciousness separate from material phenomena, or do our minds actually participate in creating that physical reality? What theories can be made based on what we observe and how can we test them?

By making a flyover of some of the most influential and hotly debated concepts in today's new quantum theory of reality, nonscientists can also get a glimpse of what's behind the scenery. Be forewarned: Physicists themselves refer to many of their discoveries as "absurd," "bizarre," and "like crazy science fiction." At the same time, many of these "spooky" theories can be supported either mathematically or in lab experiments.

The brief summary of quantum theory undertaken here is not meant to provide the reader with a complete understanding, but rather to lay some groundwork for the startling, almost fantastical concepts that might shake a doubter's certainties about the impossibilities of UFOs, interstellar travel, and paranormal phenomena such as ESP and telepathy. These theories just might give us some good ideas about ways in which these beings may truly come from "behind the scenery."

In my readings in the strange, elusive world of quantum physics, hyperspace, string theories, time travel, and other dimensions, it's clear that most philosophers and physicists—faced with their own inexplicable findings at the quantum level—are experiencing the same squirmy uneasiness that I feel in attempting to deal logically with UFO cases that contain some element of the paranormal. Einstein coined a phrase that expressed his distaste and discomfort for certain offshoots of his own work that he couldn't explain. "Spooky action at a distance" was his term for the inexplicable connectedness or "communication" that was shown to exist between widely separated photons. For bizarrely dressed thespians who appear briefly, practically waving to catch our attention, then vanish, we might coin an analogous term: "weird encounters at the fringe."

Making Unforgettable Memories

The appearance of beings in bizarre costumes or archaic styles of dress have turned up in many UFO investigators' cases. The man in white formal attire in Spain, the bronze-skinned man in the restaurant with a flamboyantly colored jacket and fedora, some of the "Men in Black" appearances in suits, and in an earlier case reported by Jerome Clark,[2] a troupe of four-foot-tall men dressed in nineteenth-century breeches coming through a cornfield—these are just a few of the more memorable ones. It seems quite posssible that these beings not only are seen and want to be seen, they want to be *memorable*. Thus, the outrageous dress and strange behavior.

To see a possible method in their madness, first let's imagine the effect on one viewer who reads or hears about such a character as described above. Next, let's take another viewer who will actually *see* the being. The difference in impact would be considerable, and for good reason: Whether written or oral, our language process is linear and left-brain, and utilizes symbols quite specifically. But language is also slow and inefficient in expressing our internal map of reality.[3] Visual imagery, on the other hand, speaks directly to the prelinguistic parts of the brain that give us access to the subconscious. A striking visual image first evokes *emotional* reactions, not analytical thought. The body also provides a means for us to hold on to these vivid images longer. Recently, in *Nature Neuroscience*, researchers reported that a region of the brain called the amygdala facilitates the long-term memory of emotionally charged events, especially those that are traumatic and frightening.[4]

Notice that the strange characters in the last cases never spoke to the witnesses. They simply showed up, straight from some wardrobe department "behind the scenery" and decades later the witnesses are still telling the stories.

Quantum theory, which burst into existence in 1925, actually turned Einstein's theory of relativity—according to which gravity is a warping of space-time and light always travels at a constant speed—on its head.

Before and after the acceptance of Einstein's theory, physicists such as Planck, Heisenberg, and Schrödinger were evolving a quite different view of the universe. They discovered that matter is made up of tiny, random, and unpredictable particles—that all possibilities exist simultaneously and that we can never know anything to be certain. In nearly every way, quantum theory is the opposite of what had become Einstein's model of the universe.[5] His theory of general relativity tells of a cosmos where the stars and galaxies are held together by the smooth fabric of space and time.

In contrast, quantum theory begins at the microcosmic level. Here, subatomic particles hold sway, dancing in an unseemly and jittery way "on the sterile stage of space-time, which is viewed as an empty arena, devoid of any content."[6] Undeniably, these two theories propose two such different ways of understanding the world that they could be described as "hostile opposites," as was often the case between the scientists who championed one theory over another.

Fairly rapidly, quantum theory began to win over its opponents, even some scientists in the early 1920's who still denied the existence of "atoms." If something couldn't be seen or measured directly in the laboratory, the holdouts ridiculed, it didn't exist. Perhaps ufologists should take heart after all: It seems that debunkers—people who *need* to disbelieve in any revolutionary concept—have been around for quite some time.

Over the past eighty to ninety years, as quantum theory began to offer a comprehensive framework within which to describe the visible universe, it brought about a profound change in human understanding of how the world works. It also introduced what has been called alternately "the greatest scientific problem of all time" and "the Holy Grail of physics." It's the quest taken up by a new generation of physicists to find a way to unite the new quantum theory with Einstein's more established theory of relativity and gravity, largely because each theory offered valid explanations of certain aspects of the universe that the other didn't allow. In short, the problem that has frustrated and eluded some of the greatest minds of our century is an attempt to reconcile opposites into a simplified and beautiful construct called "the Theory of Everything."[7]

Don't Bother Me with Physics: I'm Only Interested in UFOs.

Why should these scientific struggles be of interest to people who occupy a very specific niche in the hinterlands of science—those people gripped with the need to understand UFOs, abductions, and other paranormal phenomenon? As you probably know, in the field of UFO research, there's a great deal of talk about the need for a new scientific paradigm that would go beyond the usual methodologies of working only with material evidence that's quantifiable, repeatable, measurable. What is currently left outside the tent of science are the millions of anomalous (i.e., "unscientific") experiences people have had since the beginning of recorded history. In ufology, there are also calls for UFO researchers to attempt linkages with mainstream science in order to attract the expertise of people trained in specialized sciences, as well as their access to labs and funding. In order to make that link, writers like Jerome Clark, Charles Emmons, Richard Hall, and Steven J. Dick ask ufologists to restrain themselves from putting forward "high strangeness" cases without any hard evidence and to be cautious in trying to fold all anomalies under the UFO umbrella. Insistence on inclusion of such "anomalous anomalies" tends to alienate mainstream science even further from considering a serious study of the UFO phenomenon.

Returning to why UFO researchers should care about physics: There are at least two answers to that. First, perhaps we can learn something from watching the physicists' halting progress toward that grand unified theory. Many ufologists are following a similar path, as unlikely as that might seem at first glance. They, too, are deeply committed to a single grand theory—one that unites a vast array of anomalous and inexplicable phenomena, such as UFOs, ETs, ESP, teleportation, psychokinesis, mental telepathy, and more. By analogy to the progress in quantum theory, perhaps we can get a sense as to whether opposites (in physics or in ufology) can ever be reconciled.

Another major reason that ufologists should and often do take an interest in quantum physics is that the theories and discoveries coming out of this field offer us the best hope of linking our own interest with that of mainstream science. The most inexplicable findings about the workings of the universe have come, and are still coming, out of quantum physics. Their otherworldly strangeness appears to be somehow related to the quasimateriality and quasiethereality of UFOs. The strangeness of the world as perceived from the subatomic level up resonates with the strangeness of the various phenomena ufologists are interested in.

A Problem of Loose Boundaries in Ufology

There are some unique difficulties that ufologists encounter in playing the science game—in other words, attempting modestly, as nonscientists in self-funded efforts, to gather credible UFO abduction reports that can eventually become data for further analytical study. One of the biggest problems in the study of UFOs is in drawing the boundaries around a subject that seems, like a magnetic force, to draw into its field *everything* inexplicable—apparitions, telepathic communication, remote viewing, etc. Standard scientific disciplines operate much like a married couple dividing up the chores of day-to-day living: The work, the inquiry within a broad field, is broken down into specialties, such as astrobiology, cosmology, astronomy, etc., with each operating on a relatively clear set of boundaries. Each discipline has a turf and specialists who know it, claim it, and learn it to the bone.

But the study of the UFO phenomenon defies boundaries. Many times, as Harvard psychiatrist John Mack has openly acknowledged, it is hard to know where to draw the line in giving credence to an abductee's accounts. People floated through walls and taken into a silent craft the size of Shea Stadium? A man who channels his Native American ancestors? A woman who has fetuses removed by humanoid beings? A college student reliving a past life in Rome in 135 B.C.? From the perspective of Western science, Mack says, all of the above are considered absurd. In his book *Abduction: Human Encounters with Aliens*, Mack believes that our culture suffers from a deeply held belief in the "total separation of the spirit and physical worlds."[8]

And so it does. But the question still stands for everyone fascinated by UFO reports: Where do we draw the line before a field of inquiry begins to bleed into the chaotic inclusion-confusion of a commercially driven pop culture?

Quantum studies, for instance, suggest that interstellar travel *is* possible for ETs, not by breaking the speed limit, but by finding shortcuts through the universe—shortcuts discovered on the new map of the universe being drawn from a quantum perspective. These new studies also show how microcosmic and macrocosmic worlds touch and echo one another in ways we've never dared to dream of; that the universe is passingly strange; and that anyone who is both humble and has a mind that is prepared to apprehend the intangible isn't likely to go away disappointed.

Oddities of the Subatomic World

Even before mid-century, the equations of relativity simply couldn't handle the growing realization of physicists that, on an extremely fine scale, space-time—and reality itself—becomes grainy and jumpy, like the "snow" on a badly tuned television set. At the subatomic particle level, relativity's logical laws of cause and effect break down. Not bothering to "make sense," particles of matter jump from point A to point B without actually traveling through the space between the two. (Hold that thought for future discussion about UFOs.)

Another disturbing detail about the quantum world is that photons, the quantized energy packets that make up light, are not clearly, unambiguously, distinct entities with specific traits, like your cocker spaniel, for example, or your brown loafers. Photons have the seemingly capricious ability to show themselves as either particles or waves, and that state is related to whether you are observing or measuring them or not. It's as if the shoes that you dropped—ker-*chunk*—on the floor last night also had the ability to become liquid and flow underneath your bed when you weren't looking.

Yet another oddity of the quantum world is that bunches of photons act in concert with one another even after they are separated into different spaces. They somehow are either communicating instantaneously across space in order for this coordinated action to occur, or they stay "nonlocally" connected as a unit that can get things done even after they are separated (another idea we'll come back to in relation to UFO properties).

Starting as it does way down at the micro level of life, quantum theory warns us that the world of apparent solidity around us is an illusion.

The particles that make up matter are so tiny that we humans can't possibly perceive the constant interactivity and interconnection of it all. For instance, things that we assume to be solid, like doors and rocks and people, are constantly exchanging quanta, or particles of energy, between them. Everything is in motion; nothing is actually solid. It's only our rather gross sensory perceptions that make them *seem* that way.

Quantum physics is the stuff of genuine intellectual revolution. Anyone who even partially understands quantum reality can never walk through life in quite the same way again. All certainties about the basic materials and processes of life are gone. In this new quantum world, you can only calculate what will *probably* happen next. As physicist Michio Kaku states, the earlier, more orderly "picture of the universe was now replaced by uncertainty and chance. Quantum theory demolished, once and for all, the Newtonian dream of mathematically predicting the motion of all the particles in the universe."[9]

Some Other New and Weird Ideas for Understanding the Universe

Superstring Theory

Theoretical physicists have developed a framework that seems like the best hope yet of integrating Einstein's theory of gravity with nature's other fundamental forces. In fact, the theory's significance lies in its power to unify all known physical phenomena in an astonishingly simple model. Popularly known as "string theory" or "hyperspace," it posits that the smallest, irreducible components of the universe are tiny loops that resemble vibrating strings.[10]

The strength of this concept is that it can explain the nature of both matter and space-time and answers a series of puzzling questions about the large number of particles in atoms. No one could understand why matter needed so many. But when we magnify each particle down to its smallest level, we can see that it's not a point at all but a vibrating string about one hundred billion times smaller than a proton. According to this theory, matter—the stuff of you and your cocker spaniel—is nothing but the harmonies created by these vibrating strings.[11]

Other Dimensions

But string theory, for all the questions it helped resolve, offered scientists additional complications. To work as scientists believe it does, super string theory requires the *existence of six or seven dimensions in addition to the four we know about* (height, width, length, and time). Many physicists now believe that our four-dimensional model of the universe is simply too small to describe how our universe works. It's now thought that conceiving of our universe with six or seven more dimensions will bring clarity and simplicity to the picture. Michio Kaku uses this example: Weather, to the ancient Egyptians, was a total mystery. Why did it get warmer as they traveled south? What caused the seasons? Why did the winds usually blow in one direction? The Egyptians couldn't possibly understand the weather from their vantage point, because to them Earth appeared flat, a two-dimensional plane. But imagine the enormous change of perception if the Egyptians one day boarded a rocket and set off on an orbit around Earth. *By going up one dimension,* they could see Earth as a whole, a globe covered with shifting clouds, storms, ever changing as it orbits the sun.[12]

In a similar way for us today, the laws of gravity and light seem impossibly different: They obey different physical laws and different mathematical constructs. No one has ever been able to unite these two major forces of nature under one theoretical roof. But if we add one more dimension—a fifth dimension—then the laws that govern gravity and light fit together like pieces of a jigsaw puzzle. From this higher perspective, light emerges as the warping of the geometry of higher dimensions, just as Einstein showed that gravity (electromagnetism) also warps space-time. In this way, the fifth dimension has simplified the life of many a physicist—even if it's not yet experimentally verifiable.

When we move on to a ten- or eleven-dimensional world, we find it's filled with weird objects called branes. The strings of matter are called one-dimensional branes, while membranes are two-dimensional branes. But at the higher levels, the branes are so small that they can curl and fold into infinitesimally small shapes that we cannot see. Each one, though, represents another dimension of the universe about which we currently know almost nothing.

If Only You Were in the Fifth Dimension:

You'd walk through walls without getting splinters.

You'd float toward a closed window that has bars and you'd just be curious, detached, seeing the black iron start to vibrate, your body vibrating and shimmering, too, and as you reach the window, everything "solid" opens, the tiniest particles separate at just the right time to allow one another to pass, and you're through and intact again.

Instead of walking up three flights of stairs to go to bed, you'd just vanish from your studio and rematerialize in the bedroom.

You'd know exactly how your aunt in Manila redecorated your cousin's room after he died last year, even though you never returned to the Philippines.

You'd be considered a master surgeon, able to pass directly through a patient's skin without making cuts and perform the delicate operation.

Nobody could keep secrets from you, nor you from them. (The consequences of this have not yet been fully considered.)

You'd know where all the treasures on Earth are buried. Bodies, too, most likely.

What sort of being would you have to be to have such God-like powers? A being from the fifth dimension, just one level up from where we now perceive ourselves to be. Although the rest of us here in our 3-D world (plus space-time) would regard your powers as magical, you'd realize that it's just having a more advantageous perspective that makes such a difference. Some extraterrestrials somewhere may already know how to manipulate spacetime, although it's far in advance of anything we on Earth know how to do. But in the realm of hyperspace, all of these things are theoretically possible.[14]

Might these dimensions that scientists say are there but cannot be seen represent the "scenery" behind which our alien visitors come and go? Some physicists speculate that these extra dimensions might indeed account for paranormal phenomena. In this way, they could have a relevance to UFOs. One reason that UFOs seem to appear and disappear in and out of thin air (among the other possibilities explored earlier in this book) might be that they enter and exit our 3-D space by moving in another spatial dimension.[13]

Michael Murphy, in *The Future of the Body,* states that these hyperdimensional models of the universe "have a resonance with esoteric accounts of extraspatial worlds in which our familiar existence is embedded, and from which phantom figures, luminosities, odors of sanctity, and other extrasomic phenomena materialize, and through which highly developed spirit-bodies move. Might our present movement abilities be analogous to those of early amphibians that had not learned to breathe or move freely on land?"[15]

Many Worlds

As early as 1957, the possibility was raised by physicists that during the evolution of the universe, it repeatedly split in half, each split like a fork in the road. If this is correct, the number of universes we might have to take into account are literally infinite. And each universe would be linked to every other at the points of the forks in the road. The "many worlds" theory allows that all possible quantum worlds exist. For example, in some worlds, humans exist as the dominant life-form on Earth. In other worlds, chemical reactions took place that prevented human life from evolving, and on this same planet another very different life-form is the reigning species.[16]

Parallel Universes

Physicist Stephen Hawking's theory of "parallel universes" takes the "many worlds" theory a bit further: He believes that there are an infinite number of self-contained universes and that *wormholes offer the possibility of tunneling between them.* But it's not likely that you'll soon be able to open a door and step into another, parallel universe where your boss never heard of you and your family doesn't know who you are. The connecting wormholes, which are now quite respectable topics of study for science, are thought to be extremely small, about the size of a Planck length—close to a one hundred billion times smaller than a proton.[17] People who hate cramped travel situations might want to opt out of a trip to the neighboring universe until the technical details get worked out and a little more legroom is possible.

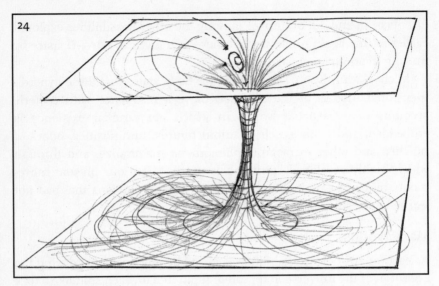

Multiple worlds are not thought to interact on a regular basis. Certain events, however, may cause tubes or wormholes to open up between them. Communication and travel between universes would then be possible.
(Drawing by Budd Hopkins)

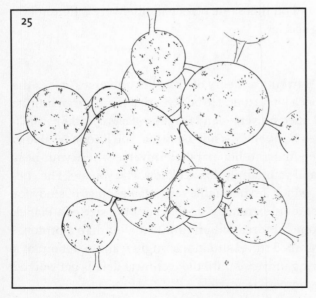

Many physicists currently use quantum theory and experiments to describe the whole of reality as a *multiverse* that contains vast numbers of parallel or multiple universes.
(Drawing by Budd Hopkins)

Wormholes through space could also be prime candidates for explaining how UFOs travel from one universe or solar system to another. Having mastered the difficulties of hyperspace, the UFO occupants (or their higher-intelligence leaders) would use these multiple tunnels constructed by nature to take a shortcut between their world and ours. The old argument "You can't get here from there" would no longer be valid.

Harvard's colorful physicist Sidney Coleman has built upon Hawking's work, constructing mathematical arguments that, if correct, suggest that wormholes through space are essential to all physical processes; they're not just the stuff of fantasy. Wormholes, it seems, rather than being science fiction, are the connecting arteries between worlds. These tubes, or tunnels, are essential to keeping our universe somewhat stable, in the same way that rope and pegs hold a tent in place.

But at this point, on the human level, the issues are mainly theoretical. What we don't know is whether any other intelligent life has found a way to work with the enormous amount of potential energy available in the near vacuum of empty space. As Kaku says: "Any civilization that masters the energy found at the Planck length will become the master of all fundamental forces."[18] They will be the masters of hyperspace.

Nonlocal Connections

Former Apollo astronaut Edgar Mitchell, raised in a Southern Baptist family and later trained in the Western rational, linear mode of thinking at MIT, has spent the last twenty-five years of his life working to integrate the different ways of "knowing" available to the human consciousness. These ways of knowing, unfortunately, are often separated by Western thought into two opposing states: that of religion (all miracles and faith) and that of science (allowing in only what is material, measurable, and testable). Mitchell left NASA in the early 1970's to found the Institute of Noetic Sciences, where he initiated research into areas of study that are neglected by mainstream science. Using scientific methodologies, Mitchell began experimenting with paranormal phenomena such as extrasensory perception, telepathy, and telekinesis. What Mitchell eventually proposed was a new "dyadic" model of reality that found a common ground between science and the spirit.

Making the Earth Larger

English essayist Thomas Browne thought of man as "that great and true Amphibian whose nature is disposed to live, not only like other creatures in diverse elements, but in divided and distinguished worlds.[19] [Browne, *Religio Medici*] In other words, we humans exist on many levels at once, moving through different domains and modes, minute by minute altering our role, electrified in dreams, meditative in everyday thoughts, shot through with emotions and sensory events, even straying at times into interior spaces that seem remote from any recognized human existance.

We might suggest that this is the normal human condition, not the anomalous one—not an existence that has to be sought in a nunnery, a zendo, or total absorption in UFO phenomenology. It is conceivable and desirable, Michael Murphy, the originator of the Esalen Institute, points out, to broaden our horizons in *this* world and open ourselves more and more to the world we now perceive, rather than disengage from it. Perception of new dimensions of the physical world can actually stimulate our evolutionary advance "by revealing new territories for the human race to explore and inhabit."[20]

By a willingness to explore and inhabit these new dimensions of our physical world, we might be able to truly understand the meaning of a being who appears in C. S. Lewis's space trilogy *Perelandra* as a thirty-foot giant, burning white-hot, and says to the astonished protagonist: *"I am not here in the same way you are here."*[21]

Other scientists, most notably physicist David Bohm, have developed a concept of the world and the human brain that was based on holographic principles. Perhaps you have seen the fascinating displays of laser technology that produce three-dimensional images of objects or beings that seem eminently physical. Yet, if you reach out to touch these laser projections, your hand passes right through them. Edgar Mitchell was involved in a great deal of research indicating that the human brain manages information in a similar way: taking triangulated "snapshots" of the image before us and storing them away until we need to recreate them again as realistic, 3-D images.[22]

Mitchell points out that the brain and every cell of the body is a quantum entity, which means they have both local (particle) and nonlocal (wave) properties. The nonlocal information in our experiences are those that continuously resonate and vibrate with the underlying, infinite, and unstructured energy of the universe. At this point of connection, our individual being contributes its own unique information and experience into that larger force, just as a stream trickles into the river and then into the ocean. Quantum theory attempts to deal with the issue of how these particles stay connected and somehow "know" what the others are doing. Some physicists refer to that underlying and connective force as the "zero-point energy field."

But the most useful idea is this: that at extremely subtle levels, the quantum energy given off by every individual carries with it *the information of that person's entire inner experience.* Not only do you carry around in the essence and atoms of your body all the life experiences of your former years, but those energetic particles of your life are also stored in the shared consciousness of the universe. It's a bit like discovering that your own personal information—address, name, phone number—is tucked away in the massive Manhattan telephone directory or in the largest search engine or databank on the Web. You didn't ask to be there, but there you are, accessible and equal to all other conscious beings who know how to tap into the resources of the nonlocal information system.

Further, Mitchell states that it's this mysterious nonlocality that brings new insight to many of the most puzzling and subjective aspects of human consciousness—telepathy, for example. If that is indeed true, perhaps some day none of us will know what it is to live a truly private life—not after the human race masters or reintegrates what are evidently inherent, if unused, abilities within us. Perhaps that's one of the things the aliens are demonstrating on a very small, incremental scale, one abductee at a time: a way of knowing that effortlessly taps into the largest databank available, the centralized energy field of the universe.

Think back to Budd's case of Lisa, a young woman going on a job interview with a man, "Mr. Nelson," who seemed to know far more about her than was humanly possible. Although she had never met this man before, he knew the secret of her sexual abuse as a child; he knew her emotional state when her father left the family; he knew that she had had sex with her boyfriend for the first time the day before in a locked house with the bedroom door shut. Since he later drove her to an encounter with aliens in a landed UFO, he was also evidently aware that Lisa had ongoing abduction experiences.

If the holographic model of the universe and the individual brain operates along the lines of the thinking of Edgar Mitchell, physicist David Bohm, and writer Michael Talbot, among others, it's not mystical or magical at all to conceive of "Mr. Nelson" having access to all of Lisa's personal experiences. According to Mitchell:

> Quantum holography as a carrier of nonlocal information is then available to the individual. Some individuals seem to make this shift of awareness more naturally and easily than others. They are able to consciously perceive nonlocal information, as their brain quells the noise and focuses on the signal.[23]

Lisa even recalled an unusual experience within her own consciousness, almost as if "Mr. Nelson" had accessed or "touched" her retrieved memory in some way. As she got into his car and he began to comment on what he knew of her most secret moments, Lisa said she suddenly felt very *tiny* inside herself, the size of a needle's point. But her body felt huge.

There's a suggestion here of something close to an out-of-body experience, in which the person is there but peering through a narrow lens at her own experience. Edgar Mitchell observes that such an event ". . . would indicate that more of the body/brain is involved in the resonance and one's entire attention more narrowly directed."[24]

Time Travel—If You Dare

Is it physically possible to follow pathways into the past? It's a question that's been much joked about and researched and is still highly controversial. Einstein's equations do allow you the ability to travel into the past, but until recently physicists thought that time travel would lead to the sorts of paradoxes whereby if you traveled into the nineteenth century and accidently killed your great-grandfather, you'd never be born. But the influential physicist David Deutsch argues that quantum effects, not relativity, would be dominant in time travel. In fact, on a quantum level, past-directed connections are continually forming, spontaneously and naturally, with no time machines involved.

But, of course, humans would want to get in on the action too. To them the physicists say: Be patient. If physics continues to develop at the rate it currently is, past-directed time travel is merely "a technological problem that will eventually be solved."[25] However, it's my duty to point out to the intrepid voyager that past-directed time travel requires the manipulation of black holes or wormholes—and some very violent gravitational disruptions of the fabric of time and space. It's a little like locating an airline, then a shuttle, followed by a bus, to take you back to Normal, Illinois, from New York City in the middle of the worst ice storm of the millennium: You might be able to do it, with some grief and frustration, but would you want to?

Future-directed time travel, Deutsch believes, only requires more efficient rockets, and they are on the foreseeable technological horizon. Once we have built a time machine, he says, we can expect visitors (or messages) from the future to emerge from it. But what can they tell us? Not news of our own future. They can't know the future of our universe any more than we'd know theirs. What they could tell us is about the future of their own universe, whose past would be identical to ours. If their culture made several disastrous decisions, they could warn us about them. Maybe we'd follow their advice, maybe not. What we could greatly benefit from, though, is access to knowledge from the creativity of minds in other universes.

To their credit, ufologists of the "positivist" school seem to sense the cornucopia of riches that would spill lavishly from that sort of interstellar cultural exchange. Each new morsel of advance knowledge that we would receive from the "time machine" or time travel will have had an author somewhere in the universe, but it may benefit untold numbers of different universes. If time travel is achieved one day, Deutsch assures us that it shouldn't require any fundamental change in our worldviews—that all the connections it would set up between past and future, the connections we'd begin to see between apparently unrelated events, will not be disturbing and paradoxical to us. They'd all be quite comprehensible. We just don't have the vantage point to see and appreciate those connections yet.[26] But there's that fifth dimension popping up again. Does that mean it isn't going away—that we're actually going to have to deal with this strange idea?

Can the Curtain Come Down Now?

With quantum theory and its various offshoots summarized—or should I say, summarily buzzed over—we begin to sense whether these abstract, mathematically driven arguments explain anything at all about UFOs and aliens and alien abductions. The topics above are, to be sure, still considered somewhat exotic scientific arenas. A decade ago, most self-respecting physicists would not want to be caught attending a conference with such titles as "Wormholes through Space" or "Beyond Hyperdimensionality." However, today physicists who once considered these ideas quite ridiculous are now taking them extremely seriously. The scholarly papers, books, conferences, and simplified *Nova* television versions of the theories are proliferating like mice on fertility drugs.

All of this should be good news to people interested in UFOs. Mainstream science, as represented by some of the most influential quantum physicists today, is finally focused on a model of the universe that just might leave margins for some of the anomalous subjects we believe should be included under the banner of scientific research.

Having unexpectedly discovered that so much fascinating territory was actually on the map of mainstream science, I should have been content to present here the theoretical concepts and go rest on my rooftop garden. Nothing proven, but nothing lost or negated by the findings, either. But the sense of futility is hard to shake. Having slogged through so much cutting-edge research, what outcome was I hoping for? Certainly not this ongoing sense of feeling like the frayed and muddy rope in a tug-of-war between two adversaries—the model of standard science and the inexplicably bizarre personal experiences reported by individuals. How credulous it was to have thought of pulling one truth out of that round of mud-wrestling! It was, in effect, a zero-sum game to play: using one unproven theory (quantum reality) to support another unproven theory (UFO abductions).

The truth looks more like this: The characters and incidents from the previous cases *might* have emerged from almost any one of these theories of quantum reality—perhaps from a higher dimension, some parallel universe, or as a holographic projection. It's also possible that not one of those scientific constructs comes close to explaining the source of what our witnesses saw and experienced.

Chapter 23

ANNE–MARIE AND THE ELUSIVE MR. PAIGE

A S ONE MIGHT GUESS after reading a few of the individual abduction cases I've presented, people who report such experiences belong to a wide range of racial, religious, and ethnic groups, and run the gamut of sexual orientation, socioeconomic class, and level of intellectual and professional accomplishment. They also come in all sizes, shapes, and personality types. One man I worked with, for example, highly successful in a creative profession, appeared not only to have very few friends but seemed even to lack a gift for friendship. Edgy, suspicious, and isolated, he struck me as being as profoundly unhappy an individual as any abductee I ever worked with, and the only reason I mention him is because he represents virtually the polar opposite of "Anne-Marie," a wonderfully warm, appealing abduction-experiencer from a large and supportive Italian-American family.

Unlike the man I just described, Anne-Marie makes friends wherever she goes, enjoys a loving relationship with her parents, brothers, and sisters, and even among casual acquaintances radiates kindness and a gift for sympathetic understanding. For both Carol and me, she has become a close and cherished friend. And though one can sense an undercurrent of the sadness that seems to afflict most abductees, Anne-Marie's sunny demeanor and generosity of spirit dominate her friendships.

Anne-Marie lives alone in a small, beautifully appointed house in the woods on Cape Cod, surrounded by tall pines and flowering shrubs and attended by amazingly tame hummingbirds that frequent her well-stocked bird feeders. Since Anne-Marie's natural altruism extends into other realms of the animal kingdom, she has become active in an organization devoted to rescuing the unfortunate whales and dolphins that sometimes find themselves stranded on Cape Cod beaches. She carries her boots and wet-weather gear in the trunk of her car, ready to help at a moment's notice.

I first met Anne-Marie in 1988 when, after having read *Intruders,* she called me to ask if I could refer her to someone in Paris to help her explore her own abduction recollections. At the time, she was working in England in the film industry, but when she phoned me she was visiting her family on Cape Cod. As I was nearby in my summer studio in Wellfleet, I suggested she drive up so that I could interview her. Our subsequent conversations and hypnotic sessions revealed a life-long series of UFO encounters, and in a recent conversation with her brother "Peter," Carol, and me, she described some of her childhood recollections:

I remember waking up, feeling myself just landing in bed, dropping down and stopping suddenly, with wet, freshly cut grass all over my feet. The bottoms of my pajamas were all wet because I'd been outside. I would come down on the top bunk where I slept, because Peter slept on the bottom bunk.

This was in our big bedroom at Nana's house. We all shared a room. [My sisters] Mary and Ellie had the big bed. I had the top bunk because I was the oldest, and Peter was on the bottom. And I remember flying in through the side window. In fact, I have an extremely vivid memory of seeing that house from a bird's-eye point of view, up above the roof. It was a big house, but I remember always coming in that same window and flying right onto my bed, the top bunk, and then I would throw up because of the motion sickness. I'd feel as if I'd just been going really fast and then all of a sudden slow, and I'd throw up, and then I'd go into our mother and father. I'd wake them up. I'd say, "I just threw up." I remember telling my mother I'd been floating through the air [Laughs] and she would say, "Oh, yeah, right. It must have been a dream." That was her stock answer to everything. But you want to say, and you don't have the words, "No, it wasn't a dream. It was real." As a child you don't have the words to express that it was real, so you just kind of stop telling it after a while, and then you internalize everything because they're not going to believe you anyway.

Carol and I had this conversation with Anne-Marie and her brother, who was about two years younger, in the winter of the year 2000. For Anne-Marie, the most surprising thing about the evening was hearing Peter describe for the first time some of his strange but similar childhood experiences.

"I remember floating around, too," he said, to his sister's astonishment. I asked where he was when he remembered flying.

I was doing it in my bedroom and I was doing it at "Eric Avallar's" house. Vicki's brother. I'm flying around his room. That's right. I remember that, in the bedroom. I can even tell you what it feels like. I think I was watching, *I Dream of Jeanie*. No. *Jeanie* wasn't on yet. But I honestly do remember floating around [Laughs] in our bedroom and also over at Eric Avallar's house, floating around their house. It was a kick. I know what it feels like to be flying around. I'd be way up there too. I'd be almost at the ceiling. But I don't think I was steering or in control.

A little earlier Peter told us about a UFO sighting he had made as a young boy, a dramatic incident that Anne-Marie remembered his describing to her at the time:

We were living in East Bridgewater, and I was about ten years old or so, and I went out one night with my friends . . . to do, you know, whatever kids did at seven o'clock at night. I'm standing near the police station, and remember, the police station was near the high school. They were side-by-side and I was over near the police station, and I saw what looked like a spaceship land behind the high school.

So we ran over from the police station. It probably took us a minute or so to get in back of the high school, and we expected to see it sitting there. We got there, and it's, like, "Where did it go?" It was gone. I mean, it was that fast. Then we ran back to the police station, where we'd just been, and went in. I can remember the desk being right up there, we're looking at the policeman, and he's saying, "Oh yeah? Yeah? Tell you what: Bring me a picture." So the next week we're out there with a little Kodak camera. For a week we were looking for it.

Anne-Marie added her recollection of the incident:

I remember that day, Peter, when you came home, because you know it wasn't really *dark* dark. It was dusk, it wasn't quite dark yet, and I remember you came home, and you were saying, "Oh, my God, oh my God!" You came in, you and Ernie, wasn't it? Yeah. They came running in the house and said, "You're not going to believe what we saw." They were really scared and excited.

Peter resumed his account:

This thing was big and close and had lights around it like the movies. It was real. I actually expected, when I went around the corner, I expected to see something there. I mean, this thing came right down. It was round and it had lights, orange lights and bright lights. It was probably about three hundred yards away or so.

The other boy, I think it was Ernie, I haven't seen him in years and I have it in the back of my mind when I see him I'm going to ask, "Do you remember?"

Anne-Marie confirmed his recollection. "It was Ernie. I remember I thought, *Wow, he went to the police and told the police. That means he really saw it.*"

Peter continued:

I was out there the next week with the camera, so I obviously didn't dream it. I can see it right now, in my mind. It came down and it was moving slow. I wasn't scared. I was a ten-year-old kid, you know, and when you're that young, you're ignorant and you don't fear a whole lot.

Though Peter described a few more highly suggestive encounters that might reward further exploration, he is not interested in doing so at the present time. This is, of course, a judgment in which I concur. If an individual's life is going well—if he or she is relatively happy and successful, and has few sleep problems or episodes of anxiety—then it is best to leave well enough alone. To explore and thus possibly to uncover a history of traumatic UFO abduction experiences is to unnecessarily disturb calm waters.

Anne-Marie, however, had a different attitude toward her own partially recollected UFO abductions. Between 1988 and the present, I helped her look into a number of such incidents. In two encounters, separated by several months, she experienced periods of missing time, each of which was followed by her discovery of a fine, scalpellike cut at the center of the very top of her scalp. Photographs of these wounds exactly match photos of scalpellike cuts in other abduction cases, with the wound located at the very top of the head in precisely the same place. In several of Anne-Marie's abductions she was with friends who experienced the same puzzling periods of missing time and the sense of "coming to" in an area a mile or so from the location of their last conscious memory.

But it is not this collection of Anne-Marie's UFO experiences that are to be discussed in the following pages, fascinating though they may be. Almost from the beginning of our friendship, my interest was caught by her description of a very strange man who lived in the same house with Anne-Marie's family and who became the abiding focus of my interest. His name was Mr. Paige, and this is his story.

At the age of three, Anne-Marie, her parents, and her baby brother Peter were living in a capacious three-story frame house in eastern Massachusetts. They shared the house with Anne-Marie's grandparents, who owned the building. And then one day—out of the blue, one might say—Mr. Paige arrived. He was to stay with them for almost a decade.

Mr. Paige's odd physical appearance has been described by various members of the family. Peter recalls:

When I first remember him I was five years old—four, five, six years old. Mr. Paige seemed to be at least ninety! [Laughs] Now I would say early fifties maybe, maybe forties. But you know, here I am, five, six years old. Maybe he could only have been in his thirties, but he appeared to be a lot older. However old he was, he was definitely a very gentle man. I kind of compare the way he looked to the face in the movie *The Wizard of Oz* when they go in to visit the wizard and there's that big head with the flames and the smoke: "I am the wizard." He kind of looked like that. His head was rather large, [his] forehead rather large and kind of veiny. You'd see the veins in his forehead. Very pale-looking, he always wore white painter's pants and a white T-shirt, right? Like Mr. Clean, he was always in white.

His hair was gray and white. Yeah, that's why I think he was older. He was very thin, a very, very thin guy. His arms were really skinny. His height? I would guess he was probably around five-eleven maybe, something like that. Maybe six feet, yeah. But he was probably only 145 pounds, 150 pounds. Really thin.

I asked Anne-Marie and Peter if today, at their present ages, they were to see Mr. Paige for the first time, would they think he was an odd-looking person. Peter answered first:

Yes, I would. In fact, when we moved to Cape Cod, I was a teenager and I saw Mr. Paige on his bicycle two, maybe three times on the Cape. I was out with my friends and we were hanging out at a gas station where one of the guys worked when he went by. I was too embarrassed to say that I knew the guy because he looked odd, you know? I saw him drive by on his bicycle but I didn't say, "Hey, I know that guy." I didn't say anything. I felt embarrassed that I knew this guy because he was so odd-looking.

A moment later Anne-Marie also answered my question:

If I were to see him now, I'd think he was odd-looking, too. Just the way his head went up: It was like he had a long chin. He had a prominent forehead and a very long chin. He had really bushy eyebrows, too, I remember that. And when he smiled, his whole face lit up because of his eyes. And when he spoke, he didn't have any kind of accent. He didn't seem to have any family or any friends, and he owned almost nothing. It was like he was an island. When I was little I asked him several times where he came from, and he answered by pointing his finger straight up to the sky and saying, "From up north."

During a later interview, which included "Nicolle," Anne-Marie's mother, Nicolle said, "Mr. Paige never seemed to age. His skin and hair color was "always gray, grayish-white, as if he'd once been a blonde. If anything, he would have seemed like a Norwegian or a Swede or something like that. That's the feeling I get. He certainly wasn't Italian," she laughed.

In addition to his appearance, it was Mr. Paige's mysterious behavior that drew attention. He arrived at Anne-Marie's grandparents house looking for work. He was hired as a handyman and given a place of his choosing in their large, twenty-two-room house, but to everyone's surprise he chose quarters in the basement, next to the furnace. Unlike the upstairs rooms he had been offered, which were near bathrooms, he picked a room with no running water.

But there are many other oddities. He simply walked into the yard one day with no references, no identification—in fact, with no visible connections with the outside world. He had no driver's license, no credit cards, no apparent family. For the next eight years he lived with Anne-Marie's family, disappearing at irregular intervals for months at a time. With no prior warning he would simply walk away, carrying a small satchel, after refusing a lift to the local bus or train station. He never said where he was going or why, and gave no information when he returned. He received no mail or phone calls and lived an extremely simple, almost hermetic existence down in his basement quarters, which were directly under Anne-Marie's first-floor bedroom.

And Anne-Marie adored him. From the beginning her mother allowed Mr. Paige to take her little three-and-a-half-year-old daughter off for hours for a "nature walk" down to a beloved cow pasture nearby. What occurred there on these nearly daily outings, what made them so magical, Anne-Marie to this day cannot remember. She recalls that Mr. Paige would put her on his shoulders and carry her as she clasped her hands around his neck and over his prominent Adam's apple. Nicolle now wonders why she was so trusting toward a man about whom she knew absolutely nothing, but she thought of him at the time as being completely honest and trustworthy around her little daughter: "He seemed almost like a monk."

Anne-Marie recalls Mr. Paige's basement quarters.

> The thing I remember most about him is, he lived down in the cellar. I don't think he had running water down there. It was a large cellar. My grandmother had a room where she made her lye soap, another room she had for canning, and he lived near the furnace, where it was warm. I have great memories, believe me. I lived in this house since I was very little and I have great memories of this house and Mr. Paige too. The town where we lived was sleepy. But there were cow pastures, barns, and a real town, a thriving little downtown area.

In our earlier interview, Peter had added his recollections:

> What I remember most about Mr. Paige is going down in his little room down there in the cellar and eating soft-boiled eggs. He used to boil them up . . . he had a little hot plate or something and he used to boil up soft-boiled eggs. He was such a gentle guy. Friendly. It was fun to go see Mr. Paige. He made it so special when he brought you down there.
>
> Another thing that I remember is, he used to serve water with his soft-boiled eggs or hard-boiled eggs, and you'd usually get two eggs. They had some salt and pepper on them and he used to serve water with them, which he poured because he had no running water downstairs and so he used to have milk bottles of water. And he would pour the water in a certain way. We'd be sitting around a little table or something and he'd hold the bottle of water about two feet from the glass and he'd say, "Okay, now, when you pour the water, make sure when you hold it up here so the air can get to the water and aerate the water and purify it." And that's how he used to pour his water. "Now, make sure when you do that . . ." Every time you'd have a glass of water with him, he always said, "Now make sure . . ."

Anne-Marie remembered the same ritual. Carol asked if during these visits there was sometimes a group of children down there. "No,"

Anne-Marie answered. "Outside he played with groups of us neighbor-hood kids, but down there in his room usually it was one-on-one."

I asked if she knew where Mr. Paige went to use the bathroom.

"Where did he go?" she puzzled, trying to remember. "Did he go up to the second story? I'm not sure where he would go. I don't know, I don't know. I don't remember running into him upstairs at the john. I don't ever remember, no. There was an outhouse on the property, behind the barn.

"And that outhouse," she added with a laugh, "was our clubhouse."

I was curious to know how, under the circumstances, Mr. Paige bathed. Earlier both Anne-Marie and Peter had said that he always seemed extremely clean, and that neither ever recollected running into him in an upstairs hall with a towel under his arm.

"The only thing I remember him doing was taking turpentine to wash the paint off his hands," she recalled.

That's the only thing I ever remember him doing as far as cleaning. But you know what, Peter? There was a sink in Nana's soap room. There was a sink in there. I think it was only cold water. I think it was like a soapstone sink, wasn't it? He could have gotten washed down there, now that I think of it.

It's strange: The day he came, my grandmother gave him a tour of the whole house, and then he asked to see the cellar. I remember there was a perplexing kind of thing going on, like *Why the heck does he want to see the cellar?* And then he goes down there and picks out the room and it's under my bedroom. That room was exactly under my bedroom. And he lived there from '56 to '71 or so. Almost fifteen years. We moved from there in '64, so I was eight years with him.

So far in our account of Mr. Paige he could easily—perhaps not *easily* but at least plausibly—be seen as an elderly eccentric with a Pied Piper-like effect on children. As Anne-Marie said, "He was such a gentle per-son that none of us ever made fun of him." But there were other aspects of his behavior that add real mystery to the situation.

There is, for example, the matter of his writing. During his long absences he occasionally wrote to Anne-Marie's grandmother, his actual employer, and yet his letters made no real sense. Anne-Marie's mother Nicolle described his letters this way:

> You couldn't make out the writing. The sentence never started and ended. It was very strange, because it isn't like the way he spoke. He never said where he was in the letters, and he wrote very rarely, to let my mother know he'd be coming "one of these days."
>
> My mother would hand it to me and say, "Can you make sense of this letter?" And I'd read it and I'd say no. He never told anybody where he was going or when he was going. All of a sudden, he'd be gone. And he never told anyone when he was coming back. He'd just arrive suddenly. We missed him when he went away because he was like a Mr. Fix-it. He'd know how to fix everything. My mother put him to work because he was living there downstairs for free. He would be fixing toasters. . . . He'd always be fixing something.

Carol returned the subject to Mr. Paige's letters. "I'm interested in what that communication was. We all get letters from people whose handwriting is illegible. I write many of them myself," she joked.

Nicolle pointed out:

> It wasn't that the handwriting was illegible; it was just that the words were all thrown together. And he didn't speak that way. He spoke quite well, like an educated person. His letters were never written the way he spoke, and my mother would always show them to me because she thought there was something wrong with her: "Can you make sense of this letter?"

I thought for a moment that it was as if Mr. Paige had learned, as a child, how to speak but had never been taught how to construct rational sentences on a page. He was like an expatriate who has acquired oral competency in a foreign language but has no mastery of the structure and syntax of the written language.

But then Anne-Marie brought up a surprising fact completely new to her mother: Mr. Paige had written a book and had had it published, presumably at his own expense.

"I didn't know anything about a book," Nicolle said, astonished. "How did he ever have anything really published?"

"Well,' Anne-Marie replied,

The Cape View Press or someone like that did it. I don't know where the books are that he gave me. I think they might be at your house in the bookcase. You can see them but you're not going to make much sense out of them. I have two of them and they make absolutely no sense at all. It's like some kind of stream-of-consciousness writing—just a bunch of mumbo jumbo.

He must have paid to have them printed. I'm sure it was like one of those little local vanity presses. . . . It was in Hyannis and they don't exist anymore. I remember the title of one of the books was *The Long True Promised Life from the West*.

What Mr. Paige gave me was . . . they looked to me like rough galleys or something, just pasting, cutting and pasting, like getting something ready for press. But a very . . . I don't know, just a very unprofessional kind of job. I guess this was his thing, that he was going to publish these books and get his word out because he had an opinion on everything, from marriage—and here is somebody that we never thought had anyone else in his life, if he ever did, but he had his own ideas on marriage as well as on what to eat and what not to eat and how this causes that. All of this was in the book, in the headings he had. I just think, you know, he was a little weird. At the time there with him, if you said something that he didn't agree with, he'd go, "Ha, ha, ha," and leave. [Laughs] He'd never argue with you. He'd go "Huff" and leave. He wanted everybody just to be happy. But those books of his didn't tell you much.

Nicolle again expressed her amazement: "How could anybody carry on a perfectly clear conversation with you sometimes and then write the way he did?"

Anne-Marie replied with her own theory about Mr. Paige's strange style:

I think some of it was what he thought was channeled writing. I remember how he sometimes spoke. It was weird, like a kind of stream-of-consciousness, like he was channeling and writing down everything he heard. I talked enough with him to know that you could have a normal conversation. He could put sentences together. They made sense—I mean, grammatically they made sense when he talked—but some of the stuff that he believed in I didn't, and so we didn't argue about it. He believed in what he wanted and I believed in what I wanted.

But Anne-Marie had another, more significant recollection about Mr. Paige:

When I was eleven through about sixteen, when we had moved and he was still living at my grandmother's, he would write to me and sometimes I got three letters a week from him. That was when I was living in East Bridgewater. I didn't understand them, but in a way I did. Well, I did and I didn't. I could understand part of them, I could sometimes get the gist, but then . . .

When he was living there or about to leave on one of his long trips and I would be very sad, he would tell me to send him my thoughts and feelings and he would know. And I did send him my thoughts. I would tell him in my mind about something that happened in school, for instance, and he would write to me and say he understood what had happened to me in school, as if he really *had* received my thoughts. It was the strangest thing.

All of his letters would be typed. He had this old typewriter. He would type something and then leave a space. I told you about this. He would leave a space, a gap in the sentence, and he would write in all these symbols instead.

The symbols that he drew in his letters to Anne-Marie are an aspect of the Mr. Paige saga I had been interested in from the moment she first mentioned them to me, and for a very important reason: Over the decades, various abductees I've worked with recalled having seen remarkably similar sets of symbols during abduction experiences. Sometimes they were on the walls of the ship, occasionally on the edge of the examination table, and often on flat, booklike or tabletlike surfaces. I have no idea what these symbols mean—one can speculate that they are an alien notational system of some kind—but they are so similar as to fall outside the realm of coincidence or chance. I have never published these symbols because, so long as they remain unknown to the public at large, they offer an excellent way to validate the testimony of people who recall abduction experiences.

These "alien" symbols are not often reported by abduction experiencers. Among the hundreds of abductees I have worked with, perhaps only one in twenty—like Anne-Marie—recalls having seen examples of a possible notational system, but those who do recall them describe extraordinarily similar images. It is difficult to know whether or not the presence of such symbols is as rare as eyewitness testimony suggests, because there are several factors that might limit an abductee's observational powers.

First, of course, is the issue of fear. A paralyzed man or woman lying on a table and undergoing a possibly painful, quasimedical procedure is not always an objective, wide-ranging viewer of his immediate surroundings, and thus a row of symbols some distance away might be easily overlooked. Then there is a second issue, mundane in the extreme, that I have encountered many times. Nearsighted people, abducted at night with neither eyeglasses nor contact lenses in place, often say they can only see clearly what is close to them. Conversely, for farsighted abductees, a closeup view of a page of symbols would likewise be a blur. And yet a third limiting factor has to do with the fact that investigators often neglect to ask abductees if they recall having seen anything resembling writing or a notational system during their abductions.

If these are generalizations about the basic issue of an alien notational system, Mr. Paige's involvment in the issue is both very specific and extremely suggestive. Though none of his letters survive—a mystery I will soon address—after a hypnotic session Anne-Marie said the symbols he included in his letters were very similar to those she recalled seeing during a UFO abduction experience. Thus Mr. Paige apparently noted down many of the specific alien symbols with which I am familiar, placing them into preplanned gaps in his typewritten letters to the very young Anne-Marie, *as if he assumed she would know what they meant.* But why would he assume such a thing, and how did he know about these symbols in the first place?

From a very early age Anne-Marie recalled his mentioning "flying saucers." They were real, he told her, but she was not to be afraid of them. If Mr. Paige were only a mystically inclined eccentric, his embrace of flying saucers would hardly be surprising or unusual. But because he was familiar to some extent with the appearance of an alien notational system and communicated these symbols to Anne-Marie—who, we recall, was experiencing her own UFO abductions—we can infer that Mr. Paige might himself be an abductee. Either that, or that he had some kind of ongoing special connection with the UFO phenomenon. If the latter is true, many things about his strange behavior fall into place. Anne-Marie's description of him as being like an island in our extraordinarily interdependent normal world makes perfect sense. Despite how odd it sounds to say so, one can at least hypothesize that Mr. Paige belonged to neither world completely—neither to our familiar, quotidian existence nor to the enigmatic alien world of telepathy, paralysis, UFOs, and human abductions. This complex view of Mr. Paige is one that Anne-Marie has gradually come to hold.

My friend and colleague Stanton Friedman has long employed a useful expression—"my 'gray basket,' " to describe those reports of UFO sightings, abduction accounts, propulsion systems, whatever, that at present do not belong to any distinct, repeated pattern. But if the source of such an anomalous anomaly seems credible, Stan does not automatically reject it but instead drops it, metaphorically, into his "gray basket" for later consideration. Mr. Paige, it is safe to say, virtually dwells in my "gray basket."

But there are still more strands to this mysterious fabric.

Central to Anne-Marie's connection to Mr. Paige were the "nature walks" that he took her on, from the time she was a three-and-a-half-year-old child. They led through the woods to the cow pasture that she ever after remembered as magical. She describes it this way:

> When he took me for the nature walks, he would tell me the Latin names for flowers and weeds that we passed: "That is a blah, blah, blah weed or flower." He'd say, "Now repeat after me," and I'd repeat it. It didn't mean anything to me. I can't recall any of them now. Sometimes, when I've looked at the Latin names of flowers, some sound familiar to me, but I didn't memorize any of them. It's not like he said there's going to be a test next week. [Laughs] I

remember one time he gave me a little lecture about praying mantises, which I had been afraid of, but he told me how they eat the bad bugs and do good for the environment, and he actually made me feel comfortable around them.

Years later, when I was seventeen and living on the Cape, Aaron White, my old boyfriend, and I went back to visit because I wanted him to meet Mr. Paige. We stayed overnight at Nana's, where he was still living. I said, "Mr. Paige, I want you to take us down to the cow pasture. I want you to show me the pasture and I want Aaron to see it." So we go down there and I said, "Now, I want Aaron to take a picture of the two of us." Mr Paige says, "No, no, no. I don't want my picture taken," and this went on for a few minutes. Finally, I said, "Mr. Paige, this means a lot to me. I don't have a picture of you." So finally he relented but he didn't like it and you could tell in the photograph that he was feeling uncomfortable and awkward. It was me in this black and white wool coat and we had our arms around each other and he was looking straight at the camera and I was so happy when that picture came out because I finally had a picture. But I had to beg him. That was the only picture of him I ever had and it disappeared with a box of my things in Paris. Someone must have broken into my apartment and stolen only my photo album and my file of old important letters and papers, including the letters he had sent me. Nothing in the file or album [was] really valuable, but it broke my heart to lose that picture.

I asked Anne-Marie why, when she was seventeen, she wanted to show her boyfriend the cow pasture. She replied:

I don't know. It was almost like I wanted, as a young adult, I wanted someone else as an adult to see the cow pasture with me because it held this magical feeling for me in my head, and I wanted to know, was it really there? I wanted to go back. Is it really there? Is it like I remembered it? When I was little, it was when we got in the woods near the cow pasture that it was the best. There were mushrooms. I remember there was a tree there, there was a shady tree in the middle of the cow pasture. It was a beautiful space, with woods all around the place—all around it except for one row which went by one side of it, I think, with an electric fence or some kind of fence. But it was a dirt road we're talking about, a path through the woods, that we would take. And there was a big rock that was there in the field. It wasn't flat. It was just sort of a big . . . no, no, it was huge. It was like something left over from a glacier.

The whole place felt magical. I remember we would go and see the skunk cabbage that was in the woods. I remember there was a very marshy wet place. . . . There was a pretty little brook that ran through there. Maybe that's why they have the cows there, because they could drink from this brook. But there was definitely some marshy stuff back there, because I remember getting wet and I remember the skunk cabbage. There was a lot of skunk cabbage, and that only exists in marshy areas. Skunk cabbage smells like skunk.

However magical the cow pasture seemed to Anne-Marie, she could not remember what she and Mr. Paige did when they got there, though sometimes they were gone for most of the afternoon. To me, it seemed that her walk *down to the pasture* was not only the most exciting part of the adventure, it was, oddly, the only part that she recalled with any clarity.

Around the time Anne-Marie and I first met, she told me about a disturbing incident in the pasture involving herself and another little girl, her friend "Myra." It was an experience that cast an unpleasant shadow over her memories of that enchanted place, and its most baffling aspect is her uncharacteristic attitude that day toward her friend. In fact, all of her life Anne-Marie has suffered from guilt feelings about her behavior, which she regards as completely unlike her and inexplicable in its tinge of brutality.

I have known Anne-Marie for nearly fifteen years and I regard her as one of the kindest people I have ever met. In light of the love and consideration she instinctively bestows upon family, friends, and even casual acquaintances, her behavior toward Myra in this simple childood incident strikes me as incomprehensible.

She describes what happened:

I decided one day I was going to take Myra to the cow pasture and show her around. She had never been down there before. We were both about nine years old at the time. So we get down to the cow pasture and then all of a sudden I suggest that we play hide-and-seek. I planned it. I told her she was "it" and she had to count by the big rock. I ran off and hid, and I watched her from behind a tree where she couldn't see me. I watched her for a long time, searching for me and calling me. I watched her finally freak out and start crying. She was so frightened. She didn't know where she was or how to get home. She was lost and I had abandoned her.

When she was really upset and crying and afraid, I came out and she was so furious at me. She said, "I'm going to tell my mother on you." She was really upset and we went home together. Sally, her mother, was visiting with Mom. They were in the kitchen and Myra comes running in, "Mom, Mom," and she told them what I did and I got punished for it. I got sent to my room or put in the corner or something.

But I had such a sense of shame and also bafflement. I thought, *Why did I do that to my friend who I love? Why did I torture and victimize her like that?* I couldn't understand it. It was always a mystery to me but something that always stayed in my mind as an act of cruelty I did as a child, but I couldn't understand why I did it. Why did I do that? And I felt so guilty.

We became friends again, thank God. I apologized and everything, and we became friends again, but I never forgot it. It was always something, like a major incident from my childhood that I didn't understand.

I set up the whole thing. I took her there and suggested the game. I never, never played hide-and-seek with just one other person. It was no fun with just one. We used to play hide-and-seek with the whole neighborhood. Playing hide-and-seek with one is like playing tag with just one person. That's another reason this whole thing seems so strange.

Carol asked Anne-Marie now how she explains what she did. Anne-Marie said,

I've spoken to Budd at length about this, and I know some strange things happened down there in the pasture with Mr. Paige. UFO-related things. I just have a feeling about it, and I think what I was doing with her was, I was reenacting what I felt when I was left alone or I was lost down there, and I just needed to reenact it with somebody else. Like I was playing a trick. It was not like me, because I was the kind of kid who, if there was a kid being picked on in the neighborhood, I would be standing up for the kid, like little "Rosemary Dennison."

But then, I also told Budd about another incident. There were two incidents where I was the instigator of something a little cruel. The other one, I think Peter was part of it. In the field behind Nana's house. . . . Up high on the hill with apple trees. There was tall grass around the trees. I remember we all formed a circle around little "Rosemary Dennison" and she was the victim, and we were all poking at her and teasing her. She was crying. Kids didn't do things like that in our neighborhood. We didn't have that kind of neighborhood. Kids got along. But I orchestrated this too! I remember being in a circle of kids—Peter, probably Mary, Ellie, and those kids next door, Bobby and Willie. But also I remember two other kids too—the kids who had the little playhouse in the backyard next to us, across the street. Their house was between us and the Dennisons. Well, they were part of this thing, and we were all around Rosemary. The "Dennisons" were the poor kids of the neighborhood, and I remember we were poking her and she was just sitting there. She was too afraid to move, I think. We were all around her. It was just weird. And then finally she started to cry, and then right away it was like, "Okay, let's stop this." But it was as if we were seeing how far we could go.

I was the oldest of the kids and she was the youngest, and we were seeing how far we could go, you know, before she broke. It wasn't really pain-inflicting. We were just kind of poking her and making fun of her. Nothing terribly physical.

I asked if this poking had a sexual component.

No, no, no, nothing like that. No, it was just sort of poking her and saying whatever, "You're dirty," or "You smell," or something like that, because they were a dirty, poor family that lived in our neighborhood. But I used to go over to their house all the time and clean their house and do anything I could for them, you know. I remember Mrs. Dennison would say. "All right, Anne-Marie, enough is enough. You really don't have to clean our house." But I wanted to help them. I'd bring them cookies. I felt bad for this family.

It wasn't like I was a mean kid, because I felt for them because they were poor and I wanted to help them. I remember giving my doll clothes to the daughter. I mean, I'd give just anything I could give that was my own, which isn't a lot when you're eight or nine years old.

I asked Anne-Marie if her generosity to the family came after the incident with Rosemary. "No," she replied,

This went on all during the years. So, during this time, this incident with Rosemary happened, and why would I have done it? That was another thing I couldn't figure out, because why would I do something like this to a little girl who I was trying to help otherwise? And that was a big guilt thing for me. Those two things stand out more than anything from my childhood, and they were both about victimizing somebody else who was helpless. I was the ringleader. I saw it as being my thing, and that at some point I could call it off, and when I called it off, it was stopped.

Now I think that since I'd been poked and prodded when I was being taken—abducted—that that was what this was about. I was probably reenacting something, to try and get it out.

I reminded Anne-Marie that it is a basic tenet of psychological theory that if someone was abused as a child, sexually, verbally, or physically, that person as an adult will tend to abuse his or her children too. She replied that, "of course, in my family, no victimization happened. So it's not like I was acting out because of something that happened at home. And I had Mr. Paige as my guardian angel. He was very protective of me."

I explained to Anne-Marie how I felt when she first told me about these two abusive childhood incidents. "The thing that struck me is how strange they seemed to *you*, your own behavior being so out of character at the time. I always pay attention when somebody says, 'This is weird for *me* to have done.' And when something that in a way is actually as minor as these incidents is recalled with guilt years, decades later . . ."

"I'll never forget it," she said. "I was very ashamed of myself."

Only once, in 1988, did I try to conduct a hypnotic regression session on Anne-Marie's trips to the cow pasture with Mr. Paige. The results were both emotionally moving and ambiguous—and worth describing. I set the scene, with Anne-Marie as a little girl riding on Mr. Paige's shoulders. She vividly relived the sense of being high up on his back— he was, as I remembered, nearly six feet tall—and being carried down the path that led to the magical pasture. She described her arms around his neck and the feel of his prominent Adam's apple against her steady- ing hands. He was perspiring slightly as he walked, but he continued telling her about the plants and flowers they were passing by.

And then there was a pause in her account—a long pause. She began to cry softly and spoke no more. After a few minutes I asked if she wanted to end the session, and she nodded. I counted from five down to one, my usual way to end the relaxed trance state, and she opened her eyes.

Anne-Marie lay on the couch and wiped away her tears. She said that Mr. Paige's presence had seemed so real that many memories flooded back. It was unmistakable to me that on some very profound level she adored him, whatever his role in her life had been—or, per- haps I should say, whatever *roles* he had played in her life. Because she later said something to me that indicated she did not really want to find out exactly what happened down in that pasture during all the many times Mr. Paige took her there.

She was certain that he never physically harmed her, nor abused her sexually or in any other way: That much seems clear. But I am left with other, equally disturbing scenarios in my mind. Did Mr. Paige regularly deliver her, a young and helpless abductee, to the occupants of a landed UFO? Did he abandon her in the cow pasture, frightened and alone, in the same way that she later took little Myra down to the pasture and abandoned her, inflicting her own terror on another little girl?

Who was Mr. Paige? Why did he exist as an "island," as a man of total mystery, apparently lacking a home, a family, a past, or even the simplest ability to connect rational sentences together on the written page? Why did he maintain the strictest secrecy about his life, with-holding every single detail, even from those like Anne-Marie whom he apparently loved? When he left so abruptly on his long trips, declining even a free ride to a bus station, where did he go?

Anne-Marie's mother, Nicolle, once hypothesized that perhaps somewhere else there was another family like her own that took care of him during these times, paying him as a handyman and allowing him to live in *their* basement. Obviously she could only see Mr. Paige in a mirror image of their own situation, because to imagine him leading a normal life elsewhere, with a family, a job, and a home, was impossi-ble. "I can't imagine he could ever hold down a regular job," she told me. "He was too weird. No one would ever hire him."

Anne-Marie tells of the last time she saw Mr. Paige. It was 1970. She was living on Cape Cod with her parents and siblings. Two years before, Mr. Paige had also moved to the Cape, apparently to be closer to Anne-Marie. Her parents provided him a place to live in part of a duplex apartment they owned, much as Anne-Marie's grandmother had let him stay in the basement of her large house in Attleboro. In the past, each time he had gone away on one of his mysterious trips, he had told Anne-Marie the day before that he was leaving. Worried, she would look into his eyes and ask if she would see him again. He always returned her gaze and said that he would be coming back; she would see him again. But this time, when seventeen-year-old Anne-Marie asked if he was coming back, she saw that he lowered his eyes and murmured an unconvincing yes. She knew she would never see him again. And she didn't, nor did any member of her family, nor did any-one ever receive a letter from him. He disappeared from their family life as mysteriously as he had entered it years before.

As one listens, bewildered, to Anne-Marie's account, one can only speculate helplessly about the nature of Mr. Paige's view of himself, of his role in the world, and, above all, the source of his allegiances. After spending so much of my life investigating the extraordinary complexity of the UFO phenomenon, I no longer see it as schematically as I did twenty-five years ago. The UFO phenomenon is not a simple "us"-and-"them" situation in which distant aliens in spaceships drop down to Earth from time to time to abduct and study our citizens, taking the biological samples they need to accomplish their as yet not fully understood program of genetic manipulation. Case after case leads me to the idea that there are already transgenic beings, sharing human and alien characteristics, living and functioning among us. And it is not inconceivable that some of these beings may not be fully aware of their own complex genetic makeup, and thus do not so much represent an ominous fifth column of infiltrators as they do an emotionally ill-equipped, confused, externally directed group of quasiservants wending their way through daily life, understanding little and deprived of a great deal.

Who in this sad story do we feel more sympathy for—Anne-Marie and her close-knit family, or the awkward, uncommunicative, strange-looking Mr. Paige, even if he might often have been the agent who dutifully—and duplicitously—carried Anne-Marie to her waiting abductors?

Chapter 24

THE LUCKIEST LITTLE ABDUCTEE

WHEN BUDD AND I WENT to interview Anne-Marie on Cape Cod in February 2000, she took us for a drive one evening along Airport Road near her present home. Used mainly by local people, the road was a narrow blacktop that wound its way eventually into a wooded area. There were no streetlights or houses along this stretch of road. As we rounded a bend half hidden by scrub oak trees, Anne-Marie pulled over and stopped the car, leaving the headlights on.

"Right up there," Anne-Marie said, pointing. "You couldn't miss it. I just remember a *whoosh,* and it stopped on a dime right over the woods. It was hovering so low over the road, about treetop level. My heart was pounding. I don't know what was going through my mind."

With Anne-Marie showing us how the hovering craft extended beyond the road slightly, Budd approximated its size to be about thirty-five feet across. This event, as I mentioned briefly in an earlier chapter, happened to Anne-Marie in 1973, when she was nineteen and driving alone at night. It was her first conscious memory of sighting a UFO, and she remembers little about what happened after the initial shock. But in 1988, when she'd first begun to explore her experiences with Budd, he regressed her back to that moment and that stretch of road. Under hypnosis, Anne-Marie recalled being taken inside the craft, which had landed in the woods, and made to undergo what seem to us now to be rather standard medical procedures. Standard for aliens, that is.

It was on this same night that the UFO occupants handed Anne-

Marie a thick tablet that was covered with symbols. She remembers bracing to accept its weight, but was surprised to find it light as a feather. As her eyes scanned the odd symbols, Anne-Marie knew she'd seen them many times before, during her childhood and, we assume, during earlier abductions. Although she believed that the beings had once taught her to recognize individual symbols, she'd never before seen them this way, put together as a seemingly integrated text. Then for a few seconds Anne-Marie could read and understand what the tablet said. Horrified and shocked by what she'd read, she raised her head to stare at the aliens, and when she looked down again her ability to read the text was gone. She cried out: "This is so terrible! You have to tell us about this. . . ." In the small vehicle the beings were quite close to Anne-Marie, and she's not certain how they communicated that her sudden loss of memory was all right, but her sense of what they "said" was: *You've seen and you'll remember when the time is right.* She also sensed that the aliens wanted her to know she'd be called on to play a role in whatever cataclysmic event that would unfold in the future. To this day Anne-Marie has no idea what the symbols or the text meant.

As Budd mentioned, after the session Anne-Marie drew an approximate version of some individual symbols she was shown. They have a distinctive appearance that first brings to mind Egyptian hieroglyphics or Chinese iconography. Yet, the symbols don't fit either of those categories, nor, as far as we know, do they resemble any other known written human language. I've gone through Budd's collection myself and have seen how closely Anne-Marie's drawings compare with remembered alien notations drawn for Budd by other experiencers—people abducted in other decades, other countries, and under completely different conditions from Anne-Marie's.

For me, these symbols constitute some of the most noteworthy clues of this case. Having never been made public, they're the touchstone of credibility that links Anne-Marie with other abductees' experiences and observations while on board the craft, and they also are among the small but significant details that link Mr. Paige to Anne-Marie's UFO experiences. In his rambling typewritten letters to the girl during his long absences, Mr. Paige left blank spaces in which he handwrote *symbols that he believed she would understand*—symbols virtually identical to the ones she recalled being taught by the aliens. In this arena their lives overlapped and their knowledge was secret and shared only by the two of them, he seemed to think. Unfortunately for Mr. Paige, it was as if he'd underestimated the memory-blocking specificity of the aliens. Seeing the symbols, Anne-Marie knew she *should* know or *had* known them but didn't know what Mr. Paige was trying to say exactly.

The Significance of Anne-Marie's Case

There was something profoundly moving and ambiguous to me about the fifteen-year involvement of the enigmatic, gentle Mr. Paige with Anne-Marie's family—first on a Massachusetts farm and later on Cape Cod, that narrow isthmus of land curling out into the Atlantic Ocean. In particular it was this monklike, unworldly man's benevolent influence over young Anne-Marie—as well as, paradoxically, his probable role in her abduction experiences—that struck me as entirely new material to attempt to understand in the context of this phenomenon.

There was a deep affection and bond that lasted for years between Anne-Marie and Mr. Paige, the oddball handyman with the huge forehead and long, pointed chin who showed up in her life as her mentor, teacher, protector, and surrogate father when she was three and a half years old. Whether told from Anne-Marie's highly subjective point-of-view, or from her brother Peter's somewhat less subjective recall, or from her mother's fairly objective viewpoint, the account of their long relationship holds within its telling a mutuality that is unique in both its commitment and its high paranormal quotient. Anne-Marie and Mr. Paige had one of the most rewarding relationships that we currently know of and deal with in these pages between a human being and what we might infer is a transgenic or "normal" being with alien characteristics.

Is this a large speculative leap about Mr. Paige? Perhaps. But let's take a look at the aspects of his and Anne-Marie's overlapping lives in terms of what we would ordinarily refer to as "normal" exchanges.

Telepathy

Apparently, Mr. Paige had some form of telepathic resonance with Anne-Marie, even when he was away on one of his trips. Before leaving, he told her to think of him, essentially sending him her thoughts, and he would know them. Anne-Marie can recall at least one instance of a schoolroom situation that made her very unhappy. When he returned from the trip, he mentioned the incident, and on several occasions he seemed to know events that had happened to her while he was away. But whether this is the sort of informed guesswork that some fortune-tellers use or whether he actually did pick up some specifics of Anne-Marie's distress is unclear, since the letters no longer exist.

What we do have to acknowledge is that among certain scientists—the group at Princeton Engineering Anomalies Research, Hal Puthoff, Edgar Mitchell, Fred Alan Wolf, and Nobel prizewinner Kary Mullis, among others—the subject of the paranormal is not at all off limits. The possible connection between the paranormal and UFOs eventually also fascinated Dr. Allen Hynek, an astronomer and former Air Force consultant hired to debunk UFO sightings, who eventually came to take the phenomenon quite seriously. In a 1978 lecture at a Mutual UFO Network conference, Hynek suggested the possibility that somewhere in the universe existed a supercivilization that had discovered how to utilize

> ESP, psychokinesis, teleportation, *mental telepathy* [emphasis added] as part of their everyday technology as we incorporate transistors and computers in ours. . . . UFOs could well be the product of such a technology. To such a technology, the idea of building nuts and bolts spacecraft and blasting them off from some space Cape Canaveral would seem archaic and childlike. Perhaps all they have to do to get someplace is to think themselves there, projecting a thought form, or a force field[,] to any part of space they want and causing it to manifest there, on that plane.[1]

Speaking of everyday technologies: Mr. Paige also might have been able to continue supervising Anne-Marie from a remote location if she had been outfitted with one of the "implants" or chips that we discussed in earlier chapters. With little effort Mr. Paige would have been able to track his protégée, monitor her emotional peaks and valleys, log her physiological data, such as her fertility cycle, perhaps even watch her from any distance—on planet or off. The Veri-Chip (or some future cousin thereof) would keep right on ticking.

Floating

Both Anne-Marie and Peter have childhood memories of "floating"—
not your ordinary childhood anecdote. Anne-Marie's experiences were
always associated with either being taken out through a wall or window
or returned downward through space, inside a craft, very quickly, and
then quite suddenly slowing down in order to reenter her room and
drop onto the top bunk, where she promptly became sick. Either emotional stress or motion sickness would be equally valid reasons for her
vomiting. If the craft was putting out a certain level of radiation at the
time, that could also account for the nausea. What is harder to account
for on a logical basis is the fact that most of Anne-Marie's memories of
her childhood home and ground are *from a bird's-eye point of view*. She
literally recalls her grandparents' sprawling house and farm from an
aerial perspective. In memory she sees the roofs, the overall layout of
the house and outbuildings, the woods and pastures—as if she'd been
floating above it all.

Science can now achieve a sort of levitation or "floating"—although
they prefer to call it "diamagnetism." This recent discovery takes
abductees' floating reports out of the magical realm. In experiments a
frog in a small container had a large magnetic force placed above it.
The magnet caused all of the atoms inside the frog's millions of cells to
alter their motion to repel the exterior force. The frog's disturbed elec-
trons had created their own magnetic field to repel the magnet seeking
to pull it upward, while at the same time the weak force of gravity
pushes it downward.

At that point, the frog has reached a type of stasis as the forces
equalize out.[2] Mr. Frog might just as well *enjoy*; after all, he's floating
freely in a diamagnetic field that his own body has helped to create. We
believe a similar process could be what floats small children and sizable adults out windows and, with some tweaking of magnetic and
gravitational forces, lifts them gently into a craft that is also, possibly,
hovering in keeping with the same principles.

Or perhaps the frog would agree with a child who once wrote in a
science exam that gravity was the principle of "no fair jumping up
without coming back down." As far as we know, frogs—and
abductees—*do* come back down.

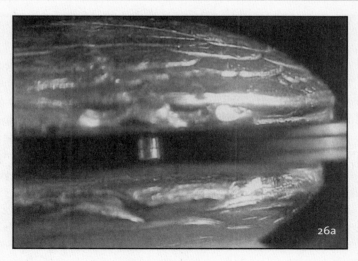

Electromagnetic levitation has been used for years in various industrial and transportation systems. To work, these systems need a source of energy at all times or the levitation will end. Physicists predicted that stable levitation of a magnet was impossible. Today's science, however, achieves *real* levitation that can last forever and has no energy input. This is possible through the use of certain materials that are surprising in their diamagneticism, meaning that when they are exposed to a magnetic field, they induce a weak magnetic field, or force, in the opposite direction. Diamagnetic materials include water, carbon graphite, and bismuth—even human fingers, frogs, and fruit. In the photo above, a cube magnet is suspended between two carbon blocks. Pictured below is another small magnet floating between two carbon blocks. In both cases, material not considered to be magnetic conductors are providing permanent, stable levitation. (Photos courtesy of Forcefield at www.wondermagnet.com)

"I Thought Everybody Floated"

Many abductees' reports include the seemingly impossible feat of "floating." Molly, for instance, remembers that she and her brother floated out their window into the bright beam above. Anne-Marie's brother Peter, a businessman on Cape Cod who is now in his late thirties, also recalls floating as a child. But he remembers only the exciting novelty of floating near his bedroom ceiling. Unfortunately, Budd suspects that might be the prelude to an as yet unexplored abduction.

Another case that Budd and I investigated involved a television anchorman-turned-entertainer, "Spencer," a genuinely funny but extremely phobic man in his late-thirties. On a Friday night in September 1984, Spencer and his wife experienced an abduction in the Adirondacks as they were driving back from a Borscht-belt comedy gig at a major hotel there. The sightings that night were numerous, and the following day, contrary to its usual policy of ignoring such reports, *The New York Times* featured a major "Metro" section story about the upstate sightings by multiple witnesses.

In a preinterview before hypnosis, Spencer told us something he'd never told anyone else. When he was a little boy, he said, his family lived in a large three-story house. It was his peculiar habit at certain times to run down one flight of stairs, then race across a hallway toward another flight of stairs that led to the lower floor. On the landing of that stairwell, he recalls, an extremely bright light would be shining through the windows. "I'd hit the landing," Spencer said, "and I swear to you that I'd float up *over* that landing. Sometimes I thought I'd hit the ceiling. But then somehow I'd end up down at the bottom of the stairs without ever having walked down them. At a certain point in my life it happened a lot. I didn't make anything out of it. I just thought I was at, you know, *the floating stage*." As we were all laughing Spencer threw up his hands: "I didn't know. I was a kid. I thought *everybody* floated!"

Origin

As a child just meeting Mr. Paige, Anne-Marie saw the world through the eyes of a small girl in the embrace of a large family. To her, everybody in the family and neighborhood, the plants and animals, all seemed connected with one another and with her. But Mr. Paige, Anne-Marie recalls, "seemed like an island." Only a child who felt fully encompassed and nurtured by human relationships would be likely to consider him in quite that way. Mr. Paige seemed to have no past and no connections he would discuss. When she asked where he came from, Mr. Paige simply pointed up toward the sky and said: "From up north."

From what we can tell, he wasn't simply making a humorous remark about his origins. Evidently, Mr. Paige believed he did come from the ambiguously stated "up north"—but whether that referred to Toronto or outer space, we don't know. Anne-Marie and her mother are certain that Mr. Paige could not be accounted for by any of the usual means: no driver's license, no Social Security number, no bank account, no incoming mail. If we are to attempt to explain this man by speculating he was in hiding from the law or his past—certainly a possibility—it would be hard to reconcile that idea with both his scrupulous honesty and his commitment to Anne-Marie. In fact, one of the amusing stories about Mr. Paige is that when he worked for Anne-Marie's grandfather, who was an occasional auctioneer, he could be counted on to hold up a less-than-stellar used implement or tool and quite candidly demonstrate the object's flaw to the audience. The story goes that Grandpa was neither impressed with nor amused by such honesty. But Mr. Paige stayed on and repeated his rigorously honest performance on the very next occasion.

The Teacher-Mentor Role

If Mr. Paige was indeed a "normal," or transgenic alien-human, he evidenced qualities of personal commitment to Anne-Marie and an empathy with human emotions that far surpasses those of any other possibly transgenic beings whom we present in these pages. For instance, when he and Anne-Marie's grandfather spent an afternoon killing rats in the barn, Mr. Paige was adamant that Anne-Marie not be witness to the butchery. He taught her the Latin names of the flowers they passed on their trips through the woods to the cow pasture; he taught her "health-food consciousness" long before most of the nation caught wind of the idea; and regaled her with his ideas about all aspects of life, including a more sensible form of currency and the conditions of a proper marriage, as well as the need to aerate one's drinking water.

Preemptive Strikes against Phobias

When Anne-Marie was still quite small, she recalls, Mr. Paige directly raised the issue of flying saucers with her—again, an unusual subject of conversation with a child in the early 1960's. He assured her that UFOs were real but there was no reason to be afraid of them. In a similar fashion he taught Anne-Marie not to be afraid of the praying mantises, a big-eyed green insect they often came across in the field near her house. Years later, UFO investigators compared notes and found that many abductees had a phobic fear of the praying mantis. In numerous cases abductees have reported that enormous mantises (along with "reptilian" aliens) are among the stranger forms of intelligent alien life aboard a spacecraft. In retrospect, Mr. Paige's behavior might be seen as a preemptive strike, an inoculation to prevent the most common and often crippling phobias that his abductee-protégée might develop.

But at that point in UFO and cultural history, the 1960's, how would this handyman be aware of common abductee fears that would not have surfaced in a major way in public arenas like books, films, and TV until the late 1980's? Obviously he would if he himself was an abductee, as Budd has suggested is a possibility, or if he was somehow working in conjunction with the UFO occupants and given the task of calming this human child's inevitable fears. Perhaps the aliens—or some more enlightened group of aliens—had learned by then what human primatologists who study the great apes have learned: that the more the subject's stress and fears can be allayed, the truer will be the results of the tests given to the subject and therefore the more valid the experiment's conclusions.[3]

"Mother"

One of the more bizarre—if not downright comic—incidents of alien attempts to ingratiate themselves with an abductee was told to Budd by Karla Turner, a writer, abduction researcher, and abductee. In one of her first conscious memories, she was outside alone in the middle of the night. She was five years old and looking up at a six-to-seven-foot-tall praying mantis towering over her. When she cried out that she wanted her mother, the creature said to the child: "I *am* your mother."

Very few children, I suspect would find that a comforting remark to hear. We have to speculate what is happening in instances like these: Perhaps the aliens are testing the human limits of tolerance at seeing them in their actual, physical form. Or perhaps the mantis was a screen memory, an image generated in the child's mind to soften an even more disconcerting sight. Another possibility that increasingly strikes me as credible is that *the alien beings may have no set form at all*. If they are, instead, holographic or thought projections from either another dimension or another planet, they could literally take material form of any kind, any species, even as discrete beings that we don't recognize as living beings and therefore might not even see.

If you knew Anne-Marie, you'd see how effectively Mr. Paige must have planned his strategies to keep her whole, no matter what her experiences aboard UFOs would eventually entail. If you knew the arrested, fearful, not-fully-realized quality of the majority of abductees that pass through our front door or e-mail or write or call, you'd also see why it is that Anne-Marie is truly one of the luckiest little abductees.

She had a Mr. Paige to help, someone who, even on a subconscious level, she *knew* understood her experiences—just as he knew she would recognize the alien symbols in the letters he sent her. Even if parts of the abduction experiences were traumatic, Anne-Marie had an ally during fifteen of her most vulnerable years. Other child abductees at that same period in their own lives generally have no one who believes their experiences are anything but fantasy or bad dreams.

When the beings arrive and the children cry out, there is no rescue by Mom or Dad: They're quite likely to be "switched off" and ignorant of their child's abduction in the next room. It's easy to see how an abducted child without an ally would tend to develop deep feelings of distrust and abandonment that follow her around the rest of her life and manifest in all her relationships.

Incomprehensible Letters from Mr. Paige

One of the most puzzling issues to Anne-Marie, her mother, Nicolle, and the grandmother, Mr. Paige's employer, was the enormous contrast between the handyman's verbal abilities and his written communications. The three members of Anne-Marie's family whom Budd and I most recently interviewed—Anne-Marie, her mother, and her brother Peter—unanimously agreed that Mr. Paige

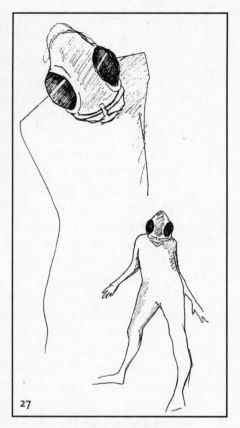

27

An abductee's drawing
of a grasshopper-like being she
encountered during a UFO experience.
(From Budd Hopkins's archive)

spoke quite well, "like an educated person." There was no trace of a regional accent. Yet, the letters he'd occasionally send during his long absences were nearly incomprehensible. Anne-Marie's grandmother would hand them off to Nicolle, not being able to make heads or tails out of his run-on sentences and garbled thoughts. Nicolle couldn't understand them, either, except for a sense that he was returning sometime soon. As for Anne-Marie, who was still receiving letters from Mr. Paige as she grew into her teens, she could only partially comprehend their meaning—and those were the sentences he'd typed in English! The interspersed handwritten symbols in the letters she vaguely recognized but still could not recall their meaning. Several years ago Anne-Marie also loaned Budd a manuscript that Mr. Paige had published at his own expense, and Budd found it no more explicable than anyone else had.

There are several things we might infer from this drastic difference between Mr. Paige's verbal and written skills:

- **An organic problem.** A language disorder called agraphia describes a person's *acquired inability* to write understandable prose and is usually due to a brain lesion. In other words, the affected person once knew how to write coherently, but the brain disorder eliminated that function. Verbal skills may remain intact.

- **A breakdown in the normal process of human acquisition of language skills.** According to linguistic experts: "The acquisition of the ability to read and write is quite different from learning to speak and understand speech. Normally, a considerable amount of explicit instruction is needed [in learning to write], and the more skilled and erudite writers have usually gone through many years of rather intense training. Thus, the acquisition of written language belongs to the so-called *secondary socialization,* in which school and other cultural institutions play a very important instrumental part."[4]

  Since educational opportunities everywhere are uneven and unequal, spoken language is the one thing that's everyone's property. Even illiterate people speak and carry on their lives quite effectively. And because verbal expression is inherently dynamic and interactive, one-on-one, it's more likely to be fluid, changing according to the speaker's feedback from his or her listener.

  But, worldwide, written language belongs to relatively few people. It's associated with often abstract and specialized knowledge that's quite separate from "the world of direct experience." In that workaday world, any inherently intelligent but not formally educated person has a better opportunity to "pass" in social and educational situations in which he'll be judged mainly by the repeated practice of and feedback about his verbal language ability.[5]

Given these facts, what is it about the gap between Mr. Paige's oral and verbal skills that might shed light on his background, his place of origin? \

A bright man from humble origins. It's possible that Mr. Paige was simply an eccentric but intelligent man who came from poor means, had no formal education, and therefore had no way to hone his writing skills, which would have been used mainly in private arenas or business transactions. As a loner, perhaps with no family he wanted anyone to know about, it's conceivable that a person like Mr. Paige might have learned to speak well from reading and listening to others, as well as getting the subtle kinds of feedback that we all get when we make a social or lingual gaffe—in person and in the immediate moment. That instant feedback is one of society's most powerful tools for developing behavior (and spoken language) that conforms to the norm.

The main problem with this possibility is that a person from a lower socioeconomic background without the intervention of formal education usually has his region, his ethnicity, and his upbringing stamped all over his verbal expression. You'd expect a strong regional accent, nonstandard grammar, and less constraint in terms of the rules and conventions followed by people with a higher level of education. But Mr. Paige had none of those markers in his speech.

A transgenic human with ties to the aliens. Keeping in mind Mr. Paige's other idiosyncrasies, let's consider the idea of a transgenic ("hybrid") human with alien genes—or a genome manipulated by aliens—growing up literally *off-planet*. Where that would be, and how all these alleged transgenic offspring seen aboard ships are raised are questions beyond our scope right now. Let's assume that Mr. Paige, along with others like him—passable as humans but answerable to other beings—was raised in the company of aliens. Astronomer Seth Shostek and science historian Steven J. Dick, who philosophize about such matters, invariably attribute a much larger than human neural capacity to even theoretical aliens—more computational brain power, with a likely ability to download enormous amounts of data into their brains (such as all the linguistic rules of every known human language). So the alien creators of Mr. Paige would easily be able to teach him, a modified human, an oral language by downloading data, as well as by any of these additional means: (1) programmed recordings of human verbal exchanges; (2) watching or listening to human radio and/or TV signals from Earth (which, of course, has been the astronomy program Search for Extra-Terrestrial Intelligence's (SETI) major premise of the way that extraterrestrial life would locate us; (3) being put into a human society at certain points in development to "pass" among us. During that trial period, the transgenic being or, as Budd calls him, the "normal" would interact and learn language skills as most humans do, by speaking, getting feedback, and further refining the skill.

But if a person's written language proficiency *does* grow out of prolonged "secondary socialization," such as school and other cultural institutions, as experts indicate, it's not likely that Mr. Paige was a beneficiary of such socialization—nor did his observed social skills, as Anne-Marie and her family would attest, seem to indicate that experience. If transgenic beings like Mr. Paige or Stewart or the "interviewers" are gradually eased into our society after periodic practice sessions with humans, they might well have not lived in our world for the prolonged period it takes to develop such skills as writing—not to mention the finessing of a sexual proposition, something quite different from "Mr. Nelson's" ham-handed attempt to get intimate with Terry. In that incident, "Mr. Nelson's" social abilities rank him at about the twelve-year-old male human stage.

Here's another thought about why Mr. Paige, as the partly human, partly alien-modified being, wouldn't be able to write coherently: If he was raised with beings whose primary source of communication, as witness reports indicate, was *telepathic*—in both long-distance (remote) and up-close transactions—he would have had little need to write. Scant practice, little feedback, not even Christmas thank-you notes to send. Eons ago, a civilization of telepaths would have dropped the heavy reliance on the reams of paperwork that encumber our own lives.

Alien Ombudsman—Or Betrayer?

It is certainly possible, with all of the elements of Anne-Marie's story considered together, to understand Mr. Paige as the mentor and helper that he seemed to be to Anne-Marie and her siblings. But we also can't forget Anne-Marie's own strong sense that Mr. Paige's repeated trips with her to the cow pasture were somehow related to UFO experiences. If you recall, Anne-Marie clearly remembers riding on Mr. Paige's shoulders, feeling his Adam's apple and his moist skin, and repeating the names of the flowers after him as they went down the path. But Budd's attempt to regress Anne-Marie to one of those seemingly idyllic field trips ended right at the point where the man and child came to the opening, the meadow encircled by trees with the giant rock in the middle. She began to cry and wouldn't say another word. After the session ended, Budd had the clear sense that Anne-Marie didn't really want to know any more about what had happened there.

Why? Would Anne-Marie betray Mr. Paige if she acknowledged, even to herself, that the man she trusted was ultimately delivering her to the occupants of a landed UFO waiting for them in the cow pasture? Or was it Mr. Paige, the guide and mentor of this bright and sensitive child, who was the real betrayer? I suspect that the truth was far more complex and subtle than these either-ors. It's simply easier for us to identify with the child's feelings than with Mr. Paige's. And as for the partly human, partly alien-concocted being, if that's what he was, we can only speculate about the obligatory but possibly agonizing limbo in which he now found himself.

Torturing Myra

What did happen to Anne-Marie in the pasture? There's no sign that sexual abuse occurred with Mr. Paige—although it can't be completely ruled out. But we can discover something about the child's emotional state from the incidents that an eight-year-old Anne-Marie herself initiated at about the same time as the Mr. Paige visits to the pasture, which Budd detailed earlier. The incident Anne-Marie still sees as deeply shameful, unnatural to her own character, was deliberately staged by her: running away from the small friend unfamilar to the woods and pasture and watching as the child grew increasingly afraid and wept, frantic to be taken home.

In recent years a body of research has been presented about the "acting out" behavior that invariably accompanies a child's or adolescent's post-traumatic stress disorder (PTSD). The acting out, which might consist of antisocial or cruel acts, violence, self-harm, and hostile behavior, are considered to be PTSD symptoms of a traumatic event that the child can't process. According to Dr. M. J. Horowitz in a 1986 study, the person "is likely to continue to re-enact the original trauma until it is therapeutically worked through . . . The act may serve to medicate the emotional pain of the original trauma. . . ."[6] Anne-Marie's torturing of Myra suggests that she was reenacting a distinct traumatic event that had happened to her in that isolated yet lovely place. And it doesn't suggest sexual abuse, but something closer to abandonment in the face of fear.

The Shadow Side of the Story

Anytime we're given a life story of a loving person who lives a rich and varied life—one full of deep attachments to family members and friends, a life filled with accomplishments, all obstacles overcome—we would be right to suspect that that life sounds too good to be completely real. Even in biographies that are relatively sunny (a rarity, unfortunately), you can count on finding a deep pool of shadows that have gathered protectively around some alcove in that person's life. Perhaps, for some, the profound loss or sadness in that one area can be encapsulated, withheld from spreading any further. Those individuals are the lucky ones, the ones given the gift of acceptance rather than bitterness.

The partial chronicling of Anne-Marie's life, in which we selected the aspects that we believe relate to the UFO abduction phenomenon, has mainly been a sunny account of a "lucky little abductee." Now comes the hard part: the shadow of loss in Anne-Marie's life that appears to be directly related to the repeated UFO abductions throughout her youth.

Anne-Marie is a warmly maternal woman—a quality that's sensed by both men and women, not to mention all of the children in her life. She spent years as a preschool teacher, nurturing other people's children and developing strong attachments to her sisters' and brother's children. Several years ago, when a younger sister, mother to two small boys whom Anne-Marie adored, moved out of state with her family, Anne-Marie was shaken to her roots. She mourned the loss of those boys as if they'd been her own. It was as if what she once told Budd, in tears, had actually come true.

In her twenties, Anne-Marie had been married for several years. During that marriage, Anne-Marie once told Budd, she'd considered having children of her own, but something held her back. Then, breaking down, Anne-Marie told Budd that she was afraid to have a baby. Gently, seeing her profound grief, he probed a bit deeper: Was it the responsibility? The concern over "not doing it right"? What was the basis of her fear?

Anne-Marie took a moment to compose herself. Then the pent-up anxiety spilled out in very specific terms: "I'm afraid to have a baby because I know it will be taken away from me," she said.

As it turns out, there is some possibility that her worst fears had actually happened, over and over again.

What the Surgeon Found

From her first menstrual cycle on, Anne-Marie experienced an extraordinary flow, closer to hemorrhaging than to normal menses. When she was in her late thirties, her gynecological problems became severe. An ultrasound indicated large fibroids in her uterus. Fibroids are generally benign and involve smooth muscle tumors of the uterus. They're also often associated with endometriosis—abnormal tissue growth and unusual bleeding.[7] With her biological clock ticking away, no acceptable partner in sight, and her hesitation about having any children at all, Anne-Marie decided on a complete hysterectomy. The operation would be the end of a dream—but also the end of a nightmare. She was able to accept both sides of the equation.

Her mother Nicolle waited outside the surgical unit while the operation was performed. After some time had passed, the surgeon emerged, looking for the patient's mother. Nicolle said he seemed stunned, unable to explain what he'd found. What he said was: "What on earth happened to your daughter? It's a mess in there. I've never seen ovaries and tubes with so much scar tissue."

The surgeon also confirmed what he had already suspected: the presence of large fibroids on Anne-Marie's uterine walls. But there's nothing paranormal about fibroids: They're quite common in women of both childbearing age and older. Fibroids could also be responsible for extraordinary bleeding. But Anne-Marie's medical records further state: "The right ovary was scarred down to the posterior broad ligament with fairly thick adhesions."[8] The records also refer to "multiple scarring" of tissues adjoining the uterus, and considerable "adhesive tissue." As we know from our own surface cuts and wounds, the body's natural reaction is to cover a raw area with scar tissue, also called adhesions. The surgeon likely attributed such severe scarring to past pelvic infections of which Anne-Marie may have been unaware. However, if we put Anne-Marie's lifetime history of abduction experiences together with what we do know is an unusual aspect of her gynecological history—the ovarian and fallopian tubal scarring—it suggests that we might look to current science for further possibilities.

As we'll see in more detail later, women in in vitro fertility clinics often undergo laparoscopy in order to retrieve their eggs. In this procedure, a long hollow needle is inserted through the woman's abdomen until it reaches the ova, the nearly ripe eggs in one of her ovaries. The instrument penetrates the ovary and sucks up the eggs, which can then be fertilized later in a laboratory setting. Similarly, if abductees are called upon to be involuntary egg donors over and over, as they seem to be, it's reasonable to assume that over a certain amount of time these procedures would result in scarring and/or adhesions on the surface of the ovaries. Referring to surgery on a blocked fallopian tube, Dr. Russell A. Foulk at the Nevada Center for Reproductive Medicine, confirms that post-operative adhesions— either scarring or an inappropriate fusing together of tissues—occur after even microsurgery or laparoscopy.[9]

Let's further speculate as to what might be happening to an abductees' fallopian tubes. As the long muscular canals leading from the ovaries down into the uterus, the fallopian tubes receive the woman's ripe eggs from the ovaries. Hopefully, at just the same time, sperm have entered the woman's vagina and are starting a valiant swim up through the uterus and into the fallopian tubes from the opposite direction. It's a movie moment: An especially dashing sperm meets up with a lovely egg inside one of the fallopian tubes and the deed is done—fertilization and the beginning of new life. In a normal pregnancy, the fertilized ovum continues its passage into the uterine cavity, where it implants itself in the uterine wall and begins to develop into an embryo. But in cases of ectopic (or tubal) pregnancy, the fertilized ovum remains inside the fallopian tube and begins dividing and growing into a preembryo. Since this is a dangerous situation for the mother, surgical intervention is called for: a process called salpingotomy, in which the tube is incised, or cut, with pinpoint scissors or a laser. Then "the ectopic gestation is gently expressed through the incision" and the tiny ball of preembryonic cells is sucked out by an aspirator.[10] It's at this point that trauma to the tube may happen: When the aspirator is introduced into the incision on the tube, the tissue sometimes tears.

Back to Anne-Marie and the alien agenda: In the fallopian tube, immediately after the egg is fertilized and before it has implanted itself in the uterus—even before the mother knows she's pregnant—might be an ideal moment for ET's intervention: to abduct the woman (whose hormonal cycle is easily monitored) and suck the newly fertilized ovum from the fallopian tube. The abductee might be left with some internal scarring, and the aliens would have the makings of a malleable, preembryonic cell mass, ready for genetic manipulation. A nearly invisible theft.

There's one other case that bears mentioning in this context—that of "Phyllis," a middle-aged woman in New Hampshire, who gave birth to only one daughter, now in her late twenties. In the mid-1980's, Budd had worked with Phyllis over a three-year period, gradually uncovering at least two decades of repeated abductions. Troubled by conscious recollections common to experiencers, under hypnotic regression Phyllis would also recall certain vaginal procedures, but their purpose remained vague to her. She didn't know whether something was being inserted or removed. Budd was unable to get her to take a more specific look at the procedures she was undergoing. And so much of Phyllis's abduction experiences remained in Budd's "gray basket," where all interesting but unclear phenomena end up.

But recently, when gynecological problems similar to Anne-Marie's caused Phyllis to also undergo a complete hysterectomy—in a different state, in a different hospital, with a different medical team—her surgeon's reaction to what he found was nearly as blunt and uncomprehending as in Anne-Marie's case. Without quite using the phrase "It's a mess in there," he was startled enough to show Phyllis the pictures of her uterine lining. As she told us: "The walls of my uterus were scarified up one side and down the other—and in folds of the lining where you'd never expect to see scarring. The doctor said, and he wasn't joking, 'It looks like you've had forty or fifty pregnancies.' "

Dr. Richard M. Neal Jr., who has explored the elusive issue of the "missing embryo/fetus syndrome," states that he has not been able to find medical evidence to confirm that any pregnancies are taken during abductions. However, Dr. Neal goes on to say that if a real pregnancy *were* removed from a woman's uterus, it would leave obvious marks, since such a procedure would require "intervention/invasion."[11]

Any Conclusions?

At this point we certainly can't draw any definite conclusions about who or what Mr. Paige was. There are the anecdotal and tangential clues that he might well have belonged to a subpopulation of "normals"—an emotionally and ethically more humanized "model," if you will. But for a new breed in a new world and a new atmosphere, perhaps yearly departures from human society would be necessary. Perhaps it would be the fragility of this subgroups' genetic makeup, or perhaps the intensely stressful internal conflicts of acting as drones for the aliens, delivering up their human contacts. But whatever the reason, a more advanced "normal" like Mr. Paige might have to return on a yearly basis to the environment of his birth for purposes of maintenance, debriefing, or downloading what he's learned from his stay on Earth—a debriefing for the benefit of whoever is directing this play, this universal drama in which human beings seem to play a largely unwitting and passive role.

If Mr. Paige was one of the best bioengineered human-aliens that had been developed, it would be logical to clone him. By now there may be thousands of Mr. Paiges strategically planted around the world as human helpers, acting as mentors for young abductees. Bonding with their wards, the odd "normals" could be put in charge of acclimating human youths to repeated abductions and genetic tinkering. In the process, both the child and the transgene would build a trusting and mutually caring relationship.

If so, we're in a more ambiguous position than most people will be comfortable sustaining for long. In Anne-Marie and Mr. Paige's case, their fifteen-year friendship led to a strong emotional attachment that she feels is largely benevolent. That's in spite of the fact that she refused to go forward with hypnosis and find out what actually happened in that meadow. All things considered, though, it might make a great deal of sense to not risk losing the benefits of those close emotional ties with someone for whom Anne-Marie was "the special one." Contemporary sociology and psychology are replete with examples of the benefits to young professional women of having a male mentor—an older male, more experienced in the field—who can help the younger woman hold her self-esteem intact and navigate the larger world from which he comes. In Anne-Marie's case, we'd have to say she was protégée to a benefactor of quite extraordinary capabilities and insights. What young woman would willingly give those up by having to disclose, even to herself, the ambiguous and shadowy side of that cherished relationship?

What Mr. Paige came away with is another issue completely. It's impossible not to feel empathy for a creature, like Frankenstein's monster, who might have been made for someone else's purpose, yet developed with many of the seemingly independent, idiosyncratic sensibilities and ties and loyalties that we humans like to think are exclusive to us. If Mr. Paige was created to value those things, as humans do, while still maintaining an allegiance to alien beings, then where is his own home, his own world, his people, his mate? Where is his own integrity of choice?

Chapter 25

DAMOE AND THE UNMARKED HELICOPTERS

IN EARLY JANUARY 1986, while working on my book *Intruders*, I received a remarkable letter from a Wisconsin man whom I shall call "Will." Will wrote that he had just watched me on a TV program discussing UFO abductions, and certain things I had said so closely paralleled several of his own experiences that he felt compelled to write to me. Because of the highly detailed and dramatic content of his letter, I telephoned him at his home, a small farm in a sparsely populated rural part of the state, and began an investigation.

Will recalled pieces of many different UFO encounters, some of which included periods of missing time as well as conscious recollections of alien beings, landed spacecraft, and physical examinations inside these craft. In some instances these memories had floated into his conscious mind years after the event, but in others they had been present from the moment of the experience. In answer to my request, Will, an unskilled and reluctant typist, sat down before a small tape recorder and spoke about his recollections at length.

A few months later, in the spring of 1986, I was able to travel to Will's modest white clapboard farmhouse, where I met his family and conducted extensive interviews and several hypnotic sessions. The investigation ultimately revealed one of the most powerful, compelling, and, in its own way, tragic abduction cases I had yet confronted.

Significantly, Will's account includes several meetings with a strange man of normal appearance who later seemed to mediate between Will and the UFO occupants. It is also important that this young man, whom Will called by the name Damoe, very closely resembled one of his own sons.

Damoe had first approached Will while he was toiling in one of his fields, and they had had a normal, somewhat philosophical conversation. Will had no idea where this young man lived, but assumed he must be staying at one of the neighboring farms. Damoe appeared on a number of other occasions, and each time he joined the older man, he seemed to "just wander up out of nowhere," as Will put it, with no sign of a car or any other means of transportation. Will was clearly drawn to him and was fascinated both by his unusual intelligence and the striking resemblance to his own son.

Also, as Will explained, there was the odd business of his wristwatch. Shortly after he met Damoe, he discovered that his watch was missing—something that seemed highly unusual, since he only took it off his wrist when he slept and bathed. A week or so later, as he was working alone in one of his fields, Damoe suddenly appeared again and handed him his watch, which he claimed to have found in a nearby field. The instrument seemed to be clean and in perfect working order, and though Will was puzzled by the circumstances of its disappearance and reappearance, he was grateful to Damoe for having found it.

This matter of the watch may not be connected in any way with Will's ongoing abduction experiences, but it is part of a curious pattern that I have noticed with several abductees. In these cases, personal, cherished objects—a wedding ring, a favorite bracelet, a particular article of clothing—seem to vanish and then reappear under highly unusual circumstances. For example, while washing her hands one night, "Kathie," the central figure in *Intruders,* placed her wedding ring on the rim of the washstand, but when she reached for it to put it back on her finger, it had vanished. Knowing that the ring was too wide to have slipped down the drain, she began searching for it on her hands and knees, but it seemed to have disappeared. Several days later, while vacuuming an upstairs bedroom, she noticed a small bulge under the thin, tacked-down carpet. Since the bulge, which felt ringlike in shape, was close to one of the bedroom walls, she was able to pull up the tacks and, miraculously, found her ring. There was no sign of the carpet's having been tampered with, so the problem of the ring's reappearance remains a mystery. Other abductees have reported similarly "impossible" lost-and-found stories, and though nothing can be established with any degree of assurance, the pattern is intriguing enough to deserve mention.

In the long tape recording that Will sent me, he included an experience that had always bothered him because it not only involved a period of missing time but seemed to have a profound—ultimately critical—effect on his wife, "Melissa." In a slow, careful, unmistakably sad voice, he related his story:

I have a date in my mind for an incident that took place—1974—but I don't think that's right. I don't think it was in 1974; it was more like 1968 or 1969. I could be more accurate if I checked some records, but I don't think it's real important. So instead I'm maybe going to just continue along and look at this 1968 or 1969 thing, which I have never talked about before, and I'm very hesitant to talk about right now. And I don't believe I would, except for that which happened to my wife, which is very real. That's recorded, so we'll go back to I believe the month of August of 1968 or 1969. And as we talk I may say 1974, because that date's strongly in my mind, but I don't believe it's correct.

At this time we were milking a herd of cattle and our farming was stretched out. We had property south of us six miles and we also had some six or seven miles north of us. On this particular day we were going to finish up some haying. And I took my wife and went to the north hay field. The equipment was there; we just simply drove the pickup over there. The day was dry and we had low humidity. There had been some hay previously raked. Not a whole lot, perhaps two hundred or two hundred and fifty pounds. So we proceed to bale this small amount of hay and we made a stack. I would now rake and roll some more hay which had been cut previously. As we finished baling this hay, ah, I suggested to my wife to take a short break, and I would rake the hay. At this time in her life she was a very cheerful person, very commonsense, very down-to-earth. Very conservative—conservative family-wise, that is—and we had enough money. And so when I said, "Take a break," she took the canvas with her and slid it across some hay bales that was laying on the ground.

Now, baling hay is very dusty, it's very dirty; you get filled with chaff, and it's very uncomfortable. You get very itchy and sweaty. And we were in a very remote area, the closest house was, oh, perhaps more than a mile away. And so she removed her work clothes, leaving nothing on except for her panties, and she stretched out on the canvas.

I now continued on to rake the hay, which was in sort of a second meadow. Between the point where she was and I was was a long stretch of woods laying in a piece of lowland. As I was raking I heard a sound, and glanc[ed] toward the area where Melissa was, and she really wasn't that far away from me—I would think a maximum of a thousand feet—but there was a small stretch of woods between us. I glanced in that direction and I noticed a helicopter. We have a National Guard base, "Fort Longley," which is between "Mason Creek" and "Morgan," and so I had seen helicopters before. It's not unusual. This helicopter I glanced at several times because I did not see the normal markings. Then two more helicopters appeared. They gathered together and they hovered over the exact area where Melissa, my wife, was. They then settled down to the field, probably 350 feet [from] where she lay. I saw again that the two other helicopters had no markings on them, but when they settled in the field I got a little upset. I thought of these very young GIs being away from home, and I know full well my wife was laying there with nothing but her panties on. And with a little feeling of hostility I stepped from the tractor, pulled the pin out of the rig, and left. I was going to the area where my wife was at.

Between my wife and myself was an area of mud that was always difficult crossing. I don't remember crossing the mud. I remember walking up to my wife. I don't remember crossing the mud. I do not remember the helicopters leaving. I guess at this point I want to stress one thing: They was helicopters. They was not saucer-shaped in any form. They was helicopters. As I walked up to my wife, there was nobody present, nobody was around except her, and she laid asleep where I had left her. The helicopters was gone. I don't know what happened to them. As I walked up to her I said, "Are you okay?" and she looked up and says, "Yeah, everything is just fine." She had a strange look in her eye. I said, "Is everything okay?" She says, "Yeah." She says, "Who was here?" And I says, "I don't think anybody was here, because when the helicopters showed up, I came over and it couldn't have taken more than three minutes to get here." And she says, "What helicopters?" She said, "There was no helicopters." She remembered no helicopters. And I thought, *That's weird: Nobody could sleep with three helicopters hovering over your head.*

As I sat down on the hay beside her, I couldn't help but notice a small amount of blood right on her navel. And I asked what happened, and she goes, "I don't know." She says, "probably a needle from a thistle." And that is very logical, since thistles will make you bleed. I remember taking my finger in my mouth and a little bit of saliva and dabbing it on the small amount of blood and then wiping it off with my palm.

It must have been early in the day when we went over there and baled, and in my mind it should not have been more than about one P.M., but yet, after this happening, I went back and hooked up the rake and something was strange there. I don't remember what it was, but there was something strange. I knew I'd made one round and I felt, *Well, it's time to go home and do the milking.* This was probably about five or six P.M. So it sounds so insane, but right in here is a period of time I should be able to account for, and yet I cannot.

I wouldn't even talk about this, but as I stated, what happened to my wife makes me talk about this. I was somewhat confused by her lack of memory. She didn't remember the helicopters. She had a feeling somebody was there. The incident was just dropped: We never discussed it, we've never talked about it. Within the past year I tried to ask her on several occasions about it, and she has no memory whatsoever in regards to this incident.

In about I think it was 1978, my wife began to have nightmares. She would scream, "Take it out, take it out!" and I would wake up and say, "What's wrong?" and she would say, "They have that thing in my belly button and it hurts, it hurts." These nightmares continued. They got worse. She became very moody. She related that somebody had sex with her and she didn't know where. She began to have nightmares and she'd viciously tear at her forehead just above the bridge of her nose. She would say, "It hurts, it hurts, take it out." This was complete insanity. It made no sense.

The situation got worse. At times she would make gouges, cutting herself above her nose. I had no choice but to seek medical help for her. When I mentioned medical help, she became very violent. It took two ambulance people and a nurse who gave her a shot which virtually knocked her out before they could handle her. When they talked to her about this, she said that it wasn't that she was afraid of the ambulance people but that she didn't dare to go outside, because if she went outside "they" would see her: "They would come and take me away." She continuously used the word "they"; "they" would do her harm; "they" would take her away. I don't know why, but she developed a great fear of the color yellow. I had a yellow car and it scared her to death. One of my sons bought a yellow car and she didn't want nothing to do with that car. I had some yellow sheets and she refused to use them.

She spent a small amount of time at the hospital, and then she came back under heavy medication. She was here only a short time, then pretty much the same thing happened. She refused to leave the house because "they" would see her. She was on the nose thing a bit; she was on about the navel thing and about some kind of sexual encounter. She began to hear voices. She was very concise [*sic*] about the voices: She could relate everything that was said to her, and, very honestly, most of it didn't make too much sense.

However, I guess at this time I deliberately spoke to her about a person I knew, and in my mind I deliberately thought of him doing things he simply was not doing. And she related to me that this person was doing things exactly the way I was picturing in my mind. This sounds bizarre, but really and truly, for the few minutes she talked, she was reading my mind. I do not understand this.

She was hospitalized on two occasions—when I think about it, three occasions. The people at the hospital related the same things that she had related at home. She had great fear of somebody coming after her, that she was a prisoner, that somebody had violated her. "They" had placed a large needle in her navel. "They" had put something up her nose. "They" had given her a complete examination. And that stuff is on record. If it were not for that record existing, I don't think I would have mentioned any of this.

Will's account was long, filling both sides of a sixty-minute audio-tape. This helicopter incident was only one of a number of encounters he described, as well as being the one with the fewest conscious memories that would tie it to the UFO phenomenon. However, there were so many parallels to missing-time cases that I had looked into over the past decade—nasal probes, painful navel insertions, and invasive genital procedures—that I felt almost certain that further investigation would reveal a full-fledged UFO abduction. And because of Melissa's serious emotional problems that Will associated with that incident, it seemed to me that finding out what had really happened that day might be helpful to everyone concerned: husband, wife, family, and the appropriate mental health professionals.

Will's spoken account had been immensely touching to me. His slow, sadly resigned tone of voice and the innocent simplicity of his phrasing made the actual events even more powerfully affecting. I resolved to visit him, to meet his wife, to explore their experiences, and to see what I could do to help ameliorate their debilitating problems. Will and I exchanged letters and phone calls, but it was not until May that I was able to travel to his Wisconsin homestead.

Around the family dinner table in the small frame farmhouse, I talked to Will, three of his grown children, and Melissa. Will himself was a quiet, serious man with a rounded, careworn, melancholy face. He appeared to be in his early sixties but was probably ten or fifteen years younger. His hair was thinning, and both his stoop-shouldered posture and his slow-moving body betrayed the fact that he was in ill health. Bib overalls were obviously his standard dress, though his wife, Melissa, made an attempt to brighten her appearance, an effort made more poignant by her depressed, almost vacant expression. She spoke very little and seemed alone in her own world, leading me to suspect she was still under heavy medication.

Will, I soon realized, was highly intelligent though poorly educated. He informed me that he had only had the benefit of a seventh-grade education. Nevertheless his interests were surprisingly broad, and he seemed to have a special aptitude for physics and mathematics. Of his personal honesty and credibility, and that of his family, there could be no doubt: He wanted nothing from me except whatever help I could provide in exploring his years of nagging memories.

I spent three days with Will's family and carried out numerous interviews, extended philosophical conversations, as well as three hypnotic sessions. It was during the third session, on May 24, that we approached the 1968 (1974?) experience in the hay field. After the induction I set the scene, describing the hot, dry summer day, the tractor, the baling and stacking, and Melissa relaxing on a piece of canvas on the bales of straw:

BH: *What's the first odd thing that you notice?*

Will: I see three craft.

BH: *What do they look like?*

Will: They're not helicopters. Why did I say helicopters?

BH: *Let's not worry about that. Just tell me what they look like.*

Will: They're like two soup bowls together and a ring around them . . . like Saturn. I thought they was helicopters! They're . . . they're slowly moving to the ground. They're below the trees. I can't see 'em. They're right by Melissa. I pull the pin on the rake. I open the tractor wide open and put the gear high. I come to a mud hole: I hit it so fast I almost tip over. I come out of the mud hole and down between me and Melissa is a grove of trees.

BH: *Are you still on the tractor?*

Will: Yeah. And there's a person I know: Damoe. He calls me over, and he waves to me. I don't want to stop. I know there's somebody by Melissa. But he holds his hands up and I stop. I don't want to stop. I get off the tractor. He says, "Don't be concerned, Will. Everything is all right." And I say, "No it isn't." And he says, "Everything's all right." He insists that I talk with him, but I turn and I start running. I'm out of breath. And he's running alongside of me and he keeps saying, "Everything's all right."

I turn the corner by the trees and my heart stops. I don't know what happened. One craft is sitting in the middle of the field. It's sitting on the side of a big rock. And I look for Melissa. She's laying on the hay wagon. There's people around her. I'm scared. I'm screamin'. Damoe's talking to me and I tell him, "Go to hell!"

I'm gasping for air. I'm running. There's about six people. What are they doing? I'm running. When I get to the hay wagon I bump into one of them and he goes flying. Without stopping I jumped the wagon. Frantically, I looked around. I want a club or stick. And there's a log chain laying across the back of the wagon. What was they doing? Melissa's completely nude. I grabbed the chain and I'm standing over her. I'm swinging it over my head. I can hear it. I'm swearing at 'em; I'm screamin'; I'm full of rage. What did they do?

They hurt her. She won't answer me. I call her and she won't talk to me. I know these people. I've seen 'em before. Damoe has backed off. I thought he was my friend. I'm cryin'. [His voice breaks] I'm screamin'. I'm going to tear their heads off. [In a whisper:] I'll kill 'em. They just back away and look at me. I tell 'em, "Come on! Come on!" My hand's getting sore from the chain.

Damoe speaks. He's moving his lips! He says, "Will, put your weapon away. You may hurt yourself or your mate."

I'm cussin' at him. I'm swearin'. I say, "Get near me, you bastard, I'll show you who I'm going to hurt."

There's a sound from beneath the wagon. I've heard that sound before. It's a monotone. Damoe speaks some more. He says, "We did not want you to do this. We merely wanted you to witness what has taken place. We did not want you to be angry." And then another voice speaks but I don't see anyone talking. And they say, "Put your weapon down and come off of that wagon." And I have to do it. I stopped swinging the chain and I come off the wagon. Damoe says, "Sit down. Just relax."

I'm holding on to the chain. He says, "You don't have to put up your weapon. Just don't use it." I pull the chain up and I'm holding it and he comes over and helps me lay it across my shoulder. He says, "Sit down. No one is going to hurt you and they're not going to hurt your mate."

I'm very mad. I'm very angry. I was so helpless. What can I do? They're by Melissa. They're doing some of the same things to her they've done to me. They're looking at her hair. I didn't know women had hair on their breasts. They're pulling hairs off the nipples of her breasts! How can that be? They're scraping her with something like a square instrument, like a squared knife. They're looking at her fingernails and toes. And then they tell her they're going to turn her over. And they lay her on her stomach. There seems to be someone who knows what they're doing, like a doctor. They're very careful in looking at her spine. They move her legs. They look at the bottom of her feet. They point to something on her neck. I don't know, what are they pointing at?

They've got some of the stuff [equipment?] I've seen before. Then they turn her over again. She seems to do everything they ask her to do. She's laying on her back. They've got a long needle. I'm cussin' at 'em. I've seen that needle before. I've seen 'em use it on another woman. They place it in Melissa's navel. She's hollerin' and screamin.' I can't help her. [Crying] I can't help her. I'm mad at Damoe. He lied. He said no one would be hurt.

What are they going to do now? Damoe said, "It's just instruments. They just want to check her. She won't be harmed." Melissa's cryin'. Oh, if I could just help her! They're spreading her legs They seem to be taking . . . like . . . wiping her with something. Melissa's cryin' and she says, "Don't . . . don't. Take it out. Take it out." What are they doin' to her?

[Crying:] They're putting Melissa's panties back on and she's crying, saying, "Dumb shits! Assholes!" Then they come over to me now and they look at Damoe. I says, "Get your creepy fuckin' hands out of here, you bastards!" And Damoe says, "We will leave it the way it is."

Somebody takes Melissa by the hand. It must be very strong. They . . . he lifts her up as if she didn't weigh anything. Someone picks up the canvas and lays her back on the bales of hay. And then he lays Melissa down. And then Damoe talks. He says, "We wanted you to see this. We wanted you to know what happens. But," he says, "you become angry."

They're leaving. Damoe says, "Your wife will waken. But don't talk to her until we're gone. It'll be best that way."

They're walking away as if nothing has happened. The craft lifts gently in the air and very slowly moves across the treetops. I want to go to Melissa but I can't move. I gotta go back to the tractor. I don't want to go back to the tractor. I got to. I go back to the tractor and I climb up top and there's that sound again. Where the hell's that sound coming from? I let the clutch out of the tractor and I drive as fast as I can. I come up to Melissa and I jump off the tractor. I go out there and I says, "Melissa?"

She opens her eyes. I says, "Is everything okay?" She says, "Yeah, everything's just fine."

I says, "You're sure you're okay?"

She said, "Who was here?"

"There's nobody here," I said. "There was some helicopters but they left and I just come to see if everything was okay."

She says, "They come down to the ground, didn't they?"

And I said, "No, no, they was just overhead. I thought they come to the ground, but I think they just moved away." I sat and talked with her. She seems very calm. There's some blood on her navel. It's dryin' a little bit. I put a finger in my mouth and take some saliva and I wash it and wipe it away with the palm of my hand. And I says, "You cut yourself here somehow."

"Yeah," she says, "you know how it is, baling. It was probably a thistle."

I don't want to bale hay anymore. Melissa quickly gets dressed and we decide, let's just go home for the day and be with the family. As we're drivin' away in that old junk pickup, she looked at me and smiled and she says, "I was dreamin' about you." And I says, "What were you dreamin'?" And she says, "I dreamt you had sex with me three times." I laugh at her and say, "I'm good, but I'm not that good!"

We laugh a little bit and we drive home. I don't feel like talking. I don't think she does, either. She seems a little down in the dumps. And we come home and everything's all right.

After this long, harrowing reliving of his ordeal, I wait awhile for Will to rest and process the experience before I resume my questioning. I feel so sorry for this good, loving man that I almost decide to end the session without any further questions. But I know that if I stop here, later we will both regret it.

When I finally do resume, I speak very gently, hesitant to disturb him in any way:

BH: *Will, when is this happening?*

Will: This is the twenty-second of July. It was 1974. We just bought that old hay wagon.

BH: *You said they put something in Melissa. They wiped her and put something in her vagina? I don't understand.*

Will: I don't, either. She kept sayin', "Take it out. Take it out." But she said that when they put that needle in her navel too. But . . .

BH: *Did it appear that something was actually in her, or did they just wipe her?*

Will: I couldn't see. I could see they was wipin' her but I couldn't see what else they was doin.'

BH: *Was Damoe the man you had been friendly with?*

Will: Yes.

BH: *Is he big or small? What is he in size?*

Will: He looks like my son. Blond hair. The same build.

BH: *Is he the one who found your watch?*

Will: Yes. But he had the watch before this.

BH: *How about the other men around Melissa? What do they look like?*

Will: They're very small. They're very agile. They're . . . sort of greasy-lookin'.

BH: *Does it seem that like they're holding equipment and stuff around Melissa?*

Will: Some of 'em. Not all of 'em. Maybe two of them.

BH: *And how close were you to her while this was going on?*

Will: When I first got there, I jumped up on the wagon. Then they made me leave. I was about fifty foot away.

BH: *So you couldn't make out a lot of it?*

Will: No.

I continued, pursuing a different set of earlier recollections Will had told me about, concerning an incident from his youth. The details of this abduction, though intriguing and important, need not concern us here. Damoe, the object of our immediate interest, was apparently not involved in any way in this earlier event.

After we had explored that second experience, I gave Will a series of positive posthypnotic suggestions and then slowly counted him out of the hypnotic trance state. When the long, emotional session finally ended, he opened his eyes, wiped away a few tears, and glanced around. "Where's Melissa?" he asked, anxious to see that his wife was safe. "Melissa's not here," I answered gently, "but she's all right. You just lie there for a while. We're going to try to pick up the pieces. This is going to be a new start for the two of you."

The session had been almost as rich in information and insight into alien methods and tactics as it was in powerful, resonant emotion. For example, in Will's initial taped letter to me, describing the National Guard helicopters, he had been emphatic: ". . . I want to stress one thing: They was helicopters. They was not not saucer-shaped in any form. They was helicopters." Under hypnosis he seemed amazed that he had ever thought the three hovering UFOs could have been heli-copters, since he had so strongly pressed the point that they were not. One might speculate that the aliens imposed this screen memory image more forcefully than other images, since it led Will at the outset to define his experience as being of conventional origin rather than alien. One may also wonder how many of the later "black helicopter" references and so-called military abduction reports that some abductees have made might also, under hypnosis, be transformed in the same way.

Of equal interest is the fact that Will seemed able to act freely at some points in his narrative, frightening Damoe and the small, "greasy-looking" aliens with his whirling chain, and yet at other moments he was forced to obey by what appears to be telepathic control. "Put your weapon down and come off of that wagon," a voice tells him. And Will says that, despite his extreme rage, ". . . I have to do it. I stopped swinging the chain and I come off the wagon." The mysterious sound that Will said came from beneath the wagon, a sound he had heard before, precedes the periods when he no longer has control of his own actions, and thus may be a significant factor in the aliens' mind-control process.

In an analogous way, Melissa is almost unconscious most of the time, silent and doing exactly as she is told. But at two points, when instruments are inserted in her nose and in her vagina, she is conscious and cursing: "Take it out," she cries. "Take it out! . . . Dumb shits! Assholes!"

So how does alien mind and behavior control operate? Do these examples of its intermittent efficiency show that it is a flawed and inexact alien science, or perhaps that it is a fully operative technology that can be switched on and off during an abduction, as necessity dictates? Or were the inconsistent results in the case of Will and his wife at least partially due to their own reactions, to their fierce human will and degree of anger? Any answer at this point is speculative, though these particular examples of seemingly erratic efficiency are far from rare within the case reports.

Will's account also offers a rare insight into what one may call "alien stagecraft," their systematic and effective restoration of the abduction scene to the way it appeared to the participants at the very beginning. Will's conscious memories of the incident included seeing the descending "helicopters" and driving frantically on his tractor toward his resting wife, who was stretched out, nearly nude, on a sheet of canvas thrown over some bales of hay. And yet, under hypnosis he remem-

bered jumping off his tractor and running up to Melissa, now surrounded by alien beings and lying on the canvas, which is atop the *hay
wagon,* not the bales of hay. At the incident's conclusion, Will, still
under hypnosis, described the aliens lifting Melissa from the wagon,
moving the canvas sheet back to the hay bales, and then placing her
upon it so that everything looked to him exactly as it had at the beginning of the encounter. And in the end Will himself was made to leave
the wagon and his wife and was sent back to his tractor, so that when
his conscious memories resumed, he and his wife were precisely
where they had been at the outset.

Considering the aliens' careful, detailed restoration of "the set"—the
abduction site as it was at the outset—together with the vivid images of
American military personnel and army helicopters—which, it would
seem, they deliberately implanted in Will's memory—one can see the
Machiavellian cleverness and efficiency of the aliens' covert operations.
It should not be surprising, therefore, that a number of UFO abductees
have been left with confusing images of traumatic "military" abductions and a resulting distrust of their fellow human beings. Often in
these imposed scenarios the aliens are either entirely nonexistent or
appear as kindly, benevolent presences, in contrast to the "evil" military
personnel. That Will declined to blame his fellow human beings—
those "young GIs . . . away from home"—for his wife's later severe
emotional problems is a tribute both to his innate common sense and
the fact that he recalled having had similar UFO abduction experiences.

Another interesting aspect of Will's fruitful recollections involves
Damoe's use of language—in particular his frequent use of generic
terms. Thus, he orders Will to "put down your weapon," not "your
chain." Melissa is referred to as Will's "mate," not his wife. Few married people characteristically refer to their husbands or wives as their
mates, but in the context of the aliens' interest in human reproduction
and genetic experimentation, *mate* is a useful term. In the mid-1980's,
before I had published *Intruders,* I dealt with a young single woman in
New York City who reported similar phrasing. During an abduction
she was told by an alien—who she was supposed to believe was her
mother—that she should "find a mate and begin to breed." These are
hardly the words a mother would use to urge a daughter to find a

boyfriend or to begin thinking seriously about marriage, but for the aliens these phrases may be handy generic shorthand for the human reproductive process.

For our purposes here, the most significant aspect of this ultimately tragic experience of Will and Melissa is the presence of Damoe himself. He is a physically normal-looking male who resembles Will's son, is able to exert mind control over both Will and his wife, and ultimately seems to belong more to the alien world than to our own. Unlike any rational human being, Damoe seemed surprised by Will's rage, saying, "We merely wanted you to witness what has taken place. We did not want you to be angry." Apparently he assumed that if Will saw what the aliens were doing to his wife, he would understand and take it all in stride—hardly the judgment of someone who understood human love and protectiveness.

But despite possessing obvious paranormal abilities and lacking basic psychological insight into human relationships, Damoe seems able to move through normal society unnoticed, as if he were as fully human a being as any of the rest of us. Taken together, I find this non-human mix of disturbing psychic powers, unexceptional appearance, and deeply flawed emotional understanding to be as ominous as anything I have learned so far about the UFO phenomenon.

A final, more personal observation: When I joined Will, Melissa, and several of their sons at the family dinner table the night I arrived at their farm, I vividly recall my feelings of intense sadness. Melissa, Will told me earlier, had once been vivacious, humorous, and happy. But now, sitting silently at the dinner table, her hands resting limply in her lap, she behaved as if her intellectual, spiritual, and emotional energies had been drained away, almost to the point of nonexistence. There is no way of knowing if her blank, unresponsive, melancholy demeanor was partially due to medication or even, conceivably, the result of electroshock treatment administered during her hospital stays. But I am certain of one thing: However drastic the medical treatment she received, one of its central causes was the severe trauma of that afternoon a decade or so earlier. The physical and psychological suffering she endured at the hands of Damoe and his alien cohorts virtually destroyed her life.

Cases like this—and this is only an extreme version of hundreds of other similar cases I have explored—leave me with barely concealed fury at those who would paint the aliens as benign saviors here to help us by spreading higher truth and demonstrating "unconditional love." The only unconditional love I saw in this tragic affair was Will's enduring and luminous love for his profoundly damaged wife.

Chapter 26

HUMAN RESOURCES: OURS OR THEIRS?

IN BUDD'S TELLING OF Will and Melissa's story and in the flat mid-western cadence of Will's voice on audiotape, I soon sensed that this case—and its tragic outcome—was, on the surface, nearly the polar opposite of Anne-Marie's UFO abduction experiences. It would turn out to reveal one of the darkest sides of the phenomenon, in terms of its lasting effect on an entire family. Twelve years later it is still moving to hear Will speak about the drawn-out, tortured, breaking apart of a marital bond.

Is There a Scientific Explanation for Melissa's Experience in the Field?

Beginning with the now famous Betty and Barney Hill abduction in September 1961, women have reported that the UFO occupants punctured their abdomen with long needles, entering near or through the navel. Years before the commonly used procedure of amniocentesis, Betty Hill was told by the alien beings that they were testing her (nonexistent) pregnancy. In her own highly distraught state, Melissa referred repeatedly to a needle entering her navel and how much it hurt. Moments after the actual incident in the hay field, though, Will says she seemed to have no conscious recall of the event, even though they both noticed the spot of blood near her navel. It must have been a thistle, she said, and Will dabbed it away with a little spittle on his fingertip.

Over a decade later Will, in hypnotic regression, narrated his memory of that day step by step, from the landing of three discs (not the helicopters he consciously recalled) to seeing Melissa nude, surrounded by "greasy-looking" people who were clearly involved with reproductive procedures of some sort—wiping her vaginal area and inserting a long needle directly into her abdomen. Although Will did see both of these procedures, he had been virtually immobilized some distance away when Melissa cried out about what was evidently a third part of the procedure: Something was being inserted into her vagina.

It's a given that often in memory retrieval, there's likely to be some element of distortion, filling in, or blotting out of certain details. But a huge needle piercing a woman's abdomen is an extremely vivid and specific image, one that's not a standard part of all abductions. However, enough researchers have documented these incidents that it qualifies as another abduction pattern. Unfortunately, the scenario does seem to come straight out of a movie genre that could be called Let's Go Mutilate a Bunch of Women. Do doctors really do such invasive things to pregnant women or in the course of a gynecological exam?

Laparoscopy

The answer is yes, but mainly in the process of *in vitro* fertilization. A multitude of fertility clinics have sprung up around the world since the birth of the first "test-tube baby," Louise Brown, on July 25, 1978, at a hospital in England. Most private fertility clinics do a brisk and largely unregulated business with infertile couples willing to undergo various and repeated medical interventions to achieve a pregnancy. In the earlier years of this work, a process called *laparoscopy* was the mainstay for ovum recovery. It involved the use of a long hollow needle inserted near the woman's navel and pushed down to a certain depth that would allow the instrument to retrieve her ova, or nearly ripe eggs, from the follicles in the ovary. The needle actually aspirates or sucks up the eggs, which are whisked off to a laboratory setting and checked for viability. Six to eight hours after that, the eggs are inseminated in a test tube with the male's sperm. If an eight-celled blastomere, or "pre-embryo," develops normally for about forty-eight hours, one or more will be implanted back in the mother's uterus or in a surrogate's womb.[1] Eventually there will be an additional option, now being researched in Japan: an artificial womb.

So it's not hard to see how the "huge needle in the navel" aspect of Will's account seems quite relevant to the UFO occupants' evident reproductive manipulation of human beings. Since the laparoscopy also helps the user (alien or human) to check the overall condition of the woman's reproductive system, the "greasy-looking guys" with the needle were either determining Melissa's viability as a potential egg donor or actually retrieving her ova for their own purposes. In any case, they didn't ask her permission or explain their purpose.

As to Melissa's vaginal procedure, we can only speculate what might have been happening on the basis of our own developing technologies.

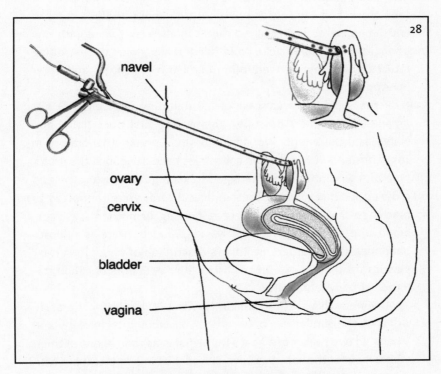

Medical illustration of a laparoscopy performed
for ovum retrieval. (Drawing by Charles Foltz)

Artificial Wombs

Some of us humans may find the new developments in science that we've discussed so far shocking or distasteful. Interspecies mingling through the technology of transgenics, the cloning of genetic replicas of ourselves, the bioengineering of our food, and the use of embryonic stem cells to create spare body parts are technologies that may be considered disturbing on several levels. However, abductees' eyewitness testimony indicates that the ETs seem to have mastered these technologies long ago.

Then along comes another hard-to-process human innovation—partly shocking in the way it radically changes our concept of human life, and equally startling in the way it confuses and blurs the lines between "their" advanced technologies and "ours." Four prominent abduction researchers—Budd Hopkins, David M. Jacobs, John Mack, and Ray Fowler—have written about multiple cases in which people recall specialized rooms in alien craft lined with row upon row of small, clear, fluid-filled tanks holding developing fetuses. These reports were often derided by scientists and other investigators.

Perhaps it's the usual case of life imitating . . , well, *life*—but Japanese researchers have just created the first operational and viable artificial womb. Working in a small research laboratory in Tokyo, Yosinori Kuwabara and colleagues have developed the prototype of a womb that has managed to keep goat fetuses alive and growing for three weeks. Their umbilical cords were connected to machines that acted as placentas, feeding in nutrients, oxygen, blood and siphoning out the waste products. Here is philosopher–medical writer Jeremy Rifkin's description of the unit: "A clear plastic tank the size of a bread basket, filled with amniotic fluid stabilized at body temperature."[3]

Anyone with a passing familiarity with UFO abduction literature will spot the similarities between our developing technology and "theirs" in two shakes of a goat's tail—that is, as soon as one of them makes it out of the baby box alive. The goal, of course, is to make artificial wombs viable and popular for human use.

The aliens may well have been using a more refined version of follicular aspiration, which, you'll be glad to hear, does away with the horse needle through the belly. Ultrasonic rectal probes (more later on their use in men) are now used to locate a woman's egg-bearing follicles so they can be aspirated through the vagina with a mere syringe. Vaginal ultrasound is also used in in vitro procedures to measure the size and number of follicles, to determine whether they're ready to be harvested. In fact, according to the Alta Bates In Vitro Fertilization Program, women generally receive five or six vaginal ultrasounds for each pregnancy attempt.[2] It's doubtful that ETs would need or bother to work at what probably seems to them a very crude level. Most likely, their monitoring of the intended mother is so precise in transmitting hormonal and chemical levels that they could move in at the right time and simply extract the ripe eggs. It would be hard to imagine that ETs, like our fertility experts, would patiently check and recheck every twelve hours a woman who was near ovulation. That's a lot of abductions.

An additional possibility is that, unaware of it, Melissa was actually pregnant at the time with a genetically modified embryo implanted in her several weeks earlier by these same individuals. If that was the

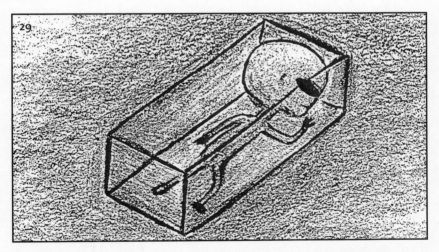

Tiny fetus floating in a nursery tank, as drawn by female abductee B.C. in 1991. Compare this sketch to the 1997 Japanese development of an artificial womb: "A clear plastic tank the size of a bread basket, filled with amniotic fluid. . . ." (From Budd Hopkins's archive)

case, they might first have used the needle to check the embryo's viability, then proceeded through the vagina to detach the weeks-old embryo from the wall of her uterus and extract it.

Enter Unwilling Male Subjects, Stage Left

If, as we suggested in an earlier chapter, the UFO occupants are deliberately creating a transgenic species that blends our humanness with some recessive (for the time being) traits of their own—or if they are simply manipulating the human genome toward a direct goal—where does the human male fit into the picture?

Just as with the "hybrid" baby phenomenon, in which researchers stubbornly continued to report what the abductees said they experienced years before the science was in place to justify or validate what they were saying, the same holds true for certain alarming and painful medical problems that have been experienced by some male abductees over the years. From two cases originating in the 1970's, Budd collected some very odd data without having any distinct medical condition as an explanation. In completely unrelated cases, one in Arizona and one in Tel Aviv, two boys who were between fifteen and seventeen years old at the time of their abductions had each begun to pass blood in their urine. This happened the day after each boy, respectively, had missing-time events and each had scattered memories of a trauma. When the passing of blood continued for several days, the boys' parents sought medical advice and testing, but no explanation was ever found. In the case of "Moshe," an Israeli man now in his late thirties, his own father was a physician who quickly became alarmed and took his son to a urologist in Tel Aviv. Hospitalized for several days of extensive testing, including a cystoscopy, Moshe never received any diagnosis or reason for the bleeding.

Now we have a few scientific clues as to what may have caused such bleeding in male abductees. In in vitro clinics, sperm is usually collected by masturbation or vibratory stimulation of the penis. But if neither of these methods work, electroejaculation stimulation (EES) is recommended. It's performed in a medical setting in order to closely monitor the patient for changes in blood pressure and pulse. The procedure involves an anal probe that reaches as far as the prostate; a low level electrical current is then applied. Although sperm might be collected as a normal antegrade (exterior) ejaculate after such a technique, there's often the unfortunate consequence that EES produces a retrograde (internal) ejaculate back into the bladder. The procedure then becomes even more invasive. Using other instrumentation, the bladder is washed out afterward so that the sperm present in the retrograde ejaculation can be retrieved. At the Center for Male Reproductive Medicine in Las Vegas, where men with spinal injuries and differing degrees of paralysis are often treated for infertility, EES is frequently employed.[4]

For male abductees just taken aboard a UFO, under stress and/or with parts of their nervous system shut down to make them malleable, electro-ejaculation stimulation would seem to be an effective tool for the aliens to acquire sperm as well. In our own medical practice, if the invasive procedure of retrieving sperm from the bladder is also involved, a man can be expected to pass some blood in the urine for several days, until any small lesions heal.

Over the years, Budd has had many other cases of male abductees who report, with discomfort and embarrassment, that some sort of anal probe had been used on them. Currently there's not enough specific information to do more than speculate about the purpose of these more benign probes, which left no known aftereffects. Perhaps these men's sperm was collected in a normal external ejaculate—either with EES or without it.

Primates as Test Animals: Both Human and Nonhuman?

There are some striking parallels between alien handling of abductees and our own scientists' treatment of nonhuman primates used in research. In May 1997, the European Convention for the Protection of Vertebrate Animals Used for Experimantal and Other Scientific Purposes (EUPREN) met to consider the best ways to house and handle nonhuman primates—great apes and monkeys. Because of their close relationship to humans, these animals are considered excellent models for researching man's central nervous system and other crucial areas of biomedical research. Human vaccines and medications have also been developed by employing primates as test animals.[5] In other words, our scientists are using *them* to find out about *us* It's conceivable that ETs are utilizing humans for a similar purpose.

Take a look at some of the following concerns addressed by scientists at the EUPREN convention. They may seem eerily familar to anyone knowledgeble about UFO abduction reports:

- It is best to study the "behavioral repertoire" of the species *in their natural habitat*. That way, researchers will gather the most reliable data about normal behavior, such as breeding activities, social needs, pair bonding, etc. Captivity causes stress, which skews the data.

- A *reuse policy* states that animals should be treated with care so that they can be used over and over in experimental procedures—possibly for a lifetime. This is cost-effective, saving on the number of animals bred and kept for research.

- Animals should be *trained to cooperate* with experimental procedures—leading to less stress and more accurate physiological, biochemical, and behavioral measurements.

- Regarding *implants* in research primates: "The use of preinvasive implantable radiotelemetry has revolutionized the collection of physiological data under stress-free conditions"[6] These devices are used for remote monitoring of the animals in which they are implanted.

- In many studies—including pharmacological and behavioral studies—scientists need to follow the progression of a disease or the effect of a new drug over months to years. Thus *the same individuals must studied over time.*

In a vein similar to that of the EUPREN protocols, the United States Department of Agriculture captions the photograph of these three piglets: "Piglets are one of the main subjects of ARS animal behaviorists. These scientists study behavior of pigs and cows 'round the clock with the goal of improving animal handling practices to reduce stress on animals and lower production costs." (Photo courtesy of the Agricultural Research Service, U.S. Department of Agriculture)

It's also possible that the anal probes are part of a routine health checkup for the abductee, who has usually been part of the aliens' "program" for many years, if not since birth. Notice that Will definitely recognized the beings in his hay field, having seen them on earlier occasions; he was also familiar with the needle going into Melissa's navel because he'd seen them do it to other women, presumedly aboard an alien craft. Regular physicals for abductees would make sense, in the same way that our own research scientists do routine checkups to ensure that his or her experimental animal subjects are in good health. After all, in both the alien and human cases, there has been a significant investment made over time in that living subject. Kept alive and healthy, the animal or human subject pays off with the dividends of ongoing collection of medical data or results from long-term experiments, including offspring. Aliens often tell people they're "just checking." As Damoe assured Will, "It's just instruments. They just want to check her. She won't be harmed." Abductees have heard that line so many times, and it's rarely true. Often there *is* pain and discomfort; there *is* nearly always mental anguish; and, in a few cases there is permanent physical damage. But perhaps, in "the higher interest" of science, neither the alien nor the human researcher considers that this constitutes *harm* to the subject.

Monkey Number 14609

At the Oregon Health and Science University's Primate Research Center, nearly every day monkeys and other nonhuman primates are strapped down by human technicians and have electric shocks applied to their penises to obtain sperm for reproduction experiments. In 1999 this painful procedure was caught on hidden video, as "Jaws," monkey number 14609, a twenty-one-year-old rhesus macaque, underwent electroejaculation, the same procedure that extraterrestrial researchers apparently use on human abductees. Jaws is a veteran of this procedure, and former primate technicians say his penis has been shocked hundreds of times. An animal rights group, along with Dr. Jane Goodall, is working to eliminate such abuse of primates in research centers around the world.[7] The irony of many concerned citizens and scientists working on behalf of our animal friends can hardly be lost on the abductees, who are virtually on their own.

What you'd expect alien researchers—or miners of our resources—to be interested in are all the ways that human males could be used in transgenic modification of either our species or that of the ETs—or both. As you look over the possibilities below, keep in mind that Damoe fascinated Will by his close resemblance to Will and Melissa's own son, as well as by his intelligence. How is it conceivable that the ETs could develop Damoe as a "normal" who resembled Will's son, yet who clearly acted as an intermediary for the aliens and their reproductive missions? Here are just a few possibilities:

- Will might have been an unknowing donor of a nucleus from an adult cell by undergoing a simple procedure that scoops off skin or other external tissue. That adult cell of Will's could be used to clone a genetically identical copy of Will. Or, if Will's son had also been an abductee, Damoe might have been an actual clone of that son. Although genetically nearly identical, each boy's appearance and self-expression would be somewhat different, according to what we assume would be a great disparity in their upbringing and socialization—one in Wisconsin, one in outer space.

Theoretically, before developing any cloned embryo from a cell, it would be modified in some way consistent with alien goals. This could be done by inserting a certain set of genes— say, alien immune-antigen-producing genes—into the human DNA. The resulting offspring would seem to be human in every sense except for the markers that are only seen by the human's immune system. But it's a good first step for gradually introducing more and more alien genetic material into the human male without his body's rejecting the foreign genes.[8]

Currently we can't do such sophisticated cloning, says Henry T. Greely, codirector of the Stanford University Program in Genomics, Ethics, and Society.[9] He's considered a leading expert on the ethics and law surrounding issues of cloning, genetic manipulation, and genetic farming. But Greely cites many cases in which researchers are working toward previously unimagined types of cloning achievements. Inserting human genes into pigs, for example, is a hotly competitive field right now, with different biotechnology firms hoping to eventually be able to transplant a pig's organs into the original human cell donor. The body's immune system would recognize its own genes in the pig and wouldn't reject the transplanted organ.

- Will might have also have been an involuntary sperm donor in the aliens' program. A recent procedure that was developed in fertility clinics offers us one possible way that his sperm might have been used. Called intracytoplasmic sperm injection (ICSI), the technology is able to isolate an individual sperm—the best and brightest, no doubt—by means of microinjection pipettes. Using techniques called micromanipulation, doctors can inject a single sperm directly into the egg's cytoplasm.[10] If aliens have found a way to reliably cross species' boundaries, Will's sperm could be used as an in vitro fertilizer for extraterrestrial eggs— if they do have such sex cells—or even for cross-breeding with another species.

Using Will's sperm in this way is essentially "directed evolution," where the purpose is to make genetic variants that are completely new organisms. Greely cautions, however, that genes work together in ways that are unforeseen. Since genes may have multiple functions, how well they perform in their transplanted organism (a gorilla or an alien or a squid) also depends greatly on the genetic environment around them. Greely adds that, given our current (human) knowledge:

> It would be really risky to take a gene from one species and move it into another. There's a very good chance it wouldn't work as you expected. . . . Double that risk if you're talking about genes that have never been seen before and don't come from any existing organism, and that we've made up by scrambling up the genes. Then we really have no idea how it's going to play out.[11]

- If Will had already become a transgenic individual, courtesy of the alien visitors, he would be to the aliens what transgenic mice or chimpanzees are to us: powerful tools for solving human gene puzzles. In other words, he'd be a walking, talking alien experiment, just as Melissa seems to have been. By "turning on" or "turning off" certain genes in Will, the ETs would be able to better understand the complexity and diversity of gene expression in humans. Perhaps also in themselves.

- There's another way in which Will or any abductee's bodily tissues might be used by the aliens for cloning. Since it involves a human donor cell being incubated in a cow egg, the complexity of the issue will be explored in the following section.

Cow Egg Cells as Ideal Incubators for Cloning: Another Look at Cattle Mutilations

In a recent twist in mammalian cloning research, we may have discovered an intriguing connection between the alien breeding program and the as-yet-unsolvable grisly mystery of cattle mutilations. Although these animal mutilations have a long and complex history,

I'll briefly review the phenomenon for those unfamiliar with it. For nearly a century, though most prominently in the decades between 1960 and 1990, ranchers and farmers have reported sporadic cattle deaths that seemed straight out of the Twilight Zone. There was nothing conventional about the deaths of these livestock. The animals were found in remote locations with certain body parts—an anus, an eye, an udder, a cheek—cored out cleanly or excised by an instrument producing extremely high heat. The cell walls were literally cauterized. There was no blood, no tooth marks, no tracks of any kind leading into or out from the kill. Predators would not touch the dead cow. Ranchers and law enforcement remain either baffled or attribute the deaths to natural causes, predators, or, on some occasions, to occult groups practicing some sacrificial rite. No proof on any side has been persuasive.

But according to Dr. John Altshuler, a Denver physician and pathologist who has done extensive field and microbiological investigation of the cases: "These animals are often found within hours of having been seen alive at a time of unusual observed aerial phenomena." Along with the abnormal pathology of the animals' tissues, the absence of the expected marks of predators or hunters, and witness reports of both daylight and nighttime sightings of unusual craft nearby, Altshuler believes that extraterrestrial forces must be considered a possible suspect.[12]

Over the years, many reports, some substantiated, some not, insistently connected the animal deaths to UFO sightings. Several people claimed to have seen a bawling cow hauled up a beam of light into a hovering craft. Linda Moulton Howe's television documentary *Strange Harvest,* brought even more attention to the subject when it aired as a Fox Special in 1993. Since then Howe has followed a trail that she and others believe is strewn with convincing evidence linking the slain livestock (or "mutes") to UFOs and their occupants.[13]

The main problem with the theory is *why.* Ufologists haven't offered many solid motivations as to why aliens would kill cattle and selectively harvest animal body parts. The theories have ranged from a Christian orientation that "mutes" are a sign that the Earth "is under a curse" to Howe's own explanation that bovine tissue is similar in genetic makeup to humans' and offers the aliens a way to sample pollutants and other harmful substances from the environment that accumulate in living tissue.[14]

Here is another suggestion: It relates to new discoveries in cloning that use cow eggs to produce clones of embryos from completely different species. Those findings could shine another light on alien motives for animal mutilations. In January 1998, Dr. Neal First from the University of Wisconsin, Madison, published the startling results of cloning experiments in which cow eggs (oocytes) shot to the top of the list of preferable experimental cloning material. According to a 1998 paper by Dr. Lawrence Roberge, "cow oocytes are cheap, plentiful, and relatively easy to handle."[15] That becomes a significant issue when you look at the conclusions of the University of Wisconsin research.

The major findings of the study show that even after an oocyte is stripped of its own bovine nucleus and DNA, the cow egg still retains a small amount of genetic material in the cytoplasm (a thin inner structure) of the egg—and that cytoplasm carries a powerful punch. When the nucleus of other *adult* mammalian cells (from monkeys, rats, pigs, and sheep) are inserted into the emptied cow oocyte, its cytoplasm literally reprograms the "alien" nucleus back into its infancy. That ability to turn back the clock on a adult cell—to regress it—is so significant that Roberge and others suggest that *"cow oocytes might provide a cheap source of oocytes to accelerate human cloning experiments."* [emphasis added][16]

Let's take a closer look at how the scientists used cow oocytes to reach such a conclusion. First, the scientists stripped the bovine eggs of their own nuclei (the DNA at the cells' centers), which is one of the standard cloning procedures. Next, skin cells from five different species of animals, all adults, were scooped from the surface of their ears. (Remember the abductees' "scoop marks"?) These would become the sources of donor nuclei, or DNA that's specific to a species—and, of course, specific to an individual, containing the full set of necessary chromosomes. It was the same technique used by Scotland's Roslin Institute to create the famous sheep Dolly. (Her genes, though—in the interest of giving equal credit to different body parts—came from an udder cell of an adult sheep.) Fused into the outer shell of the cow egg, the adult ear cells of the monkey, rat, pig, sheep, and cattle took their cue from "Mama" cow. The cow egg was actually able to *reset* the other animals' genes back into an earlier embryonic state—before they differentiated into ear cells. In the final stage, when the cow egg with the monkey nucleus, for example, is implanted in a surrogate mother or artificial womb, theoretically we'd expect *the birth of that monkey's cloned self* several months later.

Before Dolly, many scientists didn't believe it was possible that adult, fully specialized cells (skin, heart, lung, etc.) could be reset to produce embryonic clones of those very same animals.

The cow oocytes turned out to be more than gracious hostesses to a Noah's ark–like parade of cells from other species. The enucleated cow eggs actually functioned as a sort of cradle to hold and nurture the DNA of these different animals. The University of Wisconsin study showed that all of the species' somatic cells seemed to feel right at home in the tiny artifical "womb" of the cow cell. Each one of the species began the cell cleavage process and cell division that leads to the earliest stages of the embryo.[17] After being transferred into surrogate mothers, the biogeneticists claim, no pregnancies from these experiments were allowed to be carried to term—possibly for fear of pushing the wrong public and political buttons too early in the game. What the study did establish, though, was that the cow egg cytoplasm seemed just as accepting of a nucleus from a three-year-old male rat cell as it was toward the nucleus of a ten-year-old female monkey.

Cow oocytes, then, seem to be truly equal opportunity cradles. In fact some scientists refer to them as possible *universal recipients* for many other animal species—including humans. And if it does turn out that we and even a single species of ET once came from a common source, those cow eggs could be ideal cloning incubators for our alien visitors as well. Incubators for them or us or some combination of the two.

Meanwhile, Back at the Ranch

If the perpetrators of the cattle mystery killed only cows, not bulls, or excised only the ovaries and uterus, we'd have an interesting theory going: that extraterrestrials had known, long before we did, that cow eggs were the universal "wombs" for cloning species of all kinds and that they were harvesting our cattle for that purpose. But, as usual in ufology, the answer doesn't come that neatly packaged. Certainly cow reproductive organs are among the parts taken (making eggs available), but somatic, external cells of cattle are also taken—in rectal coring or excising of tongue and cheek cells.

Here are some informed guesses about what those cells might be used for, according to the brand-new, constantly changing state of *our own* knowledge in this field of cloning: (1) food or nutrients of some kind that have nothing to do with cloning; (2) harvesting of many different organs and tissue samples purely for experimental purposes; and (3) *they're actually manufacturing something from these raw materials*. To do that, the ETs would have to know something we don't yet know: how to decode the chemical signals that tell stem cells to differentiate into specific tissues and when to do it.

We know that one chemical signal says to an embryonic cell: "Go, become a liver cell," while at the same time a different chemical is calling to other cells: "You, there, take your buddies with you, head for the surface, and start making the epidermis." Although research labs are making significant headway on the problem, we aren't certain which signal does what—or what the built-in timing cues are, either. It wouldn't be good to have the baby's hair turn white at six months, or for a little girl to develop breasts at age two. But once the decoding is done, scientists would then have the ability to create off-the-shelf living creatures built to anyone's specifications.

The potential of our own current bioengineering technologies makes Dr. Frankenstein's rough assemblage of miscellaneous body parts seem positively primitive. As a metaphor, though, its power is alive and well. In the first decade of the twenty-first century, watch what happens in the public, political, and religious psyches of the world as the general public seriously begins to come to terms with bioengineering's implications. We can expect to see the Frankenstein monster get up off the table again and walk stiffly along the shores of our fear.

The Use and Reuse of "Mute" Body Parts

Maybe there's a method to the madness of cattle mutilations, if aliens are indeed the ones cutting them up. Perhaps these beings have the essential need to experiment, just as we do, before the project turns out right. If the taking of cattle tissue relates to cloning procedures or creating something out of bovine raw materials, let's say, certain groups of alien visitors may be quite recent explorers of Earth's treasures. They may be in the process of building their own data bank about us—one that maps the complex inner workings of every living organism on Earth. It doesn't matter how fast their supercomputing big brains are: Some things just have to be tried.

For example, a newly cloned kitten named "Cc:" could offer a possible reason for the excision of somatic (exterior) cow cells, rather than just oocytes, or eggs. When scientists at Texas A&M University began their work on animal cloning, they started with the use of cheek cells from an adult cat.[18] After inserting the cheek cell nuclei into enucleated cat egg cells, eighty-two cloned embryos were implanted into surrogate mother cats. But only one pregnancy resulted, and that fetus died. Cheek cells—not a good idea.

In their next try, the Texas A&M team took nuclei from cumulus cells clustered around the original cat's ova. This time after only *five* embryo implantations, a successful pregnancy occurred, and so Cc: was born. She was a lively, normal-looking kitten, according to the February 21, 2001, issue of the journal *Nature*. Somebody should tell the ETs to "stop already" with the cattle cheek excisions.

The Essence of Womb Time

In continuing to look at the issues related to what seems to be an ET program of genetic manipulation of human beings, the abductees' reports of row upon row of stacked "incubators" seen aboard spacecraft are worth some additional pondering. The clear liquid-filled cubicles that house "hybrid" or transgenic fetuses bring up profound questions about the psychosocial and character development of a human (or reengineered human) fetus that gestates almost exclusively in an artificial womb. Is womb time really necessary, or are we (and the ETs) technologically advanced enough to handle all substantial concerns about the future child's well-being? What might go lacking in a fetus gestating in a plastic box—even a sophisticated box that handles all the fetus's physiological needs of nutrients, oxygen, blood, and waste disposal? That seems, after all, a rather a mechanical process. Nutrients in, waste out, temperature regulation. Why not mechanize this part of our lives, too, freeing up women's human potential to do more complex and interesting tasks? Actually, the answer to that question has a great deal of bearing on what the aliens and the "normals" primarily seem to lack: the depth of human emotion, including intuitive responses of love and empathy with another being. Damoe, for instance, just didn't get it: *Why was Will so upset at seeing what the UFO occupants actually did to Melissa?* Seeming to want Will's help and cooperation in these medical procedures on his wife, Damoe was genuinely puzzled at Will's fury. After all, Damoe seems to have been following our own scientist's EUPREN protocols: Encourage and train the primate to co-operate with the procedures.

In *Intruders,* Kathie Davis relived under hypnosis the terrible moment of realization that the aliens were actually extracting a living fetus from her. On audiotape you can hear her sudden screaming and sobbing: *"It's not fair! It's mine! I hate you!"* Later, after a great effort to calm down, Kathie told Budd: "I screamed it at [him]—and the fucker looked *surprised.*"

If we think back to the wooden, detached behavior of the "interviewers" and recall how often abductees frequently report, "They don't care about me; they're just working," Mr. Paige stands out head and shoulders above the others. He apparently had a full range of human emotions, the only "alien among us" that we know of who does. What we seem to face is a growing number of day-to-day encounters—in our jobs, our homes, our schools and parks—with this subpopulation of normal-appearing humans with alien traits. If that's what they are, these artificially gestated transgenic beings have abilities that give them a great deal of power over us. "They can hear what you're thinking," as one child told Budd. Their minds seem capable of controlling our very actions, thoughts, and perceptions. They seem to appear on our plane of reality "out of nowhere," no transportation needed. And, at the aliens' bidding, they can deliver us up at any time, anyplace, like an involuntary subject in a clinical trial.

So how do artificial wombs or gestation tanks have anything to do with these often affectless, detached beings? There's still a great deal scientists don't know about the development of a fetus's emotional life, its sense of safety or distrust about the outside world. But we do know, in measurable chemical and physiological interactions, that between the fetus floating in the dark womb and its mother is a subtle, delicately sensed choreographic bond. In the first few months the fetus receives all of its "messages" through the mother's placenta or through even more subtle ways of communication that we can't quite define.[19] About halfway through the pregnancy, though, the process changes. As its sense organs bud, the embryo actually begins to learn through sensory input from *outside* the womb. It feels motion and its mother's heartbeat, hears (or feels) Mozart and Louis Armstrong. Through placental interchange and primitive sense organs, it senses its mother's moods and emotions, as well as emotional stimuli in the larger environment around the mother. At this point, the embryo is, in some senses, "teachable," according to Thomas Verney in *The Secret Life of the Unborn Child*.[20] He suggests there is evidence that even in the womb, the infant is learning about fear and nurturance and trust.

In the British newspaper *The Guardian*, Jeremy Rifkin writes of his troubling concerns about the kind of child that would be produced from a plastic chamber.[21] What will fill in for the critical role of the mother's sensory input on the child's development? He questions whether gestation in an artificial womb can possibly turn out children who are normal in motor functions and emotional and cognitive development. Depriving an embryo of all external and internal stimuli, withholding from it the subtle interactions with the mother, he suggests, isn't likely to produce a mentally balanced child: "We know that young infants deprived of human touch and bodily contact often are unable to develop the full range of human emotions and sometimes die soon after birth *or become violent, sociopathic or withdrawn later in life*" [emphasis added].[22]

It seems to many UFO abduction investigators that the latter remark describes precisely what seems to be lacking in both the ETs and in the transgenic beings we believe they are "coproducing" with our involuntary help. The evidently cloned children with alien-human appearance that Jen saw on the playground seemed passive, expressionless, and unused to the simplest of sensations—like the feel of sand trickling through one's fingers. It's no wonder these transgenic children seen aboard craft might be described as having the "failure to thrive" syndrome. They seem thin, listless, and nonresponsive. Do the aliens expect these children to take their places in our society as Mr. Paige and Damoe evidently did? Or do these children represent an interim stage in an overall alien plan to develop beings more like us in many ways—with our vital genetic diversity and our emotions, which actually have a survival purpose in our society. Or perhaps we flatter ourselves with this speculation, and all the ETs are interested in is getting the technical part right. They seem to have gone a long way toward producing serviceable facsimiles of humans who answer to them. The models seem to be getting better and better.

The old debate still rages on over what is the most powerful influence to shape human beings (or any sentient being): Is it nature or nurture? But it's possible that both our great human vulnerability and our strength lies in our ongoing desire to attend to both equally. We earthlings value our science; we don't mind tinkering with nature if it seems to confer some genetic advantage on us, rather than the next guy; we're even drawn to some of the more radical new abilities of genetics to make designer babies free of defects. But we know that nature won't paint the whole picture, either—that these small bundles of neurons, muscles, blood, and bone, these offspring of ours, will also grow out of the environment we create and the examples we set. We will need to intentionally nurture our children into becoming loving, empathetic, and ethical adults, responsible to the rest of society.

But what happens to a species like ours that might become infiltrated by a subpopulation of bioengineered people who never knew the nurturance side of the equation? ETs may be on the way to creating an increasingly perfect facsimile of a human being, but we don't yet see convincing evidence that they understand what lies behind the scenery of a fully fleshed-out human existence—qualities such as emotional openness, the courage to act independantly as a moral being, the desire to nurture others as you were once nurtured—or to nurture another person *even if you were not.* We don't know if this new variant species of mankind, intentionally created by "the Other," is here to offer us earth-lings fresh knowledge and profound insights from the farside of the cosmos, or whether it intends to deliberately betray us into the service of its own extraterrestrial creators.

In the meantime, it seems that all we can do is to continue to bear witness and offer modest emotional support—through conversations, letters, phone calls, and writing—to the thousands of people undergo-ing these experiences. We, as well as the abductees, look toward the day that it dawns on the scientific, political, educational, and spiritual insti-tutions of this small planet that their understanding and guidance are terribly lacking in dealing with this strange experience that touches every dimension of what it means to be human.

Chapter 27

A FEW FINAL WORDS

For the reader who has patiently labored through these "incredible accounts from credible people" (a much overused but still apt phrase) and the related activities of contemporary science, it is time to pause for a moment to put things into some kind of perspective. The first goal we shared was to make a persuasive case that the "paranormal" alien technology described by thousands of witnesses has far more in common with advanced *earthly* science than anyone may have previously thought. We've tried to drain the stigma of magic from the conventional perceptions of both scientists and the public toward alien activities by showing how seemingly impossible aspects of the UFO abduction reports—such as practical invisibility, levitation (or diamagnetism), mind control, the dropping of barriers between species, and mass cloning—are already within the realm of human accomplishments.

In the last quarter century, scientists have moved into territories previously thought to be either disreputable or literally impossible. In the biological arena, the sequencing of the human genome, among other innovations, has given scientists unprecedented control over the very processes of life itself, in ways that include the mixing and matching of species' genes. In the world of physics, the mainstream acceptance of quantum reality has left philosophers and physicists of all stripes pondering how little is actually known about the makeup of the universe. Starting from the basic level of the atoms in us all and moving out to the cosmic level, physicists acknowledge that as much as 90 percent of all matter that makes up the universe has never yet been seen or defined.

It's our contention in *Sight Unseen* that these achievements and realizations alone should radically alter the attitude of mainstream science to the UFO phenomenon. The vast distance we have come in the past quarter century can be illustrated in the context of an incident Budd Hopkins observed in 1976. During a television program on the subject of UFOs, Dr. Robert Jastrow, an eminent astrophysicist then serving with NASA's Goddard Space Laboratory, took the accepted skeptical position while astronomer Dr. J. Allen Hynek, a seasoned UFO investigator, presented case material supporting the physical reality of the phenomenon.[1]

Dr. Hynek discussed reports he had gathered during his twenty-year stint as the Air Force's scientific consultant on UFOs and subsequently as director of the Center for UFO Studies, while most of Dr. Jastrow's presentation against the physical reality of UFOs was of a theoretical nature: "You can't get here from there; they wouldn't be doing what people claim they can do; the occupants wouldn't look like that," and so on. After the program ended, Hopkins spoke to Dr. Jastrow and remarked that the debate had been interesting in that it had essentially pitted Hynek's data against Jastrow's theories. Dr. Jastrow had presented virtually no data bearing on any UFO report; such accounts, he implied, had to be rejected out of hand because, in 1976, scientific theory had no place for them. The existence and behavior of UFOs as described by witnesses was *at that time* theoretically, and thus to him actually impossible.

Despite this opinion, long dominant among mainstream scientists, undaunted UFO researchers have for decades gone on to investigate UFO sightings, photographs, ground traces, and abduction cases, weighing their credibility at each step of the way and searching for significant patterns. Year after year this "Damn the theories, full speed ahead!" scientific openness and curiosity has led to many important insights into alien methods and intentions. Significantly, the vast majority of these insights have stood the tests of time. The beleaguered skeptics, on the other hand, have seen their once-certain concept of reality and its attendant theories—dikes to hold back the threatening waters of "irrational" UFO acceptance—erode away in the face of new discoveries in astronomy, cosmology, quantum physics, and molecular biology. As we can see now, twenty-six years later, many of the theories that Dr. Jastrow must have seen as both immutable laws and as powerful arguments against the reality of UFOs have had to be discarded or radically altered.

As one example, it was a widely held belief by many astronomers that planetary systems such as our own were probably quite rare in our galaxy. But since the deployment of the Hubble telescope and the development of new, subtler systems of measurement, many other solar systems have been discovered. Although astronomers remain divided on this issue, many now believe that planetary systems like our own are probably quite common, vastly increasing the chance that life exists elsewhere.

As a corollary to this expansion of belief in the likelihood of extraterrestrial life, Carol Rainey discussed how the theory of wormholes through space-time or as connectors between worlds has recently become a legitimate area of study. Even time travel, traditionally relegated to science fiction, is seriously regarded by respected physicists such as Kip Thorne, David Deutsch, and Stephen Hawking—though each of the three holds a different view of it, varying from highly likely to at least marginally possible. It is theories such as these, then, that even allow for the possibility of UFO occupants arriving here from our own future.

Collectively, these relatively new concepts, although not definitively proven, have enormous implications for our understanding the universe in completely unprecedented ways. All along, it seems, previously derided "fringe science" has been slowly making its way into the mainstream. In many of the most exotic precincts of physics and biology, the heavy wooden doors that skeptics labeled "Impossible!" have now been flung open, never again to be securely nailed shut. UFO research is inadvertently gaining credibility as more prominent scientists begin to espouse ideas analogous to the once heretical concept that "stones actually do fall from the sky."

As we have detailed in these pages, it is in some of science's more material achievements—as well as in the heady rush of strong, new theoretical models of the universe—that we find the greatest hope for the future of UFO research. In the strange world of quantum reality, where paradoxes abound amid dark matter and "funny energy," and where things happen that aren't *supposed* to happen, we see the best hope of linking up the investigation of UFOs and their occupants with the concerns of mainstream science. Between our concerns and theirs lies a common resonance, a certain layering of the quasimaterial and the quasiethereal, a hint of some deeper and stranger world than any of us could ever have imagined, existing back there somewhere "behind the scenery." With some cooperation and openness on the parts of both scientists and UFO researchers, it is possible that a joint investigation into the UFO phenomenon could reveal an astonishing fact: that there aren't two opposed sides here, us and them; there is only a very large, presently incomprehensible mystery that no single "side" or team or individual could possibly understand all alone. But each of us is capable of understanding some part of the mystery, and together *we* just might begin to make some sense of the greatest scientific and cultural mystery mankind has yet had to face.

To make this point clear in *Sight Unseen,* we chose, within the mass of complex UFO abduction reports, to concentrate upon two patterns that have previously received almost no serious, systematic attention: the technology of temporary invisibility and, in greater depth, the presence on our planet of what seem to be partly alien "human" beings. In 1987, a decade and a half before the completion of this present book, Hopkins published *Intruders,* in which he recounted many abductees' reports of apparent sperm and ovum sampling, artificial insemination, and the presentation of part-human, part-alien "hybrid" infants and small children. *Intruders* was criticized on theoretical grounds by a number of scientists who insisted that "hybrids" such as the abductees described could not be produced, that they would not result from merging male and female reproductive cells of two different species, that cloning was a virtual pipe dream, and so on. In other words, it was "You can't get here from there" all over again. Conventional theory was invoked to trump unconventional data.

But as we've explored in *Sight Unseen,* with astonishing advances being made almost daily in genetic research, cloning, and transgenics, the barriers between species are beginning to fall. Tomatoes that withstand cold weather contain genes from salmon, artificial wombs are being developed by Japanese scientists, and the cloning of mammals in large numbers is a technique that offers the additional promise of pro- ducing, in the body of the transgenic animal, drugs and/or organs for human use. In other words, the human creation of an "alien" animal containing human genes within the DNA of its own species.

Now, in the new millenium, the alien reproductive procedures that abductees reported to investigators in the early 1980's not only seem plausible but, in hindsight, provided a foretaste of a well-developed technology we have begun to understand and to employ ourselves in test animals.

The late Carl Sagan, a brilliant man and, in Hopkins's dealings with him, a principled gentleman, was a committed if somewhat conflicted skeptic about the reality of the UFO phenomenon. But had his untimely death not occurred, he might have found it disturbingly ironic that in the new millenium, instead of being a bulwark against the UFO phe- nomenon, advanced science has actually helped us to make an even stronger case for UFO reality. A large caveat remains, nevertheless. Though *science* has inadvertently become our ally, too many individual *scientists* remain mired in past attitudes. Indifference to an objective consideration of the mass of available UFO data is still the norm. It is our profound hope that *Sight Unseen* will alert open-minded members of the scientific community to the need to join in this crucially impor- tant investigation.

Our second goal in writing this book is to provide enough specific information about the aliens' behavior on our planet to enable readers to form their own judgments about its intent and its future course. We have presented nearly a score of UFO abduction cases and provided many verbatim transcripts of the abductees' interviews, letters, and hyp- notic sessions. As most of our readers are probably aware, the actual range of this firsthand testimony is far more consistent than the bewil- dering range of opinions theorists have issued about the meaning of it all. On one end of the scale is what we might call the ultraparanoid inter- pretation: that the aliens are demons, beings who have come here to capture and devour our children, to use human body parts as replace- ments, and to feast upon what General Buck Turgison in *Dr. Strangelove* called our "vital bodily fluids." There is not, in our opinion, a scintilla of evidence supporting such a dire and melodramatic reading of the data.

On the other end of the spectrum is the idea—*hope* is perhaps a better word—that the aliens are here as quasi-godlike beings to help us with our problems, to heal our damaged planet, and to offer what has been called, with a straight face, "unconditional love." No one who reads the accounts we have been presenting can come to such a rosy— and simplistic—conclusion. The truth is, of course, that we do not know the future. We do not know the aliens' ultimate intentions, nor do we really know what their options are.

As the reader may have discerned, Hopkins and Rainey have somewhat differing views about alien intent. We do not share the same balance between hope and pessimism. On the one hand, Rainey suggests:

"What the ETs may be creating are not hybrids at all but transgenic human beings. It is both biologically possible and would best fit the profile of a secretive, invasive force that might be intent on conquering us from within—or equally possible, healing or altering the genes that no longer work for us in our present environment. The change could happen one genetic code word at a time—or an entire chromosome at a time. Either way, if the genes to be modified were carefully and expertly selected over thousands of years, we might never notice what was happening. The Hollywood-style massive destruction and cultural devastation seen in the movie *Independence Day* would never have to be played out. Biologists tell us that an entire species can do most of its changing internally, with new species traits only gradually manifesting themselves in outward appearance and behavior. If this is indeed occurring, will these alterations be good for the humans—or bad for the humans?

This is a difficult issue to take in both emotionally and intellectually: The subtle but inexorable alteration of the human species. But it may very well be that a culture several million years in advance of our own has already mastered the technology of bioengineering. The basic building blocks of life—proteins, amino acids, sugars, etc.—appear to be the same throughout the universe. The question is: How different are the issues and problems of altering the life-forms on Earth from those of other planets—or even, perhaps, in other dimensions? On Earth, as most biologists will tell you, the process is complex, intertwined with other systems, and not yet well enough understood to be predictable and safe for human use. With no federal or institutional support at all, and with only a handful of mainstream scientists willing or able to risk ridicule and loss of funding, people worldwide who are experiencing the UFO abduction phenomenon firsthand have little choice. They can only hope and pray that these alien beings know what they're doing.

On the other hand, Hopkins cautions, in such a transaction the odds favor us losing and the aliens gaining. He states:

> The twenty-seven years I have spent working with abductees, listening to their traumatic encounters, and trying to help them heal a lifetime of psychic damage, have left me hardened to reassuring talk of "beings of light" practicing benevolent "tough love." I have seen too much pain to allow myself more than a life-sustaining modicum of hope. And yet, I may be wrong. Though abductions inevitably leave the abductees scarred, emotionally and psychologically, there is no sign that this kind of psychic damage was intended. In fact, there are many indications that the UFO occupants try to minimize the pain and emotional damage their activities naturally inflict. *Amoral* is a useful word in this context, less brutal than other terms I could use with equal justice.
>
> And yet . . . the future is still the uncertain future, and the alien mind is still mysteriously alien. We do not know their real attitude toward our own humanity as it is now, with most of Earth's population as yet untouched by forced genetic manipulation. We do not know how the aliens view our inherent qualities of spirituality, physical diversity, romantic love, humor, and sexuality. Or our intensely protective love for our children, our rich artistic expressiveness, and our willingness to sacrifice our own selves for the greater good. How many of these basic human qualities—attributes in which the aliens seem so sadly deficient—do they truly envy and wish to append to their own narrow natures? Might they be willing to complete their program of genetic manipulation, successfully merging their ominous "paranormal" abilities with our frail but splendid human characteristics, and then leave to populate another place, to seed another developing race of intelligent beings?

What *are* their ultimate intentions? Are we merely a race of modern Aztecs hoping that the Spaniards will either get back in their boats and sail away or turn out to be benevolent gods? Do we, like the ancient Mexicans, need to turn a blind eye to the third possibility: that our alien visitors will instead turn out to be the ultimate conquistadors? For myself, I carefully nurture the seed of a fragile optimism. Admittedly it's a tiny seed, threatened on every side by inhospitable conditions, but I feed and water that tiny seed every day, and quietly hope it grows.

How to Report a Suspected UFO Experience

If you feel you may have had the kinds of experiences dealt with in this book, please write your recollections in detail to:

Budd Hopkins
c/o I.F.
Box 30233
N.Y., N.Y., 10011

E-mail: IFCENTRAL@aol.com

Our website is: www.IntrudersFoundation.org

As time permits an investigator will be in touch with you. All communications will be kept strictly confidential.

NOTES

Introduction

1. Temple University history professor David Jacobs, in his book *The Threat* (New York: Simon and Schuster, 1998), presents a disturbing hypothesis that the aliens are operating as infiltrators, using the genetic engineering implicit in their covert abduction program to produce "hybrid" beings who are physically more like humans but who retain alien paranormal abilities. The evidence supporting Jacobs's theory is compelling, though he has said again and again that he profoundly hopes that he is wrong.

Dr. John Mack, a psychiatrist who teaches at the Harvard Medical School, and author of *Abduction: Human Encounters with Aliens* (New York: Scribner, 1994) takes an opposing view. He has stated in various lectures that the aliens' interactions with humans may, in his words, represent a benevolent "outreach program to the spiritually handicapped," and though he admits the traumatic nature of UFO abductions, he has found witnesses who describe their experiences as enlightening in a virtually religious sense. In my view, when abductions are viewed in terms of their physical and emotional after-effects, the evidence clearly supports Jacobs's more ominous hypothesis rather than Mack's more optimistic one.

2. The earliest such examples in my files date from the 1920's.

3. Budd Hopkins, *Missing Time* (New York: Marek/Putnam, 1981), Chapter 8.

4. The most tragic such case involves the late atmospheric physicist Dr. James McDonald, who strongly defended the scientific relevance of the UFO phenomenon but was bitterly attacked by some of his colleagues for doing so. He was asked to testify before the Congressional Committee on Appropriations in 1971 to discuss not UFOs but the potentially harmful effects of supersonic transport aircraft (SSTs) on the atmosphere, a subject on which he was an acknowledged expert. For two days of hearings the congressmen who did not agree with him baited him with remarks about his "believing there are little men flying around in the sky" and so forth. Apparently this public humiliation was the final straw in a series of personal and professional crises: He committed suicide in June 1971.

5. *New York Times,* July 25, 2000, D3.

6. Ibid.

7. Salvatore Guido, " 'Your Wish Is My Command': Human Communication with Magical and Mechanical Agencies in Norbert Weiner's

Cybernetics," in *Being Human: The Technological Extensions of the Body*, edited by Jacques Houis, Paola Mieli and Mark Stafford (New York: Agincourt/Marsilio, 1999), p. 392.

PART 1: UNSEEN

Chapter 1:
The Alien Abductors Hiding and Sometimes Showing Off

1. John Fuller, *The Interrupted Journey* (New York: Dial Press, 1966).

2. Budd Hopkins, *Witnessed: The True Story of the Brooklyn Bridge Abductions* (New York: Pocket Books, 1996).

3. Travis Walton, *Fire in the Sky* (New York: Marlowe, 1996).

Chapter 3:
Uncovering Clues to the Science Of Invisibility

1. Major Donald Keyhoe (Ret.), *The Flying Saucer Conspiracy* (New York: Henry Holt, 1955), pp. 221–224.

2. Leonard G. Cramp, *UFOs and Anti-Gravity: Piece for a Jig-Saw* (Kempton, IL: Adventures Unlimited, 1966), pp. 143–144.

3. Steven J. Dick, *Life on Other Worlds* (Cambridge, U.K.: Cambridge University Press, 1998), pp. 266–270.

4. Gerald Feinberg, *Solid Clues* (New York; Macmillan, 1986), p. 95.

5. http://sciencenow.sciencemag.org/cgi/content/full/301/0

6. George Johnson, "Hardly Dead, Physics Lives Out a Permanent Revolution," *New York Times*, Science section, June 20, 2000, F1.

7. Ibid., F6

8. http://sciencenow.sciencemag.org/cgi/content/full/2001/208/1

9. David Deutsch, *The Fabric of Reality* (New York: Penguin, 1997), pp. 44–49.

10. Ibid., p. 51.

11. Ibid., p. 48.

12. Michael Talbot, *The Holographic Universe* (New York: HarperCollins, 1991), p. 163.

13. http://imagine.gsfc.nasa.gov (NASA website)

14. Ben Bova and Byron Preiss, in Michael Klein, ed., *Are We Alone in the Cosmos?* (New York: Pocket Books, 1999), p. 165.

15. Based on information from NASA website: http://imagine.gsfc.nasa.gov/cgi-bin/print.pl

16. Jennifer Lee, "An Audio Spotlight Creates a Personal Wall of Sound," *New York Times*, May 15, 2001, F4.

17. www.discovery.com/area/technology/b2/stealthintro.html

18. Paul Hill, *Unconventional Flying Objects: A Scientific Analysis* (Charlottesville, VA: Hampton Roads Publishing, 1995), pp. 316–17.

19. www.nasatech.com/briefs/AugOO/NPO20706.html

20. http://physicsweb.org/article/world/15/10/8

Chapter 5:
The Perpetual Photographer

1. Hill, *Unconventional Flying Objects: A Scientific Analysis* (Charlottesville, VA: Hampton Roads Publishing, 1995), p. 8.

2. Ibid., pp. 312-13.

3. Jacques and Janine Vallee, *Challenge to Science: The UFO Enigma* (Chicago: Henry Regnery Company, 1966).

4. Coral and James Lorenzen, *Flying Saucers: The Startling Evidence of the Invasion from Outer Space* (New York: New American Library, 1970).

5. *Nature*, Science Update, July 20, 2000.

6. Hill, op. cit., pp. 57–58.

7. http://www.kodak.com/cluster/global/en/service/tib/tib5201/shtml

8. Marc Davenport, *Visitors from Time: The Secret of UFOs* (Tigard, OR: Wildflower Press, 1992).

9. http://www.voicesweb.org/voices/sn/radioneuro3y2k.html

10. Barbara Opall, "U.S. Explores Russian Mind-Control Technology," in *Defense News*, 11–17, January 1993, p.29.

11. Jim Keith, *Mind Control, World Control* (Kempton, IL: Adventures Unlimited Press, 1998), p. 220.

12. Charles F. Emmons, *At the Threshold: UFOs, Science and the New Age* (Mill Spring, NC: Wildflower Press, 1997), p. 147.

13. David Deutsch, *The Fabric of Reality* (New York: Penguin, 1997), pp. 108-10.

14. Budd Hopkins, *Witnessed: The True Story of the Brooklyn Bridge UFO Abductions* (New York: Pocket Books, 1996), pp. 98–99.

15. www.wired.com/wired/archive/9.08/assist.html

16. Ibid.

17. www.explorezone.com/archives/99_08/26_ns_micro_bugs.htm

Chapter 6:
The Strange Case of the Reluctant Faucets

1. Katharina Wilson, *The Alien Jigsaw* (Portland, OR: Puzzle Publishing, 1993).

Chapter 7:
How to Explain Katharina?

1. Willis Harman, quoted in Michael Talbot, *The Holographic Universe* (New York: HarperCollins, 1991), pp. 2–3.

2. Ibid.

3. James Ganz, "Scientists Bring Light to Full Stop, Hold It, Then Send It on Its Way," *New York Times,* January 18, 2001, p. A21

4. Ibid., p. A1

5. http://observe.ivv.nasa.gov/nasa/education

6. http://www.phys.virginia.edu/classes/252/black_body_radiation.html

7. Norbert Weiner, *The Human Use of Human Beings: Cybernetics and Society* (London: Sphere, 1950), p. 35.

8. Talbot, op. cit., p. 187.

9. Kenneth Chang, "From One Quantum State to Another, It's Shades of 'Star Trek,' " *New York Times,* September 1, 2001.

10. www.newscientist.com/news, February 21, 2002.

11. Chang, op. cit.

12. Ibid.

Chapter 9:
Maggie's Holgraphic Body?

1. Paul Hill, *Unconventional Flying Objects: A Scientific Analysis* (Charlottesville, VA: Hampton Roads Publishing, 1995), p. 122; quote from Frank Edwards, *Flying Saucers: Serious Business* (New York: Bantam, 1966), p. 175.

2. Coral and James Lorenzen, *Flying Saucers: The Startling Evidence of the Invasion from Outer Space* (New York: New American Library, 1970), p. 60.

3. Hill, op. cit., p. 122.

4. Ibid., p. 130.

5. Michael Talbot, *The Holographic Universe* (New York: HarperCollins, 1991), p. 54.

6. Ibid., p. 55.

PART II: SEEN

Chapter 11:
Aliens Here and Now

1. Budd Hopkins, *Missing Time* (New York: Marek/Putnam, 1981), pp. 25, 26.

2. John Fuller, *The Interrupted Journey* (New York: Dial, 1966).

3. Author's conversation with Betty Hill, 1981.

4. Budd Hopkins, *Intruders: The Incredible Visitations at Copley Woods* (New York: Random House, 1987), pp. 82, 83.

5. Coral and Jim Lorenzen, *Encounters with UFO Occupants* (New York: Berkley, 1976), pp. 61–87.

6. Jerome Clark, *UFO Encyclopedia* 2nd ed. (Detroit: Omnigraphics, 1992), pp. 392–95.

7. In one case I've investigated, a New Jersey woman had her fetus disappear in the seventh month. She subsequently sued her obstetrician for malpractice and lost her case. The judge correctly pointed out that although she had proved she had been pregnant with a living, viable fetus, she had not proved that anything the doctor had done had contributed to its disappearance.

8. Hopkins, *Intruders,* pp. 154–63.

Chapter 14:
The Breakdown of Barriers between Species

1. Lawrence Krauss, *Beyond Star Trek* (New York: Basic Books, 1997), p. 64.

2. http://sciencenow.sciencemag.org/cgi/content/full/1999/526/1

3. Ibid.

4. Michael Swords, "Extraterrestrial Hybridization Unlikely," MUFON (Mutual UFO Network) *UFO Network Journal,* no. 247, November 1988, p. 6.

5. http://sciencenow.sciencemag.org/cgi/content/full/1997/530/3

6. Nancy Jones and Linda Bevington, "Human/Animal Transgenics: When Is a Mouse Not a Mouse?" Paper for the Center of Bioethics and Human Dignity, spring 2000.

7. Swords, op. cit., pp. 6–10.

8. Personal conversation with Dr. John Altshuler, May 2002.

9. http://sciencenow.sciencemag.org/cgi/content/full/2001/816/1

10. http://www.news.wisc.edu/view.html?get=3315

11. Swords, op. cit., p. 9

12. Ibid.

13. http://animalscience.ucdavis.edu/faculty/Anderson/research. htm

14. Swords, op. cit., p. 9.

15. *Environmental Health Perspectives*, vol. 101, no. 4, September 1993.

16. http://animalscience.ucdavis/edu/faculty/Anderson/research.htm

17. Michael Specter, "The Pharmageddon Riddle," *The New Yorker*, April 10, 2000, pp. 58–71.

18. Gina Kolata, "Monkey Born with Genetically Engineered Cells," *New York Times*, Jan. 12, 2001, A1, A20.

19. Specter, op. cit., p. 66.

20. http://www.dpz.gwdg.de.eupreycage.htm

21. http://jama.ama-assn.org/issues/v288nb/full/jbk0814.3.html

22. "Sweet Spot Found in Asteroid Belt," *Nature*, Press Release, Vol. 414, No. 6866 Dated 20/27, December 2001.

23. http://animal/science.ucdavis.edu/faculty/Anderson/research.htm

24. Ian Wilmut, Keith Campbell, and Colin Tudge, *The Second Creation: The Age of Biological Control by the Scientists Who Cloned Dolly* (London, U.K.: Headline, 2000).

25. Gina Kolata, "Babies in Fertility Method Have Genes from 3 People," *New York Times*, May 5, 2001.

26. Ibid.

Chapter 15:
The Man Who Knew Too Much

1. Travis Walton, *Fire in the Sky* (New York: Marlowe, 1996), pp. 36, 37.

2. The author's files contain extensive investigations into two different cases that involve *seven* people each in simultaneous abduction experiences.

Chapter 18:
Vulnerable in a Thousand Ways

1. Philip Morrison, quoted in Steven J. Dick, *Life on Other Worlds* (Cambridge, U.K.: Cambridge University Press, 1998), p. 261.

2. Seth Shostak, "Alien Abilities and Behaviors," in *Being Human: The Technological Extensions of the Body*, edited by Jacques Houis, Paola Mieli and Mark Stafford (New York: Agincourt/Marsilio, 1999), pp. 481.

3. Ibid.

4. *New York Times*, Feb. 8, 2001, G4.

5. http://cac.psu.edu/~pgsg109/qs/emo2001.html

6. http://uphs.upenn.edu/ihgt/info/whatisgt.html

7. David Jacobs, *The Threat* (New York: Simon and Schuster, 1998), pp. 132–36.

8. Michael Swords, "Extraterrestrial Hybridization Unlikely," MUFON (Mutual UFO Network) *UFO Network Journal,* no. 247, November 1988, p. 6.

9. Lawrence F. Roberge, paper presented at the October 22, 1998, Society of Catholic Social Sciences Conference: http://pages.map.com/lroberge/cloningpaper-2.html, p. 13.

10. Clifford Pickover, *The Science of Aliens* (New York: Basic Books, 1998), p. 174.

11. http://www.pbs.org/wgbh/nova/transcripts/2612time.html/, p. 17.

12. http://sciencenow.sciencemag.org/cgi/content/full/2001/112/2

13. Pickover, op. cit., p. 174.

14. http://www.framingham.com/heart/backgrnd.htm

15. www.wired.com/wired/archive/9.11/aging.html

16. Ibid.

17. www.wired.com/wired/archive/9.06/mustread.html?pg=5

Chapter 19:
First You See Them, Then You Don't

1. Jerome Clank *Unexplained* (Detroit: Visible Ink, 1993); various articles.

Chapter 20:
The Phantom Support Group, Stewart and Other Mysteries:

1. MUFON is the acronym for the Mutual UFO Network, 9862 W. Unser Ave., Littleton, CO 80128.

2. A typical example is the Herbert Schirmer abduction of Dec. 3, 1967, in Ashland, Nebraska. Schirmer, a police officer on duty in his patrol car when the abduction occurred, recalled being asked by one of the UFO occupants, "Are you the watchman over this place?" To an armed, uniformed police officer, the lowly job of "watchman" is like that of a busboy to a waiter or a maître d'. In the security professions it is a slightly degrading term that I doubt Schirmer would have ascribed to himself. And, as we shall see shortly, aliens have often referred to the wife of a male abductee as his "mate," and have referred to a female abductee as being ready to "breed."

3. In many abduction cases the abductees were returned with their clothes on backward or inside out, as if they were dressed hurriedly and incorrectly after the quasimedical procedures were completed. In one case I investigated, a man and his wife were driving one night when their car stopped and a UFO hovered above it. The pair stepped out of the car on opposite sides to observe the UFO and, in what seemed an instant, found

themselves standing on the same side of the car, barefoot. The UFO had disappeared and, to their amazement, their shoes and socks were resting neatly, side by side, on the fender next to them.

4. In one of the most harrowing hypnotic sessions I conducted with Sally, we explored a childhood event in which she was literally raped by Stewart at the age of six. Since Sally's memory of the incident had been blocked, and since her mother had not seen Stewart, she ascribed her daughter's injuries to some kind of unfortunate accident that occurred during play. My colleague David Jacobs, in his book, *The Threat* (New York: Simon and Schuster, 1998), recounts a number of violent sexual assaults by so-called hybrid beings.

5. One of the most commonly reported endings to an abductee's initial recollection is that of "going to sleep," even though countless investigations have shown that this really means the end of conscious memory. Examples: "I woke up and the room was filled with light and there were three small, black-eyed figures standing next to my bed. And then I just went to sleep"; "The engine in my car died and we looked up and saw a huge UFO about twenty feet over us, and then I guess the three of us just went to sleep." In such cases as these, the last thing anyone would do would be to fall asleep in the face of such a dramatic, frightening, adrenaline-infused scene.

Chapter 22:
Behind the Scenery

1. William James, "The Gospel of Relaxation," in *Talks to Teachers* (New York: W. W. Norton, 1958), pp. 140–141.

2. Interview between Jerome Clark and Helen Anderson, April 27, 1978.

3. Edgar Mitchell, *The Way of the Explorer* (New York: Putnam, 1996), p. 191.

4. http://sciencenow.sciencemag.org/cgi/content/full/1999/224/2

5. Michio Kaku, *Hyperspace* (New York: Anchor/Doubleday, 1994), p. 113.

6. Ibid.

7. Ibid. p. 136

8. John Mack, *Abduction: Human Encounters with Aliens* (New York: Scribner, 1994).

9. Kaku, op. cit., p. 115.

10. J. Madeleine Nosh, "Unfinished Symphony," *Time*, December 31, 1999, p. 86.

11. Kaku, op cit., pp. 152–53.

12. Ibid., viii.

13. Charles F. Emmons, *At the Threshold: UFOs, Science and the New Age* (Mill Spring, NC: Wildflower Press, 1997), p. 123.

14. Kaku, op. cit., pp. 45–48.

15. Michael Murphy, *The Future of the Body* (New York: Putnam 1992), pp. 217–18.

16. Kaku, op cit., pp. 263–65.

17. Ibid., p. 267

18. Ibid., p. 269.

19. Thomas Browne, *Religio Medici,* quoted in Michael Murphy, *The Future of the Body* (New York: Putnam, 1992), p. 214.

20. Murphy, op. cit., pp. 135, 215.

21. Murphy, op. cit. p. 215.

22. Mitchell, op. cit., pp. 177–80.

23. Ibid., 180.

24. Ibid.

25. Deutsch, *The Fabric of Reality* (New York, Penguin, 1997), pp. 311–18.

26. Ibid., pp. 318–19.

Chapter 24:
The Luckiest Little Abductee

1. Allen Hynek, quoted in Jerome Clark, ed., *The UFO Encyclopedia,* 2nd ed. (Detroit: Omnigraphics, 1998), p. 704.

2. www_hfml.sci.kun.nl/levitate.html

3. J.M.F. van Vlissingen, Biomedical Primate Research Centre, Rijswijk, The Netherlands, in abstract of EUPREN/EMRG (Multilateral Consultation of Parties to the European Convention for the Protection of Vertebrate Animals Used for Experimental and Other Scientific Purposes) Discussion paper, May 1997.

4. http://eserver.org/langs/linell/chapter02.html, p. 4.

5. Ibid.

6. www.familytraumaservices.com/articles/artparks.htm

7. www.centerforendo.com/QandA.htm

8. Medical records for "Anne-Marie," Budd Hopkins's case files.

9. www.Nevadafertility.com/education/hydrosalpinx.htm

10. American Society for Reproductive Medicine, on-line technical bulletin, www.asrm.org/Media/Practice/ectopic, p. 3.

11. Richard M. Neal, "The Missing Embryo/Fetus Syndrome," *MUFON 1992 International UFO Symposium Proceedings* (Sequin, TX: MUFON, 1992), pp. 214–29.

Chapter 26:
Human Resources: Ours or Theirs?

1. http://obgyn.upenn.edu/IVF/ARTsyllabus.html

2. http://www.abivf.com/html/ivf_primer.html

3. Jeremy Rifkin, "The End of Pregnancy," *The Guardian* (London) January 30, 2002.

4. www.malereproduction.com/19_electroejaculation.html October 26, 2000.

5. EUPREN/EMRG (Multilateral Consultation of Parties to the European Convention for the Protection of Vertebrate Animals Used for Experimental and other Scientific Purposes) Conference, May 1997.

6. Ibid.

7. http://www.boycottohsu.com/animal-abuse.html

8. Henry T. Greely, on-line interview,
http://www.maxmuscle.com/cutting_edge/cloning/cloning_page.html

9. Ibid., p. 7.

10. http://www.obgyn.upenn.edu/IVF/ARTsyllabus.html

11. Greely, op. cit.

12. John Altshuler, quoted in Jerome Clark, ed., *UFO Encyclopedia,* 2nd ed. (Detroit: Omnigraphics, 1992), p. 116.

13. Ibid., pp. 112–117

14. Ibid., p. 117

15. Lawrence F. Roberge, paper presented at the Oct. 22, 1998, Society of Catholic Social Services Conference: paper-2.html.,
http://pages.map.com/lroberge/cloning

16. Ibid.

17. http://www.news.wisc.edu/view.html?get=3315

18. www.sciencenow.sciencemag.org/cgi/content/full/2002/214/0

19. http://home.earthlink.net~whizkidz/design07.html

20. Thomas Verney, *The Secret Life of the Unborn Child,* quoted in ibid.

21. Jeremy Rifkin, "The End of Pregnancy," *The Guardian* (London) January 17, 2002.

22. Ibid.

Chapter 27:
A Few Final Words

1. *The Stanley Siegel Show,* Channel 7, New York, NY. The guests included Dr. J. Allen Hynek, Dr. Robert Jastrow, former astronaut Dr. Edward Mitchell, and UFO witnesses George O'Barski and Betty Hill.

INDEX